T5-BAR-270

HARVARD STUDIES IN
MONOPOLY AND COMPETITION

---

1. CORPORATE SIZE AND EARNING POWER
William Leonard Crum

2. THE CONTROL OF COMPETITION IN CANADA
Lloyd G. Reynolds

3. UNFAIR COMPETITION
John Perry Miller

HARVARD STUDIES IN
MONOPOLY AND COMPETITION

LONDON : HUMPHREY MILFORD

OXFORD UNIVERSITY PRESS

UNFAIR COMPETITION

A STUDY IN CRITERIA FOR THE CONTROL OF TRADE PRACTICES

BY

JOHN PERRY MILLER

ASSISTANT PROFESSOR OF ECONOMICS IN YALE UNIVERSITY

CAMBRIDGE · MASSACHUSETTS

HARVARD UNIVERSITY PRESS

1941

COPYRIGHT, 1941

BY THE PRESIDENT AND FELLOWS OF HARVARD COLLEGE

PRINTED AT THE HARVARD UNIVERSITY PRESS

CAMBRIDGE, MASSACHUSETTS, U.S.A.

380.18
M648u

HD
3626
U6
M5
1941

Ne 22 D47

16 MY 47 SUS 3.20 (Econ,)

355523

To
MY MOTHER AND FATHER

EDITOR'S NOTE

This is the third of a series of monographs on selected aspects of the general problem of monopoly and competition, reporting specific studies in the research program of a special committee of the Harvard Department of Economics. The investigation leading to the present monograph was financed in part by a grant from the A. W. Shaw Fund and the Harvard Committee on Research in the Social Sciences.

Edward S. Mason

PREFACE

PROBLEMS of monopoly and competition have been in the center of public discussion in the United States perennially since the Civil War and bid fair to remain so. The ways in which the problems have been visualized at various times have differed, but running throughout the discussions has been a concern with various competitive practices generally referred to as "unfair methods of competition." It is fair to say that many have felt that unfair competition is the crux of the monopoly problem and that if unfair methods of competition could be prevented, the monopoly problem would be resolved and an effective or workable form of competition in industry would be assured. Economists need not be reminded that the legal and popular approaches to these problems have been seriously hampered by an oversimplified conception of the dichotomy between the two categories of monopoly and competition.

The terms "unfair competition" or "unfair methods of competition" are normative terms used in the field of public policy to distinguish legal from illegal practices. They are also terms which, since they are applied to economic phenomena (i.e. rivalry in the market), have economic connotations. It is to a study of the legal meaning of these terms and to the economic significance of these legal categories that this study is devoted. An attempt is made to distinguish the general lines drawn by the courts between fair and unfair competition; more detailed studies are made of certain practices which have bulked large in discussion and public policy. The later part of the book is devoted to a consideration of proposals for self-government in industry; one of the chief purposes of these proposals is to develop voluntarily rules of fair and unfair practices which would change substantially the existing rules of the game.

There have been those who believed that the regulation of competition would be a sufficient approach to the problems of monopoly and competition. It is a principal thesis of this book that the advocates of this view grossly oversimplify the problem. On the one hand, this view exaggerates the significance of competitive practices as promoting monopolistic conditions at the expense of certain other factors such as the corporate law, the patent law, the concentration of ownership of natural resources, etc. On the other hand, they underestimate the need for the regulation of trade practices in the broader sense as against competitive methods which may be considered "unfair." The purpose of a law of trade practices is to make the economic system work; to do this our legal system must take adequate account of the variety of market conditions which exist. Moreover, the test of legality of trade practices must be economic results. When this is recognized, the task is seen to be much more complex than has in general been recognized previously.

This study was originally undertaken as a doctoral thesis submitted at Harvard University, but it has subsequently undergone extensive revision not only in detail but in general structure as well. I am deeply indebted to Professor E. S. Mason, who first suggested the study to me, for advice and encouragement at all stages. He has read the manuscript on several occasions. I should like also to express my indebtedness to the participants in the Price Policy Seminar held at the Littauer School of Public Administration at Harvard during the years 1937–39. The discussions of these groups under the leadership of Professors J. D. Black, E. S. Mason, and D. H. Wallace contributed much to the formulation of the issues and the revision of the early draft of the book. Professors D. H. Wallace of Williams College and A. M. McIsaac of Princeton University each read the manuscript at an intermediate stage and gave me extensively of their counsel. For this I am deeply grateful. I am also indebted to Dr. C. D. Edwards, now with

the Anti-trust Division of the Department of Justice and
formerly Economist for the Federal Trade Commission, who
read the manuscript and gave extensively of his advice.
I am also grateful to my colleagues Professor H. F. William-
son and Dr. H. M. Oliver, Jr., of Yale University, each of
whom read a chapter. Messrs. R. W. Dittmer, C. A. Bemis,
and N. Zolot of Yale University have aided me heroically in
the tedious task of editing the manuscript for the printer.

J. P. M.

Silliman College
Yale University
October 1940

CONTENTS

UNFAIR COMPETITION

Instead of the world of light, order, equality, and perfect organization, which orthodox political economy postulates, the commercial world is thus one of obscurity, confusion, haphazard, in which, amid much destruction and waste, there is by no means always a survival of the fittest, even though cunning be counted among the conditions of fitness. "The race is not to the swift, nor the battle to the strong, nor yet riches to men of understanding; but time and chance happeneth to them all." T. E. C. LESLIE, *The Known and the Unknown in the Economic World*

CHAPTER I

THE PROBLEM AND ITS SETTING

THE DEVELOPMENT of an effective system of control of trade practices and competitive relations has long been one facet of public policy in the field of industrial organization. Recent legislative developments and the current studies of the Temporary National Economic Committee alike suggest that the problems of trade practices are still an important issue of public policy and will continue to bulk large in the visible future. Since the demise of the NRA, itself a gigantic effort to develop codes of fair competition, federal legislation regulating trade practices has been extensive. It has taken such forms as the Robinson-Patman Act, dealing with discrimination; the Miller-Tydings Act, exempting contracts under the State Fair Trade Laws from the Sherman Act; amendments to section 5 of the Federal Trade Commission Act dealing with unfair methods of competition; the Wheeler-Lea amendments dealing with false advertisements; and the Guffey-Vinson Act regulating the pricing of bituminous coal. Recent activities of the Anti-trust Division of the Department of Justice suggest that the Department is evolving a new and significant approach to the problem of trade relations. Moreover, there are numerous current proposals for further changes. These range from proposed legislation concerning block-booking in the motion picture industry, the basing-point system of price quotation, and design-piracy, to proposals for a change in content or administration of the anti-trust laws so as to permit joint action by industrial groups for the promotion of efficient marketing under public scrutiny.

The issues raised by previous policy and current proposals are various and perplexing. The problem was traditionally viewed as that of developing a law of *unfair competition*. More recently the problem has been viewed as requiring a more positive approach, the establishing of standards designed to promote *fair competition*. The development of doctrines of fair and unfair competition in the United States has not been one of linear progression. It has presented paradoxes and apparent inconsistencies. However, in the development down to the early 1930's certain general categories of competitive practices had been delineated. Distinctions have been made between practices in competition and practices in restraint of trade.[1] Unfair practices in competition have been distinguished from other competitive practices. Unreasonable restraints of trade have been distinguished from reasonable restraints. The bases of distinction have not been articulate. The classifications have been developed pragmatically, by case law, legislative action, and Commission decision. These in turn have been influenced in some degree by business practice and the discussion of business groups.

It is important to view in perspective the function of a system of restrictions on competitive practices in modern industry. The principal force which has been relied upon in the United States during the last century for the organization of economic activity has been the competition of individuals or groups of individuals in the market under a system of free private enterprise. The system was based upon the institution of private property, and upon recognition of the freedom of the individual to employ his property and his effort as he wished and to enjoy the fruits or suffer the losses of such employment. The rivalry of individuals or firms and of associations of individuals or firms, which expressed itself in voluntary exchange in the market within the general legal structure of free private enterprise, was accepted as the prevailing method by which the

---

[1] It appears that in the development of American law "to monopolize or attempt to monopolize" is equivalent to restraint of trade.

economic problems of the society should be resolved. This rivalry and exchange meant an elaborate structure of prices determined by competition.[2]

The competitive economy was the economic counterpart of the broader political and philosophical movement generally referred to as liberalism, the essence of which lies in its emphasis upon the rights, dignity, and sanctity of the individual. The moral precept of the doctrine urged that "all relations between men ought ideally to rest on mutual free consent, and not on coercion, either on the part of individuals, or on the part of 'society' as politically organized in the state."[3] As A. N. Whitehead has pointed out this "liberal faith of the nineteenth century was a compromise between the individualistic, competitive doctrine of strife and the optimistic doctrine of harmony."[4]

In its extreme forms this philosophy took a nihilistic attitude toward the state. And as a matter of historical fact the fervor of liberal doctrine was long directed at the medieval and mercantilistic schemes of restriction upon the individual in both his spiritual and social activities. In the economic sphere liberalism became associated with *laissez faire*. But it is generally agreed that no leading liberal economist or political scientist took an extreme position on the function of the state. It was recognized both in theory and in practice that the state was responsible for establishing and regulating a large series of economic and social institutions, such for example as the system of money and banking or the various legal forms of

[2] By competition in this context is meant rivalry. We need not for the present distinguish kinds and degrees of competition.

[3] F. H. Knight, "Ethics and Economic Reform, I: The Ethics of Liberalism," *Economica*, VI (1939), 5.

[4] *Adventures of Ideas* (New York: The Macmillan Co., 1933), p. 41. *Cf.* the discussion of J. M. Clark concerning the conflict between the ideas of "rights" and "liberties," *Social Control of Business* (New York: McGraw-Hill, 1939, 2d ed.), chap. V.

business organizations. The state was generally held responsible for certain lines of endeavor in which private enterprise might prove ineffective, e.g. police, army, certain public works, and education. Moreover, it must supervise in various ways the conditions under which rivalry is to be pursued. It must prevent fraud and coercion in competitive relations. It was recognized that freedom might be used not only for rivalry but for coöperation and that the limits must be determined within which the freedom of the individual might be restricted by contract or used to further joint action.

These problems were all recognized early in the history of liberalism. It is true, however, that the emphasis was upon the negative responsibilities of the state. The traditional law of contract and property were looked upon as "natural law," while proposals for progressive readjustments of these institutions were looked upon as exceptional if not questionable interferences with business relations. The problem of evolving effective institutions within which political liberalism might be a reality and free private enterprise might be effective was relatively neglected, particularly by the popular expositors.[5] Increasingly, however, the sphere of necessary governmental action was recognized. The reasons compelling action varied. It became evident that some of the results of free private enterprise, as we knew it, were unacceptable, that is, the logic of free private enterprise was unacceptable in some cases however perfect or harmonious the system within itself. In other cases it appeared that the existing institutional frame work, the existing rules of the game, were incompatible with the logic of the system.

Of particular relevance to us was the development of various strands of thought concerning the efficacy of the freedom of the individual or the firm to act as it chose in the market. The lines

---

[5] J. M. Keynes, *The End of Laissez-faire* (London: The Hogarth Press, 1926), *passim.*

of approach were various. Freedom in the market might lead to monopoly in several ways: by agreement of individuals to withdraw from the market, by the elimination of individuals through merger or combination, by agreement of potential rivals to follow joint market policies, or by the practice of exclusive or coercive policies in the process of rivalry on the part of some firms against others. Competition might, then, breed its antithesis, monopoly. Practices leading to this result are of concern to public policy. In consequence, limits must be drawn between tolerable and intolerable practices or between practices in pursuit of competition and those in restraint of trade.

More than this, it was conceivable that competitive practices while not involving monopoly or restraint of trade (in the legal sense) might nevertheless be *unfair*. There were recognized to be types of competitive practices or types of rivalry which distributed the rewards or penalties of the competitive process in a manner which violated the inner logic of competitive enterprise or were in some other manner unacceptable to public policy. These practices might involve relations of a business unit with its customers, relations with sources of productive factors including labor, or direct relations with competitors. Legal theories of unfair competition were developed. As we shall see, they were in their origin ostensibly concerned with the effects of practices upon the competitor. These developments were based on the inarticulate assumption that consumers were to be protected by the preservation of competition and that competition would be protected if besides being freed from restraint of trade it were freed from unfair methods. A distinction was recognized between competitive injuries which were compatible with the logic of free private enterprise and those which were not.

Here, then, we have the problem as it has been traditionally viewed, the problem of preserving competition by preventing it from turning into its antithesis, monopoly (in the legal sense); by preventing its infection with practices which violate its inner logic; by promoting such practices as will positively promote effective competition; and finally by rechanneling or curbing competitive efforts in those spheres where the logic of competitive enterprise and the objectives of policy conflict.

NATURE OF COMPETITION

The nature of competition as it actually functions in industrial markets has only recently been subjected to detailed study. Competition is a very complex phenomenon. It may take any one of several forms. It may become a rivalry in buying factors of production of better quality or in buying factors on more favorable terms. It may consist in an endeavor to organize and utilize factors more effectively in producing goods and services, this involving a rivalry in technological processes as well as in economy in the use and organization of men and materials. It may take the form of rivalry in attracting customers. This in turn may be done in various ways: by price competition, by informative or competitive advertising, by differentiation of product or of the many ancillary terms and conditions of sale, or finally by effective choice and control of the channels of distribution. In a purely competitive market competition becomes simply a matter of efficiency in organization of production and the correct determination of the quantity to be produced. But such conditions are rare. It is doubtful whether there is any market in which neither the demand nor the supply is significantly affected by monopolistic or monopsonistic forces.

Not only may rivalry take many forms, but the intensity of rivalry may vary. There are different degrees of competition depending upon the particular blend of monopolistic and competitive elements which may be present in the market. The existence of significant monopoly elements means that there are areas of choice within which the firm may, at least in the short-run, operate. Buying and selling becomes a matter of policy. To be sure the individual firm is affected in its decisions by the action of rivals, but to a greater or lesser extent it can affect the market perceptibly. The form and the intensity of competition will vary depending upon market conditions and market policies. These policies it is within the power of the firms acting either individually or jointly to modify.

Consider as an example the question of price making. The price of a commodity is not a simple thing. The ways in which prices are made are manifold. For example, in some markets prices are customarily made by higgling; the price is remade with every individual sale. At the other extreme are those prices, set by administrative action, which are publicly announced and subject to no variations. This is illustrated by the one price policy of most of our retail stores. In other cases there is some mixture of these policies, i.e. public announcement with deviations in some instances determined by individual bargaining.

Of equal importance is the procedure by which price changes are introduced in those markets where price administration is customary. In various markets conventions have been developed for the initiation of changes in administered prices. In some industries it is customary to announce publicly all price changes, making them effective to all buyers at one time. This public announcement may be made through the press, through publication of revised price lists, through the activities of the sales force, or through a formal system of open-price filing effected through the joint efforts of the industry. In other industries price changes are initiated by offering special or secret concessions to particular customers which then spread, finally being recognized by the publication of new price lists. In many industries there are certain customary times at which price changes are announced. This is especially true of commodities whose sale has a seasonal pattern. For example, carpet prices are customarily announced at the annual shows, and automobile prices are announced with the introduction of new models. In these cases it is not customary to change prices except at more or less stated periods. In the steel industry prices are announced in advance for each quarter of the year. In the sugar industry price changes are customarily made at about monthly intervals at the time of sugar "moves." These customs are not always uniform for a particular industry. Often more than one procedure is in effect at a given time. Moreover, the customs change with the passage of time. The policies and changes in policies of one firm may have repercussions upon others. These differences in procedure in making and changing prices, and these changes in procedure have many repercussions on the fortunes of business rivals and give rise to innumerable conflicts between competitors or groups of competitors.

Another source of conflict lies in the complexity of the concept of price itself. The word *price* is conventionally used by the economist to refer to the whole complex structure of prices which the individual firm charges. However, price may vary for different classes of customers, for customers buying in different quantities, and for customers located at various points. Moreover, price may vary according to the type of contract, whether based on individual sale or for all purchases over a period of time. Differences in the time and conditions of delivery or payment may also be occasions for different prices. Whether this be interpreted as differences in price or differences in product is immaterial. Such considerations suggest that the question of price is one of the whole structure of prices. The relations between these various specific prices of a firm are of concern to the consuming public and to business rivals alike. Differences in the price structures of rival firms and changes in these price structures give rise to conflicts between business rivals. In an economic system such as ours where imperfections and monopolistic elements are usual the relations between the various prices in the price structure of a firm are not independent of the desires, interests, whims, inertia, or policies of the firm. So far as these price relations are of significance to the effective functioning of the price system as a regulator of our economic system the public has an interest therein.

Competition, then, may take many forms. In its pursuit a host of trade practices have been developed. It is within the power of particular firms or groups of firms to affect these practices significantly. The form which rivalry takes and the practices by which it is pursued will clearly affect the parties concerned. This has induced business to attempt to develop a code of ethics, i.e. a code of practices to be forbidden, on the one hand, and those to be sponsored on the other. At the same time public policy has attempted to develop its code of fair and unfair practices presumably in the interest of effective economic organization. It is to a study of the criteria involved in distinguishing fair and unfair methods of competition in this country and the economic significance of the existing restrictions on competitive practices that the following chapters will be devoted.

SIGNIFICANCE OF COMPETITION

It is pertinent as a prelude to the discussion of policy with reference to the control of competition to inquire as to what difference the form and character of competition makes. What is the significance of whether competition is intense or limited, pure or monopolistic, fair or unfair? What does it matter whether prices are high or low, flexible or rigid, uniform or discriminatory? The answer is to be found in the functions which competition and the price system perform in a system of private enterprise.

It is, of course, obvious that the character of competition and price policies has much to do with the success and failure of established business concerns. Changes in prices and competitive practices will affect appreciably the relative profitability of established firms. This fact explains many of the pressures for control of competitive methods and price policies. Entrenched firms seek protection of their position from injury by certain methods. But the waxing and waning of business firms is a normal incident of capitalistic enterprise which we expect and even welcome, though the rules of the game prevent the use of certain tactics (e.g. deceit and predatory practices) to influence the process. The firm, however, is simply an instrument through which the economic affairs of society are administered. Firms grow and then disappear, while the individuals and often much of the capital values which make up the firm remain. Of course, the individuals who comprise the firm and the owners of the capital values represented therein may be injured through loss of income, but while public policy may be concerned with the incidence of such losses on individuals, the protection of established firms is not the function of competition nor even the controlling purpose of public policy.

The functions of competition and the pricing system are to be found in another direction, namely in serving to marshall the scarce resources available for the satisfaction of man's desires. From an economic point of view the significance of competitive methods and price policies is to be found in the effectiveness with which this task is performed. This effectiveness will depend upon several factors:[6]

1. The level of employment of resources. Other factors being equal the greater the average level of employment of available resources the more effectively our desires will be satisfied.

2. The efficiency with which resources are organized in

---

[6] For a somewhat different but related classification of the issues *cf.* D. H. Wallace, "Industrial Markets and Public Policy: Some Major Problems," *Public Policy* (Cambridge: Harvard University Press, 1940, edited by C. J. Friedrich and E. S. Mason), p. 100.

producing particular goods. By use of the best combination of various factors of production in plants of optimum size and in the best location costs per unit of output may be minimized, and at any given level of employment a maximum output of goods will result.

3. The allocation of factors between alternative uses. In so far as resources are allocated to various alternative uses in proportion to the urgency of the demand for the alternative products, the effective desires of the community will be satisfied to a maximum at any given level of employment and efficiency.

4. The allocation of claims to share in the total income between various individuals. Competition and the price system by determining the rewards to the various factors determine individuals' claims to share in the national income. Criteria of a good or just distribution of income are difficult to formulate, but it is sufficient to note that public policy has customarily recognized the desirability of alleviating extreme inequalities.

5. The adaptability of the economic system to innovation and to changes in tastes or in cost conditions. Receptiveness to innovation is the basis of economic progress, and adaptation to change in tastes and costs is a prerequisite for the most effective utilization of resources.

6. The incidence of gain and loss which results from the adaptation of the system to innovation and change. Gains and losses are a natural concomitant of change, and unless controlled their incidence may be arbitrary.

These are the economic functions which must somehow be performed in any society. In this country chief reliance is had upon free private enterprise working through the price system and under the impulse of competition, such as it is. In the absence of countervailing considerations (e.g. national defense or political expediency) the economic effectiveness of a system of organization is to be judged by the way in which it performs these functions. The economic significance of market structures, competitive practices, and government policies is to be found in these directions. Competition, i.e. rivalry within the institutional framework of capitalistic enterprise, is a means by which these functions are performed more or less effectively. Does a method of competition foster full employment of labor and other productive factors, effective allocation of resources, efficiency in their organization, justice in the distribution of income, adaptability of the system to innovation and change, and a reasonable allocation of the gains and losses incidental to such change? These are some of the questions which will be raised in the following chapters.

CHAPTER II

REGULATION OF TRADE PRACTICES BEFORE 1914

COMMON LAW

WHILE the regulation of competitive practices in the United States first came into public notice with the discussions incident to the passage of the Federal Trade Commission and Clayton Acts in 1914, there were already rather definite restrictions on competitive practices arising from three sources. There was, first, the law on unfair competition which had developed out of the consideration of trade-mark infringement, in which the legal basis of action was a private injury coupled with deceit or fraud.[1] In the second place, there were developing at common law precedents by which certain practices, in themselves legal, might be condemned when exercised by business enterprises having a predominant position in the market, i.e. where the market had become potentially seriously monopolistic.[2] Finally, under the Sherman Act certain classes of contracts or competitive practices were enjoined as tending to establish a restraint on trade or as constituting an attempt to monopolize.[3] The first group of decisions did not involve any problem of monopoly in a legal sense; the second group concerned practices illegal because of the actual prior existence of a seriously monopolistic market condition; while the third group of decisions involved monopoly or restraint of trade within the meaning of the Sherman Act.

[1] J. E. Davies, *Trust Laws and Unfair Competition* (Washington: Government Printing Office, 1916), chap. VII; H. D. Nims, *The Law of Unfair Competition and Trade Marks* (New York: Baker, Voorhis and Co., 1929, 3d ed.), chap. I.

[2] A. M. Kales, *Cases on Contracts and Combinations in Restraint of Trade* (Chicago: Callaghan & Co., 1916, 2 vols.), p. 89.

[3] *Ibid.*, chap. VIII.

Unfair Competition at Common Law. The term "unfair competition" has a common law meaning which must be distinguished from the use of the same or analogous expressions in discussions of the trust problem or of the NRA. It is believed that the first use of the term "fair competition" (or its antithesis "unfair competition") was in an English case, *Hogg v. Kirby*,[4] in 1803, although the legal question involved, which was the copying of a trade-mark, had a history going back at least to 1742, when Lord Hardwicke refused a request for injunctive relief in a case of trade-mark piracy.[5] However, it soon became established that "passing-off" by pirating a trade-mark was illegal and would be enjoined. The ground of the action was injury to a competitor through deceiving the public. As Lord Langdale, writing in 1843, expressed it, "two things are required for the accomplishment of a fraud such as is here contemplated . . . in the first instance, to mislead the public, and in the next place, to secure a benefit to the party practicing the deception by preserving his own individuality."[6]

The early decisions apply only to trade-marks, but by analogy legal relief was gradually extended to other situations both in England and in the United States so that by the end of the nineteenth century the courts recognized the right to equitable relief from a series of practices analogous to trade-mark piracy, which practices were designated in England by the term "passing-off" and in the United States by "unfair competition." In this group of practices were included the simulation of trade-names and trade-signs, the use in trade of personal or geographical names which had come to have a secondary meaning to the public and use of which by others

---

[4] 8 Vesey, Jr., 215 (1803). Nims cites this case as probably the first use of the expression (*op. cit.*, p. 7).

[5] Case of *Blanchard v. Hill*, 2 Atk. 484 (1742), cited by F. I. Schechter, *The Historical Foundations of the Law Relating to Trade-Marks* (New York: Columbia University Press, 1925), p. 134 and Nims, *op. cit.*, pp. 7–8.

[6] *Croft v. Day*, 7 Beav. 88–89 (1843), cited in Nims, *op. cit.*, p. 11.

might divert trade through misleading the public, and the simulation of the dress or color of a competitor's goods.[7] But in the United States, at least, the process of broadening the meaning of unfair competition was not confined to practices which might be included under the phrase "passing-off." The concept was extended to include cases involving the disclosure of trade secrets,[8] bribery, misrepresentation of all sorts, interference with a competitor's contracts, or any malicious interference with a competitor's business.[9]

The very diversity of the practices falling within the common law concept of unfair competition raises the question as to what principle justifies the grouping together of such practices under one designation. Can the answer be found in the legal grounds on which the courts have based their decisions as to the fairness or unfairness of specific practices? A leading authority, H. D. Nims, concludes that there does not seem to be any single generally accepted basis for decision of the cases.[10] He notes three grounds for condemning particular practices which have appeared frequently: the promotion of honest and fair dealing, the protection of the public, and the protection of the rights and property of individuals.

One of the most recent commentators has noted that:

> Jurists have quarrelled, almost from the beginnings of these actions, as to whether the basis of relief is the protection of the property interest of the owner of the mark or name, or the protection of the public from the deception practiced by the infringer. Both theories have their adherents; both are incapable of explaining all the decisions of the courts. . . .

[7] Thus, in 1890 G. D. Cushing wrote an article "On Certain Cases Analogous to Trade-Marks," *Harvard Law Review*, IV (1891), 321.

[8] O. R. Mitchell, "Unfair Competition," *Harvard Law Review*, X (1896), 295–96.

[9] The series of legal definitions of unfair competition cited by Nims best indicates the gradual widening of the concept by the courts, *op. cit.*, pp. 16–22.

[10] Nims, *op. cit.*, pp. 25–26.

By and large, with some notable exceptions, judicial relief has depended upon the concurrence of the dual factors of a threatened diversion of trade and the probable deception of the public.[11]

The protection of the public seems to be only a minor factor in many of the cases. The essential elements in the original trade-mark cases were the injury to a competitor in his business by means of deceit or misrepresentation. The basis of action was a private injury by an unlawful means. But when the concept is widened to include such diverse practices as are indicated above, it becomes difficult to define accurately the basis of action. It is an inherent part of a competitive economic system based on the institutions of private property, individual enterprise, and freedom of contract in a free market that individuals in seeking their own interests may cause economic injury to a competitor. This is a part of the underlying philosophy of the system and is recognized by the law. The courts have noted repeatedly that ordinary competition has injury as a result and have insisted that, however much a person is actuated by malice in competing with a rival, some unfair act is necessary to warrant the granting of relief.[12]

Nevertheless, certain practices, even within such a system, are unconscionable in the opinion of most people. The most extreme doctrines of *laissez faire* assumed a certain restraint upon individuals, either moral restraint from within themselves or legal restraint from without. The right to compete was conceived as being a right to compete by increasing one's own efficiency and to gain trade by charging lower prices or by giving better quality or service than a competitor. It is only reasonable that certain competitive practices should have been condemned. That the practices listed above come under the general category of *fraud* is recognized by Nims when he says,

[11] Milton Handler, "Unfair Competition," *Iowa Law Review*, XXI (1936), 183.
[12] Nims, *op. cit.*, p. 442.

"It seems, now, that the term 'Unfair Competition' may be applied to the legal rules regulating all acts done in trade which are tainted with fraud." [13] Another writer on the meaning of unfair competition says, "Probably no exact definition of the term can be given. What is unfair depends too much upon the special circumstances and conditions of each case. According to Justice Hough, *unfair competition* consists of selling goods by means that shock judicial sensibilities." [14]

This excursion into the legal bases of unfair competition may be briefly summarized. In general an act to be *unfair* must have two characteristics. It must involve injury to a competitor or trade rival, which injury must be caused by acts which are characterized by fraud, or are "contrary to good conscience," or "shock the judicial sensibilities," or are otherwise unlawful. "Misrepresentation, misappropriation, diversion of trade, interference with trade relations, attacks upon competitors — these are the stuff out of which the law of unfair competition was built." [15] This is as near to a definition as one can arrive. Each practice is to be considered "with reference to the character and circumstances of the business." The public injury or interest is a minor factor. The essence of the matter appears to be a private wrong perpetrated by unconscionable means.

It is appropriate at this point to indicate just what remedies have existed at law and in equity in such cases of unfair competition.[16] For the most part suits for unfair competition are brought in equity where the relief is twofold, the issue of an injunction and a decree for an accounting of profits as an element of damage. Unless the evidence is conflicting and doubtful a preliminary injunction will generally be issued.

[13] *Ibid.*, p. 23.

[14] C. G. Haines, "Efforts to Define Unfair Competition," *Yale Law Journal*, XXIX (1919), 19.

[15] Handler, *op. cit.*, p. 212.

[16] For an extensive treatment of relief in these cases, *cf.* Nims, *op. cit.*, chap. XXIII.

Sometimes, in trade-mark and like cases, if a preliminary injunction is not issued, the defendant will be required pending decision to keep a record of sales in order to aid in estimating profits if the contentions of plaintiff are sustained. Injunctions will be granted to prevent threatened acts of unfair competition as well as to prevent the continued practice of such acts. Most cases of unfair competition can be pressed in a court of law for damages, as well as in equity for injunction and profits. In cases where the profits of the defendant are not considered adequate compensation for damages to the plaintiff, equity courts have adopted various devices to compensate the plaintiff adequately without forcing recourse to a second action at law. For the present purpose, the fact to be noted is that in cases arising from private action in the courts the plaintiff receives not only relief from the unfair practice but damages as well, while in cases arising under section 5 of the Federal Trade Commission Act, to be considered in later chapters, there is no accounting of profits or damages, the Commission merely issuing an order to cease and desist.

Coercion, Intimidation, and Force. The second restriction upon competitive practices at common law concerned certain practices which, while in themselves legal, were condemned when exercised by business organizations or associations which had a predominant position in the market.[17] This principle was only beginning to be recognized at law in 1914. In fact, the earlier decisions had been against interference, but with the increasing importance of large-scale combinations and associations and perhaps in response to public opinion on this subject, the courts in several states began to grant relief from various competitive practices. In particular, the courts began to grant relief from combinations formed to cut off a competitor's supplies or to destroy his market. These cases generally involved associations

---

[17] Kales, *op. cit.*, p. 89.

of manufacturers, wholesalers, and/or retailers, although in some instances a single dealer was able to accomplish his purpose alone. The details of the practices which were prohibited varied. There were agreements by associations of wholesalers and/or retailers not to purchase from concerns which were supplying price-cutters or competing firms which were otherwise considered "illegitimate."[18] There was a voluntary association of manufacturers, quarriers, and polishers of granite, whose members agreed to have no business dealings with any similar concerns outside the association, an agreement which was enforced by means of fines.[19] There was concerted action by three newspapers which refused to accept advertisements from anyone who paid the advertising charges of a fourth, whose charges were 25 per cent higher than those of the three newspapers which were in agreement.[20] Again, dealers' associations, in order to coerce "illegitimate" competitors, circularized the customers of these competitors and thus destroyed their market. Finally, there were cases where attempts had been made to force competitors to comply with the demands of an association by interfering with their labor relations.[21]

The general basis of the decision in these cases was that the practice involved coercion, intimidation, or force. One of the more interesting of these decisions from the point of view of the economist was *Martell v. White* in which Judge Hammand pointed out that if one is to plead the right to compete as one wishes on the doctrine that "the great public are best subserved . . . it is manifest that the right of competition furnishes no justification for an act done by the use of means which in their nature are in violation of the principle upon which it rests."[22]

[18] *Brown & Allen et al. v. Jacobs' Pharmacy Co.*, 115 Ga. 429 (1902).

[19] *Martell v. White*, 185 Mass. 255 (1904).

[20] *State ex rel. Durner v. Huegin*, 110 Wis. 189 (1901).

[21] See Davies, *op. cit.*, pp. 395–403 for instances of these various practices.

[22] 185 Mass. 255, 260–61 (1904).

Here is a recognition of the fact that competition is something more than an end in itself.

That in some jurisdictions the common law was beginning to deal with a narrow class of practices which become unfair when exercised by an association occupying a predominant position in the market cannot be doubted. But the movement was slow. With respect to this type of practice, more was to be hoped for under the state and federal laws on restraint of trade and monopoly.

INTERSTATE COMMERCE ACT

Statutory regulation of trade practices and competitive methods in the United States did not originate in 1914. On the contrary, the regulation of trade practices has been intimately associated with our trust policy from the very first. The beginning of a legislative policy by the Federal Government with respect to large-scale industry may be dated by the passage of the Interstate Commerce Act of 1887. Although the principal subject of legislation was the railroads, an important motive for this legislation was the desire to curb large industrial enterprises which were enjoying railroad rebates.[23] The primary problem was not excessive earnings of the railroads, but rather the inequity to the public of discrimination in one form or another. It was seen that certain forms of discrimination, forced on the railroads by the trusts, tended to impair railroad earnings and furthered the development of monopoly. The problem of railroad discrimination and its tendency to foster monopoly continued to be an important subject of legislation until 1910.[24]

[23] J. D. Clark, *The Federal Trust Policy* (Baltimore: Johns Hopkins Press, 1931), chap. II.

[24] I. L. Sharfman, *The Interstate Commerce Commission* (New York: The Commonwealth Fund, 1931), I, 52 *et seq.*

SHERMAN ACT: CONGRESSIONAL INTENT

The Sherman Act of 1890 was couched in general legal terms and was aimed at monopoly and the restraint of trade. Just what was intended by the act we need not consider at this point. It is sufficient to note that no great amount of discussion was devoted to the economic meaning or purpose of the act. However, the record does show that the Congressional leaders did intend that the act should reach certain practices which *prevent competition* and *restrain the freedom to compete.* Specific mention was made of railroad rebating, local price-cutting, and resale price maintenance contracts.[25] The evidence seems conclusive that the sponsors of the Sherman Act in the Senate were especially interested in regulating practices in competition. In fact, the original Sherman bill introduced in the Senate was directed at "all arrangements, contracts . . . made with a view or which tend, to prevent full and free competition. . . ."[26] After the bill went to the Senate Judiciary Committee for revision, it emerged as a bill condemning "restraint of trade," but there is no indication that a change of purpose was intended.[27]

[25] See the discussion by Senator Culberson, *Congressional Record,* XXI (1890), 4089.

[26] S. 1, 51st Cong., 1st Sess. (1889), reprinted in *Bills and Debates in Congress Relating to Trusts,* I, 69. (Three volumes compiled by the Attorney General. The first volume was published as *Senate Document* No. 147, 57th Cong., 2d Sess. This and the two subsequent volumes carrying the material down to 1913 will be referred to as *Bills and Debates.* The three volumes are paged consecutively.)

[27] See the statement of Senator Cummins on this point in 1911: *Congressional Record,* XLVII, 3187. Senator Hoar, Chairman of the Senate Judiciary Committee explained the choice of terms as follows: "We thought it was best to use this general phrase which, as we thought, had an accepted and well-known meaning in the English law, and then after it had been construed by the Court, and a body of decisions had grown up under the law, Congress would be able to make such further amendments as might be found by experience necessary." G. F. Hoar, *Autobiography of Seventy Years* (New York: Scribner's, 1903, 2 vols.), II, 364.

The explanation of the bill to the Senate by Mr. Sherman likewise bears evidence of this interest in methods of competition. Speaking of the substitute which was reported after his original bill had been emasculated, he said, significantly:

> *It* [the substitute bill, S. 1] *does not in the least affect combinations in aid of production where there is free and fair competition.* It is the right of every man to work, labor, and produce any lawful vocation and to transport his production on equal terms and conditions and under like circumstances. . . .
>
> This bill does not seek to cripple combinations of capital and labor, the formation of partnerships or of corporations, but only to prevent and control combinations *made with a view to prevent competition*, or for the restraint of trade, or to increase the profits of the producer at the cost of the consumer. . . .[28]

Again Senator Sherman said:

> I am not opposed to combinations in and of themselves; *I do not care how much men combine for proper objects; but when they combine with a purpose to prevent competition*, so that if a humble man starts a business in opposition to them, solitary and alone, in Ohio or anywhere else, they will crowd him down and *they will sell their product at a loss or give it away in order to prevent competition*, . . . then it is the duty of the courts to intervene and prevent it by injunction. . . .[29]

Finally in describing the recently developed trusts, he said:

> *The sole object of such a combination is to make competition impossible.* It can control the market, raise or lower prices, as will best promote its selfish interests, reduce prices in a particular locality and break down competition and advance prices at will where competitors do not exist. Its governing motive is to increase the profits of the parties composing it. The law of selfishness, uncontrolled by competition, compels it to disregard the interest of the consumer. It dictates terms to transportation companies, it commands the price of labor without fear of strikes *for in its field it allows no competitors.*

---

[28] *Congressional Record*, XXI (1890), 2457. The italics in this and the following four passages are not found in the original.

[29] *Ibid.*, p. 2569.

Such a combination is far more dangerous than any heretofore invented. . . .[30]

Of equal interest as evidence of concern with fair competition were the remarks by Senator Hoar in defense of the substitute bill as finally passed.

The great thing that this bill does, except affording a remedy, is *to extend the common law principles, which protected fair competition in trade* in old times in England, to international and interstate commerce in the United States.[31]

And in answer to the question as to whether an enterprise would be considered a monopoly if because of superior skill it alone received all orders for a particular article, he replied:

The word "monopoly" is a merely technical term which has a clear and legal significance, and it is this: It is *the sole engrossing to a man's self by means which prevent other men from engaging in fair competition with him.*[32]

It may fairly be concluded that the sponsors of the Sherman Act had in mind a restricted group of methods of competition which may be pursued by enterprises having a dominant position in their market to eliminate competitors or restrict the entrance of new competitors.[33] Their intention was to prohibit obstacles to fair competition. Although the meaning of the term "fair" was not explained, the general purpose seems to have been to preserve not a perfectly or purely competitive market in the economic sense, but rather the freedom of individuals to remain in or enter a particular line of manufacture or commerce without being exposed to competitive methods and

---

[30] *Congressional Record*, XXI (1890), 2457.

[31] *Ibid.*, p. 3152.

[32] *Loc. cit.*

[33] The contrary view is taken by the National Industrial Conference Board in its study, *Public Regulation of Competitive Practices* (New York: rev. ed. 1929), p. 43, note 2.

competitive powers which a monopoly position enables its possessor to exercise. The concept was vague, for the problem was new and relatively unexplored.[34]

CONGRESSIONAL CONSIDERATION OF UNFAIR METHODS 1890–1910

Further evidence that Congress prior to the legislation of 1914 had in mind the curbing of certain competitive practices is indicated by the proposed bills introduced in Congress. Many competitive practices were recognized as being closely associated with the trust problem such as agreements not to sell below a common fixed price, resale price maintenance, factor agreements and exclusive dealing arrangements, local and personal discrimination, compelling a competitor to sell out or to cease doing business, and selling one's product below cost or giving it away.[35] As early as 1903 a bill [36] introduced in the House proposed to declare "unfair and dishonest competition in trade . . . unlawful"; and still earlier, in 1888, a bill was introduced defining the term "trust" as including "a combination of capital or skill by two or more persons, firms, or associations . . . with intent to obstruct or hinder fair competition. . . ." [37] Perusal of the Congressional debates from 1890 to 1912 likewise shows evidence of increasing concern with "unfair," "oppressive," or "illegal" practices and with such tactics as discrimination, factor agreements, selling at less than cost, and giving away of product free. Consideration was given to factor agreements, local discrimination, and railroad rebates as causes of combination by the Industrial Commission

---

[34] The thesis that the Sherman Act was intended to prohibit unfair methods of competition was supported by A. A. Young, "The Sherman Act and the New Anti-Trust Legislation," *Journal of Political Economy*, XXIII (1915), 219.

[35] *Cf. Bills and Debates, passim.*

[36] H. R. 2536, 58th Cong., 1st Sess. — 1903. (*Bills and Debates*, II, 1687.)

[37] H. R. 11534, 50th Cong., 1st Sess. — 1888. (*Bills and Debates*, I, 67.)

appointed by Congress in 1898 and reporting in 1900 and 1901.[38]

THE CORPORATION COMMISSIONER

The Corporation Commission created by Congress in 1903 [39] to investigate and report on "the organization, conduct, and management of the business of any corporation, joint stock company or corporate combination engaged in commerce among the several states and with foreign nations excepting common carriers" concerned itself from its inception with the relation between the trust problem and unfair competition. In its first report, it noted that there were two legislative approaches to the problem: first, the prevention of monopoly and the maintenance of a condition of competition; second, the regulation of the methods of competition. Commissioner Garfield characterized the first as "singularly futile" and the second as "fundamentally correct." [40]

The second class of legislation, usually a part of "anti-trust" laws, but having no necessary connection with combinations or trusts, is that which prohibits rebates, discriminations, and unfair competition. This legislation is based on an entirely different principle and is entirely correct. It is aimed not at the restraint of combination as such, or the maintenance of competition, but at regulating the methods of competition. It recognizes the irresistible tendency toward combination, and its purposes are to make certain that combination is reached only through just, fair and proper means.[41]

Similar views were expressed in subsequent reports,[42] particularly by Commissioners Garfield and Smith. In the report

[38] U. S. Industrial Commission, *Report on Trusts and Industrial Combinations* (Washington: Government Printing Office, 1900), I, 20–21, 24–29, 34; XIII (1901), xxiii–xxv, xxx, xxxv.

[39] Public No. 87, 57th Cong., 2d Sess. (1903).

[40] U. S. Bureau of Corporations, *Report of the Commissioner*, 1904 (Washington: Government Printing Office, 1904), p. 41.

[41] *Loc. cit.*

[42] *Ibid.*, 1905, p. 7; 1907, p. 5; 1909, p. 4; 1912, p. 3.

of 1908 Commissioner Smith advocated the recognition of combination as inevitable and the adoption of a policy of regulation
which would include a consideration of the "intent, methods,
and effects" of combination.

> If we are to do anything effective with the corporation question, we
> must make an advance on our present legislation. The practical
> object is to see that business opportunity and the highways of com-
> merce are kept equally open to all; to prevent fraud, special privilege
> and unfair competition.
> To do this we must recognize concentration, supervise it, and regu-
> late it. We must do this positively, through an active federal agency,
> and not merely by the negative prohibitions of penal law. We must
> have coöperation with corporate interests as far as possible. We
> must have, of course, effective penal laws against specific forms of
> unfair competition, and the misuse of monopoly powers.[43]

The opinions as presented in these reports of the Corporation
Commissioner represent a significant view as to the place of the
regulation of competitive practices in a regulatory scheme. Too
much of the discussion of the problem of unfair competition
has been dominated by the view that the problem is one of
"preserving competition," of "preventing monopoly," or of
limiting the acquisition of monopoly power by certain methods.
These reports recognized the problem not as one of "monopoly"
versus "competition," but rather as the problem of the use and
abuse of monopoly power. This involves a frank recognition of
the existence of considerable concentration and the acquisition
of market positions involving significant monopoly power. Followed to its logical conclusion such a view would seek to distinguish desirable and undesirable behavior by those firms
endowed with power to affect the market by their individual
action. It would recognize that many so-called unfair methods
of competition not only lead to the acquisition of monopoly
power but also presuppose the existence of significant monopoly

[43] *Ibid.*, 1908, p. 5.

elements for their successful practice. As will develop, the failure to recognize this fact has made the problem of devising an effective public policy with reference to competitive practices more difficult. A frank recognition that we must evolve a system of regulating the use of monopoly power as a competitive weapon makes the task appear more formidable but is a necessary preliminary to any solution of the problem.

CHAPTER III

THE SHERMAN ACT AND BUSINESS PRACTICES

As WAS INDICATED in Chapter II there is considerable evidence that the sponsors of the Sherman Anti-trust Act were concerned in large part with the exclusive, coercive, or predatory practices used by large concerns as a method of obtaining size or of maintaining or extending their monopoly power. A survey of the enforcement of the act indicates that the courts have likewise interpreted it in large part as a statute dealing with competitive practices and methods. The act uses the terms "restraint of trade" and "monopolize," both of which had acquired meaning at common law previous to their inclusion in this statute. In using such terms Congress invited the courts to apply tests of legality in the general spirit of those which had been developed in the common law. While it was some time before it became clear what the courts' general line of interpretation of the act would be, it became increasingly clear that the emphasis of the courts would not be upon size *per se*, nor upon the possession of monopoly power in the economic sense,[1] nor finally upon the

---

[1] The economist in speaking of monopoly power means power over price or output. Numbers in the market or proportionate control of total output of a particular product would be possible measures. But the availability and price of substitutes, the urgency of the desire for the product are equally significant. One measure of the degree of monopoly power, which depends upon the elasticity of the demand for the product of the individual firm, is that of Mr. A. P. Lerner. He defines the degree of monopoly power exercised as equal to $\dfrac{\text{Price} - \text{Marginal Cost}}{\text{Price}}$ ("The Concept of Monopoly and the Measurement of Monopoly Power," *Review of Economic Studies*, I (1934), 157–175. For some of the limitations of such a concept *cf.* J. T. Dunlop, "Price Flexibility and the 'Degree of Monopoly,'" *The Quarterly Journal of Economics*, LIII (1939), 534). Each of these measures in its

legal form which a combination of previously competing firms might take, but rather upon the practices which a firm pursued in gaining or maintaining its market power. As one legal commentator has noted, by 1911 "The Sherman Act had evolved from an anti-trust act into an act relating to the legal control of competitive methods." [2]

The decisions involving the Sherman Act fall into two general groups, those dealing with close combinations, i.e. arrangements such as mergers, trusts, or holding companies by which additional market control is concentrated in the hands of a single unit of business, and loose combinations, i.e. agreements or other arrangements by which market control is gained through the joint action of two or more independent business units which maintain their independence of action with reference to all matters internal to the firm and most external to the firm except those definitely agreed upon as the object of the joint action. It is with the impact of the Sherman Law upon the practices of both close and loose combinations that this chapter is concerned. The policy of the Sherman Act as it has been interpreted to date has been to scrutinize the close combinations to determine whether or not there is evidence that their formation or existence interferes unreasonably with the freedom of others to enter the market, and to scrutinize loose agreements to determine whether or not such rivals as there are in the market have unreasonably restrained competition among them-

---

usual form has the disadvantage of referring to a moment or period of time. A relevant factor to consider from the point of view of public policy in a situation involving significant monopoly power in terms of any one of these measures is the probable effects of present price and profit prospects upon future conditions. This will depend upon, among other things, the ease of entry to and exit from the industry which will be affected by the legal obstacles, availability of materials and labor, ease of access to consumers, extent of consumer preference, size of investment necessary, and the practices of the entrenched firms with reference to new rivals.

[2] J. A. McLaughlin, "Legal Control of Competitive Methods," *Iowa Law Review*, XXI (1936), 280.

selves. This is but a brief and rough statement of the tenor of the courts' policies in interpreting the act, useful as a starting point for subsequent discussion.

COMBINATIONS AND THEIR PRACTICES

In dealing with close combinations whether by use of the trustee device, the holding company, merger, or consolidations the decisions of the courts have been concerned to protect the freedom of competition, that is to insure that the channels of trade should be kept open to the entrance of new firms. The courts have reiterated that neither mergers and consolidations nor the acquisition of large size or preponderance of position in the market is illegal *per se*. This became clear after the decisions in the *Standard Oil*[3] and *American Tobacco*[4] cases in 1911.

The history of the development of both of these trusts is well known. While the factors in these cases which impressed the courts with the illegality of the combinations were many, the obvious intent and policy of the trusts in question to monopolize or reserve to themselves their respective markets by exclusive, coercive, and predatory practices bulked large. Speaking of the history of the Standard Oil Companies in the period prior to 1882, by which time they had acquired control of over 90 per cent of the business of refining of oil, the Supreme Court stated:

. . . we think no disinterested mind can survey the period in question without being irresistibly driven to the conclusion that the very genius for commercial development and organization which it would seem was manifested from the beginning soon begot an intent and purpose to exclude others which was frequently manifested by acts and dealings wholly inconsistent with the theory that they were made with the single conception of advancing the development of business power by usual methods, but which on the contrary neces-

---

[3] *Standard Oil Co. et al. v. U. S.*, 221 U. S. 1 (1911).
[4] *U. S. v. American Tobacco Co. et al.*, 221 U. S. 106 (1911).

sarily involved the intent to drive others from the field and to exclude them from their right to trade and thus accomplish the mastery which was the end in view.[5]

This and other evidence were determining factors. They gave rise "to the *prima facie* presumption of intent and purpose to maintain the dominancy over the oil industry, not as a result of normal methods of industrial development, but by new means of combination which were resorted to in order that greater power might be added than would otherwise have arisen . . . the whole with a purpose of excluding others from the trade. . . ."[6]

While much was left undetermined by these two decisions of 1911 concerning the criteria of legality under the Sherman Act, it became clear that a high degree of control over the market associated with a clear intent to use this power to exclude competitors transgressed the bounds of legality. Certain practices such as rebates, local price cutting, restrictive agreements not to compete, exclusive dealing arrangements with distributors, espionage, and the sponsoring of fighting brands or bogus independents when undertaken by firms holding a dominant position appear in the guise of coercive, exclusive or predatory practices. They appear as presumptive evidence of an intent and effect to monopolize or restrain trade. It is not the individual practices in themselves which are illegal. It is the totality of the situation — the size, the intent and effect, the practices and methods — which determines the illegality of the action.

The general outlines of policy which characterized these decisions of the Supreme Court in 1911 seem with some notable exceptions to have foreshadowed the subsequent enforcement of the act. Shortly after the decision in the *Standard Oil* case, the lower courts entered a decree against the powder trust.[7]

---

[5] 221 U. S. 76.
[6] *Ibid.*, p. 75.
[7] *U. S. v. E. I. DuPont de Nemours & Co. et al.*, 188 Fed. 127 (1911).

E. I. DuPont de Nemours Company was found guilty of restraint of trade and a decree was entered breaking up the
company. The court found that from 1872 to 1902 there had
been an intent by various trade associations to dominate the
industry through agreements concerning price, output, and the
sharing of territories. Subsequently, the same purpose was
effected even more successfully by a series of corporate combinations and the holding company device. In the pursuit of its
purpose the dominant firm had resorted to rebates, local price
discrimination, and other methods designed to force competitors to submit to its desires or to enter the combination.
Dominance in the industry combined with an intent to monopolize as evidenced by predatory practices were again the distinguishing characteristics.

The decision of the lower court in the proceedings against
the Keystone Watch Company is likewise pertinent.[8] The
company had by purchase acquired control of several other
companies making watch cases and movements, some of which
were competitive with and others complementary to its own
lines. It had also adopted a distributive policy with reference
to its products involving resale price maintenance and exclusive
dealing which it enforced by threatening to refuse to sell to
jobbers not abiding by its distributive policy. In its decision
the court noted that "A merchant may without offense add one
department to another as his business prospers. . . . Size does
not of itself restrain trade or injure the public." [9] Consequently,
the court did not feel that the acquisitions by the company were
illegal, since the methods were unquestionable. But the use of
its position, however legitimately acquired, to coerce jobbers
and indirectly to deprive competitors of free access to the
market was another matter ". . . what the defendant company
did was either to close already existing and already utilized
outlets; or to narrow them materially, so far as the cases of its

[8] *U. S. v. Keystone Watch Case Co. et al.*, 218 Fed. 502 (1915).

[9] *Ibid.*, p. 510.

competitors are concerned; and we think the proposition need not be discussed that this was pro tanto a direct and unlawful restraint of trade." [10]

In the decision in the *Eastman Kodak* case the courts likewise showed concern over the use by the defendant of predatory practices in acquiring and maintaining its control of about 80 per cent of the trade in photographic supplies and materials.[11] Here the court concluded that it had suppressed competition by engrossing to itself the best supplies of raw paper stocks, by buying up competitors' plants upon condition that the vendors would not reënter the business, and finally by imposing upon dealers "arbitrary and oppressive terms of sale inconsistent with fair dealing, and suppressing competition," [12] more specifically by requiring the maintenance of resale prices by dealers and inducing exclusive dealing through a system of special bonuses. In another decision in the lower courts at about the same time the absence of evidence of a misuse of power was a ground for dismissing the case. Thus, while the court found that the American Can Company originally intended to monopolize the market, it found no evidence that the company had since its early days actually used its power in a prejudicial manner.[13] Moreover, the court noted the existence of significant competitors which were presumed to limit distinctly its power over price.

More significant, however, as an indication of public policy in anti-trust actions are the cases which have gone to the Supreme Court. Unfortunately the cases since 1911 involving close combinations which have gone to the Supreme Court have been few and the attending circumstances such as to make the meaning of the decisions inconclusive.

The first of these decisions was that in the United Shoe

---

[10] *Ibid.*, p. 512.
[11] *U. S. v. Eastman Kodak Co. et al.*, 226 Fed. 62 (1915).
[12] *Ibid.*, p. 80.
[13] *U. S. v. American Can Co. et al.*, 234 Fed. 1019 (1916).

Machinery case.[14] The United Shoe Machinery Company had been formed in 1899 by the combination of seven independent shoe machinery companies. These companies together controlled about 90 per cent of the shoe machinery produced in the United States, a control based primarily upon patent rights. The original combination was in large part a combination of firms producing different types of machines, of a complementary or non-competitive sort. Subsequently, the Company expanded by acquiring various properties and patents on rival processes from Thomas Plant and acquiring other properties for the manufacture of brushes, findings, and other products ancillary to the shoe machinery industry. The government's attack upon the combination was threefold; it challenged both the original combination and the subsequent additions as being in restraint of trade and it attacked the restrictive clauses which the company inserted in all its contracts for leasing its machinery. These restrictive clauses were of various sorts, but were all intended to insure that the lessees of the United Shoe Machinery Company would use its machines exclusively for all processes, thus enabling the Company to engross to itself the manufacture of machines for processes on which it did not have sole patent rights as well as for those on which it did have such rights.

The Court handed down a decision against the government. With reference to the original combination the Court noted that this was a combination of non-competitive firms, each of which had a dominance in its own field prior to the combination. The subsequent expansion it found was made in the normal course of trade by transactions in which sale was consummated without coercion. "The company, indeed, has magnitude, but it is at once the result and cause of efficiency. . . . Patrons are given the benefits of the improvements made by the company and new machines are substituted for the old ones without disproportionate charge. There has been saving as well in the

[14] *U. S. v. United Shoe Machinery Co.*, 247 U. S. 32 (1918).

cost of manufacture of shoes." [15] As to the prohibitive clauses in the leases the Court concluded that these were not unreasonable. It noted that there had been similar clauses in the leases of the constituent members prior to formation of the combination and that there were certain economic advantages to be achieved by using the various machines in the proper combination. It commented that a patentee had no power to force its device upon buyers and expressed an inability to find any evidence that the business of the Company had been obtained by coercion. The installations of the machines of the United Shoe Machinery Company, it believed, had been made voluntarily, on the merits of the machines. The Court was not impressed by the effect of the restrictive leases, once the dominance of the Company was established in certain lines, in limiting actual or potential competition in the production of unpatented machines or patented machines which might be used for single manufacturing processes. This is an outstanding case where the courts have failed to restrict the use of power, legitimately acquired, to cut off the access of rivals to the market. It is a case where exclusive practices of a dominant firm have been condoned. However, it is significant to note that the decision was rendered by a majority of only four Justices, two Justices disqualified themselves and three dissented. [16]

The next major decision by the Supreme Court involving a merger was that in the proceedings against the United States Steel Corporation. [17] The Corporation had been formed in 1901 by a combination of three groups of interests whose plants had achieved various degrees of integration but did nevertheless in some measure supplement one another. The combination at the

[15] *Ibid.*, p. 56.

[16] The Department of Justice in its *Brief for the United States on the Meaning of the Sherman Act* submitted in the proceeding of *U. S. v. Aluminum Co. of America et al.* (Southern District of New York, Equity No. 85–73, Sept. 1938), discounts the significance of this case for this reason.

[17] *U. S. v. United States Steel Corporation et al.*, 251 U. S. 417 (1920).

time of its inception had a preponderant control of the output of iron and steel products,[18] although this control subsequently declined. During the period from its formation until proceedings were instituted against the Corporation in 1911 there was no evidence that it had pursued any coercive, exclusive, or predatory practices with respect to its competitors. Quite to the contrary, the evidence suggested that between 1906 and 1911 the United States Steel Corporation was able to exercise control over the market only by seeking their coöperation. The industry had experienced various degrees and forms of collusion, such as the famous Gary dinners, interspersed with periods of aggressive competition.

The lower court had dismissed the case, two of the Judges finding that the Corporation had been formed with no intent to monopolize, and two others finding that although there had been an intent to monopolize, the attempt had been ineffective.[19] The latter noted that the Corporation had never misused its power against its competitors or labor. The Supreme Court, with two Justices not participating and three dissenting, likewise decided against the government. The majority of the Court, while admitting that the intent had been to monopolize or dominate the trade, found that the Corporation had been ineffective. The sporadic competition, the pools, and the Gary dinners were taken to prove the absence of monopoly power ". . . it is difficult to see how there can be restraint of trade when there is no restraint of competitors in the trade nor complaints by customers."[20] Moreover, the Court was impressed with the economies which were attained by the original com-

---

[18] It produced about 60 per cent of the pig iron used for steel making and anywhere from 40 to 83 per cent of various leading finished products. Eliot Jones, *The Trust Problem in the United States* (New York: The Macmillan Co., 1921), pp. 206–7.

[19] 223 Fed. 55 (1915).

[20] 251 U. S. 451. The Justices were agreed that there had been collusion in restraint of trade, but noted that this had terminated.

bination and by the practical exigencies of the situation. "Our present purpose is not retrospect for itself, however instructive, but practical decision upon existing conditions, that we may not by their disturbance produce, or even risk, consequences of a concern that cannot now be computed." [21]

This decision suggests that size or intent to monopolize are in themselves not illegal. In the absence of evidence of coercive or exclusive practices pursued against competitors or labor, and in the presence of evidence of sporadic competition, a declining relative position, and the expediency of not disturbing established business relationships, large size and a former but ineffective intent to monopolize were condoned. This decision, interesting as it is from many points of view, acquires significance for us because of the emphasis by the courts on the absence of predatory use of its power. The Court specifically noted the absence of a long list of practices which had been traditionally associated with the trusts.[22]

The third important case to reach the courts involving the legality of a merger was that involving the International Harvester Company.[23] This was a decision in a case instituted by the government seeking additional relief under a decree which had been entered against the Company as a result of a previous action. At the time of the formation of the International Harvester combination in 1902, it controlled about 80 per cent of the harvesting machinery in the United States. Although its proportionate control of the market had subsequently declined, during the period from 1911 to 1923 it still controlled about 65 per cent of the sales. In the decree of 1918 the Company agreed to dispose of three of the lines of harvesting machinery which it had acquired by combination and the plants in which

---

[21] *Ibid.*, p. 444. The combination was formed in 1901, the action brought in 1911, and the decision rendered by the Supreme Court in 1920.
[22] *Ibid.*, pp. 440–41.
[23] *U. S. v. International Harvester Company et al.*, 274 U. S. 693 (1927).

these lines of machinery were manufactured.[24] The decree likewise prohibited the Harvester Company from having more than one representative or agent for the sale of its product in any city or town. In many communities it had previously had several dealers, each operating under exclusive agreements or understandings. The purpose of the decree was stated to be "to restore competitive conditions." [25] The technique envisaged was the reëstablishment of rivals by the sale of production facilities and brand-names, and the opening of the channels of distribution to these and other companies by restricting the International Harvester Company to one dealer in a community. The effectiveness of the decree was questioned and in 1923 the Attorney General entered a supplemental petition for a revision of the decree. The lower court dismissed the petition and its decision was affirmed upon appeal to the Supreme Court.

This review of the decisions in cases of close combinations indicates clearly the concern of the courts in interpreting the Sherman Act to preserve the freedom of competition by enjoining the use of monopolistic power to exclude or coerce competitors. The concern of the courts in these cases has been to preserve the freedom of entrance to the trade. Size or predominance in the market *per se* are not controlling. The price and production policies of the firm are not the principal objects of scrutiny. The important factors are the intention and effect of large firms to use their position for the extension or preservation of their power by predatory practices. The act, so far as close combinations are concerned, has been enforced so as to protect competitors, actual or potential, from the arbitrary

[24] For a summary of the litigation involving the International Harvester Company and a reprint of the decree *cf.* Federal Trade Commission, *Report on the Agricultural Implement and Machinery Industry*, 75th Cong., 3d Sess., House Document No. 702 (Washington: Government Printing Office, 1938), chap. III.

[25] *Ibid.*, p. 157.

action of their rivals. In this it has much in common with the law of unfair competition, since its emphasis is upon the protection of private business interests from injuries by rivals. Within these limits the firm is allowed wide discretion in its business practices and market policies.

In certain proceedings, it is true, the courts have held combinations, mergers, and holding companies illegal quite apart from predatory or exclusive practices aimed at outsiders. But these were situations where technical and economic conditions precluded the entrance of new competitors, so that combination *per se* would eliminate once and for all every potential competitor. Such a situation might arise from the combination of two major competing railroad lines,[26] or the control of all terminal facilities affording entrance to a major railroad junction.[27] But these are circumstances of a clearly exceptional sort.

VOLUNTARY ASSOCIATIONS AND THEIR PRACTICES

In contrast to the lenient policy with reference to the formation of close combinations and their practices short of action of an exclusive sort has been the policy with reference to loose combinations and voluntary agreements. The voluntary association of independent business firms for the furtherance of their joint interests is not illegal in itself, but the courts have in each case scrutinized carefully the purposes and practices of such associations. Joint action to eliminate unethical practices or genuine waste, to promote technological advance or knowledge of market conditions, these and many other practices have been recognized as clearly legal. But the law has looked with suspicion upon any attempts to control prices or production by joint action even though this is done in the name of business ethics or the stabilization of trade. The attempts of business groups to promote industrial self-government, to promote codes

---

[26] *Northern Securities Company v. U. S.*, 193 U. S. 197 (1904).
[27] *U. S. v. Terminal Railroad Association*, 224 U. S. 383 (1912).

of ethics or of fair business practices, to eliminate "ruinous competition," and to promote stabilized market conditions have been narrowly circumscribed.

This restrictive policy is one which the courts have followed with remarkable consistency. In one of the earliest cases to be decided under the act the Supreme Court decided that an agreement upon rates and other traffic regulations among some eighteen independent railroad carriers whose lines extended from the Mississippi to the Pacific was illegal.[28] And shortly thereafter, Justice Taft, speaking for the lower court, in *U. S. v. Addyston Pipe and Steel Co.*,[29] held that a loose association among the manufacturers of cast iron pipe had violated the law by allocating customers and fixing prices. He made it quite clear that although some restraints of trade were legal at common law when they were merely ancillary to some legitimate purpose, market control of the sort in question was illegal quite apart from the reasonableness of the prices and of the allocations of customers. Arguments about the need to check ruinous competition were of no avail.

Much has been said in regard to the relaxing of the original strictness of the common law in declaring contracts in restraint of trade void as conditions of civilization and public policy have changed, and the argument drawn therefrom is that the law now recognizes that competition may be so ruinous as to injure the public, and, therefore, that contracts made with a view to check such ruinous competition and regulate prices, though in restraint of trade, and having no other purpose, will be upheld. We think this conclusion is unwarranted by the authorities when all of them are considered. It is true that certain rules for determining whether a covenant in restraint of trade ancillary to the main purpose of a contract was reasonably adapted and limited to the necessary protection of a party in the carrying out of such purpose have been somewhat modified by modern authorities. . . . But these [cases] all involved contracts in which the covenant in restraint of trade was ancillary

[28] *U. S. v. Trans-Missouri Freight Association*, 166 U. S. 290 (1897).
[29] 85 Fed. 271 (1898).

to the main and lawful purpose of the contract, and was necessary to the protection of the covenantee. . . .[30]

This interpretation of the act has been upheld repeatedly to the present time.

In 1927 in the *Trenton Potteries* decision a trade association of manufacturers controlling some 82 per cent of the business of vitreous sanitary pottery in the United States was found to have violated the act.[31] The association had established a central bureau for the circulation of information about prices and discounts and had succeeded by agreement in restricting the sale of pottery to a special group known as "legitimate jobbers" and in maintaining fairly uniform prices and discounts. In enjoining the association the Court again held that such agreements were illegal in themselves quite apart from the reasonableness of the prices; to hold otherwise the Court insisted would place an impossible burden upon the courts.

In a recent session of the Supreme Court this position was reaffirmed in two major decisions involving the gasoline industry. The first case involved the use of a patent to induce price maintenance throughout the industry.[32] The Ethyl Gasoline Corporation controlled the patents on ethyl fluid which it manufactured and sold to licensed refiners to be mixed with regular gasoline to improve its performance. It licensed the major refiners to use its product, but stipulated in its licenses that the refiners should sell motor fuel containing this fluid only to other refiners or to jobbers who had been licensed by the Ethyl Corporation. Unlicensed refiners and jobbers, then, were excluded from handling the Ethyl product. Moreover, the refiners were specifically required to maintain a prescribed differential between the prices of regular and ethyl gasoline. The crux of the matter lay in the criteria adopted by Ethyl

---

[30] *Ibid.*, p. 283.
[31] *U. S. v. Trenton Potteries Co. et al.*, 273 U. S. 392 (1927).
[32] *Ethyl Gasoline Corporation, et al. v. U. S.*, 60 Sup. Ct. 618 (1940).

Corporation in granting licenses to the jobbers. It customarily investigated each jobber to determine the extent to which he followed the "business ethics" of the industry, which meant compliance with the "marketing policies and posted prices of the major oil companies or the market leaders among them" in the jobber's locality. Among these major oil companies was the Standard Oil Company of New Jersey, which owns one-half of the capital stock of the Ethyl Gasoline Corporation. Here, then, was a scheme through which a major member in the gasoline industry was able to police the price policies of refiners and jobbers, many of whom competed with it in the retail market, through its licensing system based on patent rights. The Court held that these practices, clearly illegal in the absence of patent protection, were equally illegal in its presence.

In the other recent oil decision the Court held a scheme for stabilizing the tank car price in the spot market to be illegal.[33] There was involved here an elaborate scheme by which the major oil companies selling in the Mid-Western area agreed to buy up the distress oil offered by the independent refiners thereby raising the tank car prices in the spot markets in the East-Texas and Mid-Continent fields. The independent refiners, lacking their own outlets for oil, customarily disposed of their oil on the spot market, often depressing the price significantly. Since the usual contracts between refiners and jobbers throughout the industry tied the jobber price to the price in the spot market, the sales policies of the independent refiners were of great concern even to the major integrated companies. Consequently, as an outgrowth of the NRA code experience each of the major companies adopted the practice of buying certain quantities of distress gasoline from designated independents, euphemistically called "dancing partners."

The obvious purpose and effect was to raise the tank car prices in the spot market, and as a result of the practice of the

[33] *U. S. v. Socony-Vacuum Oil Co., Inc. et al.*, 60 Sup. Ct. 811 (1940).

major companies of selling to jobbers at prices tied to these
spot prices this tended to raise the prices to jobbers and consumers as well. The defendants urged that they had been
attempting to eliminate competitive abuses and to stabilize the
industry. Moreover, they alleged that this had been done with
the knowledge and acquiescence of certain government departments if not with their connivance. In a five-to-two decision
the Court rejected these defenses and declared the scheme
unlawful.

The elimination of so-called competitive evils is no legal justification for such buying programs. The elimination of such conditions
was sought primarily for its effect on the price structures. Fairer
competitive prices, it is claimed, resulted when distress gasoline was
removed from the market. But such defense is typical of protesta-
tions usually made in price-fixing cases. Ruinous competition, financial disaster, evils of price cutting and the like appear throughout
our history as ostensible justifications for price-fixing. If the so-called
competitive abuses were to be appraised here, the reasonableness of
prices would necessarily become an issue in every price-fixing case.
In that event the Sherman Act would soon become emasculated. . . .
Under the Sherman Act a combination formed for the purpose and
with the effect of raising, depressing, fixing, pegging, or stabilizing
the price of a commodity in interstate or foreign commerce is illegal
per se.[34]

All joint activities of business firms affecting the market have
not been enjoined, however. The courts have recognized that
certain joint activities may serve to promote competition or to
eliminate patently unfair and illegal practices. In the absence
of evidence or reasonable inference that such agreements are
merely the cloak for price or production control, the courts
have imposed no obstacles. In a relatively early decision the
Court sustained the Chicago Board of Trade which had adopted
a rule providing that no wheat should be sold between the close
of business in the afternoon and the opening on the following

[34] 60 Sup. Ct. 843, 844.

morning except at the closing price of the afternoon "call." [35] The Court found that it affected only a part of the market and in general tended to promote competition by restricting the hours of business and making more buyers and sellers available for this sort of business.

The true test of legality is whether the restraint imposed is such as merely regulates and perhaps thereby promotes competition or whether it is such as may suppress or even destroy competition. To determine that question the court must ordinarily consider the facts peculiar to the business to which the restraint is applied; its condition before and after the restraint was imposed; and the nature of the restraint and its effects actual or probable.[36]

The outstanding decision in which the Court countenanced joint activities in the market was that involving the Appalachian Coals Incorporated, an exclusive selling agency formed to dispose of the coal of some 137 producers in the Southern Appalachian area.[37] The selling agency agreed to sell all coal offered by the producers at prices to be determined by the officers of the agency. The professed purpose of the scheme was to increase the sale and production of Appalachian coal through better methods of distribution, extensive advertising and research; to achieve economies in marketing; and to eliminate various deceptive and destructive practices. In its decision the Court considered at length the depressed condition of the trade, the problems of excess capacity, distress coal, the pyramiding of orders to sell, and the depressing effect on the market of the power of large buyers. It took cognizance of the fact that though the effect might be to stabilize prices, the

---

[35] The "call" is a meeting held immediately after the regular session of the exchange at which sales for grain "to arrive" are transacted. *Board of Trade of the City of Chicago et al. v. U. S.*, 246 U. S. 231 (1918).

[36] *Ibid.*, p. 238.

[37] *Appalachian Coals, Inc. v. U. S.*, 288 U. S. 344 (1933). These producers were responsible for about 54 per cent of the bituminous coal produced in their immediate territory.

agency could not fix them. The Court felt that the industry was justified in its attempts to try to recover from its plight.

A coöperative enterprise . . . is not to be condemned as an undue restraint merely because it may effect a change in market conditions, where the changes would be in mitigation of recognized evils and would not impair, but rather foster, fair competitive opportunities. Voluntary action to rescue and preserve these opportunities, and thus to aid in relieving a depressed industry and in reviving commerce by placing competition upon a sounder basis, may be more efficacious than an attempt to provide remedies through legal processes. The fact that the correction of abuses may tend to stabilize a business, or to produce fairer price levels, does not mean that the abuses should go uncorrected or that coöperative endeavor to correct them necessarily constitutes an unreasonable restraint of trade. The intelligent conduct of commerce through the acquisition of full information of all relevant facts may properly be sought by the coöperation of those engaged in trade, although stabilization of trade and more reasonable prices may be the result. . . . Putting an end to injurious practices and the consequent improvement of the competitive position of a group of producers is not a less worthy aim and may be entirely concordant with the public interest, where the group must still meet effective competition in a fair market and neither seeks nor is able to effect a domination of prices.[38]

While it was thought at the time that this decision would clear the way for various schemes for market control and price fixing, the recent decision in the *Socony-Vacuum* case has clearly indicated that this is not so.[39] Wherein lies the difference between the two cases? In the first place, in the coal case there was established a bona fide selling agency for the conduct of market relations, while in the oil case the market functions were conducted by the individual firms by a prearranged scheme. Moreover, the Court in the coal case was very much impressed by the purpose of eliminating "unethical practices" and increasing efficiency, with the price effects only incidental

[38] *Ibid.*, pp. 373–74.
[39] *Cf. supra*, p. 44.

phenomena, while in the oil decision it was inclined to pierce the veil of professed morality only to find an all too obvious intention to raise prices. Finally, although both industries have suffered from the intensity of competition, the circumstances of the industries are sufficiently dissimilar to explain differences in judicial attitudes.[40]

Nowhere has the subtlety of the judicial distinction between lawful and unlawful restraints of trade been better illustrated than by the decisions concerning trade associations and their open-price filing systems. The ostensible purpose of such systems is to circulate among the buyers and sellers in an industry information concerning prices, production, sales, inventories, etc., in order that competition may be more informed, price changes may be more orderly, and undesirable discriminations may be avoided. Systems of various sorts for circulating information concerning prices became common in American industries in the 1920's and it was inevitable that they should be challenged in the courts. It will be instructive to trace the lines of judicial thought through several of the decisions.

The first case of a price-filing system to reach the Supreme Court was that involving the American Hardwood Manufacturers' Association.[41] The scheme adopted by this association called for extensive reports on their production and sales policies by all members. Lists showing prices f.o.b. shipping point were filed monthly and whenever changed. Daily reports of

[40] There is a striking difference in the degree of concentration of market control in the two industries. In the coal industry, the benefits of the program would be widespread. In the case of oil, the most obvious beneficiaries were the refiners, especially the major integrated companies, whose plight is not considered unduly severe.

[41] *American Column and Lumber Co., et al. v. U. S.*, 257 U. S. 377 (1921). The American Hardwood Manufacturers' Association had 400 members, 365 of these members, operating 465 mills, participated in the open-price plan. The participants, while operating only 5 per cent of the number of mills engaged in hardwood manufacture in the country, were responsible for one-third of the total production.

all sales made were filed identifying the buyer and specifying all special terms. Daily shipping reports as well as monthly production and stock reports were required. Provision was made for inspection reports by the Association to check on the grading of lumber by the members in order that the reports might be more intelligible. The Association's duty in turn was to compile the information, to communicate it to the members, and to sponsor monthly meetings. The secretary was required to send out various reports on sales, prices, production, and inventories. He also sent out monthly a summary of the price lists furnished by the members, and a letter analyzing market conditions. The scheme was held to be illegal.[42] The Court was considerably impressed with the extensive discussions in market letters and at monthly meetings of the desirability of controlling production. It noted, furthermore, that these statistical reports differed from customary reports of trade conditions published in trade journals and government periodicals inasmuch as the latter are available to buyers as well as sellers, which these were not, and the customary reports are not reinforced with the exhortations of skilled interpreters, which these were.[43]

The year 1925 saw the development of a less restrictive attitude by the courts toward open-price associations in two instances where the systems were oriented less toward price control than in the earlier cases. The Maple Flooring Manufacturers' Association was an incorporated association of twenty-two firms which were engaged in selling and shipping maple, beech, and birch flooring and all but two of which had

[42] Justices Holmes, Brandeis, and McKenna dissented.
[43] The second decision in which a price-filing scheme was held illegal by the Court involved the linseed oil industry. (*U. S. v. American Linseed Oil Co., et al.*, 262 U. S. 371; 1923.) In so far as interpretation is concerned this added little to the lumber decision. The most important difference between the two schemes was that the linseed oil plan provided for an exchange of information about all quotations, as well as about sales.

their principal places of business in Michigan, Minnesota, or Wisconsin. In 1922 the members produced 70 per cent of the total production of these types of flooring. Although the activities of the Association were various, including coöperative advertising and the standardization and improvement of the product, the government's complaint concerned only four: [44] the computation and distribution among members of the average cost to association members of all dimensions and grades of flooring; the compilation of a booklet showing freight rates on flooring from Cadillac, Michigan; the gathering and dissemination of statistics, especially weekly reports of sales, prices [45] and production, and monthly reports of inventories and unfilled orders; finally, the government complained of meetings at which representatives of the members exchanged views as to problems of the industry.

The Court disposed of the first problem of cost figures by noting that there was no evidence to prove the cost figures did not conform to acceptable cost accounting procedure. Concerning the use of a freight-rate book and basing-point formula, the Court remarked that it was common custom to quote delivered prices and the freight book served a purpose in so far as it enabled prompt quotations of delivered price. It noted that "There is abundant evidence that there were delays in securing quotations of freight rates from the local agents of carriers in towns in which the factories of defendants are located, . . . that the actual aggregate difference between local freight rates for most of defendants' mills and the rate appearing in defendants' freight-rate book based on rates at Cadillac, Michigan, were so small as to be only nominal. . . ." [46] On

[44] *Maple Flooring Manufacturers' Association et al. v. U. S.*, 268 U. S. 563 (1925).

[45] *Ibid.*, p. 573. The names of purchasers of flooring were not reported and after July 1923 the seller was not identified.

[46] *Ibid.*, p. 571.

the matter of the dissemination of trade statistics, the Court took cognizance of the fact that the data on sales and prices dealt only with closed transactions, that the statistics were given wide publicity in trade journals, and that they did not differ essentially from business statistics freely gathered and publicly disseminated in numerous branches of industry. The Court found no evidence of exceptional activities at the periodic meetings.

In reversing the decree of the District Court, which had enjoined the Association from continuing the aforementioned activities, the Supreme Court carefully distinguished the present case from the two preceding cases.[47] In the *Lumber* and *Linseed Oil* cases "The unlawfulness of the combination arose, not from the fact that the defendants had effected a combination to gather and disseminate information, but from the fact that the court inferred from the peculiar circumstances of each case that concerted action had resulted or would necessarily result in tending arbitrarily to lessen production or increase prices." [48] In the *Maple Flooring* case it found no proof of such action.

The second price-filing scheme to pass the courts involved the Cement Manufacturers' Protective Association, which had been formed to aid its members to obtain correct and sufficient information concerning credits, contracts for delivery, freight rates, production, stocks, and shipments.[49] The government charged control of prices and production on four counts: the

[47] F. A. Fetter attributes the alleged reversal of position of the Supreme Court on the legality of open-price associations to the appointment of Justice Stone, who had been a cabinet colleague of Hoover when the latter, deploring the court's position in the *Lumber* and *Linseed Oil* cases, had suggested legislative action to legalize open-price associations. *Masquerade of Monopoly* (New York: Harcourt, Brace & Co., 1931), pp. 218–20. Justice Stone delivered the opinion in both the *Maple Flooring* and *Cement* cases.

[48] 268 U. S. 585.

[49] *Cement Manufacturers' Protective Association et al. v. U. S.*, 268 U. S. 588 (1925).

restriction of delivery of cement under "specific job contracts" for future delivery by a system of reports and trade espionage; compiling and distributing freight-rate books using arbitrary basing-points; exchange of information concerning credits; and finally, collusive activities at periodic meetings. Of these charges the most significant is that concerning the specific job contracts.

The plan of the Association involved no exchange of information concerning contracts for the sale of cement for immediate delivery. The nub of the Association's activities was to be found in the specific job contracts. This form of contract had been customary in the trade. Specific job contracts for future delivery are granted a buyer where construction work will extend over a period of time and the price of the completed job is fixed by contract. The contractor when bidding desires to assure himself of a sufficient supply of cement at a known price if he secures the contract. To such a prospective buyer a quotation may be made which must be accepted conditionally within a specified number of days and by contract within a longer period, perhaps thirty days, in which time the buyer must have received a contract for the job, or, if the buyer is constructing for his own use, must have secured final plans and specifications. Problems arise when a contractor uses such a contract to secure deliveries from each of several manufacturers in full amounts required for a particular job, or to secure delivery of more than the required amount from any one manufacturer. The contractor is then enabled to divert the extra deliveries to use on jobs other than the particular one for which the manufacturer contracted to supply cement on the given terms. Since tradition in the trade has treated such contracts as essentially options and since it has been customary for the manufacturer to grant a guarantee against a decline in the market price but to assume all losses against a rise, the contractors assumed little risk in making such contracts. In a

rising market the contractor who had covered himself by
duplicate contracts might endeavor to secure deliveries of
cement under such a contract to be used on other jobs, deliveries
which the manufacturer was under no legal or moral obligation
to make.

The Association attempted to correct this situation by requiring members to report all specific job contracts in detail.
The Association through the investigations of checkers ascer-
tained the amount of cement required for each job and whether
or not cement shipped under a given contract was actually used
on the specified job. It then gave wide publicity to the facts,
and many deliveries were cancelled in whole or in part where
they were not warranted under the terms of the contract of sale.
It seems obvious that the manufacturers had a real grievance.
Accepting the custom of the trade, common sense ideas of
justice would suggest their right to some sort of protection.
The activity of a trade association appeared to be most efficacious. The Court found these activities of the Association
legitimate. Moreover, the court found no evidence that the
other activities of the Association were pursued in a manner
which restrained trade unduly.

The most recent decision involving price-filing was that
rendered by the Court in the case of the Sugar Institute, a
decision of considerable importance since it involved advance
announcement of prices.[50] The Institute was an association
formed in 1925 by some fifteen refiners producing about 80
per cent of the sugar consumed in the United States and refining
practically all of the imported raw sugar processed in this
country.[51] The ostensible purpose of the Institute, as indicated

---

[50] *Sugar Institute et al. v. U. S.*, 297 U. S. 553 (1936). The opinion of
Justice Mack of the District Court gives an exhaustive presentation of the
facts of the case (15 F. Supp. 817: 1934).

[51] The remainder of the domestic consumed sugar was supplied by the
domestic beet sugar, and foreign and insular refined sugar interests. An

by its Code of Ethics, was to eradicate an extensive system of concessions and rebates which had evolved from an atmosphere of secrecy and rumor.

In order to appreciate the significance of the price-filing system in this industry it is necessary to realize the importance of price and price differences and how prices are made in the industry. Sugar is a highly standardized product in basic chemical and physical properties; brand preferences and product differentiation are not very important. Consequently price is the vital consideration and all competition tends to concentrate on price and indirect concessions having direct pecuniary value. Small differences in price, if known, are sufficient to shift trade from one refiner to another.

The Code of Ethics of the Sugar Institute is a revealing document of the objectives which may be sought by joint action.[52] The Code starts with a general statement of its purposes:

Among the purposes for which this Institute was formed were the following: To promote a high standard of business ethics in the industry; to eliminate trade abuses; to promote uniformity and certainty in business customs and practices; and to promote the service of the industry to the Public.

The Code went on to declare that practices of an unsound and unbusinesslike nature had developed, practices resulting "in confusion in the trade and discrimination as between purchasers, with a consequent uneven and uneconomic distribution of sugar to the public."

To correct these abuses the Code recommended the adoption of certain uniform practices, all ostensibly directed to the elimination of various direct and indirect forms of discrimination. First, it recommended that all sugar be sold only upon

---

inconsequential amount of domestic cane is produced and refined in Louisiana. 297 U. S. 571.

[52] 15 F. Supp. 910.

prices and terms publicly announced. Second, it recommended that all quantity discounts be eliminated. The Code pointed out that the industry received no quantity concessions on its purchases of raw sugar and then stated that "The Institute accordingly condemns as discriminatory, and in so far as this industry is concerned, as unbusinesslike, uneconomic and unsound, concessions made to purchasers on the basis of quantity purchased." Third, the Code listed some nine trade practices stating that "The Institute condemns them as unethical except when practiced openly; as discriminatory unless uniformly employed; and in any event as wasteful and unbusinesslike."

The scheme, then, provided not only for open-prices but for an extensive standardization and simplification of practices in the industry as well. It was intended to promote uniformity and to limit the directions of competitive activity. The effect would be to give greater meaning to the published price and to center such competition as remained upon price alone.

The system of price-filing evolved was one by which all announcements concerning changes in prices or terms were exchanged through the Institute in advance of the effective date. This would seem on its face to condemn the plan as both illegal and uneconomic. But attention should be given to certain peculiar characteristics of the sugar market. The great bulk of the sugar is sold on what is known as a "move." [53] A "move" occurs whenever a price advance occurs, which is about once each month, at which time the dealers purchase their month's supply. In the interval between "moves" only small quantities are sold. To initiate a "move" a refiner may announce that his price will be raised on a given day, e.g. two days hence; or he may announce a temporary drop in price to be followed a few days later by a rise. The purpose, of course, is to effect large sales at the low price before the rise. The

[53] For a detailed explanation of the sugar "move," see the *Brief for Appellants before the Supreme Court* (297 U. S. 553), pp. 49–50.

"move" becomes effective if competing refiners follow; if the other refiners do not follow, the "move" proves abortive and the initiating refiner has to withdraw his notice. Sometimes when one refiner announces a cut to be followed by a price rise, his competitors will meet his announcement with a less substantial, or more substantial, cut. Likewise, the period to elapse before the subsequent rise may be lengthened or shortened in the announcements of the competing refiners. In any event, after one refiner starts a "move," provided it does not prove abortive, the telegraph wires are busy for a time with announcements, counter-announcements, and the withdrawal of announcements. Finally, the market settles down upon a certain price and a certain period for execution of sales at that price. It is highly significant that the District Court found that "There is no evidence that the refiners consulted with one another after an advance had been announced by one of them or that the grace period was in fact used by them, to persuade a reluctant member to follow the example set; and this, too, despite the business necessity of withdrawing an advance unless it were followed by all." [54]

The reporting system in its final form provided that when making a price change the member should first notify all members of the Institute individually, and then notify the Institute itself. The Three O'clock Notice Rule recommended that all price changes be announced not later than three o'clock. In an early draft of the Rule this was stated to mean "three o'clock of the day before the changed price becomes effective." Although this clause was eliminated from the later drafts of the Code, by common practice price changes were not made effective before the day following their announcement. This had the purpose and effect of giving sufficient advance notice of price changes to enable all buyers and sellers to become informed of a price change by any firm before the change became

[54] 15 F. Supp. 830.

effective, thus allowing others to meet the price cut before any sales could be consummated. This might be presumed to eliminate such advantage as there was in initiating a price cut for the purpose of getting a particularly lucrative order. It also assured buyers of sufficient notice to enable them to place their orders before the period of grace expired and prices were raised. The Three O'clock Rule seems to have represented some modification of practice, since in the pre-Institute days the period of grace was an uncertain one.

Another innovation made by rulings of the Institute concerned the practice of "repricing." It had been the practice to make price declines retroactive to some sales made at previous high prices. This was quite generally done for sales made on the day of the price decline but previous to the announcement, but apparently repricing was sometimes extended to earlier sales. It is clear that the practice of repricing might be abused and become an indirect method of granting discriminatory concessions. A rule of the Institute limited such repricing to sales made on the morning of the day on which price declines were announced.

The lower court issued an elaborate decree enjoining a long list of restrictive practices and specifically prohibiting the filing of future prices. Upon appeal to the Supreme Court, the lower court was sustained with respect to most of its decree but the Court, recognizing the practice of the industry in selling on "moves," reversed the lower court with respect to advance announcement of prices.

The unreasonable restraints which defendants imposed lay not in advance announcements, but in the steps taken to secure adherence, without deviation, to prices, and terms thus announced. It was that concerted undertaking which cut off opportunities for variation in the course of competition however fair and appropriate they might be.[55]

[55] 297 U. S. 601.

Designed to frustrate unreasonable restraints, [the restrictions imposed by the Sherman Act] do not prevent the adoption of reasonable means to protect interstate commerce from destructive or injurious practices and to promote competition on a sound basis. Voluntary action to end abuses and to foster fair competitive opportunities in the public interest may be more effective than legal processes. And coöperative endeavor may appropriately have wider objectives than merely the removal of evils which are infractions of positive law. Nor does the fact that the correction of abuses may tend to stabilize a business, or to produce fairer price levels, require that abuses should go uncorrected or that an effort to correct them should for that reason alone be stamped as an unreasonable restraint of trade. Accordingly we have held that a coöperative enterprise otherwise free from objection, which carries with it no monopolistic menace, is not to be condemned as an undue restraint merely because it may effect a change in market conditions where the change would be in mitigation of recognized evils and would not impair, but rather foster, fair competitive opportunities.[56]

CONCLUSION

The Sherman Act has, then, attacked business practices from several points of view. It has looked with suspicion on collusive activities of independent business organizations particularly as they impinge on "the heart of the contract." It has stood as an obstacle to many attempts to promote "fair competition" where the preponderance of evidence was that the intent was to interfere with competition in price or in other terms of sale rather than to correct clear abuses. It has refused to distinguish reasonable and unreasonable restrictions on competition in price and the conditions of sale. The act has stood as no obstacle, however, to the attainment of large size, except by combination where technical considerations precluded the entrance of new competitors, so long as size was not gained or retained by coercive and predatory practices. Otherwise the practices and sales policies of large concerns are unrestricted.

[56] *Ibid.*, p. 597.

Underlying this interpretation of the Sherman Act is the inarticulate assumption that if the freedom of competition is maintained by preventing exclusive or coercive practices and if rivals are prevented from voluntarily entering into loose agreements restraining competition between themselves, the objectives of public policy will have been attained. This policy compounded of the common law concepts of monopoly, i.e. exclusion, and restraint of trade, i.e. voluntary restriction upon one's freedom, recognizes no middle ground. Having assured certain of the necessary conditions of competition, it assumes that the task of public policy is done. It does not recognize the possibilities that competition may not develop, although these two necessary conditions are maintained, nor that the degree or form of competition may vary, nor finally that all forms or degrees may not be equally acceptable. The concern of public policy has been with the preservation of certain limited market conditions rather than with a consideration of results of the market situation. In this respect the legislature and the courts on the one hand and the economists on the other have been at variance in their approach to the problems of monopoly and competition. The latter have increasingly defined their concepts and posed their problems in terms of results, specifically the relations between prices and costs, while the legal approach has been in terms of the methods of rivalry used.[57]

[57] For further discussion of the differences between legal and economic concepts in this field see E. S. Mason, "Monopoly in Law and Economics," *Yale Law Journal*, XLVII (1937), 34–49.

CHAPTER IV

LEGISLATION OF 1914

BACKGROUND OF THE LEGISLATION

As WAS SEEN in the last chapter there were by 1914 significant precedents for a program to regulate trade practices or methods of competition. Many competitive practices were clearly illegal at common law, others were illegal in particular circumstances as elements in a scheme in restraint of trade or monopoly. There were various forces at work, however, which led to new legislation to deal with business organization and practices. To many the Sherman Act appeared inadequate because of its indefiniteness and the uncertainties incident to its interpretation. To others the rule of reason which it was widely believed had been read into the act by the Supreme Court represented sabotage of the proper objectives of the act. Finally, there were those who would recognize concentration and regulate it; to these enforcement of the Sherman Act was misspent effort. The atmosphere was ripe for additional legislation.

During the campaign of 1912, each of the three principal parties called for supplementary legislation. The Democratic platform declared "A private monopoly is indefensible and intolerable" and called for a vigorous enforcement of the Sherman Act; it expressed regret that by introduction of the rule of reason the Sherman Act had been given a judicial construction depriving it of its effectiveness and called for legislation to restore its strength. Finally, it called for a clarification by law of the conditions upon which one might engage in interstate trade.

We favor the declaration by law of the conditions upon which corporations shall be permitted to engage in interstate trade, including, among others, the prevention of holding companies, of interlocking directors, of stock watering, of discrimination in price, and the control by any one corporation of so large a proportion of any industry as to make it a menace to competitive conditions.[1]

The Republican platform urged that greater certainty be given to the law by defining as criminal offenses "those specific acts that uniformly mark attempts to restrain and to monopolize trade."[2] It also urged the establishing of a Federal Trade Commission to improve the administration of the act by assigning it some of the functions previously exercised by the courts.

The Progressive Party presented a more novel program. It started with the assumption that some degree of concentration was both inevitable and necessary, and that the problem became one of preventing the abuse of power incident to concentration and monopoly.

This power has been abused, in monopoly of National resources, in stock watering, in unfair competition and unfair privileges, and finally in sinister influences on the public agencies of State and Nation. We do not fear commercial power, but we insist that it shall be exercised openly, under publicity, supervision and regulation of the most efficient sort, which will preserve its good while eradicating and preventing its ill.[3]

For this purpose it was proposed to establish a Federal administrative commission which should enforce complete publicity and attack such problems as "unfair competition, false capitalization and special privilege, and by continuous trained watchfulness guard and keep open equally all the highways of American commerce."[4] The platform further recommended strengthening the Sherman Law by prohibiting certain unfair trade practices.

[1] K. H. Porter, *National Party Platforms* (New York: The Macmillan Co., 1924), p. 322.
[2] *Ibid.*, p. 353.
[3] *Ibid.*, p. 341.
[4] *Loc. cit.*

There was, in short, a general agreement that the law should be made more specific with reference to trade practices. To the Democrats this meant preserving competition by preventing the development of monopoly. In his campaign speeches, Woodrow Wilson made it clear that he had no sympathy for the view that a high degree of concentration was based upon efficiency and so inevitable. He believed that limits to the growth of firms would be set by the competition of rivals provided only that large firms did not obstruct smaller rivals by unfair tactics.[5] To the Progressives the proposal to clarify the law of trade practices implied recognizing concentration of power as inevitable and policing the use and abuse of this power. The Republicans, less specific in their proposals, would protect the paths of business opportunity from monopoly, assure respect for "business success honorably achieved," and secure the right of all to buy "in an open market uninfluenced by the manipulation of trust or combination."[6]

In his first annual message to Congress President Wilson urged a comprehensive consideration of the problem of monopoly. He proposed, contrary to the implications of the Democratic platform, that the Sherman Act be left unamended with all of its debatable ground but that supplemental legislation be passed which would clarify it and facilitate its administration.[7] Subsequently he submitted to Congress a special message in which he offered more concrete proposals.[8] He urged legis-

[5] Woodrow Wilson, *The New Freedom* (New York and Garden City: Doubleday, Page & Co., 1913), chap. VIII.

[6] Porter, *op. cit.*, p. 354.

[7] Albert Shaw, *President Wilson's State Papers and Addresses* (New York: George H. Doran Co., 1918), p. 42.

[8] *Ibid.*, p. 47. In addition to the proposals summarized in the text, President Wilson suggested giving the Interstate Commerce Commission power to superintend the financial operations of railroads and passing legislation which would pierce the corporate veil so as to place responsibility and punishment for illegal action, not upon the corporation, but upon the person or groups of persons who have the initiative in corporate action.

lation to deal with interlocking directorates and holding companies and consideration of the problems raised by the ownership by one person of voting power in two or more companies which ought to be independent. He argued that enough was known about the processes and methods of monopoly and deleterious restraints of trade so that these practices might be explicitly forbidden by statute, item by item. Finally, he urged the establishment of an interstate trade commission as a fact-finding body and an instrument of publicity.

PASSAGE OF THE FEDERAL TRADE COMMISSION ACT

The Federal Trade Commission and Clayton Acts of 1914 were the outcome of these proposals. President Wilson had called for a statute prohibiting the practices fostering monopoly and restraint of trade item by item. Two bills had been introduced in Congress, one establishing a Federal Trade Commission without regulatory powers, the other containing the itemization of monopolistic practices.

The original bill as reported to the House of Representatives from the Committee on Interstate and Foreign Commerce gave the Commission no powers with respect to the regulation of trade practices except the weak section 11 providing that "when in the course of any investigation . . . the commission shall obtain information concerning any unfair competition or practice in commerce not necessarily constituting a violation of law . . . it shall make report thereof to the President, to aid him in making recommendations to Congress. . . ." [9] Two members of the Committee [10] filed dissenting reports each urging the necessity of prohibiting unfair or oppressive competition on the theory that "The history of the most successful business combinations shows that the chief means these com-

[9] 63d Cong., 2d Sess., *House Report* No. 533, Pt. 3, pp. 15–16.
[10] Representatives R. B. Stevens and W. Lafferty, *ibid.*, Pts. 2 and 3.

binations have used to acquire a monopoly or partial control of the business field has been by unfair methods of competition." [11] Despite this lack of provision for the regulation of competitive methods Representative Covington had said in the majority report, "The administration idea, and the idea of business men generally, is for the preservation of proper competitive conditions. . . ." [12] The efforts of the Representatives who were sponsoring the Progressive bills,[13] and of others [14] to introduce amendments or substitute bills in the House to deal with this question of trade practices were all unsuccessful. The bill went to the Senate without any change as concerns the regulation of competitive practices.

As the consideration of the matter proceeded, however, the difficulties of listing and defining all practices which might be undesirable were impressed upon the sponsors of the legislation and it was decided to abandon this effort in favor of a general prohibition of unfair competition, with power of enforcement vested in the proposed Federal Trade Commission.[15] This, of course, represented an abandonment of the President's original plan to itemize the illegal acts and involved giving regulatory power to the Commission such as had not been envisaged.

Consequently, when the Committee on Interstate Commerce

[11] *Ibid.*, Pt. 2, pp. 1–2. [12] *Ibid.*, Pt. 1, p. 2.
[13] *Congressional Record*, LI (1914), 1866 *et seq.*, 8856, 9047–49 (Morgan); 8973–80, 9050 (Murdock).
[14] *Ibid.*, pp. 9056–57 (Dillon); 9059–63 (Stevens); 9086 (Kelly).
[15] The story of this change was later told by George Rublee. He became impressed with the difficulties of defining monopolistic practices and finally with Mr. Louis (later Justice) Brandeis and Mr. Charles McCarthy of Wisconsin obtained a conference with President Wilson, who was won over to their proposal to insert into the Federal Trade Commission bill a general prohibition of unfair competition which would cover monopolistic practices of every description. "The Original Plan and Early History of the Federal Trade Commission," *Proceedings of the Academy of Political Science*, XI (1926), 666–72.

reported to the Senate, it reported out a substitute for the House Bill, which added a section on unfair competition.[16]

Sec. 5. That unfair competition in commerce is hereby declared unlawful.

The commission is hereby empowered and directed to prevent corporations from using unfair methods of competition in commerce. . . .

In reporting the bill Senator Newlands stated that the Committee had decided against an attempt to "define the many and variable unfair practices which prevail in commerce." [17] This was the result of the change of mind by the President and other sponsors under the pressure of Mr. Rublee.

CONGRESSIONAL INTENT

What did Congress have in mind when it declared "unfair methods of competition" to be unlawful? In particular, was it intended that the phrase should include such practices as were actionable as unfair competition at common law regardless of the relation of such practices to monopoly or restraint of trade? Or was section 5 of the Federal Trade Commission Act aimed merely at practices which either would lead to monopoly or else were indicative of the misuse of monopoly power? Was it intended that a perfectly competitive market should be enforced or merely that the freedom to compete should be protected? What significance, if any, is to be attached to the use of the term "unfair methods of competition" instead of the common law phrase "unfair competition"? Were there any definite economic criteria in mind in the passing of this legislation? Questions of this sort are not capable of conclusive answers. We are necessarily dependent upon construing the statements published in Congressional documents, statements which themselves were often so phrased as to obscure the real intent of

[16] 63d Cong., 2d Sess., *Senate Report* No. 597, p. 3.
[17] *Ibid.*, p. 13.

their author and which often were made in the course of debate without adequate forethought. However, though we shall not be able to answer these questions beyond a doubt, we may proceed with reasonable assurance in the case at hand because the phrase "unfair competition" was the subject of long and serious debate by a relatively large number of senators.

In reporting the bill Senator Newlands, speaking for the Committee, had the following comment to make on the use of the term:

It is believed that the term "unfair competition" has a legal significance which can be enforced by the commission and the courts, and that it is no more difficult to determine what is unfair competition than it is to determine what is a reasonable rate or what is an unjust discrimination. The committee was of the opinion that it would be better to put in a general provision condemning unfair competition than to attempt to define the numerous unfair practices, such as local price cutting, interlocking directorates, and holding companies intended to restrain substantial competition.[18]

In the light of subsequent controversy over the purposes of section 5, this statement is of interest for several reasons: first, it acknowledges reliance upon a legal construction of the term "unfair competition"; moreover, the specific examples cited as instances of unfair practices show the wide scope which Senator Newlands evidently thought it had; finally, his examples all have to do with the exercise of monopoly power or the restraint of trade.

The Senate was not so easily convinced that the term had an accepted legal meaning or in any event that the accepted legal meaning would include those practices associated with the trust problem with which it was the common desire to deal. The debate on this section in the Senate continued for several months and shows evidence of considerable study of legal authorities.

[18] *Ibid.*, p. 13.

Senator Newlands in explaining the scope of the term on the floor of the Senate was inclined to limit the meaning of the term by appeal to the "universal conscience of mankind" and to "public morals."

> The Senator [Sutherland] objects to the term "public morals" or "good morals" as a test. I think it is a very good test. I think there are certain practices that shock the universal conscience of mankind, and the general judgment upon the facts themselves would be that such practices are unfair.

> That is a definite standard if the practice is against good morals and against public morals and tends to injury of competitors unfairly.[19]

Senator Cummins, the principal supporter of the bill with Senator Newlands, appealed to the "law of the land" and the "developing sense of the country."

> The trade commission becomes bound to declare what is or what is not unfair competition according to the law of the land, according to the improving and the developing sense of the country with respect to matters of commerce.[20]

Similarly Senator Saulsbury envisioned the section as giving the Commission a free hand to recognize commercial custom.[21] Such criteria as the "developing sense of the community," "the conscience of mankind," "public morals," and "the customs of merchants" are admittedly rather unsatisfactory criteria for an administrative commission in a democratic community.

However, more illuminating discussion of the scope of the section is to be found in the record. Senators Reed [22] and Sutherland [23] expressed the opinion that contrary to the wishes of the proponents of the bill, the term "unfair competition" would be construed narrowly to cover only those common law

---

[19] *Congressional Record*, LI (1914), 12980.
[20] *Ibid.*, p. 11104.
[21] *Ibid.*, p. 11593.
[22] *Ibid.*, pp. 11874–76, 12022, 12933.
[23] *Ibid.*, pp. 12651, 12814.

practices included under passing-off and certain analogous practices involving fraud. The expression of opinion was unanimous that the *intent* was to go beyond the common law concept and to attack practices which involved either the exercise of monopoly power or a tendency to foster monopoly.[24]

When pressed as to what the section added to the Sherman Act in respect to practices in restraint of trade, Senators Newlands and Cummins expressed the opinion that practices which were not in themselves in restraint of trade but which might lead to restraint of trade and monopoly would be checked in embryo.[25] On other occasions Senator Newlands emphasized the possibilities of the bill as affording an improved machinery for administration of traditional monopoly policy.[26] It may be mentioned that this latter view was the one taken subsequently by the Supreme Court in the *Gratz* decision.[27]

One question upon which the evidence is somewhat doubtful is whether or not it was intended that the section should apply to unfair competition in the common law sense of passing-off, misrepresentation, and allied practices involving fraud. Senators Reed and Sutherland expressed a fear that the phrase would be restricted to these practices alone.[28] Senators Newlands and Cummins did not intimate whether or not they intended that the phrase should include such practices; all their discussion, however, was concerned with the relation of unfair practices to monopoly and restraint of trade. Senator McCumber distinguished unfair competition which cripples

[24] *Cf.* statements by Senator Newlands (*Congressional Record*, LI, 11235), Senator Cummins (*ibid.*, p. 11103), and Senator Hollis (*ibid.*, p. 12146).

[25] *Cf. ibid.*, pp. 12030 (Senator Newlands), 11455 (Senator Cummins), and 12146 (Senator Hollis).

[26] *Ibid.*, pp. 11109, 12030.

[27] *Cf. post*, p. 81.

[28] *Congressional Record*, LI (1914), 11874–76, 12022, 12651, 12814, 12933.

competition and unfair competition which does not cripple competition and suggested limiting the concept to the former, to which proposal Senator Cummins would neither dissent nor assent.[29] Senator McCumber did not think "glowing advertising" was intended to be included although he thought it would be included unless the term were defined.[30] There were others who seemed likewise to favor confining the scope to unfair practices involving monopoly or restraint of trade.[31] Senator Culberson submitted an amendment which would have definitely limited the concept to acts leading to monopoly or restraint of trade.[32] On the other hand, Senator Shields noted that the law made unlawful "fraudulent or tortious acts committed by corporations whereby a competitor in the same business is injured, and this regardless of the fact whether the wrongful act prohibited tends to monopoly and detriment of the public." [33]

The indefiniteness of Congressional intent on this matter is in sharp contrast with the decision in the *Gratz* case, which specifically included the common law concepts under section 5.[34] It is also in sharp conflict with the view expressed by George Rublee, who had much to do with the insertion of section 5, and who subsequently stated that it was not the intention of the sponsors of the section to give the Commission jurisdiction over the common law categories of unfair competition.[35]

---

[29] *Ibid.*, p. 13051.   [30] *Ibid.*, p. 13114.

[31] *Ibid.*, p. 12213 (Senator Sterling) and p. 12979 (Senator Thomas).

[32] *Ibid.*, p. 12910.

[33] *Ibid.*, p. 13059.

[34] *F.T.C. v. Gratz, et al.*, 253 U.S. 421 (1920). The National Industrial Conference Board considers it "plain" that Congress meant that the act should cover the common law of unfair competition. *Cf. Public Regulation of Competitive Practices* (New York: 1929), p. 50. But the Commission itself expressed doubt on the matter in an early report. *Cf.* Federal Trade Commission, *Annual Report*, 1916 (Washington: Government Printing Office), p. 6. *Cf. post*, pp. 78 *et seq.*

[35] Rublee, *op. cit.*, pp. 669–70.

There may be some significance in the fact that section 5 as it emerged from conference and finally passed substituted the phrase "unfair methods of competition" for the phrase "unfair competition." This phraseology was insisted upon by the House Conference Committee. Representative Stevens explained that it was adopted "because we wanted to cover the specific act which would be unfair, while the course of conduct by itself might be fair." [36] However, Senators Newlands [37] and Cummins [38] both insisted in debate that there was no difference in meaning between the phrases, although in the debate preceding the sending of the bill to conference, several Senators had suggested amendments prohibiting "unfair methods of competition" or "unfair and oppressive methods of competition" ostensibly in order to restrict the term to the field of monopoly or restraint of trade.[39] Senator Sutherland had insisted that there was a difference between the terms, "unfair competition" having a restricted meaning at common law and "unfair methods of competition" having no legal meaning at all.[40]

Although most of the debate was concerned with the legal scope of these terms, there were certain remarks on the economic criteria involved. Throughout the debate it was insisted that the principal object was to maintain competition. As in the debates on the Sherman Act, this did not mean the maintenance of a perfectly competitive market for it was generally agreed that there was no desire to penalize size gained fairly.[41] What

[36] *Congressional Record*, LI (1914), 14937.

[37] *Ibid.*, p. 14786.

[38] *Ibid.*, p. 14768.

[39] *Ibid.*, p. 12655 (Senator Hollis) and p. 12726 (Senator Pomerene).

[40] *Ibid.*, p. 12814. Senators Thomas (*ibid.*, p. 12979) and Brandegee (*ibid.*, p. 13103) agreed that the two terms were not synonymous.

[41] Senator Sutherland alone saw a danger in size *per se*. "I take no stock whatever in the statement that has been sometimes made by very distinguished gentlemen that mere size is not objectionable. I think that mere size may be exceedingly objectionable." He pointed out that large size business organization is a blow to individualism and initiative. (*Ibid.*,

was desired was freedom for others who were actually or potentially in the market to compete on the basis of *efficiency.*

Fair competition is competition which is successful through
superior efficiency. Competition is unfair when it resorts to methods
which shut out competitors who, by reason of their efficiency, might
otherwise be able to continue in business and prosper. Without the
use of unfair methods no corporation can grow beyond the limits
imposed upon it by the necessity of being as efficient as any competitor. The mere size of a corporation which maintains its position
solely through superior efficiency is ordinarily no menace to the public
interest.[42]

The philosophy of those arguing for the preservation of
freedom of opportunity to compete on the basis of efficiency
was essentially that of President Wilson. As we have noted, his
belief was that there were distinct limits to the increase of
efficiency with size.[43] This school of thought believed that if
large firms were prevented from obstructive and exclusive
practices with reference to rivals, large size would usually find
itself checked by the growth of smaller firms of equal or greater
efficiency. This Wilsonian doctrine gained support from no less
an economic authority than J. B. Clark.[44] It figured promi-
nently in the writing of Mr. Louis Brandeis [45] and in two
contemporary articles by W. S. Stevens [46] which were quoted in
the Senate debates.

While it is difficult to judge from this record what the inten-

---

p. 12983.) This is quite in harmony with certain remarks by A. A. Young,
"The Sherman Act and the New Anti-Trust Legislation," *Journal of Political Economy,* XXIII (1915), 214, note 1.

[42] *Congressional Record,* LI (1914), 12146 (Senator Hollis).

[43] *Cf. supra,* p. 62.

[44] J. B. and J. M. Clark, *The Control of Trusts* (New York: The Macmillan Co., 1912 ed.), p. 103.

[45] *The Curse of Bigness* (New York: The Viking Press, 1934), pp. 115,
197.

[46] "Unfair Competition," *Political Science Quarterly,* XXIX (1914),
282–306, 460–90.

tion of Congress was in passing section 5, some things are clear. It was intended to aid in the maintenance of the freedom to compete but had no purpose to prohibit mere size. Public policy aimed to prevent an individual enterprise from appropriating to itself the whole or a preponderant share of any market by means other than superior efficiency. It was assumed either that a preponderant position in the market could not be gained by such methods, or that size so gained was not contrary to the public interest. The problems of oligopoly and price inflexibility were matters of a later day. Without any doubt, Congress intended to eradicate methods of competition which were in restraint of trade under the Sherman Act because of their tendency to develop a monopoly, although George Rublee denied any intent to include agreements in restraint of trade, since to deal with these the Sherman Act was considered adequate.[47] The new legislation was thought by some to give additional power to prevent acts in the embryo whose ultimate effects would be in restraint of trade. If this were not so, it may be said that section 5 added little to the Sherman Act beyond a new machinery of administration. There is some doubt as to whether the section was intended to cover such practices as were considered unfair competition at common law in cases where there was no restraint of trade or tendency towards monopoly in a legal sense. There is no positive evidence of a desire to include such practices, but there is some evidence of a desire to exclude them. Finally, certain extravagant statements would seem to broaden the scope of the phrase "unfair competition" to include practices which "shock the conscience of mankind," or which are against "good morals" or "public morals," or which are contrary to the "customs of merchants, manufacturers and traders."[48]

[47] Rublee, *op. cit.*, p. 670.
[48] Contrast these conclusions with the simple but dogmatic statement of the National Industrial Conference Board. "The common law doctrine

PASSAGE OF THE CLAYTON ACT

In its original form the Clayton bill for supplementing our anti-trust policy had, among other things, sought to define and declare unlawful those trade practices which had been found to be the most usual method of acquiring monopoly power. As passed by the House it had included five sections dealing with such practices.[49] The subsequent decision in passing the Federal Trade Commission Act to include a sweeping declaration that all unfair methods of competition were unlawful was believed by some to make this part of the Clayton Act redundant and, in fact, several sections were eliminated by the Senate, particularly that dealing with price discrimination. In the conference on the bill, the House conferees insisted on retaining the section dealing with discrimination and on making the section dealing with tying and exclusive contracts applicable to unpatented as well as to patented goods.[50] As finally passed, then, the bill added to legislation on trade practices by declaring discrimination and tying and exclusive agreements unlawful under certain circumstances.

Section 2 declared it unlawful "to discriminate in price . . . where the effect . . . may be to substantially lessen competi-

---

of 'unfair competition' on the one hand, and the principles evolved in the enforcement of the Sherman Act as concrete tests of monopolization, on the other, were manifestly the basic criteria which Section 5 prescribed." (*Public Regulation of Competitive Practices*, p. 50.) Our investigations likewise failed to show that the popular desire to preserve the "little-man," which is considered by some to have been the purpose of the 1914 legislation (T. C. Blaisdell, *The Federal Trade Commission*, New York: Columbia University Press, 1932, pp. 7–8) was reflected greatly in Congressional debate.

[49] Discrimination, tying and exclusive arrangements, interlocking directors, intercorporate stock control, refusal to sell by an owner or operator of a mine or of a source of power, etc.

[50] *Cf.* 63d Cong., 2d Sess., *Senate Document* No. 584 for a *Comparative Print of the Federal Anti-trust Bill*, showing the bill at various stages in its legislative history.

tion or tend to create a monopoly in any line of commerce." [51] Exception was made in the case of "discrimination in price between purchases of commodities on account of differences in the grade, quality, or quantity of the commodity sold, or that makes only due allowance for difference in the cost of selling or transportation, or discrimination in price in the same or different commodities made in good faith to meet competition."

Section 3, which has to do with tying and exclusive dealing arrangements, declared it to be unlawful in the case of either lease or sale of goods, whether patented or unpatented, to fix a price or discount which would be conditional upon an agreement not to use or deal in the goods of a rival of the lessor or seller. This again was restricted to circumstances where the effect "may be to substantially lessen competition or tend to create a monopoly in any line of commerce."

What these sections were presumed to add to the previous legislation is not clear from the Congressional debates. Uppermost in the minds of those discussing the bill seemed to be local price discrimination as practiced by the Standard Oil Trust and the restrictive leases of the United Shoe Machinery Company. It seemed to be agreed that there could be little harm in adding these specific definitions of unlawful practices to the general prohibition of unfair methods of competition, among which they might be presumed to be numbered. There were those who believed that the restriction of sections 2 and 3 to conditions where the effect may be "to substantially lessen competition or tend to create a monopoly" might weaken the effectiveness of the law.[52] On the other hand, the sponsors of

---

[51] The original section had contained in the place of this proviso the words "with the purpose or intent thereby to destroy or wrongfully injure the business of a competitor, of either such purchaser or seller." *Ibid.*, p. 4. For the effect of this change on the interpretation of the act, *cf. post*, pp. 134–36.

[52] *Congressional Record*, LI (1914), 16282.

the legislation believed these sections would be distinct additions to the power to deal with monopoly under the Sherman Act, since it would enable the Commission to proceed against these practices in embryo before the offender had proceeded to the ultimate point of restraining or monopolizing trade.[53]

[53] *Ibid.*, pp. 16318, 16341.

CHAPTER V

CRITERIA OF UNFAIR METHODS OF COMPETITION

CONGRESS in legislating upon the matter of trade practices chose to use the phrase "unfair methods of competition," leaving it to the Commission and courts to give the prohibitions of the act more specific content. It is with the criteria which have been adopted by the Commission and the courts in distinguishing lawful from unlawful practices that this chapter is concerned.

Do the prohibitions of the act include practices illegal at common law? Is it concerned with injuries to a competitor? Where is the line to be drawn between legitimate injuries to a competitor and those which are unlawful? What is the relation of section 5 of the Federal Trade Commission Act to the prohibitions of the Sherman Act? When does a practice become illegal because it is in restraint of trade or tends to monopolize? To what extent is injury to the consumer a matter for consideration in cases of alleged unfair methods of competition? This chapter seeks to answer these questions by analyzing the criteria of unfair methods of competition which have been developed by the Commission under the guidance of the courts and to assess the significance of recent amendments to section 5. Later chapters present more concrete evidence on the specific practices which have been held to fall within the scope of the general prohibitions of section 5. They likewise attempt to assess the significance of the scope of the Commission's authority with reference to particular practices.[1]

[1] Other problems such as the administrative procedure, judicial review of the Commission's orders or of its power of investigation, and legislative

The search for the criteria applied by the Commission is limited by the available materials. The Commission has given but slight attention to the abstract aspects of the problem in its Annual Reports. The published Findings and Orders throw some light, of course, on the Commission's views, but until recently in only a few instances has an analysis of the problem investigated been incorporated therein. A more fruitful source of information is found in the court decisions. The Commission has been subjected to rigorously critical review by the courts, whose decisions have indicated certain general limits to the scope of the Commission's activity which have served to guide the Commission in its activities. When reversed by the courts with reference to interpretation of the substantive meaning of the act, the Commission has usually dropped the matter. It is generally agreed that until recently the Commission has not been very active in enlarging the concept either by pressing the courts or by making recommendations to Congress. For these reasons the court cases are of primary importance. Since 1935, however, the Commission, showing renewed vigor, has pressed successfully for amendments to the Act.[2] Another source of information is the Trade Practice Conference Rules. Until recently these were dominated by the court decisions and added little to the substantive law. However, during the last few years the Commission has begun to define new rules of

---

or executive interference with the Commission's activities will not be considered. These are interesting and important but are for the most part outside the scope of this study. Several studies bearing upon these problems are available. G. C. Henderson, *The Federal Trade Commission: A Study in Administrative Law and Procedure* (New Haven: Yale University Press, 1924); T. C. Blaisdell, *The Federal Trade Commission: An Experiment in the Control of Business* (New York: Columbia University Press, 1932); Carl McFarland, *Judicial Control of the Federal Trade Commission and the Interstate Commerce Commission, 1920–1930* (Cambridge: Harvard University Press, 1933); E. P. Herring, *Public Administration and the Public Interest* (New York: McGraw-Hill, 1936), chaps. 7–8.

[2] *Cf. post*, p. 101.

unfair trade which suggest that it is about to press forward the concept of unfair competition into new fields. Some reference to these rules will be made in chapters XIII and XIV.

THE COMMISSION SURVEYS ITS MANDATE

The Commission began its activities by pointedly refusing "to define in general terms what methods of competition are 'unfair' so that 'a proceeding by it in respect thereof would be to the interest of the public.' " [3] It did venture to say that its basic principle was "sufficiently elastic to cover all future unconscionable competitive practices in whatever form they may appear." The Commission was reasonably certain that "cases in which the method of competition restrains trade, substantially lessens competition, or tends to create a monopoly are subject to a proceeding under section 5." But the Commission noted that it was in some doubt as to how far it should go in the public interest in matters of misbranding, false advertising, or passing-off.

However, the Commission stated that it sought in the enforcement of the law "to protect men in the furtherance of legitimate self-interest by all reasonable and normal methods, and at the same time to keep the channels of competition free and open to all, so that a man with small capital may engage in business in competition with powerful rivals, assured that he may operate his business free from harassment and intimidation and be given a fair opportunity to work out his business problems with such industry, efficiency, and intelligence as he may possess." [4] The Commission also noted its desire in making rulings and orders "to promote business efficiency and, within the limits of practicability, to coöperate with the business world in developing the best standards of commercial ethics." [5] After

[3] Federal Trade Commission, *Annual Report*, 1916, p. 6.
[4] *Ibid.*, p. 13.
[5] *Ibid.*, p. 26.

the war, the Commission became somewhat bolder and claimed that by the act of its creation "it was empowered to leave the shores defined by the common-law and, taking the knowledge of those decisions with it, to embark on an unchartered sea, using common sense plus the common-law for its compass." [6] This venturesome attitude was not to persist. The Commission did, however, classify cases as falling under three heads: (1) methods involving an element of moral turpitude; (2) methods which while not involving any element so clearly violative of good morals are unlawful because condemned by the common law; (3) methods involving the elimination of competition or restraint of trade to the detriment of the public.[7]

In the early 1920's the Commission became rather more articulate in stating its purpose to be the preservation of the competitive system.

It would be beneficial if the basis of the Commission and Clayton Acts — the purpose of Congress in passing them — were more generally understood. The purpose is expressed in various ways, but the fundamental object was the preservation of the competitive system.[8]

Such expressions of opinion as to the scope of the concept of unfair methods of competition can hardly be considered satisfactory. The adjective "unconscionable" has no more economic significance than "unfair" and its legal significance is less. "Embarking on an unchartered sea with common sense and the common-law" as guides is little better.

"Maintaining the competitive system" is a convenient formula, but as a guide to policy it needs more careful specification. What did the Commission hope to preserve? The *freedom* of competition? The *fact* of competition? The *results*

---

[6] *Annual Report*, 1919, p. 45. The Commission was emboldened by the decision of the Circuit Court in *Sears, Roebuck & Co. v. F. T. C.*, 258 Fed. 307 (1919).

[7] *Annual Report*, 1920, p. 48.

[8] *Ibid.*, 1922, p. 36.

generally associated with competition? The word competition is frequently used loosely to refer to any one or all of these. In speaking of keeping the channels of trade free and open and protecting the small against harassment and intimidation by the large, the Commission presumably refers to the freedom of competition. In referring to the promotion of business efficiency, it appears to be concerned with the results. Often it is assumed that given the first, the others may be presumed to follow. But it is generally acknowledged by careful students of economics that this is not necessarily so.[9] The absence of legal or private obstacles to competition does not insure that rivalry will exist. Moreover, it is quite clear that competition is a question of type and degree. It may take the form of price change, of product variation, of rivalry in service or advertising. It may be intensive, or it may be limited. It may be effective immediately, from day to day, or its effectiveness may be apparent only over significant periods of time. And from this it is clear that the results of competition will depend not only upon the freedom of competition, but upon the specific embodiment which competition takes in the particular case. Just as freedom and competition may conflict, as in the case of oligopoly with tacit agreement not to compete, so competition and efficiency may be difficult to reconcile in cases where, for example, competition leads to excess capacity or wasteful sales policies. In pursuit of its legal and administrative functions the Commission never faced these problems.[10]

That the Commission never developed a clear conception of

[9] The literature on oligopoly, price-leadership, and the trade association attest to this statement.

[10] In some of the industry studies made by the Economic Division problems with reference to monopoly and competition have been dealt with more realistically. It is to be regretted that the Commission, using the information so gained, has not taken more initiative in delineating adequate categories of market situations and practices for purposes of public policy.

the scope of its mandate nor a definite meaning for the phrase "unfair methods of competition" is indicated by the testimony of Mr. N. B. Gaskill, who was appointed Commissioner in 1920. He writes that "Everybody, the examiners, the Board of Review, the legal staff, and the several Commissioners had theories of their own and worked on them." [11] But with the first Supreme Court decision interpreting section 5 in the *Gratz* case the scope of the Commission's activity was roughly delineated. Thereafter, the Commission for over a decade eschewed further speculation, being content to reiterate the words of the court.[12]

THE COURTS DRAW THE BOUNDARIES

The decision of the Supreme Court in the *Gratz* case was long a leading factor in determining the activities of the Commission. The crucial paragraph follows:

The words "unfair methods of competition" are not defined by the statute, and their exact meaning is in dispute. It is for the courts, not the commission, ultimately to determine as matter of law what they include. They are clearly inapplicable to practices never heretofore regarded as opposed to good morals because characterized by deception, bad faith, fraud or oppression, or as against public policy because of their dangerous tendency unduly to hinder competition or create monopoly. The act was certainly not intended to fetter free and fair competition as commonly understood and practiced by honorable opponents in trade.[13]

The Commission interpreted this as a mandate "to sustain those practices which support the competitive system." [14]

[11] N. B. Gaskill, *The Regulation of Competition* (New York: Harper & Bros., 1936), p. 66. *Cf.* also p. 5 where he relates that at his first session as a member the Chairman after a few words of welcome asked, "What do *you* think unfair competition means?" Mr. Gaskill writes, "My impression that the question was open to discussion was quickly confirmed."

[12] *Annual Report*, 1923, p. 1; 1924, p. 2.

[13] *F. T. C. v. Gratz et al.*, 253 U. S. 421, 427 (1920). The details of the case are developed below, p. 83.

[14] *Annual Report*, 1924, p. 2; also 1923, p. 1.

The first group of practices designated by the Court presumably refers to practices included under the common law doctrine of unfair competition. The second group, those "against public policy because of their dangerous tendency unduly to hinder competition or create monopoly," might have implied, as pointed out above, either the maintenance of a competitive market or the protection of the freedom to compete. The latter would be in accord with the interpretation of the Sherman Act as it was crystallized in the decisions of 1911 and subsequent years.

It is especially worthy of note that this leading decision took an unequivocal stand on the question as to whether or not Congress intended the concept of unfair methods of competition to be restricted to practices in restraint of trade or tending to lead to a monopoly. The Court upheld the Commission in the view that the scope of section 5 was not so restricted but included as well that range of practices which had long been recognized as unfair at common law.

There was, however, an undercurrent of dissenting opinions on this matter, endeavoring without success to limit the scope of the section to practices directly related to violations of the Sherman Act. Indeed, in a dissenting opinion in the *Gratz* case, Justice Brandeis, who with George Rublee had much to do with persuading President Wilson to include section 5 in the act,[15] speaks of the act only as an adjunct to the purposes of the Sherman Law "to preserve the competitive system." [16] In 1923 Judge Denison of the Sixth Circuit Court vigorously upheld this position after an exhaustive study of the Congressional debates in his dissenting opinion in the *L. B. Silver* action.[17] And later in the *Raladam* decision (1930), involving alleged misrepresentation of an obesity cure as "scientific"

[15] *Cf. supra*, p. 64, note 15.
[16] *F. T. C. v. Gratz et al.*, 253 U. S. 434 (1920).
[17] *L. B. Silver Co. v. F. T. C.*, 289 Fed. 985, 998 (1923).

when such was not the case, Judge Denison now writing the majority opinion for the Circuit Court reaffirmed his opinion that "the Commission came into being as an aid to the enforcement of the general public anti-trust and anti-monopoly policy, and that its lawful jurisdiction did not go beyond the limits of fair relationship to that policy." [18] However, it appears that the contrary opinion has prevailed in the interpretations of the Supreme Court and the jurisdiction of the Commission in such cases is no longer questioned. A cursory survey of the complaints and orders of the Commission will indicate that its principal legal activities have been concerned with this class of practice. During the decade from 1925–35 significant actions involving monopoly or restraint of trade were rare.

While the *Gratz* decision served to delineate the general scope of the act, it left many unsettled issues to be determined by "the gradual process of judicial inclusion and exclusion." These had to do with three general problems: the type of practice which might qualify as "unfair," the test of injury to a competitor, and the requirement that the prohibition of the unfair method of competition be in the public interest.[19]

The *Gratz* case had involved a tying arrangement. The defendant, engaged in selling steel ties for binding bales of cotton, was alleged to have refused to sell its ties except on condition that customers buy a corresponding amount of jute bagging used to wrap bales of cotton. The Commission held this to be an unfair method of competition as against other

---

[18] *Raladam Co. v. F. T. C.*, 42 F. (2d) 430, 435 (1930). He also asserted that since his dissent in the *Silver* decision, "there has been no decision of the Supreme Court inconsistent therewith, nor any Circuit Court of Appeals decision which expressly denies that theory."

[19] This threefold classification of the tests of the Commission's jurisdiction while not explicit in the earlier cases underlies much of the controversy and finally emerged in Justice Sutherland's opinion in the *Raladam* decision (1933). *Cf. post*, p. 94.

manufacturers of bagging.[20] It was reversed, however, by the courts. The fundamental grounds for the reversal are difficult to ascertain. The lower court concluded that since there was not sufficient evidence to show a tendency to lessen competition or create a monopoly, in the sense of section 3 of the Clayton Act, the method must have been unfair not to the public generally but only in individual cases.[21] The act was interpreted as not applicable to unfair methods as between individuals. Moreover, the practice of selling ties and bagging together was judged to be a natural and prevailing custom. The Supreme Court likewise concluded that there was nothing "alleged which would justify the conclusion that the public suffered injury or that competitors had reasonable ground for complaint." [22] It denied that there was any question of monopoly. To what extent the decision in this case was due to a faulty drafting of the complaint or presentation of the evidence is debatable.[23]

In tracing the evolution of the criteria of unfair methods of competition at the hands of the courts after the dictum of the Supreme Court in the *Gratz* decision two principal groups of decisions may be followed, those involving monopoly or restraint of trade and those involving practices similar to those unlawful at common law.

The first case involving restraint of trade to be presented to the court under section 5 after the *Gratz* decision was that of the *F. T. C. v. Beech-Nut Packing Co.*[24] This was an action

---

[20] For the Commission's proceedings *cf.* 1 F. T. C. 249. The complaint also alleged that the practice violated section 3 of the Clayton Act, but after hearing the case the Commission dismissed this part of the complaint for lack of sufficient proof.

[21] *F. T. C. v. Gratz et al.*, 258 Fed. 314 (1919).

[22] *F. T. C. v. Gratz et al.*, 253 U. S. 426, 428 (1920).

[23] Henderson, *op. cit.*, p. 307.

[24] 257 U. S. 441 (1922). For the Commission's proceedings *cf.* 1 F. T. C. 516.

brought by the Commission alleging that the Beech-Nut Packing Company had been enforcing a system of resale price maintenance by refusing to sell to those not observing its suggested resale prices. In pursuit of its plan the company enlisted the aid of dealers, instituted an elaborate system of espionage, and exacted assurances from those found guilty of not maintaining prices that they would do so in the future as a condition of further supplies. In deciding this case the Commission cited the precedents for holding similar policies illegal under the Sherman Act [25] and made it clear that while the Sherman Act was not involved, it might be relevant as a declaration of public policy in determining what constitutes unfair methods of competition.

The system here disclosed necessarily constitutes a scheme which restrains the natural flow of commerce and the freedom of competition . . . which it has been the purpose of all the anti-trust acts to maintain . . . competition among retail distributors is practically suppressed; for all who would deal in the company's products are constrained to sell at the suggested prices. . . . The specific facts found show suppression of the freedom of competition by methods in which the company secures the coöperation of its distributors and customers, which are quite as effectual as agreements express or implied intended to accomplish the same purpose.[26]

For these reasons the Court upheld the Commission. The decision is important just because it frankly adopted as precedents the criteria of the Sherman Act. It is significant in the light of later decisions because the public interest in the suppression of competition among dealers was considered sufficient without any finding of coercion of or injury to competitors of the Beech-Nut Company.[27]

In 1926 the Supreme Court in *F. T. C. v. Pacific States Paper*

---

[25] For a discussion of the legal status of resale price maintenance under the Sherman Act see chap. XII.

[26] 257 U. S. 441, 454–55.

[27] Cf. *post*, pp. 93–96, 98–99.

Trade Association again had occasion to pass upon a practice of the type against which the Sherman Act has been invoked.[28] This was a proceeding against a series of local paper trade associations in the Pacific States and a regional or general association, the members of which controlled 75 per cent of the business in paper and paper products, exclusive of roll newspaper, in the Pacific area. The associations were accused of distributing uniform price lists agreed upon in the local associations, which were then used by agents of the dealers in all sales. Each local association circulated lists agreed upon by the members of the local association to be observed in its territory within the state. The secretary of each association investigated complaints of sales below the established prices, and in the case of three of the five local associations heavy fines were imposed for making such sales. The Commission alleged that while there was no requirement that these lists be used in the case of interstate sales, there was a tacit or implied agreement to do so and that in fact the lists were habitually carried and used by salesmen in making sales in other states. The Supreme Court sustained the Commission stating that "an understanding, express or tacit, that the agreed prices will be followed is enough to constitute a transgression of the law." [29] While there was no discussion of the applicability of Sherman Act tests, it is clear that the Court was following the principles which are applied in Sherman Law cases involving loose agreements or price-filing schemes through trade associations.

These occasions upon which the Commission was sustained in applying Sherman Law tests to cases arising under section 5 involved loose agreements in restraint of trade. The mere proof of attempts to reduce price competition was sufficient to invoke the law. What of practices by a single firm acting alone which

[28] 273 U. S. 52 (1927). For the Commission's proceedings *cf.* 7 F. T. C. 155.
[29] 273 U. S. 52, 62.

might lead to the monopolizing of trade? In several proceedings under section 5 the Commission has alleged that the practices of a firm tended to the lessening of competition or the monopolization of trade. In most cases there was likewise involved a charge of violating either section 2 or 3 of the Clayton Act. In those cases which finally reached the Supreme Court the Commission was reversed, as it was likewise in several others which did not go beyond the lower courts. It will throw light upon the criteria adopted by the courts to cite several of these.

In the action against the Curtis Publishing Company the Commission charged unfair methods of competition and violation of section 3 of the Clayton Act because of the use of exclusive dealing arrangements. The Curtis Company had built up an extensive system of distribution through district agents who controlled an elaborate school-boy selling organization which the company had developed at considerable expense. It entered into contracts of agency with these district agents which while allowing the agents to deal in magazines of competitors of the Curtis Company in the case of sales through retail stores, customarily forbade them to sell such magazines through the school-boy organizations. The charge of violation of the Clayton Act was dismissed on the grounds that the contract was a *bona fide* contract of agency, not one of sale, and as such the Clayton Act was not applicable.[30] The courts likewise reversed the Commission in respect to the applicability of section 5. In doing so the lower court remarked:

. . . we are not dealing with anything that has been made the subject of monopoly, sole supply, or by deprivation of which the public has been deprived of anything it desires. . . . *We note these facts because this freedom of access to the consumer, and the absence of*

---

[30] *Curtis Publishing Co. v. F. T. C.*, 270 Fed. 881 (1921) and *F. T. C. v. Curtis Publishing Co.*, 260 U. S. 568 (1923). For the Commission's proceedings *cf.* 2 F. T. C. 20.

monopoly and nondeprivation of the public, have been regarded as an important element in the decision of cases of alleged unfair business competition.[31]

Moreover, the Supreme Court was impressed by the absence of any intention "unduly to suppress competition or to acquire monopoly" and the fact that the contracts were made in the orderly course of an expanding business.

Effective competition requires that traders have large freedom of action when conducting their own affairs. Success alone does not show reprehensible methods, although it may increase or render insuperable the difficulties which rivals must face.[32]

A series of cases involving oil pump leases was another occasion for reversal of the Commission by the courts. The oil refiners were leasing oil pumps and storage tanks to dealers for a nominal sum on condition that they should be used only for the sale of the lessor's oil. The refiners were induced to insist upon such contracts for the reason that an oil pump customarily serves as a vehicle of advertising and they were interested to insure that it was not used so as to mislead the consuming public. These were not exclusive dealing arrangements in the technical sense, since the dealer was ostensibly free to handle as many different brands as he chose. The Commission noted, however, that in practice these arrangements were made only with the curb-pump dealers whose business generally did not warrant installing more than one pump. This the Commission argued might have the effect of substantially lessening competition or promoting monopoly, because the capital cost involved in providing such equipment would force some refiners and distributors from the field and because the conclusion of contracts by some precluded others from access to the market.[33]

The Supreme Court in reversing the Commission denied that

---

[31] 270 Fed. 881, 914. Italics are not in the original.
[32] 260 U. S. 568, 582.   [33] 2 F. T. C. 127.

the practice was opposed to good morals and pointed out that it was a custom adopted by many competing firms and justified by some as a means of preserving the integrity of their brands.

No purpose or power to acquire unlawful monopoly has been disclosed, and the record does not show that the probable effect . . . will be unduly to lessen competition. . . . It [The Commission] has no general authority to compel competitors to a common level, to interfere with ordinary business methods or to prescribe arbitrary standards for those engaged in the conflict for advantage called competition . . . it is essential that those who adventure their time, skill, and capital should have large freedom of action in the conduct of their own affairs.[34]

Finally, in a later proceeding the Commission was reversed by the lower court when it ordered the cessation of the practice of block-booking in the sale of moving pictures by the Paramount Famous-Lasky Corporation. The Court found that there was vigorous competition in the industry and held that

In the absence of combination or agreement, the fact that the method of negotiation as practiced by the respondent tends to exclude other independent producers is of itself insufficient to establish any probable tendency toward the creation of the evils prohibited by the Sherman Anti-Trust Act. . . . Where a practice is not inherently unlawful and unfair, and its legality depends on its effect, a finding that it has a dangerous tendency unduly to hinder competition or create a monopoly, must be based upon its effect as demonstrated upon the experience of competitors.[35]

Each of these cases involves sales policies by firms with partial monopoly powers which limit the freedom of customers and make the task of competition more expensive if not more difficult. The court has in each instance sought evidence of an effect to monopolize as evidenced by experience or of an intent to monopolize as evidenced by attending circumstances. Sales

[34] F. T. C. v. Sinclair Refining Co., 261 U. S. 463, 475 (1923).
[35] F. T. C. v. Paramount Famous-Lasky Corporation, et al., 57 F. (2d) 152, 157 (1932). For the Commission's proceedings cf. 11 F. T. C. 187.

policies which are the custom of the trade or the result of orderly development of an expanding business are given the
benefit of doubt in the absence of conclusive evidence of an
intent or probable effect unduly to monopolize trade. Business
men, it is held, must have a large freedom of action. However,
a showing of substantial interference with the access of rivals
to the market, it was implied, would be evidence of an intent or
effect to monopolize. These are the same tests which have
been developed in actions under the Sherman Act involving
close combinations or mergers. It appears, then, that as applied to the practices of either loose or close combinations in restraint of trade, section 5 of the Federal Trade Commission
Act as interpreted by the courts adds nothing to the Sherman
Act tests.

The second line of development of section 5 after the *Gratz*
decision involves competitive practices analogous to those held
unlawful at common law. In reviewing the activities of the
Commission in these proceedings the courts have illuminated
the scope of the act considerably.

One of the more important early decisions was that involving
misbranding by the Winsted Hosiery Company.[36] It had been
branding its underwear, much of which contained only a small
percentage of wool and none of which was all wool, variously
as "Natural Merino," "Natural Wool," etc. The defense of the
company was that labels such as it used had long been established in the trade and were generally understood to refer to
goods made partly of cotton. The Court rejected this plea. It
pointed out that the public had an interest in stopping the
practice since many consumers were deceived, and some retailers as well. The practice was found to be unfair as against
manufacturers of genuine all wool products and also as against
those manufacturers of mixed wool and cotton products which

[36] *F. T. C. v. Winsted Hosiery Co.*, 258 U. S. 483 (1922). For the
Commission's proceedings *cf.* 2 F. T. C. 202 and 3 F. T. C. 189.

branded their products truthfully.[37] It is interesting to note
that in this case the Court insisted upon a finding of public
interest in the practice and stressed the injury to competitors
through the diversion of trade by methods involving fraud.
These tests were applied in subsequent decisions.

The test of public interest is one which has been established
by the courts on the basis of the phraseology of the Federal
Trade Commission Act. This provision, that the Commission
shall issue a complaint "if it shall appear . . . that a proceeding by it in respect thereof would be to the interest of the
public" [38] did not appear in the first draft of the Senate bill [39]
but was added in conference presumably in order to give the
Commission considerable discretion in selecting and prosecuting
cases.[40] It might have been interpreted to facilitate the functioning of the Commission by allowing it to devote its limited
energies in the most effective direction. Instead it has been
interpreted as a limiting clause necessitating positive proof by
the Commission of the public interest in prosecuting each case
in addition to the showing of an unlawful method. This may
have had the effect of preventing the Commission from being
made the arbiter of many private controversies of a petty sort,
which may have been for the best since, as we shall see, the
Commission has been concerned far too much with injury to
rival property rights and far too little with injury to consumers.

In the proceedings of the Commission involving monopoly
or restraint of trade, no serious question of the public interest
has been raised. In proceedings involving misrepresentation

[37] The Circuit Court had held that since the practice was widespread
and any member of the trade was free to adopt it, no injury was done.
Winsted Hosiery Co. v. F. T. C., 272 Fed. 957, 960 (1921).

[38] Section 5(b).

[39] *Cf.* 63d Cong., 2d Sess., *Senate Document* No. 573 for a *Comparative
Print of the Federal Trade Commission Bill* showing the bill at various
stages in its legislative history.

[40] E. P. Herring, *op. cit.*, p. 112.

and analogous practices the question has been more vital. The decision in *F. T. C. v. Klesner* [41] is especially significant since in it for the first time the Supreme Court reversed the Commission on the ground that merely a private controversy was involved. There was involved a controversy between two individuals engaged in selling window shades in the District of Columbia under the name "Shade Shop." Sammons had moved out of a shop owned by Klesner in violation of an agreement, whereupon the latter opened up a shop in the same location and advertised it as the "Shade Shop" with the qualification "Hooper and Klesner." Five years later and after an unsuccessful attempt to get an injunction Sammons filed a complaint with the Commission. The crux of the Court's argument follows:

> But the mere fact that it is to the interest of the community that private rights shall be respected is not enough to support a finding of public interest. To justify filing a complaint the public interest must be specific and substantial. Often it is so, because the unfair method employed threatens the existence of present or potential competition. Sometimes, because the unfair method is being employed under circumstances which involve flagrant oppression of the weak by the strong. Sometimes, because, although the aggregate of the loss entailed may be so serious and widespread as to make the matter one of public consequence, no private suit would be brought to stop the unfair conduct, since the loss to each of the individuals affected is too small to warrant it.[42]

The Court added that "It is not claimed that the article supplied by Klesner was inferior to that of Sammons, or that the public suffered otherwise financially."

While sympathizing with the view that the Commission should not become "a petty traffic officer in the great highways of commerce," one cannot help but wonder whether such an

---

[41] 280 U. S. 19 (1929). For the Commission's proceedings *cf.* 5 F. T. C. 24.

[42] *Ibid.*, p. 28.

interpretation of the "public interest" clause does not overlook the intention of the sponsors of the act to prevent practices at their incipiency or, if you will, to prevent unfair "acts" before they become customary "practices" or "methods." It is possible that recent amendments to section 5 may serve to relieve the Commission from such restrictions.[43]

In the *Winsted* decision in addition to the matter of public interest the courts had investigated the question of injury to legitimate competitors. This test of an unfair method was destined eventually to become a necessary condition for jurisdiction of the Commission, thereby creating such a restriction upon the scope of the act as eventually to induce Congressional amendments. In the first case involving section 5 to get into the courts, the Circuit Court had been incautious enough to state that "the commissioners are not required to aver and prove that any competitor has been damaged." [44] Moreover, in the *Beech-Nut Packing Co.* decision the court sustained the Commission in a proceeding against an elaborate scheme of resale price maintenance although no claim was made that any direct competitor of the manufacturer pursuing the practice was injured. In an early proceeding involving alleged discrimination, however, the lower court raised the question of injury to competitors.[45] This involved a system of trade discounts which the Commission alleged violated section 5 of the Federal Trade Commission Act and section 2 of the Clayton Act as well. The National Biscuit Company gave volume discounts to a chain grocery based on total purchases of the whole chain, although it solicited orders and made deliveries on an individual store basis, but refused to grant similar privileges to coöperative or pool buyers. This was presumed to be unfair to the

---

[43] *Cf. post,* p. 101.
[44] *Sears, Roebuck & Co. v. F. T. C.,* 258 Fed. 311 (1919).
[45] *National Biscuit Co. v. F. T. C.,* 299 Fed. 733 (1924). For the Commission's proceedings *cf.* 7 F. T. C. 206 and 218.

independents, so far as the discounts were not based on differences in cost, and to the coöperative and pool buyers. In reversing the Commission the Court remarked concerning the applicability of section 5, "It is very apparent that no cracker manufacturer could be prejudiced by the refusal of his largest rival to satisfy customers or prospective customers by granting the discount desired." [46]

The issue came to a climax with the reversal of the Commission by the Court in its proceedings against the Raladam Company. The latter was engaged in selling a preparation for internal use as an obesity cure. It represented this as a scientific method of treating obesity which was safe and effective. The Commission alleged that among the ingredients was thyroid which will not act uniformly with all persons and cannot with safety be prescribed without constant consultation with a competent medical authority. The lower court reversed the Commission and in this was sustained by the Supreme Court. The decision of the higher court in this case is important.[47] The opinion was written by Justice Sutherland, who as member of the Senate had had much to say about the possibility that the phrase unfair competition would receive a narrow interpretation by the courts. In introducing his argument he gave a terse outline of the prerequisites for a proceeding under section 5 which colored most of the succeeding decisions prior to amendment of the act in 1938.

By the plain words of the act, the power of the Commission to take steps looking to the issue of an order to desist depends upon the existence of three distinct prerequisites: (1) that the methods complained of are *unfair*; (2) that they are methods of *competition* in commerce; and (3) that a proceeding by the Commission to prevent the use of the methods appears to be in the *interest of the public*.[48]

[46] 299 Fed. 733, 738.
[47] *F. T. C. v. Raladam Co.*, 283 U. S. 643 (1931). For the Commission's proceedings *cf.* 12 F. T. C. 363.
[48] 283 U. S. 643, 646. Italics are in the original.

The order in question was reversed because of a failure to show that it was a method *of competition*. "Findings of the Commission justify the conclusion that the advertisements naturally would tend to increase the business of respondent; but there is neither finding nor evidence from which the conclusion legitimately can be drawn that these advertisements *substantially injured or tended thus to injure the business of any competitor or of competitors generally*, whether legitimate or not." [49] The Commission was reversed because of an inadequate presentation of evidence on the matter of injury to competitors. The Court, however, did not set up the requirement of a showing of particular injury. ". . . it is not necessary that the facts point to any particular trade or traders. It is enough that there be present or potential substantial competition, which is shown by proof, or appears by necessary inference, to have been injured, or to be clearly threatened with injury, to a substantial extent. . . ." [50] The absence of proof or necessary inference that there were honest competitors, present or potential, who would be injured was the controlling factor in the Court's decision.

This interpretation, of course, leaves considerable latitude to the Commission in establishing its jurisdiction in a particular case, but it does subordinate the consumer or public interest to the property rights of business rivals on the somewhat incomplete theory that the public interest is adequately served by protecting private property from injury by fraudulent or

---

[49] *Ibid.*, p. 652. Italics are not in the original. "It is impossible to say whether, as a result of respondent's advertisements, any business was diverted, or was likely to be diverted, from others engaged in like trade, or whether competitors, identified or unidentified, were injured in their business, or were likely to be injured, or, indeed, whether any other anti-obesity remedies were sold or offered for sale in competition, or were of such a character as naturally to come into any real competition, with respondent's preparation in the interstate market." (*Ibid.*, p. 653.)

[50] *Ibid.*, p. 651.

unfair methods. Moreover, it increases the burden of the Commission in obtaining and presenting evidence. It was considerations of this sort which led subsequently to amendment of the act.

This decision did little to illuminate the scope of the term *unfair*, though Justice Sutherland did review the Congressional debates and made it clear that the intention was to stop unfair methods at their incipiency. He pointed out that section 5 was intended to have a wider interpretation than the phrase unfair competition at common law, but how broad was not clear. He did, however, envisage section 5 as connected with the broad purposes of the Sherman and Clayton Acts and suggested the applicability of Sherman Law criteria. "The paramount aim of the act is the protection of the public from the evils likely to result from the destruction of competition or the restriction of it in a substantial degree." [51]

The *Gratz* and *Raladam* decisions had established beyond much doubt that those types of practices which were unfair at common law because injury was caused to competitors by fraud or by interference with a competitor's business relations and those practices which were contrary to the Sherman Act because of restraint of trade or a tendency to monopolize were clearly forbidden by section 5. However, this apparently restricted the Commission to a prohibition of acts already illegal under previous law. The early hopes that the Commission would do pioneering work in raising the morals of business and improving competitive relationships appeared to have come to naught. One may look through the orders of the Commission in 1930 in vain to find any significant new directions in which the prohibitions of section 5 had been expanded beyond the prohibitions of previous law.

In 1931, however, the Commission issued an order to cease and desist against a firm selling penny candies which used

[51] 283 U. S. 647.

certain lottery and gaming devices in the sale of its products. The order was appealed to the courts and the objection raised that the practice did not fall under any of the classes of unfair methods which had been held to be within the Commission's jurisdiction. The Supreme Court, however, upheld the Commission and made it clear that the limits of the phrase "unfair methods of competition" were to have some flexibility and that the determinations of the Commission as to what falls within the prohibitions of the Act are to be given some weight by the courts.

But we cannot say that the Commission's jurisdiction extends only to those types of practices which happen to have been litigated before this court. Neither the language nor the history of the act suggests that Congress intended to confine the forbidden methods to fixed and unyielding categories. . . .

The act undoubtedly was aimed at all the familiar methods of law violation which prosecutions under the Sherman Act had disclosed. . . . But as this court has pointed out it also had a broader purpose. . . . Congress, in defining the powers of the Commission, thus advisedly adopted a phrase which, as this court has said, does not "admit of precise definition but the meaning and application of which must be arrived at by what this court elsewhere has called 'the gradual process of judicial inclusion and exclusion.' " . . .

While this court has declared it is for the courts to determine what practices or methods of competition are to be deemed unfair, . . . in passing on that question the determination of the Commission is of weight.[52]

This decision has raised new hopes that the Commission may be able to extend the prohibitions in appropriate circumstances in order more effectively to preserve competition.

In the particular case the Court found good grounds for holding the practice an unfair method of competition. It noted that when one seller adopts such policies his competitors are presented with the dilemma of facing a loss of business or of

---

[52] *F. T. C. v. R. F. Keppel & Bro., Inc.,* 291 U. S. 304, 309–14 (1934).

descending to a practice "which they are under a powerful moral compulsion not to adopt, even though it is not criminal."

It is true that the statute does not authorize regulation which has no purpose other than that of relieving merchants from troublesome competition or of censoring the morals of business men. But here the competitive method is shown to exploit consumers, children, who are unable to protect themselves. It employs a device whereby the amount of return they receive from the expenditure of money is made to depend upon chance. Such devices have met with condemnation throughout the community. Without inquiring whether, as respondent contends, the criminal statutes imposing penalties on gambling, lotteries, and the like, fail to reach this particular practice in most or any of the States, it is clear that the practice is of the sort which the common law and criminal statutes have long deemed contrary to public policy. For these reasons a large share of the industry holds out against the device, despite ensuing loss in trade, or bows reluctantly to what it brands unscrupulous. It would seem a gross perversion of the normal meaning of the word, which is the first criterion of statutory construction, to hold that the method is not "unfair." [53]

While the *Keppel* decision appears to have opened the door to broadening of the Commission's activity in some directions the *Raladam* decision had implications which led inevitably to a challenging of the Commission's jurisdiction in cases of price fixing by voluntary agreement and other analogous cases. While the courts had admittedly applied Sherman Act tests concerning loose agreements and resale price maintenance, the question might reasonably be asked how any competitor could be injured by a policy of voluntary price control on the part of a group of firms. The question was posed to the court in a proceeding by the Commission against the members of the California Rice Industry who had entered into price fixing agreements enforced by a system of penalties for violations.[54] It was pointed out that there were no sellers outside of the

[53] *Ibid.*, p. 313.
[54] *California Rice Industry et al. v. F. T. C.*, 102 F. (2d) 716 (1939). For the Commission's proceeding *cf.* 26 F. T. C. 968.

agreement, and therefore no competitors to be injured. Had the *Raladam* decision narrowed the scope of section 5 to include something less than all violations of the Sherman Act? The Circuit Court, upholding the Commission, was led to give a wider interpretation to the meaning of the phrase "unfair methods of competition" than in any previous decision.

The Agreement has destroyed the freedom to compete by the sanction of the fine on any one of the price fixers who may seek at any time a greater economic advantage because of his superior energy, ability and resources to process more than his permitted quota of the crop of rice and making larger sales at smaller profits. Each petitioner is a potential competitor who, if freed, would renew the desired norm of free competition with the others. That is to say, each petitioner, through the price fixing Agreement, prevents each other from the free use of his economic power and ability. It is the "potential" as well as the immediate competitor whose competition the Act seeks to keep free. . . .

A method is "an unfair method of competition" if it does not leave to each actual or potential competitor a "fair opportunity" for the play of his contending force engendered by an honest desire for gain.[55]

Whether the Supreme Court would sustain such a definition of an unfair method remains to be seen; and if so, what change this might make in the range over which the Commission might work is not clear. However, there seems little question but that practices violating the Sherman Act are violative of section 5. The Commission, however, was concerned by the requirement that injury to competitors, actual or potential, must be shown and requested that section 5 be amended to prevent unfair or deceptive acts and practices where injury could not be shown or where, because there was a monopoly, no competitor could be injured. This request was granted in recent amendments to the Act.

[55] 102 F. (2d) 720–21.

SUMMARY OF CRITERIA BEFORE 1938

Before outlining recent amendments to the Act and proceeding with a closer consideration of specific practices enjoined by the Commission, we may summarize briefly the general criteria established by the statute as judicially construed, which stood as guides for the Commission's activities until 1938. First, the methods to be enjoined must be unfair. What methods were unfair was to be determined by the judicial process of inclusion and exclusion. The courts had construed this to include practices which involve some element of "deception, bad faith, fraud or oppression," or which are "against public policy because of their dangerous tendency unduly to hinder competition or create monopoly." They clearly included the tests of unfair competition at common law and of restraint of trade under the Sherman Act. Second, there must be some injury or probability of injury to some competitor of the person pursuing the practice or to a potential competitor. An exception was made in cases involving loose combinations in restraint of trade, in which category the courts by analogy classify resale price maintenance. Finally, there must be specific and substantial public interest in enjoining the competitive method in question. In cases involving monopoly or restraint of trade, that fact alone was considered sufficient evidence of public interest. In cases involving misrepresentation or passing-off, it was sufficient evidence of public interest in a proceeding before the Commission to show that the practice would result in the purchasers' getting goods of a different sort or origin than they wished; it was not necessary to show inferiority of goods or other financial injury to the public. In cases involving schemes of merchandising by lottery, the public interest and "fairness" alike were found in the protection of consumers from exploitation by a morally reprehensible artifice which had been generally condemned by statute. Private controversies between two rivals in which no significant section of the consuming public was involved were beyond the Commission's jurisdiction.

AMENDMENTS OF 1938

The Commission in its final report on its investigation of chain-stores submitted to Congress in December 1934 recommended for the first time substantive changes in section 5.[56] These recommendations were renewed in subsequent Annual Reports of the Commission. The specific suggestion was to declare unlawful all *unfair or deceptive acts and practices* in commerce as well as *unfair methods of competition.*

The Commission had several purposes in view. In the first place while it was possible in most of the proceedings with which it was concerned to prove injury to some competitor, this often entailed considerable trouble and expense. Moreover, in cases where there was a complete monopoly or where the practice was universal in an industry, it was difficult if not impossible to show injury to the competitors. However, such unfair or deceptive practices clearly led to injury of the consumer. The proposed amendment, so the House Committee on Interstate Commerce stated, would make the "consumer, who may be injured by an unfair trade practice, of equal concern, before the law, with the merchant or manufacturer." [57] Moreover, the prevention of unfair *acts* as well as *practices* and *methods* might enable the Commission to proceed before a type of conduct became general, thus enabling the Commission to avoid the restrictions incident to the court's interpretation of the public interest clause. It was intended, then, to expedite the work of the Commission on the one hand and to give more attention to the protection of the consumer on the other.

---

[56] Federal Trade Commission, *Chain-Stores: Final Report on the Chain-Store Investigation* (1934); 74th Cong., 1st Sess., *Senate Document* No. 4, p. 97.

[57] 75th Cong., 1st Sess., *House Report* No. 1613, p. 3.

With the passage of the Wheeler-Lea Act in 1938 this amendment of the substantive provisions of section 5 and other amendments concerning procedure were incorporated into the law.[58] Section 5 (a) now reads:

> Unfair methods of competition in commerce, and unfair or deceptive acts or practices in commerce, are hereby declared unlawful.

The Wheeler-Lea Act went further, however, and added new sections to the Federal Trade Commission Act dealing with false advertising of food, drugs, devices, or cosmetics. The amendments declared the dissemination of any false advertisement an unfair or deceptive act or practice if the advertisement was disseminated through the channels of interstate commerce or if the advertisement was for the purpose of inducing or was likely to induce, directly or indirectly, the purchase in commerce of such articles. The Commission was empowered to proceed against any such advertisement by the issue of an order to cease and desist. In appropriate circumstances the Commission may appeal to the courts for a temporary injunction against the dissemination of such advertisements pending the disposal of complaints. This is a power not granted the Commission in usual proceedings under section 5.

The term "false advertisement" was defined as:

> . . . an advertisement, other than labeling, which is misleading in a material respect; and in determining whether any advertisement is misleading, there shall be taken into account (among other things) not only representations made or suggested by statement, word, design, device, sound, or any combination thereof, but also the extent to which the advertisement fails to reveal facts material in the light of such representations or material with respect to consequences which may result from the use of the commodity to which the advertisement relates under the conditions prescribed in said advertisement, or under such conditions as are customary or usual. No advertisement of a drug shall be deemed to be false if it is disseminated only to

---

[58] Public No. 447, 75th Cong., 3d Sess.

members of the medical profession, contains no false representation of a material fact, and includes, or is accompanied in each instance by truthful disclosure of, the formula showing quantitatively each ingredient of such drug.[59]

These sections on false advertising of food, drugs, devices, or cosmetics made several additions to the powers of the Commission. In the first place false advertising is made illegal if *misleading in a material respect* whether because of representations made or suggested or because of failure to reveal material facts. This should strengthen considerably the powers of the Commission to improve advertising standards. The amendment also granted the Commission the right to seek preliminary injunctions against disseminating such advertisements pending investigation and disposal of complaints; its powers under section 5 are only to issue a complaint and after hearings, if it finds violation of the Act, to issue an order to cease and desist. Finally, the amendments provide penalties for the violation of the sections on false advertisements in the form of fines and imprisonment, a type of penalty not provided by the original legislation of 1914. The general purpose and effect of these new sections on false advertisement as well as the amendment of section 5 would appear to emphasize increasingly the protection of the consumer rather than the protection of the business enterprise from injury due to its rivals' unfair practices.

[59] Section 15(a).

CHAPTER VI

COMMON LAW PRACTICES UNDER THE
FEDERAL TRADE COMMISSION ACT

THE FEDERAL TRADE COMMISSION from its beginning has been concerned with innumerable different practices. Until recently these were for the most part practices analogous to those which had been held to be unfair at common law, i.e. practices involving passing-off or misrepresentation in its manifold forms. Proceedings involving monopoly or restraint of trade were of some frequency in the early 1920's but become rare thereafter. Only after the demise of the NRA and the revivification of the Commission did practices involving restraint of trade come to be quantitatively significant. Even today proceedings involving passing-off or misrepresentation are overwhelmingly the most frequent.

The many forms which unfair methods of competition or unfair and deceptive practices may take is indicated in Table I where the major classifications of practices enjoined by the Commission under section 5 of the Federal Trade Commission Act in the year 1939 are summarized. This chapter will be concerned with the Commission's activities with reference to practices analogous to those illegal at common law; practices in restraint of trade will be considered in subsequent chapters.

MISREPRESENTATION

Misrepresentation in its manifold forms has always been the most frequent type of unfair method of competition before the Commission, and the principal significance of the Wheeler-Lea Act of 1938 lies in the extension of the powers of the Commission to deal with such practices as unfair or deceptive acts or

TABLE I

TYPES OF UNFAIR PRACTICES AGAINST WHICH THE FEDERAL TRADE
COMMISSION ISSUED CEASE AND DESIST ORDERS: 1939

Compiled from *Monthly Summaries of Work, Federal Trade Commission:*
January–December, 1939

1. PASSING-OFF OF PRODUCTS:
    a. Representing domestic product as imported
    b. Representing imported product as domestic
    c. Representing renovated product as new
    d. Representing merchandise bought in the open market as auction sale stock
    e. Representing ready-made ware as custom-made
    f. Representing aluminum alloy as a chromium alloy
    g. Representing machine-made products as hand-made products
    h. Representing old reference book as an up-to-date publication
    i. Representing material as pre-shrunk without proof that the material will not shrink further
    j. Imitating competitor's product, trade-name, or trade-mark

2. MISREPRESENTING PRODUCTS, THEIR QUALITIES OR PERFORMANCE:
    a. Misrepresenting prices and quality of work
    b. Misrepresenting origin of product
    c. Misrepresenting composition, quality, or capacity of product
    d. Misrepresenting the results to be obtained
    e. Misrepresenting certain radio sets as capable of world-wide reception when such is not the case
    f. Misrepresenting correspondence schools (necessary training period, certainty of receiving positions)
    g. Misrepresenting financial returns to purchasers (to be derived from purchase and use of service or commodity)
    i. Falsely representing a product as approved by United States Government
    j. Use of fraudulent methods in obtaining magazine subscriptions
    k. Dispensing labeled containers to drug trade without restrictions as to contents to be placed therein

3. ADVERTISING:
    a. Passing off a comparative analysis of competing products that is paid for in part by the manufacturer of one of the products as an authoritative, unbiased analysis made by a disinterested party
    b. Using misleading puzzle advertisements to contact purchasers
    c. Failing to disclose harmful potentialities of product

4. MISREPRESENTING METHODS AND TERMS OF SALE:
    a. Refusing to carry out terms of contract
    b. Misrepresenting terms under which coupons are redeemed
    c. Misrepresenting financing plan in connection with sales made on a deferred payment basis
    d. Misrepresenting usual prices

TABLE I (*continued*)

5. MISREPRESENTING NATURE OF THE FIRM:
   a. Representing distributor and bottler as manufacturer and distiller
   b. Representing dealer as refiner
   c. Representing distributor as grocer
   d. Representing dealer as manufacturer
   e. Representing retail dealer as wholesaler dealer

6. MISREPRESENTING AFFILIATIONS:
   a. Falsely claiming to be affiliated with United States Government
   b. Passing off a commercial enterprise as a Government-controlled project
   c. Exploiting a commercial enterprise by use of military photographs and titles, and Government reports
   d. Passing off commercial enterprise as an educational institution or as a "Foundation"

7. MISREPRESENTING TO PROSPECTIVE AGENTS:
   a. Misrepresenting facilities afforded agents
   b. Exaggerating financial returns to be expected by agents

8. DISTRIBUTING OR USING LOTTERY METHODS OR DEVICES

9. APPROPRIATING COMPETITORS' PROPERTY VALUES:
   a. Appropriating trade-name and trade dress of competitor
   b. Stimulating trade dress of competitor
   c. Disparaging products or methods of competitors

10. COERCIVE METHODS AND COLLUSION:
    a. Combining in restraint of trade
    b. Price fixing and collusive bidding
    c. Coercive methods against competitors

---

practices. The types of action which the Commission may take in these cases are several. Having established the fact of misrepresentation or false advertising it frequently offers the party in question the opportunity to sign a stipulation concerning the facts and an agreement to cease and desist. This is its most informal procedure and is adopted where it appears that the violation was not in bad faith or where the party in question indicates his complete willingness to abide by the law henceforth. In more serious cases, or in proceedings in which the facts or the law are in dispute the procedure followed is the more formal one provided by the original law of issuing a complaint, holding hearings and issuing finally, if the facts warrant, an order to cease and desist. In cases involving the false advertising of food, drugs, devices, or cosmetics the Commission under the Wheeler-Lea Act has the further power of bringing a suit for the issuance of an injunction in a District Court pending issuance and final disposition of a Commission complaint.

A review of a few specific cases handled by the Commission will illustrate certain problems which are faced in cases of misrepresentation. It will also give some idea of the variety of forms which misrepresentation may take. One of the earliest cases involving misrepresentation to reach the courts was that in which Sears, Roebuck and Company was ordered to cease representing that its sales of sugar below current prices were based upon its buying economies, when in fact it was using sugar as a loss leader; and from representing that it maintained a special purchasing representative in Japan who personally went into the tea gardens and supervised the picking of such tea, whereas in fact 75 per cent of its tea was bought from wholesalers and importers in the United States and there was no evidence that its representative in Japan was qualified to make or did make such selection; finally, from representing that it bought its coffees direct from the plantations when in fact it did not.[1]

The Commission has dealt with many cases involving misrepresentation by the simulation of trade-names and trade-marks. Thus, the "Juvenile Shoe Company" was enjoined because it had adopted a name and mark similar to that of an established competitor, the "Juvenile Shoe Corporation."[2] The Lighthouse Rug Company was enjoined from using the word "Lighthouse" in its corporate name because the Commission found that the use of the word in connection with rugs had acquired a secondary meaning, indicating rugs made by the blind in institutions.[3]

Several cases involving the misrepresentation of the char-

[1] 1 F. T. C. 163 (1918), *Sears, Roebuck and Co. v. F. T. C.*, 258 Fed. 307 (1919).

[2] 5 F. T. C. 105 (1922), *Juvenile Shoe Co., Inc. v. F. T. C.*, 289 Fed. 57 (1923).

[3] 12 F. T. C. 192 (1928), *Lighthouse Rug Co. v. F. T. C.*, 35 F. (2d) 163 (1929).

acter of the defendant's business and of the relation of dealers to manufacturers or mills have been prosecuted by the Commission and sustained by the courts. In the case of the Pure Silk Hosiery Mills Company, the lower court sustained the Commission in its ruling that the purchase of 240 out of a total of 1,363 shares of capital stock in a mill from which it bought a portion of its hosiery and the fact that its treasurer was one of the directors of the mill did not warrant the Pure Silk Hosiery Company using the word "mill" in its corporate name.[4] In a later decision Justice Sutherland made it clear that "If consumers or dealers prefer to purchase a given article because it was made by a particular manufacturer or class of manufacturers, they have a right to do so, and this right cannot be satisfied by imposing upon them an exactly similar article, or one equally as good, but having a different origin."[5] In another case, where the respondent, engaged in a mail-order business, advertised that it sold direct from factory to consumer, whereas in fact it only manufactured a limited number of the items which it sold, the Commission's order to cease and desist was sustained.[6]

Innumerable orders have enjoined misrepresentation of the constituents of a product or of its method of production. The Masland Company was ordered to cease using the term "Duraleather" as a trade-name on their imitation leather, on their stationery, or in their advertisements of the product, and "from using the word 'leather' or any other word or combination of words in such manner as to import or imply that such products are real leather."[7] A perfumer which imported concentrates

[4] 5 F. T. C. 245 (1922), *F. T. C. v. Pure Silk Hosiery Mills, Inc.*, 3 F. (2d) 105 (1925).

[5] *F. T. C. v. Royal Milling Co.*, 288 U. S. 212, 216 (1933). This was a reversal of the decision by the lower court, 58 F. (2d) 581 (1932).

[6] *Brown Fence & Wire Co. v. F. T. C.*, 64 F. (2d) 934 (1933).

[7] 12 F. T. C. 351, 358 (1929); *Masland Duraleather Co. et al. v. F. T. C.*, 34 F. (2d) 733 (1929).

from abroad and then blended and diluted them to make perfume in this country was enjoined from advertising that its products were "imported perfumes." The court sustained the Commission in its findings that the blending and diluting which was done in this country is the essential step in the manufacture of perfume and that this should be determining in establishing the place of manufacture.[8] The principal order which was sustained by the courts on the matter of misbranding was that in the case of the Winsted Hosiery Company. It was found to be branding underwear as "natural merino," "gray wool," "natural wool," "natural worsted," or "Australian wool," which underwear was partly cotton.[9]

In proceeding against misrepresentation, passing-off, and false advertising the Commission has not been without its troubles. In the cases cited above, and in hundreds of the Commission's orders and stipulations involving misrepresentation in one form or another there were involved no very technical problems in deciding whether or not the advertising claims, the labels, the trade-names, or brand-names were misleading. In most cases there was evidence of a technical or conventional meaning of the terms used against which alleged violations might be tested. But other cases involved delicate judgments of the difference between "puffing" and "misrepresentation," or difficult determinations of scientific and customary usage.

This is especially true of the therapeutic claims made for various drugs and devices. In the *Raladam* order the Commission enjoined the respondent from representing its obesity cure, Marmola, as "a scientific and accurate method for treating

---

[8] 26 F. T. C. 806 (1938), *Fioret Sales Co., Inc. et al. v. F. T. C.*, 100 F. (2d) 358 (1938).

[9] *F. T. C. v. Winsted Hosiery Co.*, 258 U. S. 483 (1922). For lower court decision, see 272 Fed. 957 (1921). For the Commission's order, 2 F. T. C. 202 (1920) and 3 F. T. C. 189 (1921).

obesity," or as representing its cure as a treatment for obesity "unless such representation is accompanied by a statement that 'Marmola' cannot be taken with safety to physical health except under direction and advice of competent medical authority." [10] The order was ultimately set aside by the Supreme Court on the ground that there was no evidence of competitors who were injured.[11] But in the lower court much attention was given to differences between fact and opinion, and the basis against which misrepresentation might be measured. The court noted "that the adjectives 'scientific' and 'safe' have ordinarily no absolute meaning." [12] The witnesses for the respondent pointed to accepted medical theories that thyroid extract, the principal ingredient of the remedy, supplements the effect of the patient's own thyroid gland and causes an increase in the metabolic rate, thus increasing fat elimination. Witnesses for the Commission countered with the reply "that no treatment for obesity — or in fact for anything else — is 'scientific,' and no remedy can be scientifically prescribed or be considered itself scientific, unless there is first a thorough examination of the patient, to learn his condition in all respects." [13] This order raised two fundamental questions. What weight is to be given to the Commission's findings of fact? Could the Commission require the statement of material facts such as the desirability of using the remedy only under medical supervision?

Several cases which have reached the courts have involved the use of trade-names with a technical significance. In the *L. B. Silver* case,[14] one of the problems facing the Commission was what constitutes a difference in the breed of hogs. The Silver Company claimed that its Ohio Improved Chester

[10] 12 F. T. C. 363, 369–70 (1929).
[11] *F. T. C. v. Raladam Co.*, 283 U. S. 643 (1931).
[12] 42 F. (2d) 430, 432 (1930).
[13] *Ibid.*, p. 433.
[14] 4 F. T. C. 73. *L. B. Silver Co. v. F. T. C.*, 289 Fed. 985 (1923).

(O.I.C.) was a breed distinct from the Chester White Hog. The antecedents of the Silver Company had developed the O.I.C. from Chester White stock. There was a tradition that in their initial efforts to improve the Chester White Hog they had crossed it with a Mammoth White English Hog. This claim, however, could not be verified since it was based only on oral tradition. In any event, after the initial efforts breeding was entirely with Chester White stock. There was no question but that the O.I.C. was an improved stock; the question at issue was whether or not it could be considered a *different* breed from the Chester White. From 1870, when L. B. Silver made public his claim that the O.I.C. was a distinct breed, until 1916 this claim was not challenged. Opinion was solicited from professional writers and practical breeders. The evidence was conflicting, or so the Circuit Court concluded when it dismissed the Commission's findings that the O.I.C. was not a separate and distinct breed.

There have been numerous cases before the Commission involving the correct designation of lumbers, which also involved technical questions of nomenclature. One of these enjoined the use of the term "Philippine mahogany" which was used quite generally in the trade to designate certain woods imported from the Philippine Islands.[15] Upon the legality of such nomenclature there was difference of opinion within the Commission itself and, in fact, a change in the ruling opinion due to a change in the balance of power within the Commission incident to a change of personnel. The issue concerned the difference between the botanical and commercial uses of the term "mahogany." It was determined that "Philippine mahogany" is not at all related botanically to the tree family Meliacese, from which

---

[15] *Indiana Quartered Oak Co. v. F. T. C.*, 26 F. (2d) 340 (1932). For the Commission's proceedings *cf.* 10 F. T. C. 300 (1926). *Cf.* also *In the Matter of Gillespie Furniture Co.*, 15 F. T. C. 439 (1931). There were numerous other firms involved in similar proceedings.

family "true" mahogany comes. It was also found that the Philippine government had officially objected to the use of the term "mahogany" in relation to such wood. However, the Philippine wood has certain characteristics which make it feasible to use it for many uses to which "true" mahogany is put, although the Commission in its first order claimed that the absence of certain other characteristics prevents the substitution of this wood for some uses where mahogany is called for. Commercially the wood had been widely advertised and sold as "Philippine mahogany." It had been recognized by this name in the specifications and classifications of some government agencies. While the importers knew that this was not true mahogany, it was an open question as to what the public thought. The cases were tentatively settled by each respondent company signing a stipulation to the effect that it would not use the word "mahogany" in connection with the advertising and sale of this wood, or articles made therefrom, without the modifying word "Philippine," but the orders have recently been reopened by the Commission.[16]

The problem of standards against which to measure alleged misrepresentation and misbranding is one which has frequently impeded the Commission in the pursuit of its work. Where there are established trade terms, where medical or other expert opinion agrees, where the preponderance of buyer understanding can be established no serious problems arise. But there is a wide area in which discretion must be exercised. Until quite recently the Commission has been hampered by the courts in its exercise of this discretion. Recently, by the establishment of standards of product or labeling in industry trade practice

---

[16] *Press Release*, January 27, 1940. In connection with this case, see the case of *Algoma Lumber Co. et al.* for a Commission order enjoining the use of the word "white" in conjunction with the word "pine" in the sale of Pinus ponderosa. 15 F. T. C. 139 (1931); 64 F. (2d) 618 (1933), 291 U. S. 67 (1934).

conference rules the Commission has pointed toward a possible solution of this problem. It has gone a good distance in establishing labeling standards, especially in the case of textiles where confusion has been as rampant as anywhere.[17] The further development of standards of product and labeling by the Commission and other agencies should go far to alleviate this problem.

The Commission's activities in the field of misrepresentation have for the most part been confined to the prohibition of positively false representations, by trade-marks, labels, advertising, etc. But misrepresentation may be equally the result of failure to disclose material facts. With this the Commission has only recently begun to deal. In recent trade practice conference rules it has not only established positive standards for the marking and advertising of goods, but it has also declared the failure to identify products or to disclose material facts to be an unfair practice. This is presumably done under the amended powers of section 5. This represents a real gain which followed from the revivification of the Commission and amendment of the Act. Moreover, under the Wheeler-Lea Act, in the case of food, drugs, devices, and cosmetics, the omission of any material fact is specifically declared to be an unfair act or practice. Here then the law and the Commission appear to be proceeding slowly toward the solution of problems faced in the early days of the law. The burden of sellers to inform the buyer correctly and adequately seems to be in process of replacing the old rule of *caveat emptor*.[18]

---

[17] *Cf. post*, pp. 277–79.

[18] *Cf.* the statement of Justice Black in *F. T. C. v. Standard Education Society et al.*, 302 U. S. 112, 116 (1937). "The fact that a false statement may be obviously false to those who are trained and experienced does not change its character, nor take away its power to deceive others less experienced. There is no duty resting upon a citizen to suspect the honesty of those with whom he transacts business. Laws are made to protect the trusting as well as the suspicious. The best element of business has long

Cases of misrepresentation do not generally involve monopoly in the legal sense of the term. To be sure the markets in which such practices occur are not purely competitive.[19] In general the markets concerned are those in which products are differentiated with respect either to the quality of the product, trade-name, or trade-mark. This means that the demand curve for the product of the individual firm is not perfectly elastic. The markets in question may be characterized by varying degrees of freedom of entry. But one may hazard the guess that the typical case of misrepresentation with which the Commission deals involves a relatively high elasticity of demand for the product of the individual firm and substantial freedom of entry into the general market so that profits tend to be reduced to normal.[20] One of the outstanding factors in these markets, however, is the comparative ignorance of the consumer. Within broad limits, the average consumer is unable or unwilling to make independent judgments. He depends upon a brand-name, trade-name, trade-mark, or some other identification to establish the nature and quality of a product. Sometimes price itself is taken to indicate quality. Advertising is depended upon by the layman to inform him of the properties and uses of particular products. These are the factors which often lead to misrepresentation.

Product differentiation and limited consumer knowledge, both factors which lead to a less than perfectly elastic demand for the product of the individual firm, provide an incentive to the firm to try to increase its net revenues by changing the

---

since decided that honesty should govern competitive enterprises, and that the rule of caveat emptor should not be relied upon to reward fraud and deception."

[19] E. H. Chamberlin, *The Theory of Monopolistic Competition* (Cambridge: Harvard University Press, 1933), chap. I.

[20] This is what Fritz Machlup calls "perfect monopolistic competition." *Cf.* "Monopoly and Competition: A Classification of Market Positions," *American Economic Review*, XXVII (1937), 449.

elasticity or intensity of the demand. Since the individual firm will often be producing under conditions of decreasing average cost, there will seem to be additional benefits to be had from increasing volume. Product differentiation, advertising, and other sales efforts are the usual practices of free industry, but limited knowledge on the part of the consumer offers an opportunity for the firm to affect its demand by sales methods which are untruthful or misleading. In many instances where entry to the field is unobstructed and consequently profits of the firm tend to be no more than normal, it is increasingly difficult for a firm to resist such practices where its competitors are resorting to them. In short, market imperfections in the form of monopoly elements and limited knowledge on the part of consumers are the root causes of misrepresentation.

In assessing the economic significance of misrepresentation it is convenient to make a twofold classification of misrepresentations which distinguishes those instances in which a seller tries to identify his product with that of another or of others from those instances in which a seller tries to differentiate or distinguish his product from a general group by claims of its distinctive character or superiority. This distinction is chiefly interesting because of differences in the effects of the misrepresentation upon consumers and competitors. The first type may be further classified according to whether the seller simulates (a) the product of a particular seller or (b) a general class of product.

Where the seller by means of misrepresentation simulates the product of a particular seller by imitating his trade-name, trade-mark or other identifying characteristics, the injury to the competitor is quite specific and falls directly upon the one whose product is simulated. This is the type of case with which the common law deals under the category of unfair competition. In such cases if the products involved are essentially similar, the consumer may not suffer any significant injury. But the practice will tend to increase the elasticity of demand for the product simulated thereby injuring its producer. This practice may be illustrated by the cases prosecuted by the Commission in which certain flour dealers indicated in their firm-names and by their advertising that they were "milling" concerns whereas in fact they did not do any grinding of grain but merely mixed the flours. However, insofar as there is simulation of the product of a particular seller where the products are not substantially similar, the consumer may suffer injury as well as the producer of the product imitated.

Simulation of a general class of product is a type of misrepresentation with which the common law of unfair competition is powerless to cope. This type of case is best illustrated by examples of misbranding. When a concern sells part-cotton underwear as "all-wool," or "Philippine mahogany" furniture as "mahogany," it is trying to pass off its product as being of superior class or quality. The incidence of this type of misrepresentation is less specific. The burden falls upon all others producing the general class of product who brand their goods correctly. Evidence of particular injury may be hard to prove. This, and the fact that the incentive of any one producer to prosecute at common law is negligible, explains why the common law is inadequate to deal with such cases. In this respect, the Commission has substantially extended the common law protection to fair trade. Such practices cannot fail to inflict injury on the consumer, as well as upon the honest competitors. This follows from the fact that in the face of correct knowledge of the facts the consumer would alter his expenditure patterns.

The second type of misrepresentation, that which seeks to differentiate the product of one seller from the general group of substitute products, may be treated more briefly. This may take the form of false claims that a particular product is a "scientific" cure, that a particular product has received the approval of certain doctors or of a medical association, or that a school can guarantee a job because it has official connections with the government. Differentiation of product is, of course, a characteristic of many markets. By such differentiation the seller hopes to make the demand for his product more intense and less elastic. The differences between the particular product and substitutes are emphasized. The consequences of product differentiation have been analyzed by Professor E. H. Chamberlin.[21] It tends, on the whole, to increase costs and price by sacrificing the economies of size and stimulating sales efforts. But if it may be assumed that buyers really prefer the differentiation, it may lead to an equilibrium adjustment which, to quote Chamberlin, is "a sort of ideal." [22] However, where the demand is affected by various sorts of misrepresentation and consumer preference developed by false methods, the elasticity of the demand curve can no longer be considered an index of buyers' "true" preferences. Consumers are clearly induced to make a distribution of their expenditures which to them is less desired than the distribution which they would have made in the absence of such misrepresentation. Only in the event that their freely developed expenditure patterns, in the absence of misrepresentation, would have been irrational from the standpoint of their own desires or interests could they possibly gain by such practices.

OTHER METHODS

Other methods of competition falling in this group of practices which are illegal under the common law concept of unfair competition may be treated rather briefly. Commercial bribery, which takes the form of making gifts to the agents of customers or prospective customers without the knowledge of the employers of said agents, was enjoined by many orders of the

---

[21] *Op. cit.*, chaps. IV, V.
[22] *Ibid.*, p. 94. *Cf.* J. M. Cassels, "Excess Capacity and Monopolistic Competition," *Quarterly Journal of Economics*, LI (1937), 436.

Commission in the early years following the war. While the jurisdiction of the Commission in the case of bribery of the grossest forms has not been challenged, the courts have limited the type of practice which may be enjoined as bribery. For example, the courts have pointed out that the dining, wining, and entertaining of employees of customers has been an incident of business from time immemorial and the expenses involved are recognized as a proper deduction for income tax returns; consequently, such practices are held not to be unfair methods of competition.[23] It was likewise held that the giving of premiums or gratuities to agents of an employer with the knowledge of the latter is not illegal.[24] As a result of its investigation of cases involving genuine commercial bribery, however, the Commission was moved to send a special report to Congress recommending that legislation be passed to prohibit the acceptance or solicitation of such gifts as well as the offering and giving of them.[25]

Economically speaking bribery and other more subtle forms of salesmanship are analogous to advertising or the allowing of larger margins to dealers in that they operate on the demand schedule of the particular firm. Although the motive for pursuing this type of practice is the same as that for misrepresentation, namely, the imperfectly elastic demand curve with less than the optimum utilization of plant, its success depends upon an institutional factor generally ignored by our economic theory, a division of interest within the economic, i.e. the buying, entity. The distinction made by the courts between gifts or premiums given to an agent but made with the knowledge of the principal and secret bribery made to induce the agent to sacrifice his principal's interest is a reasonable one.

---

[23] *New Jersey Asbestos Co. v. F. T. C.*, 264 Fed. 509 (1920).
[24] *Kinney-Rome Co. v. F. T. C.*, 275 Fed. 665 (1921).
[25] *Special Report on Commercial Bribery*, 65th Cong., 2d Sess., *House Document* No. 1107 (1918).

Another practice which the Commission has from time to time enjoined is the practice of disparaging a competitor or his product. This practice may be very annoying to a concern, especially one which has not an established reputation of long standing. The Commission's power to forbid such practices seems never to have been seriously challenged. The court has held, however, that in the case of a product proved to be of varying composition and misbranded, there was no public interest in a proceeding by the Commission against a competitor who circulated the results of an independent and competent analysis among previous purchasers of the product.[26]

Orders enjoining espionage, another practice illegal at common law, have been rare, although the basic authority to do so where there is substantial evidence that the information was used to hinder or stifle competition seems well established.[27] Orders to cease making threats of suits for patent infringement in bad faith have been issued from time to time but the two cases which have been appealed have been reversed by the Circuit Court [28] on the ground that lack of good faith in making the threats was not proved by the Commission.

The Commission has proceeded frequently during the last decade against concerns which were using a lottery or prize scheme in merchandising. The Supreme Court upheld the Commission in an order against such a merchandising scheme by which inferior penny candy was sold to school children.[29] Lower courts have subsequently held that lottery schemes of merchandising may be enjoined even though the sale does not involve an inferior product and is not made to children.[30] In

---

[26] *John Bene & Sons, Inc. v. F. T. C.*, 299 Fed. 468 (1924).

[27] *Philip Carey Mfg. Co. et al. v. F. T. C.*, 29 F. (2d) 49 (1928).

[28] *Herman Heuser v. F. T. C.*, 4 F. (2d) 632 (1925); *Flynn & Emrich Co. v. F. T. C.*, 52 F. (2d) 836 (1931).

[29] 15 F. T. C. 276 (1931); *R. F. Keppel & Bro., Inc. v. F. T. C.*, 291 U. S. 304 (1934).

[30] *Cf. Hofeller v. F. T. C.*, 82 F. (2d) 647 (1936); *F. T. C. v. F. A.*

extending the concept of unfair methods of competition to this practice the Commission and courts have taken a significant step in enlarging upon the common law. It constitutes a first step in limiting the type of sales appeal which may be made to buyers. Other common law types of unfair practice have been enjoined because competitors were hurt by methods which interfered with consumers' preference: in the lottery cases for the first time the law interferes with consumer preference in the name of fair trade.

Martoccio Co., 87 F. (2d) 561 (1937); *Chicago Silk Co. v. F. T. C.*, 90 F. (2d) 689 (1937), a case involving silk hosiery.

CHAPTER VII

DISCRIMINATION. I: PROBLEM AND POLICY
BEFORE 1936

THERE is no practice which has been more consistently the
subject of concern of public policy than that of discrimination. It was in connection with the railroads that discrimination in price and service first received legislative attention.
Railroad rebates, which gained particular notoriety in the
oil industry, were generally felt to be a principal explanation
of the growth of the early trusts so that legislation on the
matter of railroad rates had as one purpose the mitigation of
the problem of monopoly in industry. The oil industry likewise provided the most notorious examples of the other form
of discrimination which early attracted public attention, namely,
local discrimination. By the turn of the century local discrimination, generally conceived as "the practice of lowering
price temporarily in one locality in order to stifle competition,
and at the same time recouping losses by raising prices in the
other markets" assumed a leading place among the iniquitous
practices which were believed to lead to the formation and
survival of monopolies.[1] It was clear by 1911 that discrimination might be one of the practices considered in determining
violations of the Sherman Act, but in 1914 new legislation was
passed empowering the Federal Trade Commission to deal with
the practice. More recently the Robinson-Patman Act of 1936

[1] Note the comment of Alfred Marshall: "The first place among unfair
methods of competition, which are denounced by the Anti-trust Laws,
is held by price discriminations; the chief variety of which is that of
malign local price-cutting." *Industry and Trade* (London: The Macmillan
Co., 1919), p. 521.

has amended and extended this legislation of 1914, while state legislation has dealt with discrimination in intrastate commerce.

MEANING OF DISCRIMINATION

The meaning of the term "discrimination" as applied to industrial practices is confused. It refers generally to differences or inequalities in price or product. Popularly, any difference in the price of a product charged by a seller to two or more buyers is called a discrimination regardless of differences in the time or conditions of the sale. Likewise when the price of a product to various sellers is the same but the quality, service or other conditions of sale differ, popular usage speaks of the situation as involving discrimination. In legal writing the term is frequently used in similar manner. Starting with this general usage, popular and legal discussion generally proceeds to distinguish between the legitimate and illegitimate reasons for discrimination, the economic and uneconomic forms of discrimination, the legal and illegal conditions of discrimination. Popular and legal usage, however, will not suffice for scientific discussion.

Discrimination in selling implies *differences* of some sort in the terms given by one seller to two or more buyers or classes of buyers. These differences may be in price, quality, service, discounts, or any of the other terms and conditions of sale. But in economic usage, all such differences are not discriminatory. If *all except one* of the variables in a sale (price, quality, services, terms, marginal cost, etc.) are identical, we may say there is discrimination. If *all* the variables are identical, we may say there is no discrimination. This is the most unequivocal use of the term. Applied to price discrimination this definition implies that if a seller charges different prices for two or more units of an identical product sold at the same moment of time and under conditions similar in all respects, there is discrimination.

But the customary circumstance is one in which *two or more* variables incident to a sale differ as between the various units of sale. In many circumstances the product is not identical, the time of sale is not the same, the conditions including costs of production, terms of sale, etc. are not the same. And yet public policy is concerned with just these price relations. For example, a tire manufacturing firm sells a product under its own widely advertised brand-name at one price and a technically similar tire under a private brand at another. The costs of production and sale vary. Is the price difference discriminatory? Or consider the differential between the price at which a company sells aluminum ingot and aluminum cable. The latter is the processed derivative of the first. Some price differential is to be expected. Some particular differential would not be discriminatory; differentials of other size would be discriminatory. Where should the line be drawn? Finally, consider the differences in the price at which two joint-products are sold. Clearly the prices per pound of cotton-seed and cotton-seed oil are not likely to be the same. A differential is to be expected. However, may not some differentials be discriminatory? Cannot the concept of discrimination be extended to apply to differentials in such sales where more than one of the variables incident to a sale differ as between the various sales being compared?

As shall be developed below, the power to discriminate implies some imperfection in the market, generally some monopoly power. Discriminatory prices are monopolistic prices.[2] This gives a clue to a more inclusive definition of discrimination by a seller. We may say that a seller discriminates if as between two sales he exercises a different degree of monopoly power. But if in the sale of two identical units of the same product, or of two variations of the product, or of units of the same product at different times, or of two joint-products he exer-

[2] The term "monopolistic" is here used in its economic sense.

cises the same degree of monopoly power, his sales policies may be said to be non-discriminatory.

For the purpose of measuring the degree of monopoly power we may take the Lerner index,[3] $\dfrac{\text{Price} - \text{Marginal Cost}}{\text{Price}}$. Assuming that price is not below marginal cost, the limits of the index would be 1 and 0. Two products selling at a price appropriate to pure competition, i.e. where price equals marginal cost, would be non-discriminatory. If two products with equal marginal costs sold at similar prices but at a price above marginal cost, these prices would be non-discriminatory since the index of monopoly power would be the same for each product.

While this definition is necessary for completeness much of the subsequent discussion will run in terms of similar products, similar costs, and similar conditions of sale. In this case there is only one variable which varies as between different sales, namely, price. Any price difference, therefore, becomes indicative of discrimination.

The problem of price discrimination viewed in terms of this definition encompasses the whole problem of the price structure of the firm. There is much elliptical discussion of price and price policies of the firm, most of which assumes that there is one product and one price. A realistic picture of the typical manufacturing firm, however, will disclose a complicated price structure composed of myriad particular prices. For any one product there may be variations in price depending upon the time of the sale, the quantity sold, the credit terms, etc. Moreover, there may be differences in the prices charged to various persons even though all other conditions of the sales are the same. Or, there are the differences in price for various qualities, grades and sizes of similar goods and for different types of goods sold by the firm, whether related or unrelated. Finally,

---

[3] A. P. Lerner, "The Concept of Monopoly and the Measurement of Monopoly Power," *Review of Economic Studies*, I (1934), 169.

there is the geographical structure of prices, which establishes the relation between the price of any product delivered at different points. The methods by which these price relations are determined are various. Discount books, extra books, basing-point formulas are part of the story. More or less arbitrary cost allocations may be important in some cases; customary differentials are important in others; while a careful calculation of demand and cost situations in a systematic pursuit of maximum profits is a principal explanation of still others.

TYPES OF DISCRIMINATION

For the purposes of analyzing the effects of discrimination and of establishing public policy with reference to the practice, it is important to distinguish certain types. Some discrimination is *systematic*, that is the price differentials are an inherent part of the price structure, while in other cases the practice is *unsystematic*. Thus, in many industries where price changes are negotiated in whole or in part by individual bargaining, price differences will often appear in the process of adjusting prices from one level to another. Price concessions are given secretly to some buyers, but gradually as they become known price settles down to a new non-discriminatory level. Another distinction is that between *temporary* and *persisting* policies of discrimination. Dumping in international trade is frequently a temporary phenomenon. Local price cutting designed to drive out competitors may likewise be of the same nature. Finally, a distinction should be made between discrimination which is pursued with the particular purpose of maximizing revenues by segregating and differentiating between markets with various elasticities of demand (henceforth called *purposive*) and discrimination which is rather *incidental* to other policies. Thus, in establishing arbitrary quantity limits for the application of quantity discount schedules some incidental discrimination will inevitably result, e.g. between two buyers who fall on either side of a quantity limit. Again any system of price control whether pursued by private industry or the government necessitates the application of some formula controlling the geographical structure of prices. It is clear that this may lead to incidental discrimination, the application of a basing-point formula or a uniform delivered price are cases in point. On the other hand, the policy of the milk industry in distinguishing between the fluid and processed milk markets is one of purposive discrimination.

Economic analysis has been concerned primarily with discrimination which is purposive, systematic, and persisting. This is perhaps the most important type from the point of view of public policy and the easiest with which to deal analytically. In studies of geographical price structures we often run into discrimination which is systematic, persisting, but incidental. The problems in this field are interesting but more difficult of analysis, and it is to be questioned whether the discrimination is the significant factor. One type of discrimination, that incidental to price changes in imperfectly organized markets, has received much attention in the literature on trade associations and open-price systems. This discrimination may be described as incidental, unsystematic, and temporary. There will be occasion to use this classification from time to time in succeeding discussions.

PREREQUISITES OF DISCRIMINATION

Someone has said that "discrimination is the better part of value," but it is also true that it is a policy which not all sellers are able to follow.[4] There are several prerequisites of the power

---

[4] The best expositions of the economic aspects of discrimination are to be found in A. C. Pigou, *The Economics of Welfare* (London: The Macmillan Co., 1932, 4th ed.), pp. 275–317, 810–12 and Joan Robinson, *The Economics of Imperfect Competition* (London: The Macmillan Co., 1933), Book 5. See also J. M. Clark, *The Economics of Overhead Costs* (Chicago: University of Chicago Press, 1923), chap. XX.

to discriminate. The first factor to be noticed is that discrimination presupposes some market imperfection which gives rise to a demand for the product of the individual firm which is less than perfectly elastic. This is generally some element of monopoly, but the imperfection may arise from incomplete knowledge on the part of some or all buyers of the character of the particular product and of substitutes.[5] This follows from our definition of discrimination. If all sales are made under perfectly competitive conditions, the degree of monopoly power will be o in all cases. Public policy, however, has seldom recognized the fact that where there is discrimination there is usually some element of monopoly. It has been concerned with discrimination, not as an exercise of monopoly power, but rather as an instrument in the development of monopoly power.[6]

A second prerequisite of discrimination is the power to separate the markets. This implies, in the first place, that units of product sold at the lesser price shall not be resold to those who have been classified in a group paying a higher price except at a cost which more than offsets the differential in price. This is one reason why in the case of geographical discrimination against buyers close to the seller, by the device of freight absorption or by use of a basing-point formula, it is customary

[5] In a market where the demand curve is tipped not because buyers acting in full knowledge "prefer" the product of one firm but because some of the buyers do not know of the alternatives, it does not seem wise to say there are monopolistic elements. It is possible to conceive of a market where there is a persistent fringe of consumers who will pay more than the going market price because of ignorance. The rest of the consumers may shift their patronage if there is the slightest price differential. A seller may be able to discriminate against this fringe. However, one would hardly characterize the market as monopolistic in the sense that monopoly means "control over supply." Much temporary and unsystematic discrimination is to be accounted for by imperfect knowledge.

[6] *Cf. post*, pp. 141, 144, 168. The conception of discrimination in our public policy is discussed more fully in the subsequent sections of this chapter.

to sell only on a delivered price basis. Otherwise, products sold at a low mill net price to a customer distant from the basing-point might be diverted to the local area in which a higher price is charged.[7] Once delivered to the distant customer, the product can compete in the local market only by incurring the cost of return shipment. Discrimination in favor of buyers located near the seller is more difficult to prevent from breaking down by resale. However, even in this case sale on a delivered basis will help especially where the freight structure favors the long-haul. One way of insuring against diversion even though the cost of diversion is not greater than the price differential is by agreement with the buyer. Sanctions in the form of a refusal to make further sales may be invoked to enforce such an agreement. In some cases, as when discrimination favors one channel of distribution as against another, the self-interest of the favored class is sufficient to prevent resale. In the case of personal services rendered directly to the customer transference of units of "product" from one market to another is most difficult.

Separability of markets also implies that no element of demand proper to one classification shall be transferred to another. Thus, where there is discrimination between processors or dealers who compete in subsequent resale, there is considerable danger of such transfer. When the Goodyear Tire and Rubber Company sold tires to Sears, Roebuck and Company at lower prices than to independent dealers, it ran the risk that the consumers would shift their patronage from the independent dealers to Sears, Roebuck and Company. If all customers knew that the tires were the same and if the only motive of the con-

[7] This is also the reason why in industries using the basing-point system it is often customary to refuse to deliver on board the customer's truck at the mill without first ascertaining beyond a doubt the destination of the product. Often the seller will not deliver f.o.b. mill to be taken away in the customer's truck on any terms for fear the product will be diverted to high-priced markets.

sumer were cheapness of price, there would be complete transference of demand and consequently discrimination would disappear. Actually, Goodyear protected itself in this case by differentiating the product with respect to nonessential characteristics and by keeping the facts of the case secret. Moreover, some buyers may be expected to prefer the convenience and service of the independent dealer and to pay a price which will cover both the additional cost of such service and the discriminatory differential. Other impediments to the shift of elements of supply or demand, then, are secrecy and the differentiation of the product sold in the different markets.

Granted the power to discriminate there will be a motive to do so, where discrimination is purposive rather than incidental, only when a further condition is satisfied, namely when the elasticities of the demand of the various markets which may be segregated differ. In the case of markets composed of final consumers, this difference is to be explained by differences in consumers' preferences. In the case of intermediate dealers, the elasticity of their demand will depend not only on the demand of the consumers whom they serve but also on their own cost of distribution and on the alternatives which they have of developing other sources of supply and of directing consumers' demand toward such substitutes. This latter factor may give considerable elasticity to the demand of large-scale distributors.

Granted the power to discriminate the general procedure will be to break up the market into as many parts as is possible and to deal with each separately. Ideally the seller would try to deal with each buyer separately, but as a practical matter he will generally be able to distinguish only a limited number of markets. Assuming the seller is producing only one standardized product and desires to maximize his profits, he will sell an output at which his marginal cost equals his aggregate marginal revenue. This output will be divided between the various markets so that marginal revenue in each of the markets is equal to the marginal cost of the whole output. The price in each market will be that indicated on the demand curve for the appropriate output.[8]

Although temporary local discrimination had been recognized by the courts in some proceedings as an exclusive and predatory practice violating the Sherman Act,[9] the legislation of 1914 was designed to settle the question beyond a doubt. While it was thought by some that section 5 of the Federal Trade Commission Act would cover the practice, there was a general desire to make certain of it by explicitly forbidding the practice in the Clayton Act.[10] Neither in the draft of section 2 as first passed by the House of Representatives nor in the form in which it was finally enacted is the prohibition limited to local discrimination. However, there has been some doubt as to Congressional intention in regard to this matter. A perusal of the Congressional reports and debates does not indicate that Congress had anything in mind other than local discrimination of the sort made famous by the Standard Oil and Tobacco trusts. The adoption of this theory of Congressional intent by the lower courts led to a reversal of the Federal Trade Commission's attempt to forbid discrimination between rival distributive channels, but a later decision by the Supreme Court

[8] *Cf.* Joan Robinson, *op. cit.*, pp. 182–83.

[9] J. E. Davies, *Trust Laws and Unfair Competition*, p. 464, 479–81.

[10] The Clayton Bill as passed by the House of Representatives previous to the final consideration of the Federal Trade Commission Bill, including section 5 forbidding unfair methods of competition, included a section making it unlawful to discriminate "either directly or indirectly . . . in price between different purchasers of commodities in the same or different sections." (63d Cong., 2d Sess., *Senate Document* No. 584, p. 4.) The Senate eliminated section 2 on the recommendation of Senator Culberson (*Congressional Record*, LI (1914), 13849). The section was reinserted in the form as passed by the Conference Committee (63d Cong., 2d Sess., *Senate Document* No. 584, p. 4).

in a case arising under section 2 to which the Federal Trade Commission was not a party reversed this interpretation.

There is no indication that Congress had a profound understanding of the various forms or possibilities of discrimination. Senator Cummins insisted that it was impossible to draft a section which would be effective and at the same time not prohibit things which it was not the desire of Congress to prohibit. "It would not be difficult to prove that a seller had discriminated in price between different localities or different buyers in the same locality, but competition cannot be preserved unless there is some discrimination." [11] In just what sense he used the term "competition" or why discrimination is necessary to preserve competition is not clear. It was on the basis of such a theory, however, that the Conference Committee, in the bill as finally enacted, made an exception in the case of "discrimination in price . . . made in good faith to meet competition." This exception was recommended "upon the ground that the enlargement will tend to foster wholesome competition." [12]

Another proviso of the section which has significant economic connotations is the clause providing that discrimination shall be unlawful only "where the effect of such discrimination may be to substantially lessen competition or tend to create a monopoly in any line of commerce." As has been pointed out in the preceding section, discrimination in the economic sense presupposes a demand for the product of the individual firm of some finite elasticity due to the existence of some element of monopoly power or some other imperfection. Public policy has not recognized this fact. This proviso is significant since it limits seriously the instances of discrimination in which the Commission may proceed.

By 1925 the Commission had issued twelve orders to cease

[11] *Congressional Record*, LI (1914), 14250 (Senator Cummins).
[12] 63d Cong., 2d Sess., *Senate Report* No. 698, p. 44.

and desist the practice of discrimination. Thereafter, no orders were issued until March 5, 1936 when it finally ordered the Goodyear Tire and Rubber Company to cease and desist from certain discriminatory practices. Its inactivity after 1925 is to be explained in part by the attitude of the courts.[13] Of the thirteen orders issued before the Robinson-Patman amendments in 1936 two were directed against simple discrimination between different customers.[14] Eight of the orders were directed against discrimination between customers who had been classified arbitrarily according to trade-status,[15] the classification in two cases being whether or not resale prices were maintained.[16] One order alleged local discrimination of the traditional sort,[17] while another was directed at local discrimination incidental to a basing-point system of price quotations.[18] The order in the tire case alleged discrimination between the mail-order house of Sears, Roebuck and Company on the one hand and the independent jobbers and dealers on the other.[19]

[13] Federal Trade Commission, *Final Report on the Chain Store Investigation*, p. 90.

[14] *Wayne Oil Tank and Pump Co.*, 1 F. T. C. 259 (1918); *Galena Signal Oil Co.*, 2 F. T. C. 446 (1920).

[15] *Cudahy Packing Co.*, 1 F. T. C. 199 (1918); *Eli Lilly and Co.*, 1 F. T. C. 442 (1919); *Mennen Co.*, 4 F. T. C. 258 (1922); *South Bend Bait Co.*, 4 F. T. C. 355 (1922); *Salt Produce Association et al.*, 5 F. T. C. 67 (1922); *National Biscuit Co.*, 7 F. T. C. 206 (1924); *DeSoto Paint Manufacturing Co.*, 5 F. T. C. 177 (1922); *Loose-Wiles Biscuit Co.*, 7 F. T. C. 218 (1924).

[16] *Cudahy Packing Co.*, 1 F. T. C. 199; *Eli Lilly and Co.*, 1 F. T. C. 442. Several actions before the lower courts to which the Commission was not a party involved discriminatory prices against those not maintaining suggested resale prices. *Great Atlantic & Pacific Tea Co. v. Cream of Wheat Co.*, 224 Fed. 566 (1915); 227 Fed. 46 (1915); *Frey & Son v. Cudahy Packing Co.*, 261 Fed. 65 (1919), 256 U. S. 208 (1921); *Frey & Son v. Welch Grape Juice Co.*, 240 Fed. 114 (1917), 261 Fed. 68 (1919). In each of these cases, however, the practice of refusing to sell to those not maintaining suggested prices except on discriminatory terms was held not to be illegal.

[17] *Pittsburgh Coal Co. of Wisconsin et al.*, 8 F. T. C. 480 (1925).

[18] *United States Steel Corp., et al.*, 8 F. T. C. 1 (1924).

[19] 22 F. T. C. 232 (1936).

Unfortunately proceedings under section 2 have not fared well at the hands of the court. The cases which have been appealed to the courts have involved discriminatory practices of a type not envisaged by the sponsors of the act in 1914, to wit discrimination by a manufacturer between various classes of customers. The Commission has been reversed by the courts in all cases brought before them, though some of the private suits under section 2 have been successfully prosecuted.[20] The inadequacy of the section as interpreted by the courts led to significant amendments in 1936.

In three cases in the early 1920's the Commission was reversed in orders charging discrimination by a manufacturer between various classes of dealers on the ground, among others, that section 2 applied only to the lessening of competition between the discriminator and his competitors, and not to lessening of competition between his customers. On this particular issue the lower courts were subsequently reversed in a proceeding to which the Commission was not a party.

The proceedings against the Mennen Company alleged discrimination between those classified as wholesalers and retailers on the one hand and the coöperatives on the other. The latter were classified as retailers, although they performed the function of wholesalers and bought in equivalent quantities. The Commission in its findings noted that this practice hindered the coöperatives in their efforts to maintain themselves on a basis of economic efficiency.[21] The Circuit Court in reversing the order [22] discarded the theory that the practice violated section 5 of the Federal Trade Commission Act on the ground that it fell under neither of the categories as established by the Supreme Court in the *Gratz* decision since there was no intimation that the Mennen Company had any monopoly of the busi-

---

[20] The Clayton Act provides that private individuals suffering injury from practices forbidden by the act may themselves bring suit in the courts for damages.   [21] 4 F. T. C. 281.

[22] *Mennen Co. v. F. T. C.*, 288 Fed. 774 (1923).

ness of manufacturing and selling toilet articles or that it had the ability or intent to acquire one.[23] Furthermore, the practice was not "opposed to good morals." As for the applicability of section 2 of the Clayton Act the court concluded that it was the intent of Congress to prohibit only practices which lessen competition between the offending party and its competitors and that the section should not be construed to prohibit the lessening of competition among purchasers. Obviously, no competitor of the Mennen Company could be injured by the latter refusing to sell to coöperatives except at higher prices.

The proceedings against the National Biscuit and Loose-Wiles companies alleged discrimination in favor of chain-stores as against independent retailers.[24] It seems to have been established that the prices charged to chain-stores were based on the quantities bought by the chain as a whole although many costs of sale and delivery to the chain were the same as to independent retailers since orders were solicited from, deliveries made to, and payment made by each of the constituent members of the chain separately. Discounts given to the chains were refused, however, to members of voluntary chains who banded together for purposes of joint buying. The court denied the significance of the price differences saying that the evidence "does not sustain the charge of price discrimination, for there is no provision in the Clayton Act, or elsewhere, that the price to two different purchasers must be the same if it cost the seller as much to sell one as it does to the other."[25] And the court affirmed the position expressed in the *Mennen* decision that the prohibition of section 2 was to be limited to the lessening of competition among competitors of the discriminating firm and did not include the lessening of competition among its cus-

---

[23] The court did not recognize the monopoly power of trade-marks.

[24] *National Biscuit Co. v. F. T. C.*, 299 Fed. 733 (1924). *Loose-Wiles Biscuit Co. v. F. T. C.*, loc. cit.

[25] *Ibid.*, p. 739.

tomers. The court denied the existence of monopoly in the legal sense despite the evidence, relevant from an economic point of view, that the National Biscuit Company controlled 40 per cent of the cracker business in the country as a whole, the percentage varying in different localities, and that on the Pacific Coast where competition was keen no such discrimination was practiced.[26] Each of these three cases involving discrimination on the basis of trade-status was denied review by the Supreme Court.

The contention that section 2 of the Clayton Act was confined to the lessening of competition between competitors on the same level as the discriminator in the process of production and distribution was subsequently denied by the Supreme Court in a suit brought by a private party alleging discrimination by the American Can Company in the sale of tin cans.[27] Justice Sutherland, delivering the opinion for the Supreme Court, rejected the position of the lower courts as expressed in the *Mennen* and *National Biscuit* decisions. He said, in part:

> These facts bring the case within the terms of the statute, unless the words "in any line of commerce" are to be given a narrower meaning than a literal reading of them conveys. The phrase is comprehensive and means that if the forbidden effect or tendency is produced in *one* out of *all* the various lines of commerce, the words "in *any* line of commerce" literally are satisfied.[28]

He then added concerning the general purposes of the act:

> The fundamental policy of the legislation is that, in respect of persons engaged in the same line of interstate commerce, competition is desirable and that whatever substantially lessens it or tends to create a monopoly in such line of commerce is an evil. Offense against this policy, by a discrimination in prices exacted by the seller from different purchasers of similar goods, is no less clear when it produces

[26] 7 F. T. C. 206, 215.
[27] *George Van Camp & Sons Co. v. American Can Co. et al.*, 278 U. S. 245 (1929).
[28] *Ibid.*, p. 253.

the evil in respect of the line of commerce in which they are engaged than when it produces the evil in respect of the line of commerce in which the seller is engaged. In either case, a restraint is put upon the "freedom of competition in the channels of interstate trade which it has been the purpose of all the anti-trust acts to maintain." [29]

This decision seemed to have prepared the way for a more vigorous prosecution of discrimination under section 2. That the Commission was disposed to do so is indicated by the complaint issued against the Goodyear Tire and Rubber Company in September 1933.[30] After extensive hearings the Commission found that the Goodyear Company under the terms of a cost-plus contract gave Sears, Roebuck and Company a lower price on tires than it allowed to other purchasers and also gave it certain secret rebates in the form of cash and valuable stock bonuses. The product, however, was identical in every respect except for the trade-mark and the pattern on the tread, differences of no functional importance. It was asserted that this discrimination was concealed from other customers of Goodyear. These practices were found to have "the effect of substantially lessening competition . . . between the said respondent and other manufacturers and wholesale distributors of said products, and between the said products, and between the said Sears, Roebuck & Company, and other retail tire dealers . . . ; and said discrimination also tended and now tends, to create a monopoly in said respondent in a line of commerce." [31]

The order of the Commission to cease and desist in this case is interesting in many respects, but especially for the criteria which the Commission used to establish discrimination and for the Commission's interpretation of the proviso that discrimination should be illegal only where the effect may be "to substantially lessen competition or tend to create a monopoly."

To determine the amount of discrimination involved the Commission took the net billing price to Goodyear dealers for each

[29] *Ibid.*, p. 254.   [30] 22 F. T. C. 236.   [31] *Ibid.*, p. 238.

of a group of representative grades of tires and adjusted this figure by deducting cash discounts, dealer and trade-in allowances, bonuses, freight on sales, and replacement losses. This adjusted figure was compared with a similar net sales price for sales made to Sears, Roebuck and Company. The difference, called the gross discrimination, was expressed as a percentage of the adjusted price to dealers. It was found that this gross discrimination in price in favor of Sears, Roebuck varied for the different grades of tires between 29 and 40 per cent of the price to dealers.[32] Another comparison was made of net discrimination after deduction from the price to dealers of the extra expense involved in selling to these dealers.[33] There was a net discrimination of between 12 and 22 per cent. This was taken to represent net discrimination on a representative sample after making "due allowance" for differences in cost due to different quantities sold and to differences in selling expenses.

In interpreting section 2 of the Clayton Act the Commission insisted that price differentials were permitted only where there were differences in cost due to differences in the grade, quality, or quantity of the product sold or differences in the transportation and selling costs and where the price differentials were no greater than the differences in cost. The Commission refused to accept an accounting procedure which would allocate to Sears, Roebuck only the additional costs [34] due to the additional volume manufactured and sold to it. To the argument that the volume obtained had value to Goodyear "in removing hazards and insuring stability by avoiding the fluctuation of profit inevitable in respondent's other business, and by casting on Sears, Roebuck and Company the risks which respondent normally bore of raw material price declines and credit losses," the Commission replied that in this case these factors were "too

[32] For the details of these computations, *cf.* 22 F. T. C. 273–79.
[33] *Ibid.*, pp. 279–85.
[34] I.e., the marginal or incremental costs.

speculative, intangible and remote to justify, or to be reasonably related to, the price discrimination." [35]

In its conclusion in the *Goodyear* case the Commission took the position that the proviso of section 2 to the effect that the prohibition of the section should apply only "where the effect of such discrimination may be to substantially lessen competition or tend to create a monopoly" was not to be taken in a "purely quantitative or arithmetical sense." [36] This proviso was taken "to mean merely that the discrimination must have the effect of imposing an unlawful restraint on competition, as distinguished from normal competitive methods . . . that the discrimination must be of a type which experience has demonstrated to be unfair. The hypothesis which underlies section 2 of the Clayton Act is that price discriminations not justified on the basis of cost and efficiency create unfair competitive conditions, and that unfair competitive methods of themselves tend toward monopoly." [37] The general tenor of this argument was, then, that Goodyear's discriminatory policy represented an unfair or abnormal competitive method since it created an unjust competitive situation as between Sears, Roebuck and Company and the independent tire dealers which "is not grounded on efficiency and cost." "Unfair methods . . . tend to monopoly." [38] The Commission implied that proof of an "unfair" or not "normal" competitive method is in itself evidence of a tendency substantially to lessen competition or to create a monopoly and that no further showing of such tendency is necessary. However, the Commission did not rely entirely on inference to establish a lessening of competition. In its Findings of Fact, much attention was given to the changes in the field of production and distribution which had taken place coincident with the Goodyear–Sears, Roebuck contracts, particularly to the increase in the share of the output which Good-

[35] *Ibid.*, p. 287.
[36] *Ibid.*, p. 331.
[37] *Ibid.*, p. 332.
[38] *Loc. cit.*

year controlled and to the high mortality among independent distributors.

The order of the Commission in this case involved one fundamental issue. Did the proviso of section 2 to the effect that "nothing herein contained shall prevent discrimination in price between purchasers of commodities on account of differences in the grade, quality, or quantity of the commodity sold" mean that *any* such differences in grade, quality, or quantity would allow a differential in price of *any size*, or must price differentials be confined to actual differences in costs due to differences in the grade, quality, or quantity sold? The Commission interpreted the act as confining price differentials to cost differences.[39] When the order was subsequently appealed to the courts, the Commission was eventually reversed by the lower court.[40] The court held the question to be solely whether the discrimination was made in good faith because of differences in the grade, quality, or quantity bought. If this were so, the court concluded, the law provided no limit to the magnitude of the price differential. On this issue alone the order of the Commission was dismissed. The question of the sufficiency of the evidence concerning the lessening of competition was not considered by the court.[41]

[39] As for sales involving different methods in selling and transportation services the act specifically provided that in such cases discriminations might make "only due allowance for differences in the cost of selling or transportation."

[40] *Goodyear Tire and Rubber Co. v. F. T. C.*, 101 F. (2d) 620 (1939).

[41] The absence of good faith had been an important factor in an earlier decision of a lower court in a case brought by a private party. The American Can Company was tried before a jury on charges of discriminating in favor of the Van Camp Packing Company by entering into a secret contract by which it made large rebates and rendered special services to the Van Camp company. The court sustained a finding that these discriminations were not made in good faith on account of differences in quantity purchased, the secrecy of the contract being considered as evidence of the absence of good faith. Concerning the lessening of competition, the court took cognizance of several facts: that the discount was a material

By 1936, two decades after Congress specifically legislated on the matter of price discrimination, almost nothing had been accomplished by way of developing an effective control of the practice. The time-honored practice of temporary local discrimination designed to eliminate competitors was clearly illegal, but this had apparently become a matter of the past. For this the Sherman Act and perhaps the legislation of 1914 might be credited. The broad problem of differentials in the pricing structure of the firm, however, was almost untouched. The explanations are various: poor legislative drafting, bungling by the lower courts in early cases, an ineffectual and unimaginative Commission, and finally a lethargic and unconcerned public. As section 2 was interpreted by the courts even after the *American Can* decision in 1929,[42] it was probably necessary to show more than an injury of competition or interference with normal competitive forces. The Sherman Act tests of monopolizing and restraint of trade were apparently to be applied to section 2. As has been noted frequently the Sherman Law tests with respect to the sales policies of large business are lenient to the latter.[43] The burden of proving a decline in numbers of competitors and an increase in the business of the firm in question is a difficult one, the more so if the practice is being followed by several large firms.

---

factor in the cost of the final product; that while for the five years preceding the contract Van Camp's business stood still, in the five succeeding years its business had increased 300 per cent, a much more rapid rate than that of the canned goods business as a whole. (*American Can Co. v. Ladoga Canning Co.*, 44 F. (2d) 763: 1930.) In two early decisions the lower courts held that a manufacturer of automobile accessories might discriminate in price between sales of original equipment to automobile manufacturers and sales to dealers for replacement and renewals. It was maintained that these are two separate markets, the members of which do not compete with one another in resale. (*Cf. Baran v. Goodyear Tire and Rubber Co. et al.*, 256 Fed. 571: 1919; *S. S. Kresge Co. v. Champion Spark Plug Co.*, 3 F. (2d) 415: 1925.)

[42] *Cf. supra*, p. 135.   [43] *Cf. supra*, pp. 41, 58.

Moreover, the approach of the Clayton Act to the problem ignored the interest of consumers in the practice where there was no injury to competitors. Section 2 of the Clayton Act like section 5 of the Federal Trade Commission Act was, and is, oriented toward the protection of private property rights from injury by rivals' discriminatory policies. It, too, is predicated upon the assumption that the public interest is best served by the protection of private property rights from unfair injury. It is clear, of course, that the consumer has an interest in preventing discrimination which injures competing business firms, but it is also true that the consumer has an interest in discrimination even where such injury is not demonstrable. It is a characteristic of public policy with reference to trade practices that it deals with injuries of an obvious and direct sort, particularly where articulate business interests are concerned, while ignoring some of the broader interests of consumers of an indirect and less obvious sort.

CHAPTER VIII

DISCRIMINATION. II: THE ROBINSON–PATMAN AMENDMENTS

THE COMMISSION was led to reconsider the problem of discrimination in its exhaustive study of the chain-store problem. In its report to Congress in 1934 it pointed out that under the original Clayton Act there were various defenses and provisos which in the light of judicial interpretation made it difficult to deal with discriminatory practices even where there appeared to be some public interest in doing so. It also noted that section 5 of the Federal Trade Commission Act had not given it broader powers to deal with discrimination since similar defenses were urged and "the later expression of legislative will in the Clayton Act dealt specifically and in detail with the subject and would therefore seem to take precedence over the more general statutory prohibition." [1] Consequently, the Commission recommended that section 2 of the Clayton Act be amended so as to eliminate the various provisos and defenses, leaving it to the enforcement agency, subject to review by the courts, to apply the principle to particular cases and situations.

After the demise of the NRA the pressure of various groups, particularly of wholesalers, jobbers and independent retailers, led to a substantial amendment of section 2 by the Robinson-Patman Act of 1936. [2] This was one result of a widespread struggle for supremacy between various elements in the distributive channels which had been pursued in the market and

---

[1] Federal Trade Commission, *Final Report on the Chain-Store Investigation*, p. 65.

[2] Public No. 692, 74th Cong., 2d Sess. (1936).

in the political and legislative arena with increasing intensity both before and after the NRA. The amendments had several general effects, first to change the defenses and provisos of section 2 with reference to price discrimination, to limit the payment of brokerage and the granting of advertising allowances or other special services (all potential sources of indirect discriminations), and finally to make it unlawful to induce or receive an unlawful discrimination as well as to grant one.

In dealing with discrimination in price section 2 (a) of the amended act declares it to be unlawful to discriminate in price either directly or indirectly between "different purchasers of commodities of like grade and quality . . . where the effect of such discrimination may be substantially to lessen competition or tend to create a monopoly in any line of commerce, or to *injure, destroy, or prevent competition with any person who either grants or knowingly receives the benefit of such discrimination* or with customers of either of them." [3]

These changes were intended to have two effects. In the first place it is now sufficient to show that any particular discrimination will "injure, destroy or prevent competition." By the introduction of these new words it may be hoped that the Commission will be relieved of the rigid Sherman Law tests of restraint of trade which were applied to the previous clause, "to substantially lessen competition or tend to create a monopoly." While this old phraseology is retained, the new phraseology may be interpreted as indicating a belief on the part of Congress that there are injuries of competition or interferences with competition which, while not leading to monopoly in the legal sense nor leading in a demonstrable fashion to a substantial lessening of competition, are nevertheless contrary to public policy. These amendments also incorporate explicitly into the

[3] Italics are not in the original.

statute the interpretation of the Supreme Court in *George Van Camp & Sons Co. v. American Can Co., et al.*,[4] namely that discriminations are unlawful if they injure competition "in any line of commerce."

It should be noted, however, that even as amended section 2 does not limit discrimination between dealers where they do not compete in resale, nor between various final consumers unless the discrimination can be shown to injure competition between the discriminator and its competitors. The law, in short, is concerned with discrimination only in so far as there are some competitive interests which are injured or potential competitors which are prevented from developing. But as has been seen discrimination generally implies the existence of some degree of monopoly power. The law, even as amended, is concerned with the use of this power only so far as it furthers the development of monopoly by exclusion or injures such competitive elements as remain. The law is not concerned with the interest of the ultimate consumers in discriminatory pricing policies except where such competitive interests are involved. Public policy, proceeding on the postulate that the public interest requires the protection of private business interests from injury by unfair tactics, has protected competitors from exclusive or coercive acts and from practices which by favoring certain groups inflict injury upon others. This is quite in accord with the view that the public interest is furthered by the freedom of competition and the freedom of business management in its policies so long as it does not transgress the freedom of others by exclusive or coercive acts or by methods of competition which inflict injury on other private interests by unconscionable means. This policy, however, leaves untouched a substantial part of the public interest in the pricing policies of concerns with monopoly power. The relation between prices at which a product is sold for non-competing uses or to various

[4] 278 U. S. 245 (1929). *Cf. supra*, p. 135.

final consumers is beyond the sphere of the Clayton Act even as amended.

Exception is made to the general rule against discrimination for "differentials which make *only due allowance* for differences in the cost of manufacture, sale, or delivery resulting from the differing methods or quantities in which such commodities are to such purchasers sold or delivered. . . ."[5] This clause is essentially the interpretation of section 2 of the original act which the Commission had adopted in its order issued against the Goodyear Tire and Rubber Company, an interpretation subsequently reversed by the courts.[6] It is designed to prevent differentials which are greater than differences in the cost of supplying the various customers. On the other hand it does not require that a seller shall grant differentials where there are cost differences. At least that was the opinion of some of the supporters of the bill in Congress.[7]

This "only due allowance" clause was designed to eliminate entirely differentials based on lower average costs induced by more nearly optimum utilization of plant with additional volume. According to a Senate committee reporting on the bill, "It is designed, in short, to leave the test of a permissible differential upon the question: If the more favored customer were sold in the same quantities and by the same methods of sale and delivery as the customer not so favored, how much more per unit would it actually cost the seller to do so, his other business remaining the same."[8] This would preclude differentials representing the cost of "particular facilities or depart-

[5] Italics are not in the original.

[6] *Cf. supra*, p. 139.

[7] 74th Cong., 2d Sess., *House Report* No. 2287, p. 10; *Congressional Record*, LXXX (1936), 3114. This is illustrative of the difference between the economic and legal or popular usages of the word "discrimination." To the economist price uniformity in the presence of cost differences is no less a discrimination than price differences in the face of cost uniformity. [8] 74th Cong., 2d Sess., *Senate Report* No. 1502, p. 6.

ments which the favored customer may not have immediately utilized, but with which the seller cannot dispense in the general conduct of his business." [9]

Another proviso stipulates that where the Commission "finds that available purchasers in greater quantities are so few as to render differentials on account thereof unjustly discriminatory or promotive of monopoly in any line of commerce" it may "fix and establish quantity limits" whereupon it shall be unlawful to grant "differentials based on differences in quantities greater than those so fixed. . . ." The implication of this clause is that differentials which make "only due allowance for differences in the cost . . ." may nevertheless be so unjustly discriminatory or promotive of monopoly that economies of large scale purchases should be sacrificed to the preservation of competition. This provision was patterned on similar policies previously adopted by the Interstate Commerce Commission and is based on the belief that there are economies which the public cannot afford since they are bought at the price of monopoly.[10]

Anyone accused of unlawful price discrimination is permitted to rebut "the prima facie case . . . by showing that his lower price or the furnishing of services or facilities to any purchaser or purchasers was made in good faith to meet an equally low price of a competitor, or the services or facilities furnished by a competitor." This proviso differs from a corresponding proviso of the act as passed in 1914 in that the latter specified no limit to discriminatory pricing for the purpose of meeting competition while the amended section permits one to rebut a *prima facie* case of discrimination by showing that the price was made to meet competition, but the price (or services) must

[9] 74th Cong., 2d Sess., *Senate Report* No. 1502, p. 6.
[10] See testimony of Mr. Teergarden who wrote the bill in its original form. House Committee on the Judiciary, *Hearings on H. R. 8442* . . . ; *To Amend the Clayton Act* (1935–1936), pp. 22, 35, 222–23.

not be more than "equally low." Moreover, the proviso in the amended section is not substantive law, i.e. a general permission to meet prices of competitors, but only a rule of evidence.[11]

The Commission has issued a large number of orders alleging violation of section 2(a). Several have been of a somewhat routine nature, dealing with particular cases of discrimination in favor of one or a few customers. Others have presented more interesting problems. Numerous orders have been concerned with discount schedules applied to an arbitrary classification of customers according to trade status. A candy company had four classes of customers with price differentials for the less favored customers for various items ranging from 12 to 67 per cent more than the minimum price.[12] There was no standard rule for classifying customers, it being left to the discretion of salesmen to decide the classification of any particular purchaser. The Commission concluded that this had the effect of discrimination between customers buying in similar quantities and under similar conditions and tended to injure or destroy competition among retailers by concentrating the retail sale of candy in the more favored retailers, who were in direct competition with the less favored.

The Commission has issued a series of orders against sellers of commercial inoculants for the inoculation of seeds of leguminous plants.[13] This is an industry in which the channels of trade were chaotic. Sales were made by producers to both jobbers and retailers, but there were few jobbers who didn't sell to final consumers as well. Moreover, some members of

---

[11] *Congressional Record*, LXXX, 9903, 9418.
[12] *In the Matter of Nutrine Candy Company*, Docket No. 3756 (order issued December 19, 1939).
[13] *In the Matter of Agricultural Laboratories, Inc.*, Docket No. 3263; *In the Matter of Hansen Inoculator Company, Inc.*, Docket No. 3264; *In the Matter of Albert L. and Lucille D. Whiting*, Docket No. 3265; *In the Matter of The Nitragen Company, Inc.*, Docket No. 3266 (all four orders issued January 12, 1938).

the industry sold through mail-order houses, and others often sold directly to farm bureaus for direct sale to consumers. Thus, there were cases where jobbers, retailers, mail-order houses, and farm bureaus might be competing with one another for sale to a particular group of consumers. The Commission concluded that the industry was riddled with discriminatory pricing not justified by differences in cost and issued a series of orders. The general effect of these orders should be either to induce a general one price policy by the seller, or to force a more clear cut differentiation of function and market between the various elements in the distributive channels.

In several instances the Commission has issued orders enjoining conspiracies in restraint of trade under section 5 of the Federal Trade Commission Act along with discrimination. The Golf Ball Manufacturers' Association and its members together with the Professional Golfers' Association and its members were ordered to cease and desist from an agreement to fix and maintain the price of golf balls.[14] And the Professional Golfers' Association was enjoined from coercing the manufacturers to discriminate in their favor in the sale of golf balls by forcing the manufacturers to enter into an agreement to pay for the privilege of using the insignia PGA on their product. The manufacturers and distributors of window glass were ordered to cease a conspiracy by which they maintained prices of window glass, and discriminated between various distributors through an arbitrary classification of buyers into two groups, "quantity buyers" who might purchase directly from the manufacturers, and "carload lot buyers" who might purchase only indirectly through "quantity buyers" at a substantial mark-up.[15]

---

[14] *In the Matter of Golf Ball Manufacturers' Association, et al.*, Docket No. 3161 (order issued February 25, 1938).

[15] *In the Matter of Pittsburgh Plate Glass Co. et al.*, Docket No. 3154 (order issued October 30, 1937).

Finally, an association of snow fence manufacturers and its members producing 90 to 95 per cent of snow fence products in fourteen Atlantic states were enjoined from agreeing to maintain an elaborate system of delivered prices.[16] They had established a price-filing system which had resulted in uniform delivered price lists for all sellers, had established discounts for various classes of distributors and dealers, had agreed upon the definitions of the various classes, and finally had agreed upon and maintained a system of resale price maintenance. The charge of discrimination resulted from the maintenance of the delivered price system. It was noted that this resulted in the receipt of varying mill-net yields on sales to different customers. The purpose of this delivered price system was clearly to aid in the elimination of price competition.

Perhaps the most significant application of section 2(a) of the Robinson-Patman Act has been to cumulative volume discount schemes based upon total purchases of a particular buyer over a period of time.[17] A customary practice in many industries has been to set up a volume discount schedule based upon aggregate purchases over a period of time, the discount increasing with the aggregate of purchases. In the case of chain-stores, the discounts customarily apply to the aggregate purchases of the chain, not to the purchases of the individual unit, even though orders may be solicited from and deliveries made to the individual store. Standard Brands Incorporated

[16] *In the Matter of United Fence Manufacturers Association et al.*, Docket No. 3305 (order issued July 13, 1938). Geographical discrimination resulting from preferential freight absorption was a factor in another order issued by the Commission. *In the Matter of Master Lock Company*, Docket No. 3386 (order issued September 14, 1938).

[17] *In the Matter of Simmons Company*, Docket No. 3840 (order issued August 25, 1939); *In the Matter of American Optical Company*, Docket No. 3232 (order issued January 21, 1939); *In the Matter of Bausch and Lomb Optical Company, et al.*, Docket No. 3233 (order issued January 21, 1939).

in the sale of its yeast based the discount on *aggregate monthly requirements* of the individual firm from whatever source, not upon monthly purchases from Standard Brands.[18]

The effect of such volume discounts is to favor those firms whose aggregate purchases during a particular period are greatest, and this is true quite apart from the question of the average size of the individual order. For example, a firm making 10 orders of 10 units apiece may receive a larger discount than one making one order of 50 units during the same time period. When based upon aggregate monthly requirements as in the case of Standard Brands' schedule for yeast it is possible that 4 sales of 10 units to one buyer might receive larger discounts than one sale of 100 units to another. Moreover, the scheme favors the chains and purchasing syndicates as against the independent retail unit, even though the individual orders and deliveries may be of the same size. In these ways it gives competitive advantages to certain groups of dealers as against others. A second effect is to concentrate the purchases of any one dealer upon one seller, thus acting in part as an exclusive dealing arrangement. In industries where limited-line and full-line manufacturers are competing for dealer patronage these cumulative volume discounts may be especially prejudicial to the limited-line seller if based on purchases of all products. The limited-line seller cannot obtain part of the business of a dealer simply by offering an equally low price as that of the full-line seller. He must offer the dealer a price sufficiently lower than that of the full-line seller to compensate the dealer for the loss of discount on that portion of his requirements which he must purchase from the full-line source.

The Commission has issued orders to cease and desist in several cases of this sort where it found the discriminations were not justified by differences in cost. The conclusions of

[18] *In the Matter of Standard Brands Incorporated and Standard Brands of California*, Docket No. 2986 (order issued June 15, 1939).

the Commission in its order against the H. C. Brill Company illustrate its basis of action.[19]

Purchasers of large annual amounts sometimes buy in larger individual shipments than do buyers whose purchases do not amount to as large a sum. Large buyers, however, also place numerous small orders and the average size of such orders is frequently less than the average size of orders placed by buyers whose aggregate annual purchases are less in volume.

Large wholesalers and chain retailers often obtain concessions in the form of cumulative discounts in the belief that their transactions, in proportion to the amount purchased, are fewer in number, take less of the time and attention of the seller, and cost the seller less. However, when such a belief is not supported by the facts the conclusion obviously is erroneous and an offer predicated thereon discriminatory.

A cumulative discount is sound only where savings have been achieved by the seller with respect to individual sales made to a particular buyer over a period of time, which savings were not reflected in the price at which the buyer purchased and which are reserved for the purpose of refunding at the end of a period of time.

The Robinson-Patman amendments went further than simply revising the provisos of section 2 of the Clayton Act. They added several sections dealing with brokerage payments, conditions of reciprocal trading, and the furnishing of special services and facilities. Moreover, in doing so, the act as interpreted by the Commission has gone far beyond a mere attempt to prevent indirect discrimination under conditions specified in section 2(a).

The broker is an institution used in many trades to bring buyers and sellers together. He may serve either the seller or the buyer. The function of a broker who represents a seller is to find customers and to sell on behalf of and as agent for the seller. The broker renders to the seller a selling service and is customarily paid by him. Oftentimes, however, a buyer

[19] *In the Matter of H. C. Brill Company, Inc.*, Docket No. 3299 (order issued February 10, 1938).

will seek out a seller directly whereupon the services of the independent broker are eliminated. In such cases the seller may pay the buyer the fee which he would otherwise have paid the broker, or give him a discount of equivalent amount. Sometimes this is done directly, then again it may be done through a dummy brokerage firm owned by and acting on behalf of the buyer. Clearly the payment of brokerage to a buyer or representative of a buyer might be used as an indirect form of price discrimination. But as such and in circumstances where it might injure or lessen competition it is unlawful under section 2(a).

The section on brokerage payment, section 2(c), as interpreted by the Commission goes far beyond a mere prohibition of indirect discriminations of the type which would be held to violate section 2(a). The brokerage section reads:

> That it shall be unlawful . . . to pay or grant, or to receive or accept, anything of value as a commission, brokerage, or other compensation, or any allowance or discount in lieu thereof, except for services rendered in connection with the sale or purchase of goods . . . either to the other party to such transaction or to an agent . . . where such intermediary is acting in fact for or in behalf, or is subject to the direct or indirect control, of any party to such transaction other than the person by whom such compensation is so granted or paid.[20]

The Commission interprets this as being a broad prohibition of the practice of paying brokerage fees to a principal to a transaction, directly or indirectly through an intermediary acting on behalf of the principal. Such practices were proscribed by Congress, in the Commission's view, not merely because they involve price discriminations but because Congress considered them to be inherently unfair methods of competition which are in themselves injurious to commerce. Payments of brokerage by one principal to another directly or through an

---

[20] Public No. 692, 74th Cong., 2d Sess.

intermediary are, it is claimed, *always* illegal. This is so whether or not there is any effect to injure or lessen competition or to create a monopoly. Nor is it a defense to show that because the seller has saved the brokerage fee the brokerage paid makes only due allowance for differences in the cost of selling. These defenses, which may be pleaded under section 2(a), are held by the Commission to be inapplicable to section 2(c). There is of course the phrase "except for services rendered." Does this mean that if an agent of the buyer renders certain services to the seller, brokerage accruing to the buyer may be paid? The Commission has concluded that this is not the case, that this is simply a clarifying phrase making it clear that brokerage payments by a seller to an independent broker acting for the seller are permitted even though the broker may in the course of his business render incidental services to the buyer.

The brokerage section of the Act has been the occasion of several orders and court appeals. The proceedings against the Great Atlantic and Pacific Tea Company provided the occasion for a most exhaustive discussion of the meaning of the law.[21] It has long been the custom of the company to locate field buying agents near its sources of supply to keep it informed of market conditions and to execute orders for the purchasing agents representing the various divisions of the company. Incidental to these services rendered the company, the field agents rendered certain services to the sellers. They exchanged information with the latter, visited sellers' manufacturing establishments giving them advice on improving the quality of their product and on size of containers, and furnished them traffic information concerning sales to be made to the company. Moreover, these agents have often called to the attention of divisional purchasing agents ways in which

---

[21] *In the Matter of The Great Atlantic and Pacific Tea Company*, Docket No. 3031 (order issued January 25, 1938).

the latter might aid the sellers when the latter were faced with the task of disposing of surpluses or of liquidating inventory to avoid bankruptcy or financial distress.

Prior to the passage of the Robinson-Patman Act the Atlantic and Pacific Tea Company had been receiving brokerage on purchases made through these field buying agents. Subsequent to the passage of the act it instructed its agents to accept no more brokerage but to make all purchases on one of three bases: (1) to purchase at a net price reflecting a reduction from the current price charged other customers of an amount equivalent to regular brokerage fees; (2) to execute "quantity discount agreements" providing for monthly payments equivalent to former brokerage; or (3) to enter agreements with manufacturers to keep a record of all brokerage which would have been paid but for the act, which brokerage would be paid when, as, and if its legality should be determined.

The Commission issued an order directing the company to cease and desist the acceptance of such price reductions or "quantity discounts," arguing that the payments were "discounts in lieu of brokerage" paid by the seller to the buyer. The company protested that the discounts were not in lieu of brokerage, that even if they were so held to be, it had rendered services to the sellers, and finally that section 2(c) must be read in light of the cost proviso of 2(a) so as to permit the passing on of brokerage savings to buyers. The court sustained the Commission, denying the company's position on every count. "We entertain no doubt that it was the intention of Congress to prevent dual representation by agents purporting to deal on behalf of both buyer and seller. . . . The phrase 'except for services rendered' is employed by Congress to indicate that if there be compensation to an agent it must be a bona fide brokerage, viz., for actual services rendered to his principal by the agent. The agent cannot serve two masters, simultaneously rendering services in an arm's length transaction to both." [22]

We . . . believe that paragraph (c) expresses an absolute prohibition of the payment of brokerage or compensation in lieu thereof to the buyer upon the buyer's own purchases.[23]

The Atlantic and Pacific Tea Company case involved payment of brokerage directly to agents of a buyer. Other cases have involved less direct methods of payment. A frequent procedure is that used by the Webb-Crawford Company.[24] This company was a wholesale grocery making purchases through the Daniel Brokerage Company, a partnership. The four principal stockholders of the one were the three partners and manager of the other. Sellers customarily allowed brokerage fees to the Daniel Company on sales made to Webb-Crawford, which fees constituted 75 to 85 per cent of the total income of the brokerage firm. Clearly the Daniel Brokerage firm in negotiating sales to the Webb-Crawford Company was acting on behalf of the latter and the brokerage fees received were accruing to the benefit of the buyers. Here then was a buyer-controlled intermediary through which brokerage was being paid by the seller to the buyer. The order of the Commission to cease these practices was sustained by the lower court.[25]

---

[22] *Great Atlantic & Pacific Tea Co. v. F. T. C.*, 106 F. (2d) 667, 674 (1939). Petition for writ of certiorari denied by the Supreme Court (60 Sup. Ct. 466: 1940).

[23] *Ibid.*, p. 673.

[24] *In the Matter of the Webb-Crawford Co. et al.*, Docket No. 3214 (order issued October 20, 1938). For similar cases *cf. In the Matter of Reeves Parvin & Co., et al.*, Docket No. 3129 (order issued April 15, 1939); *In the Matter of Quality Bakers of America, et al.*, Docket No. 3218 (order issued April 27, 1939); *In the Matter of C. R. Anthony Co., et al.*, Docket No. 3834 (order issued September 12, 1939); *In the Matter of Jake Felt, et al.*, Docket No. 3765 (order issued December 22, 1939).

[25] *Webb-Crawford Co. v. F. T. C.*, 109 F. (2d) 268 (1940).

A somewhat different arrangement is illustrated by the practices of the Biddle Purchasing Company.[26] This was a concern engaged in the business of selling a market information service and purchasing services to some 2400 distributing concerns, principally wholesalers of groceries, drugs, hardware, lumber, plumbing, automobile, and electrical supplies. It kept its subscribers informed on market conditions and on available merchandise, examined and tested manufacturers' goods, and circulated among its subscribers descriptions of goods along with price lists. Moreover, the Biddle Company would place orders for goods on behalf of its clients, which goods were delivered and billed directly to the buyers at a specified price. The sellers then paid the Biddle Purchasing Company brokerage on all such sales. For these services the clients of Biddle paid a stipulated monthly sum ranging from $25.00 to $50.00. The brokerage fees paid by the sellers to Biddle were either paid to the customers directly or credited to their account. Here, then, was a concern completely independent in point of control of either buyers or sellers which was rendering services to the buyers primarily but to the sellers incidentally. Through this intermediary brokerage fees were being paid to the buyer. The Commission was sustained by the court in ordering the parties concerned to cease and desist.[27]

It is difficult to speculate upon the ultimate effects of the brokerage provisions. In so far as it tends to prevent special treatment of particular groups the section appears likely to

[26] In the Matter of Biddle Purchasing Co. et al., Docket No. 3032 (order issued July 17, 1937). For a similar case cf. In the Matter of Oliver Brothers, Inc., et al., Docket No. 3088 (order issued December 31, 1937).

[27] Biddle Purchasing Co., et al. v. F. T. C., 96 F. (2d) 687 (1938). Petition for writ of certiorari denied by the Supreme Court (305 U. S. 634). For another decision involving similar circumstances cf. Oliver Brothers, Inc., et al. v. F. T. C., 102 F. (2d) 763 (1939).

change the balance of competitive advantage between various rival channels of distribution. But it may lead to a complete reëxamination of discount schedules, and in the process of reclassifying customers it may be that those formerly receiving brokerage will become the recipients of price concessions or discounts legal under the cost provisos of section 2(a). In still other cases it may lead to a realignment of the relations between manufacturers and distributors. The manufacturers may be led to adopt a sales policy using a particular channel of distribution exclusively, some using brokers entirely and others not at all; while the mass distributors may concentrate their purchases in large measure upon those not using brokers, thereby avoiding questions of brokerage allowances or invidious price comparisons.

Sections 2(d) and 2(e) of the Robinson-Patman Act apply to other selling practices which have been used with discriminatory effect. Section 2(d) has to do with the paying by a seller to a buyer for services rendered by the latter to the former. It is declared to be unlawful for a seller to pay a customer for any services rendered the seller by the customer "unless such payment or consideration is available on proportionally equal terms to all other customers competing in the distribution of such products or commodities." [28] This section is designed to deal with advertising allowances, the purchase of advertising space, warehouse facilities, or other services by a seller from his customer.

Section 2(e) is concerned with the extending of special services or facilities by the seller to selected buyers. It declares that it is unlawful "to discriminate in favor of one purchaser . . . by contracting to furnish, or furnishing, or by contributing to the furnishing of, any services or facilities . . . not accorded to all purchasers on proportionally equal terms." This is designed to deal with such practices as the furnishing

[28] Public No. 692, 74th Cong., 2d Sess. (1936).

of demonstrators, or missionary salesmen to selected customers while denying them to others.

These sections like the brokerage rule appear to be unlimited
by the qualifications of section 2(a). There is no need to show
that the practice lessens or injures competition or tends to a
monopoly. This effect is assumed. An offer to purchase reciprocal services or to provide special services or facilities is illegal
if not tendered upon proportionally equal terms to all. From
the wording of the act it appears that in the case of purchases
of reciprocal services, the arrangement need be offered on
proportionally equal terms only to "all other competing customers," while in the case of the supply of special ancillary
services the offer must be made to "all purchasers."

To date the Commission has not issued any final orders in
these matters. The problem faced, of course, is to determine
what constitutes "proportionally equal terms." It should prove
interesting to see how the Commission deals with this matter.
There are, of course, good economic reasons for allowing a
seller to purchase certain special facilities from a buyer. It
is likewise clear that reciprocal arrangements of this sort may
be the occasion for disguised discriminations. The effect of
section 2(d) is likely to be to induce an elimination of many
such arrangements, where their justification seems questionable. In some cases economically justifiable relations may be
abandoned in deference to the law. It may also lead to an
increase in outright price differentials, where the differentials
are justifiable under the cost proviso of section 2(a). Section
2(e), dealing with the furnishing of special services or facilities is likely to lead to a considerable revision of selling methods,
to a greater standardization of the "bundle of utilities" which
go to make up the "product" sold for a price. Both these sections are likely to reduce the variety and confusion in selling
techniques and to center the competitive process on a fewer
number of variables. Moreover, they are likely to concentrate

the attention of sellers upon price differentials where circumstances of the sale warrant different treatment under the cost proviso of section 2(a). Thus, while they reduce the possibilities that illegal discriminations will be granted by indirect methods, they also are likely in some cases to accentuate price differentials where these are legal under the provisos of section 2(a). In this respect, sections 2(d) and 2(e) like the brokerage section are as likely to effect a realignment between manufacturing sources and distributive channels, and to effect a change in sales strategy as they are to change the balance of advantage between the rival channels of trade.

CHAPTER IX

DISCRIMINATION. III: ECONOMIC EFFECTS

SYSTEMATIC AND PURPOSIVE DISCRIMINATION

To ASSESS the economic effects of discrimination in the industrial field and of the limitations which have been placed upon it by legislative action is a problem complicated by the variety of types of discrimination and the variety of market structures in which it may be practiced. It should prove instructive, however, to explore a few cases sufficiently to indicate the direction in which the economic effects are to be sought. The traditional body of economic analysis offers some help in dealing with discrimination of a systematic, purposive, and persisting sort. The simplest example of discrimination of this type arises when a seller discriminates between various consumers or classes of consumers, and it is in this form that discrimination is generally discussed in the theoretical literature. But recently in the field of public policy principal attention has been given to discrimination between distributive channels which compete in part with one another in resale. An analysis of the economic significance of the first, however, will prove a profitable introduction to an analysis of the second.

The theory of price discrimination as developed by the Cambridge School is based upon certain assumptions which should be made explicit to begin with and should be relaxed at a later point. In the first place, the demand curve for a product is assumed to be also the curve of marginal demand price or marginal utility.[1] This assumption may be granted upon two conditions: first, that each buyer appears only once in the demand schedule, having no demand above a given price and a per-

---

[1] Pigou, *op. cit.*, p. 808.

fectly inelastic demand below that price; second, that the willingness to pay for a unit is not conditioned upon the number of units enjoyed by others.[2] The second assumption of the orthodox analysis is that the demand in each of the markets into which the buyers are divided is independent.[3] This means that the demand in any one market is assumed to be independent of the price in any other. In the cases of sales to intermediate processors or distributors who compete in resale, this is obviously not the situation.

A third assumption is that the investment in the field, and therefore the intensity of demand for the product of the individual firm, is not affected by the additional profits incident to a discriminating rather than a simple monopoly pricing policy. The theory of discrimination has been developed for markets in which the demand is unaffected by profits,[4] but in practice discrimination often appears in markets in which competitive elements are intertwined with the monopolistic. If the theory of discrimination is to be adapted to the theory of monopolistic competition, allowance must be made for this possibility of the attraction of competitors by the additional profits. It appears that although competitive elements may seriously reduce the power to discriminate, this power does not disappear completely. In the limiting case of monopolistic competition emphasized by Professor Chamberlin, in which the entrance of new firms forces the demand curve of the individual firm to a point of tangency with its cost curve,[5] it appears that discriminating monopolistic competition would intensify the results of simple monopolistic competition in respect to the divergence of output and costs from the purely competitive norm. These three as-

[2] *Loc. cit.*

[3] *Ibid.*, p. 282. Joan Robinson, *op. cit.*, p. 181.

[4] This might be defined as "pure monopoly." *Cf.* P. M. Sweezy, "On the Definition of Monopoly," *Quarterly Journal of Economics*, LI (1937), 362.

[5] I.e., profits are normal. Chamberlin, *op. cit.*, chap. V.

sumptions of the accepted theory of discrimination suggest the necessity for further theoretical refinements, but this is not the place for such elaborations. It will be sufficient to bear them in mind in so far as they affect the conclusions of the accepted analysis.

The case of "perfect" discrimination, while only a limiting case, makes an interesting point of departure. By "perfect" discrimination is meant the practice of dealing with each buyer separately on such terms as will maximize profits in the given conditions of demand and cost. There are three significant cases of perfect discrimination depending on the composition of the demand schedule. There is the case where the demand schedule is the curve of marginal demand price, i.e. each individual appears in the aggregate demand schedule only once and the valuation which he places on the one unit is independent of the number of units consumed by others or the price at which others buy. If the seller can deal with each buyer separately, he will be able to exact a sum from each buyer equal to the maximum valuation of that buyer. Total revenue will be indicated by the area under the demand curve.[6] Output and, in the long run, investment will be extended to the point where marginal revenue (also marginal demand price) equals marginal cost. Output and investment will be greater than that proper to simple monopoly.[7] They will be equal to the amount proper to pure competition if the industry is one of constant costs, less in the case of increasing costs, and greater in the case of decreasing costs. The price will be raised to all who would have purchased under conditions of simple monopoly except the marginal buyer.

The second case of perfect discrimination is that in which

---

[6] In technical terms, the demand curve becomes the aggregate marginal revenue curve. *Cf.* Joan Robinson, *op. cit.*, p. 182 and p. 188, note 3.

[7] We neglect until a later point the possibility of attracting new firms because of the larger profits incident to discrimination. *Cf. post*, p. 165.

each individual enters the market demand schedule more than once, but in which the individual demand curve is discontinuous. In this case the seller will wish to sell units to any one buyer so long as the marginal valuation to the buyer is greater than the marginal costs of the seller. To get the maximum revenue he will quote the buyer a price equal to his average valuation. If the seller gauges this correctly, he will be getting the maximum possible revenue. The precise effect on output is difficult to determine. It will depend on the character of the individual valuation schedules. If the valuation schedules of all individuals are alike, there will be no discrimination and no change in output. In general, however, some of those who would be buyers at the simple monopoly price would buy more units under discrimination, some would buy less. Others, whose maximum valuation is less than the simple monopoly price but greater than the marginal cost of the discriminating monopolist, would be sold units only in the case where a discriminatory policy is adopted. The more there are of these, the more likely it is that output will be greater than under simple monopoly. Total receipts will be greater than under simple monopoly but less than the area indicated under the demand curve.

The third case of perfect discrimination is that in which the product is sufficiently divisible and consumers' preferences are such that the demand schedule of the individual consumer may be considered continuous. In this case perfect discrimination would necessitate setting a price to each indicated by the equalization of marginal revenue of the firm for each individual consumer with marginal cost of the seller. The output will certainly be less than under pure competition. Whether it will be more or less than under simple monopoly will, in Mrs. Joan Robinson's terminology, depend upon the adjusted concavities of the demand curves of the different markets and also upon the number of buyers whose maximum demand price is above marginal costs but below the simple monopoly price.[8] In these second and third cases, it is probable that the price of the product would be raised to some and lowered to others who would have bought under conditions of simple monopoly.

In general it will not be possible for a seller to deal with each buyer separately and so to achieve something approximating "perfect" discrimination. He will instead be forced to make a rough classification of his customers into a few groups, attempting to isolate buyers with a more elastic demand from those with a less elastic. Output will be determined by Mrs. Robinson's familiar theorem.[9] Marginal revenue from each market will equal aggregate marginal costs. Again output will be greater or less than that proper to simple monopoly according to the adjusted concavities of the demand curve. Where the less elastic demand curve is more convex (or less concave) than the more elastic demand curve,[10] output will be greater than that proper to simple monopoly. Mrs. Robinson suggests "that on the whole it is more likely that the introduction of price discrimination will increase output than that it will reduce it." [11] In this general case of discrimination it is probable that price will be raised to some who would have bought under conditions of simple monopoly and lowered to others. However, if marginal costs are decreasing at a sufficiently rapid rate and if the output is greater than it would be if the seller followed a simple monopoly selling policy, the price may be lower to all buyers.[12]

[8] *Op. cit.*, pp. 193–94.

[9] *Ibid.*, p. 182.

[10] The elasticity refers to the price proper to simple monopoly.

[11] *Ibid.*, p. 201. A special case in which the output of discriminating monopoly will be greater than that of simple monopoly is presented by those cases where the demand curve lies below the average cost curve but the aggregate revenue curve of the discriminating monopolist lies above it at some point. Under such conditions discriminating monopoly would yield some output while simple monopoly would yield none.

[12] *Ibid.*, pp. 204–5.

Summarizing the argument to this point, we may say that on the assumption that the additional profits do not affect the intensity of demand by attracting new firms discrimination *may* lead to an output and investment which are greater than simple monopoly and which are more nearly equal to those of perfect competition. While it is quite probable that prices will be raised to some, it is conceivable that prices may be lower to all buyers.

In so far as the additional profits incident to discrimination attract new firms, however, the demand for the product of the individual firm is likely to decrease, i.e. become less intense. Unless at the same time it becomes more elastic, this will constitute a force working against an increase in the output of the individual firm. If the firms are producing under decreasing costs, discrimination which reduced the output of the firm by attracting new rivals might lead to higher unit costs of output than would simple monopoly. This would accentuate the tendency noted by Professor Chamberlin of monopolistic competition to lead to high unit costs and diseconomies of scale.[13] Thus, while it may be true that discrimination by one firm may enable that firm to achieve the economies of large scale and to attain a more efficient utilization of plant all other things remaining the same, it does not follow that discrimination practiced by all under conditions of monopolistic competition will enable the industry as a whole to do so. Under these circumstances it is not conceivable that prices would be lower to all buyers as a result of the discrimination.

It is significant to ask what the general effect of this discrimination will be upon the utilization of economic resources and the satisfaction derived therefrom. As has been noted above, it is conceivable that discrimination will lead to plants of more nearly optimum scale and to better utilization of that plant. So far as this is the result it may induce a greater na-

[13] *Op. cit.*, pp. 116, 175–76.

tional income. But it was also noted that with freedom of entry for new firms the result might be the very reverse.

But what of the allocation of resources to the production of the various products and the allocation of income among various members of the population? From the point of view of the individual, it is the prices of various products which determine the proportion in which he distributes his income among the various uses. A rational individual who is trying to maximize the anticipated satisfaction from his money income will proportion his expenditure among various alternatives so that the addition to his total satisfaction from the marginal unit (his marginal utility) for each alternative is proportional to the price. It is a familiar proposition of economics that provided the costs represent the real value of displaced alternatives,[14] any individual will maximize his satisfaction if the marginal utilities of the various products to him are proportional to the marginal costs of producing these products. Moreover, taking the distribution of the money income as a given datum or assuming it to be the best possible, it may be shown that such a proportioning of consumers' expenditures will lead to an optimum allocation of economic resources among alternative uses in the sense that the output of one product could not be increased without sacrificing units of output of another product which are more highly valued.[15]

In a perfectly competitive economy where price would tend to equal marginal costs, there would be an approximation to such an ideal proportioning of the output among alternative products. The introduction of monopoly elements destroys this harmony. The essence of monopoly is that it raises price and

[14] L. M. Frazer, *Economic Thought and Language* (London: A. & C. Black, Ltd., 1937), p. 103.

[15] Pigou, *op. cit.*, Part II, chap. III; J. E. Meade, and C. J. Hitch, *An Introduction to Economic Analysis and Policy* (New York: Oxford University Press, 1938), Part II, chap. II.

restricts the consumption of the product in question. The consumption of a product which is monopolized is limited; the consumption of goods which are not monopolized is stimulated. Consumers are induced to change their consumption patterns so that resources are diverted from the production of one group of products of which the utility is greater, to another group the desirability of which to the consumer is less.

Discrimination is a special case of the exercise of monopoly power. Simple monopoly pricing policy restricts output to all so that in the particular industry there is a divergence between marginal utility and marginal costs for all consumers. A reallocation of resources from the competitive (or less monopolistic) to the more monopolistic industries would satisfy the consumers' desires more effectively. A discriminating monopolist exercises a different degree of monopoly power in his dealings with different customers. Those to whom the price of the discriminating monopolist is lower than it would be if a policy of simple monopoly were pursued, are benefited by the policy. The satisfaction which they receive from the expenditure of their money income is increased. Those to whom prices are raised will thereby be induced to adopt a consumption pattern which to them is less desirable than if the pricing policy of the industry had been one of simple monopoly. Only in the case where price is lowered to all or at least is not raised to any is there a clear advantage to consumers from discriminating monopoly. Except in those cases where price is either lowered to all or raised to all, some qualitative and quantitative measure is necessary which weighs the injury to the one group against the gain to the other.

So far mention has been made of two directions in which the effects of discrimination may be significant, the size of the national product and its allocation between different types of products. A third direction warranting consideration is its effects upon the distribution of the national income between individuals. Systematic, purposive discrimination is pursued in order to increase the size of the firm's profits. So far as it succeeds in this respect, the recipients of the firm's profits are the beneficiaries of the policy and participate to a proportionately greater extent in the enjoyment of the national income. The significance of this depends upon who these beneficiaries are. If they are in the high income brackets, this means an accentuation of the degree of inequality. If they are in depressed industries, this may mean a reduction in inequality. Clearly, a redistribution of income is a matter of great economic and social importance. Discriminatory pricing policies are one way by which such distribution may be affected.

Public policy, however, has not been primarily interested with these aspects of discrimination; rather it has been concerned with the impact of discrimination upon rival business interests. This is perhaps best illustrated by the recent concern with the impact of discriminatory practices of manufacturers upon the channels of distribution. As has been indicated in the previous survey of the Clayton Act and its amendments, the test of unlawfulness is the injury of competition or tendency to monopoly. The effect on competition might be either on the competitive relations between the firm which is discriminating and its rivals or upon the competitive relations between its customers. In general it has been of the latter sort, though it was pointed out that discriminatory cumulative volume discounts might injure limited-line manufacturers who were in competition with full-line manufacturers.

To what extent is the analysis given above of the effects of discrimination between consumers applicable to this problem? Is this an entirely different problem, the significance of which lies solely in the claims of rival private business interests? The author thinks not. The various channels of distribution are in part rival, that is some buyers will shift their patronage from one to another on the basis of price differences or differences in service or sales effort. Consequently, a differential in price may favor a particular channel and enable it to absorb the market. It puts that channel in a position to charge lower prices, improve its service, intensify its sales efforts, or increase its profits. So far as the channels are rival, this will clearly favor the one channel as against the other. The less favored channels will suffer financial injury if not contraction or even extinction. So far as the price differentials are due to differences in cost of sale to the alternative channels they would appear to be desirable, particularly if there is sufficient rivalry to force the sharing of these economies with consumers in the form of lower prices or better service. The consumer is doubly fortunate if the favored channel represents a more economical distributive technique. Discrimination of this type, however, would be only temporary, since if the channels were wholly rival, the one would supersede the other.

Experience shows, however, that as a matter of fact the various channels survive and price differentials persist as between them. This is explained by the fact that the various channels are not entirely rival, but to some degree complementary. They cater in part to different clienteles. Some emphasize economy, others emphasize service; some are located at central marketing points, others cater to the outlying trade; some sell for cash, others extend credit. Service differentiation is the very essence of rivalry between the distributive channels in a freely competitive economy. In consequence, the practice of discrimination does not completely eliminate the unfavored channel. Rather this channel restricts itself to that part of the consuming market where demand is least elastic. The consuming market is separated into various parts, each dealing with a particular channel, and the manufacturer discriminates purposively between them. Indirectly then, discrimination between the various channels of distribution becomes discrimination between various classes of consumers and our previous analysis becomes applicable, i.e. persisting discrimination between various channels is in effect persisting discrimination between various groups of final customers and has the same consequences. It often happens, of course, that manufacturers underestimate the transferability of consumer demand, which is to say they overestimate the elasticity of the derived demand of a particular type of distributive channel. In such cases a discriminatory policy may prove unwise.[16]

This whole problem of discrimination between various channels is best looked at as one of separating markets for purposive discrimination. Any change in policy will have effects upon the relative profitability of the various channels, inflicting injury upon those channels against which the differential is raised. It is with this latter aspect of the problem that public policy has been concerned.

Assuming there are no differences in the cost of selling to the various channels, the policy of the Clayton Act as amended would require a one-price policy where there is evidence of actual or potential rivalry between the channels. This would mean that the degree of monopoly power exercised by the manufacturer would be the same in sales between the various channels. It should be noted that one effect of this policy may be to force a realignment of the relations between manufacturers and distributors of such a nature that a particular manufacturer will distribute exclusively through a particular type channel. This may come about either by forward or backward integration of manufacturing and distribution or by the pairing-off of manufacturers with particular channels through the market. If this happens, although no one manufacturer will discriminate,

---

[16] One writer has questioned whether in formulating their discount policies manufacturers have not failed to appreciate the interdependence of the derived demand of the various channels only to be surprised by the repercussions of competition among distributors. *Cf.* E. P. Learned, "Quantity Buying from the Seller's Point of View," *Harvard Business Review*, VIII (1929), 57–68.

the degree of monopoly power exercised through various channels may differ, in which case the legislation, while eliminating differences in price by one seller, may do little to change the competitive position of rival channels or to improve the situation of the consumer.[17]

Another type of discrimination is that of a temporary, but systematic and purposive sort. One example of this is the policy used in competitive markets to dispose of surplus commodities, the two-price plans characteristic of contemporary agricultural policy. If this were undertaken sporadically and were unassociated with any restriction of supply, its principal effect would be to increase the revenues of the sellers, to penalize those to whom the price is raised and aid those to whom price is lowered. As a temporary measure, particularly in agriculture, its principal justification has been the incidental redistribution of income, which must be weighed against its effects upon consumers' expenditure patterns. When the practice becomes sufficiently established to affect the anticipations of producers, it might be expected to lead to greater investment (or if the industry is already characterized by long-run excess capacity, to a lesser withdrawal of capacity). Under these circumstances the policy means in the long-run the allocation to this industry of an amount of resources which would satisfy consumers' desires better elsewhere.

These are the principal types of systematic and purposive discrimination to be considered. The effects of temporary local discrimination designed to drive out a competitor are obvious. They are to be found in the policies of the monopoly which results. Concerning the unsystematic and incidental discrimination which accompanies price changes in imperfectly organized markets little need be said. Its incidence upon rival sellers

---

[17] *Cf. supra*, p. 159, where it was suggested that sections of the Robinson-Patman Act dealing with brokerage, reciprocal purchasing, and the supplying of special services may have the same tendency.

and buyers is likely to be haphazard. It is, of course, a factor making for flexible prices, and its principal justification is to be found in the contribution it makes to such flexibility. The next section of this chapter will be devoted to a discussion of the basing-point and other geographical price structures which are characterized by discrimination of a systematic but incidental sort.

GEOGRAPHICAL PRICE STRUCTURES: BASING-POINT SYSTEMS

One aspect of the price structure of a firm calls for special attention, namely the geographical price relations. Goods are not only sold to different buyers and in different quantities, they are also sold to buyers located at different points geographically. Every industry and every firm has some geographic pattern of prices whether this is determined by independent administrative action, by collusion, or in the market place.

The alternatives are several. One policy is to sell at a uniform price f.o.b. point of manufacture or sale, allowing the firm to take delivery at this point and provide for its own transportation. A variation upon this is to sell at delivered prices which cover a uniform mill price plus actual transportation costs. In both circumstances delivered prices would, on the assumption of uniform mileage transportation costs, rise at a constant rate as one moved away from the mill in any direction. This is the type of price structure which would characterize any purely competitive industry. If a large number of sellers are competing at one point, delivered prices would rise as one moved from the point. Any mill not located at the center of the producing area would find it profitable to sell only away from the producing center.

Another alternative is to sell at a uniform delivered price to all buyers wherever located. In this case the mill net price (i.e. net revenue from a particular sale after deducting actual transportation costs) to the seller will vary inversely with the transportation charges involved in a particular sale. In general this policy is used only in industries characterized by some element of monopoly power and in which transportation charges are small in relation to total costs. In other industries, a compromise is adopted in the form of a system of zones, with uniform delivered prices within each zone but price differentials between zones. In industries in which there are two or more sellers of a standardized product it is necessary that the zones be common to each.

A common practice, in industries in which there are several rivals located at different points, is to quote a uniform mill net price but to invade the markets tributary to a rival's plant by meeting its delivered price, i.e. by absorbing freight. In its local market area the firm has a monopolistic position which enables it to determine price within broad limits, but if it desires to invade the market area of a competitor, it becomes necessary to meet the competitor's price. It will be profitable to invade a competitor's territory so long as the mill net price realized by the seller is no less than the seller's marginal costs. This practice is called freight absorption, or market interpenetration. It implies non-uniform mill net realizations or prices. Those buyers in the market area contiguous to a firm contribute to the firm a larger net revenue per unit of product than those in the market area of a rival. In circumstances where current prices are not generally known, meeting of competition will be a very haphazard affair. In any market where sellers generally announce their f.o.b. mill prices, meeting competition with reference to a particular customer involves quoting a price at least as low as the base price of the nearest seller plus transportation charges from this latter seller's point of shipping to the point of delivery. When a firm wishes to increase its volume of sales, it may do so either by reducing its base price, thus extending its market area if rivals do not follow suit, or by invading its rival's market by freight absorption. The latter may often seem to be the most profitable, since the former means lowering price on all sales and runs the risk that the market will not be extended geographically if the rival follows suit. This practice of "meeting competition" amounts to sales in accordance with a basing-point system in which each mill is a basing-point, a practice to which the remainder of the chapter is devoted.

The typical basing-point system, such as characterizes the iron and steel and the cement industries, is a formalized system of price quoting which involves market interpenetration by means of freight absorption. Usually, however, the number of basing-points is limited, being restricted sometimes to a single basing-point, but more often multiple points are used. The difference between the basing-point system and the general practice of market interpenetration by freight absorption considered above lies in the limitation of the basing-points and the formalized nature of the system.

The essence of a single basing-point system is the quoting of all prices for a given product by all mills under the same or different managements as delivered prices composed of two elements: the one element called the base price, the other the cost of transportation from a common basing-point to the point of delivery. This second element, the transportation charge, is the same for purchases from any mill, wherever located, and bears no relation to the actual transportation costs paid for the shipment of the product except in the case of shipments made from mills located at the controlling basing-point. In some instances freight applications are not even actual transportation charges from the basing-point. The first element, the base price, may differ as between the various mills quoting on a given basing-point, although in fact it is usually uniform, allowance being made for differences in such things as credit extended and quality of the product. It is obvious why this must be so, at least for such goods as those in which the system is used where the value of individual sales is large and the buyers belong peculiarly to that class which act in conformity with rational calculations of profit and loss. If any price differences developed, all orders would go to the firm selling at the lowest price. The transportation charge being common for all mills, the base prices must be the same also if delivered prices are to be identical.

Under a multiple basing-point system, as employed in the steel industry, base prices are quoted on several points. In some cases a mill quotes on all basing-points; in other instances, a mill will quote prices on only one or a few of the basing-points. This will depend upon its desire to build up volume of sales by freight absorption. The prices quoted on a single base by different producers will in general be identical for the reasons explained above in connection with the single basing-point system. The prices quoted for different bases may be either uniform or non-uniform; this will depend upon considerations of cost and demand. If uniform, the base price for the basing-point having the lowest transportation factor to a given destination will determine the latter's delivered price. If base prices are non-uniform, as is quite usually the case, the controlling price for any point will be the lowest sum of base price and freight to any given point, the base prices of all basing-points considered.

The effect of any basing-point system as well as the effect of the general practice of meeting competition by freight absorption is a non-uniform mill net price for all mills not situated at the basing-point. That is, mill net prices (the delivered price, as quoted, minus actual transportation charges) will vary for different shipments according as the point of delivery is located at different distances freightwise from the mill whence the product is shipped. Such a difference in mill net prices is evidence of the absence of a purely competitive market situation. In a purely competitive market, each producer would seek to increase his profits by selling all of his product in the market in which net realizations are greatest.[18] However, the practice is generally defended by members of the industry as being the very essence of competition since it enables several producers to enter any market area, thus extending the area over which a seller competes, increasing the number of competitors at each point, and promoting uniform prices at each point.

Any adequate understanding of the problem of the basing-point system must recognize the similarities and relation between these various methods for determining the geographical price relations. Some discussions of the basing-point system have assumed that the only "natural" pricing system is one of a uniform mill net price for all sales by one seller. That this is the only price structure compatible with pure competition is true. The evidence shows, however, that in many markets the use of a basing-point system has been preceded by various systems giving non-uniform mill net prices; and it is highly improbable that the mere elimination of the basing-point system would restore the price structure characteristic of pure competition.

It is instructive to note certain characteristics of the markets in which the basing-point is used. It has been mentioned previously that generally the product is highly standardized and freight is an important element in the cost of the delivered product. In several of the markets in which the system is used the producing units are highly concentrated in limited geographical areas; [19] this fact induces the firms to penetrate each

[18] Jacob Viner, "Objective Tests of Competitive Price Applied to the Cement Industry," *Journal of Political Economy*, XXXIII (1925), 110.

[19] About 65 per cent of the total volume of the cast iron pipe industry is manufactured in the vicinity of Birmingham (NRA, Division of Review, *Minimum Price Regulation under Codes of Fair Competition*, Work Materials No. 56, p. 197). In the sugar refining industry refining of cane is highly concentrated along the Atlantic Sea Board, around San Francisco, and along the Gulf of Mexico (*Brief for the U. S. before the Supreme Court: Sugar Institute, Inc., et al. v. U. S.*, 297 U. S. 553, p. 29). Between 75 and 85 per cent of the volume of maple flooring is produced by

others' markets and suggests the convenience of a formalized system of quoting prices. Of equal importance is the high concentration of volume in the hands of a few sellers; [20] this makes it easier to secure adherence to the system through agreement or leadership.[21] Finally, the basing-point is often found in

---

25 mills located in Michigan, Wisconsin, and Northern Illinois (NRA, Division of Review, *The Control of Geographic Price Relations*, Work Materials No. 86, pp. 134–135). Over 30 per cent of the capacity of the oak flooring industry is located in Tennessee and a substantial additional volume in the vicinity (*ibid.*, p. 313, Table 11). In the early period, production of cement was highly concentrated in the Lehigh Valley (Federal Trade Commission, *Price Bases Inquiry*, Washington, 1931, p. 31), although it has subsequently been diffused with the result that the number of basing-points has greatly increased.

[20] The 15 members of the Sugar Institute controlled 70 to 80 per cent of the total domestic consumption of sugar (*Brief for the U. S. before Supreme Court: Sugar Institute, Inc., et al. v. U. S.*, 297 U. S. 553, p. 27). In 1935, the 21 members of the Maple Flooring Association controlled 70 to 80 per cent of the total shipments (NRA, Division of Review, *The Control of Geographic Price Relations*, p. 136). In 1919, 12 members of the linseed oil industry, which was using a zone system of pricing, were responsible for 68 per cent of the total production (*Brief for the U. S. before the Supreme Court: U. S. v. American Linseed Oil Co., et al.*, 262 U. S. 371, p. 22). Thirty-five concerns control 90 per cent of the output of the cast iron soil pipe industry (*New York Times*, March 30, 1937). Ten manufacturers produced all the corn gluten in 1919 when a basing-point was used in this industry, and one concern alone produced about 60 per cent (Federal Trade Commission, *Report on Commercial Feeds*, 1921, p. 162). In the asphalt shingle and roofing industry, which has at times been working on a basing-point system, there were in 1933 27 firms (NRA, Division of Review, *Price Filing under NRA Codes*, Work Materials No. 76, II, 512). The five largest cement firms produced during the years 1929 to 1931 between 37 and 40 per cent of the total production in the United States (Federal Trade Commission, *Cement Industry*, Senate Document No. 71, 73d Cong., 1st Sess., p. 12). Evidence of concentration in the iron and steel industry is well known.

[21] This is notoriously true of the iron and steel industry (A. R. Burns, *The Decline of Competition*, New York: McGraw-Hill, 1936, pp. 77 *et seq.*). The cast iron soil pipe industry is alleged to be "dominated to a marked degree by one individual . . . who is alleged to own foundries all over the country and warehouses in nearly all big cities." (NRA, Division of Review, *Minimum Price Regulation under Codes*, p. 198.) In the

conjunction with strong and active trade associations; the sponsorship and policing of the system is often a matter of primary concern to the association.

Why does an industry adopt a basing-point system for quoting prices? What are the motives and purposes of an industry in adopting such a system? It has been pointed out above that a firm acting on the principle of maximizing its profits by meeting competition wherever profitable may be induced to charge different prices to buyers located differently freightwise with respect to its plant. While this would explain *a* system of prices in which the mill net prices of a firm for different sales are not uniform, it would not explain a *price structure of the particular type arising from a basing-point system*. Four principal explanations have been offered for the adoption of these systems: First, it is argued that the system is of convenience to the buyer. In the lumber industry, for instance, in which there are a large number of sellers located at various and often obscure points, consumers desire to have delivered prices quoted. To quote f.o.b. mill prices would impose on the buyer an impossible task of trying to determine which price is best after transportation costs are added. This would necessitate extensive computations and much reference to obscure freight-rate books. Moreover, it is to the interest of buyers that delivered prices at any one point should be uniform, since otherwise buyers who compete in resale may compete on unequal terms. A uniform price would be an attribute of a well functioning market, but since frictions may frequently prevent uniform prices, a basing-point system, it is argued, would be a real improvement.

---

fertilizer industry, there were found to be two leaders, one in the South and another in the North, whose price policies were generally followed (NRA, Division of Review, *Fertilizer Industry Price Filing Study*, Work Materials No. 67, p. 24). Leadership has also been alleged in the cement industry (Federal Trade Commission, *Cement Industry*, 1933, p. xi).

The second explanation runs along similar lines but concerns the convenience of the seller. Granted that, in view of the substantial elements of spatial monopoly inherent in the markets concerned, the seller does not find it to its interest to sell at a uniform mill net price to all nor to increase its volume by general and uniform price reductions, nevertheless, the seller finds individual bargaining and haphazard freight absorption an expensive, confusing and time consuming procedure. When such practices prevail, a firm is never sure what its competitor is charging. Effective publicity of prices and orderly market procedure, quite aside from any question of price control, require a uniform method of quoting prices.

The third explanation, urged especially by the critics of the system, maintains that the practice is essentially one element in a scheme of price control. It is argued that in such industries as cement and steel the practice of quoting prices on a basing-point is an effective means in organizing a system of price leadership or outright agreement. Since it would not be convenient for the leader to publish delivered prices for all points of consumption or in the case of agreement to negotiate prices for all such points, the basing-point formula is a workable compromise. Since transportation costs are known and fixed (at least those of railroads), the only element which the leader must establish or which must be the subject of negotiation is the base price. Most of the industries which have adopted basing-points have been on other evidence suspected of price control activities.

Finally, the NRA showed that when price fixing under government sponsorship is attempted for an industry of the type in question, administrative efficiency dictates the adoption of some similar expedient. This was strikingly demonstrated by the attempts to prevent selling below cost in the lumber industry. To set a uniform mill net price for all firms would have seriously upset the relative volume position of the various sellers by penalizing those located farthest from the market. To set a minimum price for each seller at such a level as would have preserved such relative positions would have been administratively impossible or at least burdensome and expensive. A basing-point system with appropriate exceptions or some other formalized system of freight absorption was the compromise.[22]

The discussion of the economic effects and significance of this practice has been prolific and indeed colorful, especially in recent years. Space will not permit a consideration of the innumerable arguments which have been urged, but some brief outline of the issues will be presented.[23]

The first consideration is its effect on the geographical price

[22] The experience of the NRA in the lumber industries is developed fully in NRA, Division of Review, *The Control of Geographic Price Relations, passim.*

[23] The literature is voluminous. In the van of the critics of the system is F. A. Fetter whose book, *The Masquerade of Monopoly* (New York: Harcourt, Brace & Co., 1931) is a classic. The Federal Trade Commission has issued numerous reports critical of the practice: *cf.* especially, *Price Bases Inquiry* (1931); *Cement Industry* (73d Cong., 1st Sess., 1933, Senate Document No. 71); and two reports submitted to the Temporary National Economic Committee (T. N. E. C.), *Monopoly and Competition in Steel* (March 7, 1939) and *An Analysis of the Basing-Point System of Delivered Prices as Presented by the United States Steel Corporation* (January 26, 1940). A recent defense of the system is to be found in a report presented by the United States Steel Corporation to the T. N. E. C. and circulated privately entitled *The Basing-Point Method of Quoting Delivered Prices in the Steel Industry* (dated October 30, 1939). A comprehensive study of the pros and cons of the issue is to be found in C. R. Daugherty, M. G. deChazeau, and S. S. Stratton, *The Economics of the Iron and Steel Industry*, 2 vols. (New York: McGraw-Hill, 1937). In connection with this the review by F. A. Fetter should be read, "The New Plea for Basing-Point Monopoly," *The Journal of Political Economy*, XLV (1937), 577, and the reply by M. G. deChazeau, "Public Policy and Discriminatory Prices of Steel," *The Journal of Political Economy*, XLVI (1938), 537. *Cf.* also NRA, *Report on the Operation of the Basing-Point System in the Iron and Steel Industry* (November, 1934); Burns, *The Decline of Competition*, chaps. VI–VII; and J. M. Clark, "Basing-Point Methods of Price Quoting," *The Canadian Journal of Economics and Political Science*, IV (1938), 477.

structure. Clearly the practice results in discriminatory prices for all firms not located at the basing-point on which goods are sold, since there is a divergence between freight applications and actual freight costs which results in unequal mill net realizations. But although this discrimination is systematic, it is not purposive in the sense the word is here used, i.e. the particular system of discrimination which results is not such as would result from a careful and purposive estimate of the relative elasticities of demand of buyers located at different points. Although the discrimination is incidental to the system, it is not the explanation of the particular system.

There is no question but that the system leads to a different geographical pattern of delivered prices than would a non-discriminatory pricing system or any of several other systems which might be devised. Consequently, in industries such as steel it affects the relative profitability of various localities as areas in which to set up manufacturing plants using the product. It affects, in other words, the location of the processing industries. In the cement industry, it may have the same effect where there are two possible locations for an enterprise using cement. Where cement is sold at two points at discriminatory prices for non-rival uses, the effect is to change the allocation of economic resources. Consumption of cement-using projects is discouraged in localities where price is high and encouraged where it is low. Any change in basing-point practice — as for example a change in the number and location of basing-points, in price differentials between basing-points, or even in transportation charges — may affect significantly various rival business interests in different communities.

Quite another consideration is the effect of the practice upon the efficiency with which production and distribution is pursued in the industries using the practice. Where technical factors lead to a high concentration in particular areas, its effects may not be significant. For example, if the lumber producing firms are clustered around a particular area and the basing-point is approximately at the center of the production area, no great effect is likely upon the location of plants. In an industry such as steel where plant location is a matter of choice which depends among other things upon costs of assembling raw materials and the market price structure, the price structure of the industry resulting from use of the basing-point system may induce an uneconomic location of plant. How significant this may be seems to be a matter of debate. So little is known about the costs in even such industries as steel that quantitative verification of the assumption has been impossible. However, most of the impartial students agree that some effect of this sort of unknown quantity is probable.

Another aspect of the efficiency problem concerns the physical and economic wastes of cross-hauling of products. This is held to be the inevitable result of a system of freight absorption. On this matter of unnecessary transportation there is little or no data. That there is such wasteful cross-hauling and unnecessary freight in the industries concerned is unquestionable. How extensive it is remains unknown; many of the estimates are on the whole meaningless. But J. M. Clark believes that in the case of cement, "the waste remains substantial." [24] It is true, of course, that if the delivered price from the various sellers is uniform for any given point, a basing-point system or a system of freight-equalization removes any incentive in the form of price which a buyer might have to trade with the freightwise nearest seller. Such preference as he may have will be determined by convenience, promptness of delivery, and differences in the terms of sale or in quality.

As for the sellers, they have an incentive to maximize their average mill net prices. This means that in an industry in which every mill is a basing-point, each firm would try to reduce freight absorption to a minimum by concentrating on the area nearest its mill. This would likewise tend to reduce cross-

[24] *The Canadian Journal of Economics and Political Science*, IV, 482.

hauling to a minimum. In the case of a basing-point system, however, there is not the same incentive for the individual to minimize unnecessary transportation. Any firm located at a basing-point has no reason to prefer any customer located within the area for which the basing-point is applicable. A firm not located at the basing-point has an incentive to seek customers so located that its mill net price is a maximum. This does not mean, however, that freight costs will be a minimum, since such a firm will find it profitable to sell away from a basing-point for quite a distance rather than toward a basing-point for any distance despite higher actual transportation costs. This may mean wasteful transportation. On the other hand, if the basing-point is a center of "surplus" production and goods naturally move away from it, a firm not located at the center would even in a purely competitive market sell away from the basing-point.

It should be noted that the problem of unnecessary freight costs is wider than the problem of cross-hauling. Moreover, the charges of cross-hauling themselves need to be considered with care. Many alleged instances of this can be shown to be due to differences in the quality of the product, to greater convenience with respect to time of delivery, etc. In the lumber industry it is claimed that much which appears to be uneconomic cross-hauling is to be explained by the buying habits of contractors and retailers.[25] In any one area, due to these habits, only one or a few grades and sizes of a particular genus of wood will be in demand, but technical conditions require that a mill produce many grades and sizes. It is in consequence inevitable that lumber of a particular genus should be cross-freighted. The facts on this whole problem are not available, and the quantitative significance of the wastes is as yet undetermined.

Other sources of waste are to be found in the unnecessary

[25] NRA, Division of Review, *The Control of Geographic Price Relations*, p. 152.

extension of sales effort and the elimination of shipments by so-called "differential" transportation methods. As for uneconomic sales effort, this results from the fact that the basing-point system often leads to an interpenetration of markets, by which a particular seller seeks buyers over a wider area than he would under a system of uniform mill net prices. The wastes incident to the use of uneconomic transportation methods arise from the fact that in operation of the system it is often the practice to provide that only railroad rates be used in estimating delivered prices. Customers located so as to be served by cheaper methods of transportation, such as water or truck, are usually denied any price concession based thereon. Consequently, there is often little incentive for the buyer to ask for delivery by the cheaper and more economical methods. Moreover, it is frequently the custom to deny the buyer the privilege of taking delivery at the mill and of making his own arrangements for transportation. The reasons for these customs are to be found in part in the instability of these differential route rates and in part in the fact that to make delivery at the mill might break down the discriminatory price structure.[26] Again the quantitative significance of these wastes is in doubt.

Another aspect of the question of efficiency revolves about the size of the firm and its average rate of utilization. One of the virtues of a perfectly competitive market is that it tends to concentrate production in firms of the optimum size. One of the arguments of the proponents of the basing-point is that some system of freight absorption, some penetration into rivals' markets, is necessary for a firm in such industries in order to operate at full capacity. It is, of course, true that the limited nature of the market in the immediate vicinity of the firm may make it necessary for the firm to extend its sales geographically in order to achieve the economies of scale, but when several rivals penetrate into each other's markets, the efforts to achieve

[26] *Cf. supra*, p. 128.

the economies of scale are in part, at least, mutually offsetting. Moreover, it is possible to gain the same advantages by a system of uniform mill net prices which, if there were two sellers, would divide the market at some point between the plants where the sum of mill prices plus actual transportation costs for the two firms are equal. This might be achieved by proper adjustment of mill prices while keeping the mill price uniform for all. That freight absorption and market penetration is necessary in order to achieve the economies of scale of plant or of operation of the plant when others are following such policies is obvious. But it does not follow that other price policies, if followed by all, could not bring about the same results.

Perhaps the crux of the argument concerning the use of the basing-point revolves about the question as to whether it is a monopolistic or competitive practice. So posed the question is meaningless. The critics have clearly demonstrated that it is not a practice such as will be found in a purely or perfectly competitive market. But, of course, the market is not purely competitive and could not be, although it is conceivable that a purely competitive price *structure* could be *imposed* on the industry. By noting the similarity in the price structure resulting from a basing-point system in which each mill is a basing-point to the structure resulting from the general practice of freight absorption, it becomes clear that the same results might emerge in markets with certain basic characteristics from intense rivalry even without use of a formal basing-point system. But this does not dispose of the question of competition versus monopoly.

The opponents argue that in some industries where it is used the basing-point system is the keystone in a system of price control, that it is an important factor in making price agreements or price leadership effective. This is perhaps best illustrated by the practice in the steel industry. The industry is one which sells thousands of individual products and variations of products and stands ready to deliver any one of these products to literally millions of possible points. How can such an industry evolve a price structure which is uniform for each seller without elaborate and overt agreement upon each occasion that prices are changed?

The answer is to be found in a series of practices. First, it is the custom of the leaders of the industry to publish in advance of each quarter the prices of some forty or fifty basic products. These are announced in the press and through printed lists. How much discussion precedes changes in these prices is difficult to tell. Because of the other customs of the industry it is simply necessary for rivals to arrive at uniform prices for these forty or fifty items, either by agreement or by following the leader, in order to arrive at a price structure identical in the minutest detail. To these basic prices the prices of the other products and variations of products are tied by the application of certain "extras." The extras, which are applied to basic prices to arrive at prices for particular products, are the result of considerable discussion in the trade. They are uniform for all sellers and compiled in a book which is widely circulated. Custom decrees that in calculating particular prices the appropriate extra will be applied to the appropriate basic price. The use of the basing-point system is the final item which makes the delivered prices uniform, since the basing-point system involves the application of uniform transportation charges. By standardizing freight charges and by standardizing the book of extras for various grades, qualities, quantities, etc. the whole structure of prices is controlled by a few basic prices. The delivered price for any particular product delivered at any point is easily calculated by a clerk who is armed with the list of basic prices, the extra book, a list of basing-points, and the applicable freight charges.

Limitation of price competition becomes feasible if only by custom or agreement (whether tacit or overt) all members use the same basic prices, extras, and freight charges. How significant price control has been in the industry and how serious in its effects is in debate. It is true, of course, that at times there are divergences from the prices dictated by the customary procedure, but such divergences seem to be the exception rather than the rule. It is sufficient for present purposes to have shown the potentialities of the system in an industry where firms are few and other factors are favorable. Some formula similar to the basing-point system for stabilizing geographical price relations is a *sine qua non* of price agreement or price leadership; and it is significant that in many of the industries in which it has been found, there have been other grounds for suspecting attempts to limit competition in price.

The legal status of the basing-point system is far from clear. The courts have never dealt with the practice as such. It has come before them only incidentally as one element in an alleged scheme of market control through the medium of the open-price activities of a trade association. In two early cases the courts found nothing exceptional about the open-price activities.[27] In both cases freight-rate books were circulated showing all-rail rates from a common basing-point. In both instances the industry was characterized by a large number of firms rather highly concentrated in the area around the basing-point. In such circumstances it is doubtful whether it would affect significantly the *structure* of prices; its greatest potentialities would seem to be in affecting their level. The courts, while recognizing the potentiality of the device as part of a scheme of price-fixing, found no evidence that it was being so used. In the decision in the case of the Maple Flooring Manufacturers' Association, the Court stressed the convenience of the freight-rate books as a device for prompt quotation of delivered prices.[28]

[27] *Maple Flooring Manufacturers' Association, et al. v. U. S.*, 268 U. S. 563 (1925); *Cement Manufacturers' Protective Association, et al. v. U. S.*, 268 U. S. 588 (1925).   [28] 268 U. S. 571.

In the recent decision involving the Sugar Institute, however, the basing-point system was condemned as part of a general scheme which was held to be an agreement in unreasonable restraint of trade.[29] The case involved as part of an open-price program an agreement to quote prices according to a basing-point formula and to refuse certain differentials for cheaper forms of transportation. However, it would seem that it was not the basing-point as such which was found unreasonable. Speaking of the whole scheme of open-prices, the court said, "The unreasonable restraints which defendants imposed lay not in advance announcements, but in the steps taken to secure adherence, without deviation, to prices and terms thus announced. It was that concerted undertaking which cut off opportunities for variation in the course of competition however fair and appropriate they might be." [30] The courts, in short, have dealt with the basing-point only as one element in a general scheme alleged to be contrary to the Sherman Act. What attitude the courts would take upon the basing-point if presented as a violation of the Federal Trade Commission and Clayton Acts we cannot say.

In several instances the Commission has enjoined the practice. The most significant is the famous "Pittsburgh Plus" case involving the United States Steel Company and its subsidiaries.[31] The practice was enjoined both as an unfair method of competition under section 5 and as an illegal discrimination under the Clayton Act. The details of the charge that the practice is an unfair method of competition throw additional light on the criteria which are applied by the Commission in administering section 5. The attack was twofold. In the

[29] *Sugar Institute, Inc., et al. v. U. S.*, 297 U. S. 553 (1936).

[30] 297 U. S. 601.

[31] 8 F. T. C. 1 (1924). There are several recent orders in which the Commission has proceeded against it as a part of an elaborate conspiracy in restraint of price competition.

first place the practice was held to be part of a scheme for establishing uniform, non-competitive prices.[32] The second charge was that of unfair discrimination. It was charged that there was discrimination on the part of all mills located outside of Pittsburgh between the various customers of each mill, and discrimination between customers of the United States Steel and its subsidiaries buying from different mills. This discrimination was held unfair on two counts: first, it "prevents the customer against whom the discriminations resulting therefrom operate, from competing on an equality, or from competing at all, with their competitors in favor of whom such discriminations operate"; [33] second, "The . . . charging . . . of Pittsburgh Plus prices to their customers with whom they . . . compete, . . . is unfair to such customer-competitors, and gives the respondents an unconscionable advantage over such customer-competitors. . . ." [34] Finally, the practice was held to be an unfair method of competition because the respondents quoted and charged delivered prices "without disclosing to their customers how much they are charging for steel and how much for actual freight." [35] This order serves to emphasize further the fact that the Commission's interest in discrimination is primarily in the effects on the competitive position of private business interests; its objective is to prevent the injury of particular competitors.

In concluding this section on the basing-point, it is appropriate to raise the question as to what sort of policy would best serve the public interest. No clear answer can be given. The students disagree, and there are no facts available as to the quantitative effects of the system. Moreover, it would appear that the effects vary according to the basic market conditions of the industry in which it is used. It has been emphasized that the practice presupposes some element of monopoly, but

[32] *Ibid.*, p. 32.
[33] *Ibid.*, Par. 8, p. 28.
[34] *Ibid.*, Par. 11, p. 30.
[35] *Ibid.*, Par. 15, p. 50.

there are differing degrees of monopoly. A practice whose effects might be negligible in some division of the lumber industry, for instance, might prove serious in the case of iron and steel. For this reason it appears undesirable to pass legislation forbidding it outright. Moreover, a choice of policy must be predicated upon a consideration of alternatives, and of the costs and administrative problems of such alternative policies.

The powers of the Federal Trade Commission are limited.[36] Its powers are at the most of a negative sort, to prevent the practice. Simply to prevent the use of the basing-point system, however, will not necessarily bring into being the price structure of pure competition so long as the right to absorb freight is not prohibited. And to enforce a system of uniform mill net prices, which would bring about the price *structure* characteristic of pure competition, would not necessarily induce the price *level* of pure competition. Where sellers are few and separated geographically, each would soon learn to consider the effect of its price cuts on a competitor. While any firm by cutting its uniform mill price to all might extend its market geographically, if rivals did likewise, the initiator of the change would gain only the additional volume due to a lowering of prices in its old territory. The fact that the competitor met the cut would prevent the first seller from extending its market geographically. These considerations are only suggestive of the complications of the problem. It is clearly one to which there is no simple answer. A wise policy will vary from industry to industry. It is a matter with which the law of discrimination and section 5 of the Federal Trade Commission Act is inadequate to deal. It is a matter calling for special, discretionary legislation.

---

[36] It was generally believed at the time of the passage of the Robinson-Patman Act, that the amendment of section 2 of the Clayton Act embodied therein would not change the status of the basing-point. *Congressional Record*, LXXX (1936), 9903–9904.

CONCLUSION

The problem of discrimination is many-sided. It constitutes the whole problem of the *price structure* of a firm as opposed to the *price level*. Most products are sold to different classes of buyers and to buyers variously located from a geographic point of view. The relation between the prices charged to buyers of different classes and different location comprises the price structure of the industry. Where an industry produces goods of different qualities, the relation between the prices of these different qualities is also part of the problem. If a market were characterized by perfect and pure competition, no problems of policy would arise. These relations would be determined by market forces, and price differences would depend upon marginal costs. As a matter of fact there are substanial imperfections, generally some element of monopoly, in most markets. As a consequence, business enterprise has the power to determine these relations within certain limits. Along with the level of prices the structure of prices is administered.

Price discrimination is to be explained in some cases as the result of a systematic attempt to maximize profits by separation of markets. On the other hand, in some markets it is more or less incidental to other purposes, such as the maintenance of price stability. The basing-point system may be in this class. Finally, there is much sporadic discrimination which is incidental to price changes in markets where there is an atmosphere of secrecy and imperfect knowledge. Such discrimination is for the most part temporary. While it is disturbing to business, principally because secret price cuts to particular customers may easily become generalized, it appears that in many markets such as they are, this is the usual way in which aggressive price competition is made effective.

In our system of free enterprise the presumption has been in favor of the freedom of business enterprise to determine the price structures. Public policy as interpreted by the courts, legislatures, or the Commission has never declared in favor of a one price policy or of a general policy of limiting price differentials to differences in cost. It has been recognized that price differentials of a discriminatory sort may be used to develop monopoly or they may substantially injure certain private business interests to the benefit of others. In such cases, public policy intervenes in order to promote fair competition and to prevent it from developing into unequal competition or monopoly. In short, discrimination is illegal when it coerces or excludes competitors or when it favors one group at the price of injury to others. So long as it keeps within these bounds business enterprise is free to determine the structure of prices as it wishes.

In drawing the limits to discrimination at these points public policy has failed to consider adequately the public interest in the structure of prices. It has failed to recognize that the public has an interest in the differences in the prices of a product sold to final consumers or to dealers who do not compete in resale, i.e. it has failed to recognize discrimination as a matter of differences in the degree of monopoly power which may adversely affect the allocation of economic resources. It has likewise given inadequate recognition to the significance of such practices as the basing-point in conjunction with others in the control of price competition. Not that discrimination is in all cases undesirable. It has been seen, on the contrary, that under certain conditions of demand and of costs discrimination may improve upon a simple monopoly pricing policy. Moreover, as has been suggested unsystematic and secret discrimination may in some cases be the *sine qua non* of aggressive price competition. It cannot be emphasized too strongly that a rigid policy of requiring uniform prices to all is not ideal from an economic point of view. There are good economic reasons against such a policy. There are also reasons why this would be inexpedient from the point of view both of efficient business administration and effective public administration. There are so many ways to disguise discrimination that enforcement can at most be arbitrary. The problem of establishing legitimate differentials limited to differences in cost also rises to plague any enforcement agency. Often to permit such differentials complicates administration; while to prohibit them in the interest of administrative efficiency is to sacrifice economic efficiency.

CHAPTER X

TYING AND EXCLUSIVE ARRANGEMENTS

TYING and exclusive arrangements are usually joined for purposes of discussion although there are some differences in effects between the two practices. Both, however, are devices by which a seller reaches forward in the productive or distributive process to control business policies at subsequent stages for its own benefit. As a prerequisite to such a sales policy some element of monopoly power is necessary. In so far as a seller makes such a policy effective, he prohibits or limits the access of rivals to the market while presumably extending his own share of the market.

A tying arrangement involves the sale or lease of goods on condition that certain ancillary goods be purchased from the same source. Thus, mimeographing machines may be sold on condition that paper and ink be bought from the same seller; patented machinery may be leased subject to the condition that certain other machinery be leased from the same manufacturer or that the machinery which is leased be used only in manufacture where certain other operations are performed by the lessor's machines. Exclusive dealing arrangements are generally concluded by a manufacturer with a distributor so that the manufacturer may be assured that the distributor will devote his energies exclusively to pushing the former's product. In such cases the exclusive arrangement may be a two-way affair, the manufacturer agreeing in return to give the dealer exclusive right to sell in a given territory. Exclusive agreements may also be concluded with a buyer (usually an intermediate producer) who agrees to use a single manufacturer's product in his own production process.

Tying and exclusive arrangements, like discrimination, had a prominent place in the early history of the anti-trust laws. As was seen in an earlier chapter, Congress and the courts alike had reason to consider these practices in the period before 1910.[1] However, prosecutions of these practices had not been too successful [2] and in 1914 it was quite generally hoped to deal more effectively with them by specific legislation. Since it was considered doubtful whether such arrangements could be enjoined as an unfair method of competition under section 5 of the Federal Trade Commission Act,[3] section 3 of the Clayton Act was incorporated to deal specifically with them. This section provides that:

. . . it shall be unlawful . . . to lease or make a sale or contract for sale of goods . . . whether patented or unpatented . . . or fix a price charged therefor, or discount from, or rebate upon, such price, on the condition, agreement or understanding that the lessee or purchaser thereof shall not use or deal in the goods . . . of a competitor . . . where the effect of such lease, sale, or contract for sale or such condition, agreement or understanding may be to substantially lessen competition or tend to create a monopoly in any line of commerce.[4]

The prohibition, it should be observed, does not extend to contracts of agency. The limitation of the prohibition to those cases where the effect "may be to substantially lessen competition" is the same as appears in other sections of the Clayton Act. In addition to the power of the Federal Trade Commission to issue orders to cease and desist in the enforcement of this section, injured parties are empowered to institute proceedings

[1] *Cf.* chap. II. For a description of various cases of tying and exclusive arrangements in industry, *cf.* W. H. S. Stevens, *Unfair Competition* (Chicago: University of Chicago Press, 1917), chaps. IV and V.

[2] *Cf. supra*, p. 36, for the opinion of the courts on the applicability of the Sherman Act to the United Shoe Machinery Company's leases.

[3] *Cf.* statement of Senator Cummins, *Congressional Record*, LI (1914), 14227.

[4] Public No. 212, 63d Cong., 2d Sess. (1914).

in the courts for an injunction to restrain violations of the section and to recover threefold for actual damages suffered.

TYING ARRANGEMENTS

The Commission acting under section 3 of the Clayton Act or section 5 of the Federal Trade Commisison Act has to date issued only 4 orders enjoining the use of tying arrangements; [5] other proceedings have been instituted in the courts by injured parties.

Only one of the Commission's orders, that in the *Gratz* case, has been finally disposed of upon appeal to the courts. Since the Commission found insufficient evidence to prove substantial lessening of competition or tendency to a monopoly within the meaning of section 3, it ordered the company to cease its exclusive practices as an unfair method of competition under section 5 alone.[6] The practice involved the refusal to sell ties for binding cotton bales unless the purchaser bought a certain amount of jute bagging used to wrap the bales of cotton. The order was reversed because of failure to satisfy the criteria of unfair methods of competition developed by the court.[7] This decision made it clear that no tying arrangement that did not fall within the prohibitions of the Sherman and Clayton Acts could be enjoined under section 5.

In each of the other three orders to cease and desist a prominent feature of the findings was the dominant position of the respondent in the market for his product.[8] This suggests that a decisive factor in determining the legality of a tying contract is the predominance of the seller or lessor in his market, the

---

[5] As of June 1940.

[6] 1 F. T. C. 249 (1918).

[7] *F. T. C. v. Gratz, et al.*, 253 U. S. 421 (1920). *Cf. supra*, pp. 81–84.

[8] *In the Matter of National Binding Machine Co.*, 1 F. T. C. 44 (1917); *In the Matter of A. B. Dick Co., of N. J., et al.*, 1 F. T. C. 20 (1917); *In the Matter of Chamberlin Cartridge & Target Co.*, 2 F. T. C. 357 (1920).

implication of public policy being that a tying arrangement by a firm dominating its market is likely to tend to lessen competition further.

This conclusion is supported by several cases involving tying contracts alleged to violate section 3 which have been brought before the courts in actions to which the Commission was not a party. The most notorious of these concerned the restrictive clauses in the leases of the United Shoe Machinery Corporation.[9] The United Shoe was found to have a dominant position in the manufacture and supply of shoe machinery in the United States, a control of over 95 per cent of such business. It customarily leased its machinery to shoe manufacturers on a royalty basis. It was against the restrictive clauses in these leases that the decree of the lower court was aimed.[10] The decree preventing the continued use of such restrictive clauses was sustained by the Supreme Court, which was impressed by the dominance of United Shoe and the fact that a lessee was effectually prevented from acquiring the machinery of a competitor of the United Shoe Machinery Company, "except at the risk of forfeiting the right to use the machines furnished by the United Shoe Company, which may be absolutely essential to the prosecution and success of his business." [11]

Another interesting case arose concerning restrictions placed by the Radio Corporation of America upon the manufacturers of radio sets operating under licenses from it.[12] In these agreements R.C.A. stipulated that manufacturers producing radios under its licenses should use only tubes manufactured by

[9] *United Shoe Machinery Corporation, et al. v. U. S.*, 264 Fed. 138 (1920), 258 U. S. 451 (1922).

[10] *Cf. supra*, p. 36, for more details on the practices of the United Shoe Machinery Corporation.

[11] *Ibid.*, p. 458.

[12] *Lord et al. v. Radio Corporation of America*, 24 F. (2d) 565 (1928), 28 F. (2d) 257 (1928), 35 F. (2d) 962 (1929). *Radio Corporation of America v. DeForest Radio Co.*, 47 F. (2d) 606 (1931).

R.C.A. The courts found these licenses to be in violation of the Clayton Act. Again it is significant to note the dominant position of the party enforcing the tying contracts in the manufacture of both radios and tubes. The evidence indicates that R.C.A. and 25 of its licensees combined did between 70 and 95 per cent of the total business in radio receiving sets.[13] In the sale of tubes its position was not quite as strong due to the fact that the independents had invaded the replacement market. However, during the years 1926–1928 the Corporation manufactured between 54 and 66 per cent of the total number of radio tubes.[14] On final hearing the court concluded that the restrictive clause "not only had the effect of substantially lessening competition, but was, as well, of a character to enable the defendant, by increasing the number of its licenses containing that clause, to destroy practically all competition in the manufacture and sale of tubes." [15]

In another case the International Business Machines Corporation had leased its business machines on condition that only cards manufactured by it should be used on the machines.[16] It was found that two companies controlled the commerce in business machines in the country and that they had each agreed not to sell cards to users of the other's product. Again there is evidence of dominance in the control of both of the goods involved. Two other cases of tying contracts attacked under section 3 may be mentioned. These involved leases of patented motion picture equipment. In the one case there was a restrictive agreement providing that a motion picture projecting machine should be used solely for exhibiting films which were manufactured by the holder of the patent of the projecting

[13] 24 F. (2d) 566.
[14] 35 F. (2d) 963.
[15] *Loc. cit.*
[16] *International Business Machines Corporation v. U. S.*, 298 U. S. 131 (1936).

machine.[17] The second involved the lease of reproducing equipment on condition that repairs and replacement parts should be obtained exclusively from the lessor.[18]

A tying arrangement is a successful business practice only in the circumstance that the seller has a strong monopoly position in one or more products. In the cases mentioned above this has generally been based on patent rights, though any arrangement or obstacle limiting the development of substitutes would be a sufficient condition. This does not imply that there are no substitutes for the product, but rather that there are only poor substitutes to which, over a certain price range, only a limited number of purchasers will have recourse. In technical language the "cross-elasticities of demand" are small.[19] Given a product in which a producer has a strong monopoly position, to which we shall henceforth refer as the "patented" product,[20] the seller (or lessor) [21] then provides that the buyer shall as a condition of purchase of the "patented" good buy from the seller certain other goods, which we shall call the "tied-goods." In some cases the seller may specify the precise ratio in which the patented and tied goods shall be purchased. In the more usual case he simply specifies that the buyer shall use tied goods manufactured by the seller exclusively, leaving to the

[17] *Motion Picture Patents Co. v. Universal Films Manufacturing Co., et al.*, 235 Fed. 398 (1916), 243 U. S. 502 (1917).

[18] *Stanley Company of America v. American Telephone and Telegraph Co., et al.*, 4 F. Supp. 80 (1933). This case also involved exclusive arrangements. The equipment manufacturer produced not only the reproducing equipment used by the exhibitor but the recording equipment for the producers of film. The latter were forbidden by their contracts with the defendant to distribute films to theaters and exhibitors not using the defendant's reproducing equipment. The court permitted a preliminary injunction.

[19] Nicholas Kaldor, "Market Imperfections and Excess Capacity," *Economica*, II, new series (1935), p. 35, note 1.

[20] This does not mean that the "tied" products may not also be patented.

[21] The subsequent discussion will be in terms of purchase and sale of goods rather than lease.

buyer the determination of the quantities to be purchased. It should be noted that tying contracts are virtually exclusive contracts extended to a series of products. The monopoly position of the seller in the control of the patented good virtually assures him exclusive relations with respect to that product, and the tying arrangements extends the exclusive arrangement to the tied goods. The tied goods in turn may themselves be the subject of some degree of monopoly control by the seller, or they may be goods which in the absence of tying arrangements would be quite freely produced by others. The presumption is, however, that the tied goods are the subject of some greater degree of competition from substitutes, otherwise there would be no necessity of a tying arrangement. In technical jargon products for which the cross-elasticities of demand are high are tied to products for which the cross-elasticities are low.

The object of the owner of the patented good, if he acts to maximize his monopoly profits, will be to maximize his total monopoly profits on the various goods. In analyzing the effects of this policy, two cases may be distinguished, that in which the demand for the patented and for the tied goods are independent and that in which they are interdependent or joint.

In the first case, where the demand for patented and tied goods are independent, the output and price which would be decided upon for the patented article would, on the assumption that the cost functions are unchanged, be the same in the case of a tying arrangement as in its absence. The significance of the tying arrangement is that it gives the producer of the patented product a monopoly position in at least part of the market for the tied goods. From this market or part of the market he can exclude others, and in sales of the tied product to those dependent upon him he can pursue a monopolistic price policy. This power is limited, of course, by the available substitutes for the patented good. Thus, the use of a tying contract where the demands for the various products are independent will not affect the terms of sale for the patented goods, in the absence of effects on costs. Its principal significance from the point of view of the efficiency of the economy is in the extension of monopoly elements into the market for the tied goods. From the point of view of competitive relations and the traditional law of trade practices, its significance arises from the exclusion of actual or potential producers of tied goods and the extension of monopoly elements into these markets.

The more typical case is one where the demand for the patented and tied products is joint. It is often alleged that the effect of a tying arrangement in the case of two or more jointly demanded products is to increase the aggregate price charged for the group of goods above what it would otherwise have been and, thus, to add to the monopoly profits of the patent owner. Analysis shows that while this may be true, there are very possible cases in which it will not be so. If we assume that in the absence of a tying contract, the ancillary articles would be manufactured and sold in a purely competitive market and, further, that the manufacturer of the patented good would have the same cost functions as the independents in the event that he should manufacture these ancillary products, there would be no financial motive to institute a tying contract. Analysis shows that the aggregate monopoly profits would be the same whether the patented article were sold alone, or in conjunction with the ancillary products. The only difference would be an increase in the normal profits commensurate with the additional capital investment and enterprise necessary for the production of the ancillary products. Nor would the aggregate charges to the consumer (or intermediate producer using the jointly demanded products for further production) be any different with a tying contract than without. Potential producers of the tied product, however, would be eliminated.

It may be asked what motive there is for a tying arrangement, since the supposed beneficiary nets no greater monopoly profits, merely normal profits on an additional investment. There are four possible motives to institute a tying arrangement for complementary products, one of which is monopolized. First, there are such non-financial motives as the desire for power. Secondly, in the case of patented goods where the ancillary goods are used as a part of the patented good, it may be desired to protect the patented good from damage through the use of inferior ancillary goods (especially where they are merely leased) or to protect the reputation of the patented good for excellent performance. Probably the two strongest motives, however, lie in a violation of the assumptions of the preceding paragraph. It may be that in the absence of a tying contract, the ancillary products would not be produced and sold in a market characterized by purely competitive conditions. This being so, the owner of the patented good may find it desirable to undertake the production of these ancillary products and may add to his aggregate monopoly profits. A single firm controlling the patented and ancillary products would probably increase aggregate monopoly profits above and decrease production below what they would be if the two jointly demanded products were controlled by separate monopolies.[22] The second assumption was that the cost functions for the production of the ancillary goods by the independents and by the producer of the patented goods would be the same. It is possible, however, that the latter would have a lower cost function particularly because of lower selling expenses.

Thus, we see that the effect upon the efficiency of the eco-

---

[22] This raises the problems familiar from the studies of duopoly as to how far two sellers consider the effects of their individual actions on each other. The usual theory of duopoly considers two competitors selling identical goods. The problem in hand is that of two sellers each in control of one of two jointly demanded products. The range of solutions would seem to vary from a quantity and price proper to a single seller to a price and quantity configuration based on average costs (and below this in the short run). Cf. Chamberlin, op. cit., chap. III for a discussion of duopoly.

nomic system of a tying arrangement, where demands are interdependent, will vary. Where the tied goods would otherwise be produced under conditions of pure competition and the costs of both patented and tied goods are not affected by the arrangement, the tying arrangement would have no effect on price and output. In the absence of differences in quality or efficiency, the buyer would not be adversely affected; the significance of the tying arrangement would lie solely in its effects on rival business interests. Where tied goods would otherwise be produced under conditions of pure competition but costs are affected by the tying arrangement, price and output will be affected. Output will be increased or decreased according as the marginal cost of either or both products is decreased or increased. Where costs would not be affected by the presence or absence of a tying arrangement but the tied good when produced by independents would be produced under conditions of monopoly, there may be some additional restriction in output as a result of a tying arrangement. The less the producers of the tied and patented goods, when the goods were produced by independent firms, had considered the indirect effects of their price and output policies, the more likely is a tying arrangement to induce a restriction of output of both products. Public policy, however, has focused its attention not upon these considerations of efficiency and the degree of monopoly power exercised, but upon the effects of such arrangements in excluding competing producers of tied products from the market.

EXCLUSIVE ARRANGEMENTS

The Commission has issued some fifty-five orders enjoining exclusive arrangements, thirty-seven of which dealt with the oil pump leases. These orders were mostly issued in the early 1920's.[23] The basis of the action varied. In some instances the charge was violation of the Clayton Act alone, in others of

[23] Several have been issued in recent years.

the Federal Trade Commission Act, while in still other instances action was brought under both. The oil pump lease orders were all reversed by the courts.[24] Seven of the remaining orders have been disposed of on appeal by the courts, which reversed the Commission in four cases. In addition several actions under section 3 to which the Commission was not a party have been brought before the courts.

Manufacturers of dress patterns have been successfully enjoined under the Clayton Act from selling under contracts which forbade retailers from handling the products of competitors. The Standard Fashion Company's contracts were held invalid in an action brought by it in the courts to enjoin the violation of the exclusive clauses.[25] The courts seemed impressed by the fact that the Standard Fashion Company controlled over two-fifths of the existing agencies, a control which gave it almost exclusive access to many small communities. Subsequently, the Commission issued a successful order against the Butterick Company for selling patterns under contracts which provide for resale price maintenance as well as exclusive dealing.[26] In sustaining the Commission the court noted that the Butterick Company was one of the seven largest concerns in the industry and controlled about two-fifths of the pattern agencies.[27] In both of these pattern cases the court held the contracts to be contracts of sale and not true contracts of agency. A similar order enjoining exclusive dealing and resale price maintenance in the sale of music rolls was sustained.[28]

[24] *F. T. C. v. Sinclair Refining Co.*, 261 U. S. 463 (1923).

[25] *Standard Fashion Co. v. Magrane Houston Co.*, 254 Fed. 493 (1918); 251 Fed. 559 (1918); 259 Fed. 793 (1919); 258 U. S. 346 (1922).

[26] *In the Matter of Butterick Company, et al.*, 6 F. T. C. 310 (1923).

[27] *Butterick Company, et al. v. Federal Trade Commission*, 4 F. (2d) 910 (1925).

[28] *The Q. R. S. Music Company v. F. T. C.*, 12 F. (2d) 730 (1926). Proceedings before the Commission reported in 7 F. T. C. 412 (1924).

In the most recent case to reach the courts under section 3 upon appeal from the Commission, the latter was sustained in an order enjoining the Carter Carburetor Company from inducing dealers to handle its product solely by discriminatory price and discount policies. The Carter Carburetor Company had a predominant position in the sale of carburetors for both the original equipment and renewal markets. Success in this market depends upon having arrangements with dealers and service stations for repair and renewals. At about the time that a rival company negotiated new contracts for the use of its carburetor, Carter announced to all its dealers and customers that if they handled the competitor's product, they would no longer receive preferential discounts. The court agreed that this practice had a tendency substantially to lessen competition or create a monopoly. It refused the plea of the company that it had an interest in its dealers which it should be allowed to protect by such policies because it had given them training and instruction in servicing carburetors.

It is also true that the outlays that have been made by petitioner have given the established special service stations some advantages that they avail of when they service products of petitioner's competitors and that such competitors indirectly secure a benefit in that way. . . . But there is no way by which every bit of the fruit of such large-scale dissemination of information and knowledge as petitioner has carried on can be prevented from spreading out onto the common.[29]

The oil pump orders involving the leasing, for a nominal sum, of oil pumps and storage tanks on condition that only the lessor's oil and gasoline should be sold therefrom must be

---

[29] *Carter Carburetor Corp. v. F. T. C.*, Circuit Court of Appeals, Eighth Circuit, No. 434, June 1940. Several other recent orders of the Commission have involved the giving of the discriminatory discounts in order to induce exclusive dealing. Cf. *In the Matter of American Flange and Manufacturing Company, Inc.*, Docket No. 3391 (order issued December 12, 1938). *In the Matter of National Biscuit Company*, Docket No. 3607 (order issued January 17, 1939).

looked upon as essentially exclusive dealing arrangements.[30] These agreements were not exclusive agreements in the sense that they explicitly forbade the oil retailer to handle more than one brand of oil, since he was perfectly free to do so on condition that he used a different pump and tank. Inasmuch as an oil pump is a vehicle of advertising as well as a device for dispensing oil, the lessor has good reason for ensuring that it be not used to mislead the public as to the brand of oil being sold. The essence of the Commission's reasoning was that since this sort of an arrangement was made only with the so-called "curb-pump" dealers (garages and service stations were under different agreements), whose business in general did not warrant having more than one pump, the practical effect of such an arrangement was to prohibit the dealer from handling a competitor's oil or gasoline. This resulted, in the Commission's opinion, in a tendency to establish a monopoly in the sale of these products. The Commission was also impressed by the fact that "such leases and loans of said devices and equipment are made for monetary considerations below the cost of purchasing and vending the same, when the business of leasing and loaning said devices and equipment and the returns received thereon are considered separate and apart from the general business and sales policy of the respondent." [31]

The court, however, in reversing the Commission, was mainly moved by the fact that the dealer was *free* to sell any one or more of a number of competing oils and that the leases at nominal sums, far from lessening competition in the retailing of oils, promoted competition by enabling those who could not have afforded the initial investment to put in pumps, thus promoting public convenience.[32] A lower court, in referring to the

---

[30] For the Commission's orders in these oil pump cases, *cf.* 2 F. T. C. 26, 46, 127, 346 and 3 F. T. C. 68, 77, 78, 86.

[31] 2 F. T. C. 127, 134 (1919).

[32] *F. T. C. v. Sinclair Refining Co.*, 261 U. S. 463 (1923).

effect of the practice on competitive relations of the refiners and distributors looked upon the practice as a legitimate practice. "Competition is not an unmixed good. It is a battle for something that only one can get. . . . The weapons in competition are various. . . . Expense attending the use of the weapon, the foolishness of it, the fact that a method is uneconomical, or that the competitor cannot meet any method or scheme of competition because it will be ruinous to him to do so, have not, nor has either of them, ever been held unfair. Such things are a part of the strife inherent in competition." [33] This is a particularly instructive group of cases in which the intent of the courts to preserve the freedom of interested parties to compete was evident as a deciding factor. But it should be recognized that there is involved a trade practice which because of the expense involved goes far toward perpetuating the concentration of control in the industry.

A second type of restrictive clause which the courts have held not to contravene the Clayton Act is illustrated by the Curtis Publishing Company's agency contracts. The Curtis Company had built up an extensive system of distribution through district agents, who controlled an elaborate school-boy selling organization which the Curtis Company had developed at considerable expense. Under the customary agency agreements the Curtis Company, while allowing its district agents to deal in its competitors' magazines in their sales through retail stores, forbade them to sell through the school-boy organizations. In a private suit the courts had held that the contracts did not contravene the Clayton Act.[34] The court recognized that the agents were much more than purchasers, that the Curtis Company had built up by the use of ingenuity, labor, and capital a system which had greatly increased its sales, that for another publisher to try to avail itself of the system was

---

[33] *Sinclair Refining Co. v. F. T. C.*, 276 Fed. 686, 688 (1921).
[34] *Pictorial Review Co. v. Curtis Publishing Co.*, 255 Fed. 206 (1917).

engaging in unfair trade. However, the Commission subsequently issued an order against the Curtis Company alleging violation of both the Clayton and Federal Trade Commission Acts.[35]

Upon appeal the courts interpreted the contracts as contracts of agency and not of sale, thus eliminating the charge of violation of the Clayton Act. Considering the practice as a possible unfair method of competition, the court stressed the property right of the Curtis Company in the goodwill inherent in the school-boy organization which it had built up after much time and effort.[36] Concerning the fairness of this exclusive contract to competing publishers who desired to use the school-boy outlet, the lower court emphasized the fact that these contracts did not deprive these competitors of free access to consumers.

In three other cases the courts have refused to prevent exclusive arrangements because of failure to prove substantial lessening of competition or tendency to a monopoly. In its order against the B. S. Pearsall Butter Company the Commission enjoined a manufacturer of oleomargarine from marketing its product by exclusive dealing agreements,[37] but was reversed because it was found that there were sixty-five manufacturers of oleomargarine in the United States selling under similar contracts and that the respondent manufactured only slightly more than 1 per cent of the total output sold. These facts were taken to indicate no lessening of competition nor actual tendency to monopolize.[38]

An order by the Commission enjoining the practice of block-booking in the motion picture industry as an unfair method of

[35] In the Matter of Curtis Publishing Co., 2 F. T. C. 20 (1919).

[36] F. T. C. v. Curtis Publishing Co., 270 Fed. 881 (1921), 260 U. S. 568 (1923).

[37] 5 F. T. C. 127 (1922).

[38] B. S. Pearsall Butter Co. v. F. T. C., 292 Fed. 720 (1923).

competition was likewise reversed by the courts.[39] Block-booking is a practice quite common in the leasing of films by which exhibitors are offered a group of films at a designated lump sum and are permitted to lease all or none. The block usually includes a number which will cover the total needs of the exhibitor for the period of the contract. Under certain circumstances the exhibitor may select some individual films and reject others, but then he is required to pay prices found by the Commission in this case to be arbitrarily fixed from 50 to 75 per cent higher than the estimated prices of such films as part of the block. The court reversed the Commission on the grounds that there was no evidence that there had been a lessening of competition between film producers; in fact the evidence showed the position of the defendant in the industry, in terms of the percentage of total feature pictures released, had declined. Moreover, it failed to find that the exhibitor's freedom of choice had been unduly restrained, since as it pointed out not all films were sold in blocks. Moreover, the court held that the prices charged for films sold on an individual basis were "merely a part of the ordinary process of bargaining with the customer for the sale of one's product."

The third case arose in an action brought by private parties against the General Motors Corporation. It involved contracts with the Chevrolet and Buick dealers by which the dealers agreed to use parts manufactured by General Motors exclusively in repairing cars. The Circuit Court dismissed the case on finding the contracts were necessary to protect the manufacturer in its warranties and in its goodwill, and on finding no evidence of a lessening of competition.[40] The Supreme Court sustained the lower court upon accepting the evidence of no

[39] *F. T. C. v. Paramount Famous-Lasky Corporation, et al.*, 57 F. (2d) 152 (1932); 11 F. T. C. 187 (1927).

[40] *Pick Manufacturing Co. v. General Motors Corporation*, 80 F. (2d) 641 (1935).

lessening of competition.[41] It is interesting to note that in its findings with respect to competition the Circuit Court gave weight to the evidence of an increase in competition during the period of the contract and minimized the question of whether competition would otherwise have increased more rapidly:

. . . the record shows that competition in the sale of replacement parts for automobiles instead of growing less has substantially increased through the period during which the provisions complained of have been in force and, while it may be that competition would have increased more rapidly in the absence of such provisions, the trial court rightfully concluded that such was not the "substantial lessening of competition" which the Clayton Act was designed to prevent.[42]

Exclusive dealing arrangements represent one of a series of arrangements used by industry to acquire access to the market for the distribution of goods. They are useful only in markets where there are some elements of monopoly control in the manufacture of the product. The monopoly element is usually less than in the case of the patented article sold under a tying arrangement. The purpose of exclusive dealing is to increase the monopoly elements, i.e. to decrease the elasticity and increase the intensity of demand, by reaching forward into the channels of distribution. The alternatives which a manufacturer has in his distribution program are many. At the one extreme he may sell to any and all distributors at a given price with no conditions attached. At the other extreme, he may himself set up retail outlets owned and controlled by himself which deal solely in his own product. The exclusive dealing arrangement, along with other programs such as agency arrangements and resale price maintenance, is one of several distribution policies lying between these two extremes. In the dress pattern cases there was an attempt to use existing channels of distribu-

[41] 299 U. S. 3 (1936).
[42] 80 F. (2d) 644.

tion to push one seller's product by agreements with dealers not to handle the product of competitors. Such agreements are often accompanied by the grant to the dealer of an exclusive right to distribute within the given area. The attempt was to secure dealer coöperation in a sales program. This coöperation presumably added to the demand for the product for which substantial demand had been built up by advertising and other means. In the publishing house cases there was something more than the use of existing channels of distribution; the publishing house had built up distributive channels by the expenditure of money and effort in organizing school-boy carrier systems, which rivals were attempting to appropriate to their own use.

The effects which exclusive dealing arrangements may have on the position of the manufacturers will vary. Where one firm already has a dominant position but competes with numerous lesser substitutes, the effects of exclusive dealing arrangements may well be to consolidate further the position of the dominant firm. This is especially true where the nature of the product and its market are such that reliance must be had upon established channels of trade and where these are constrained to enter exclusive arrangements because of insistent consumer demand. The tying arrangement shuts off the customary channels of distribution for the lesser substitutes. Where the nature of the market is such that a manufacturer may develop his own distributive channels, the effects on competitive relations are not so severe. But it is clear that to develop rival distributive outlets may be a wasteful form of competition, and in any event because of the cost involved it offers a serious obstacle to entry into the industry. This is, perhaps, best illustrated by the position of the International Harvester Company in the agricultural machinery industry.[43] Where the product and market are such that a given community can sustain only a limited number of

[43] *Cf. supra*, pp. 39–40.

distributive outlets, exclusive arrangements whether based on ownership, agency, or agreement may well tend to perpetuate the position of a dominant concern.

Equally significant is the use of the exclusive arrangement as a sales policy in rivalry between a few sellers of similar importance. The dealer has a choice between each of several sellers, a choice which may be limited in part by a desire in his own interest to deal in products different from those of his immediate competitors. Any one oligopolistic seller may find the exclusive arrangement a method for the offensive in widening his market, or he may resort to it as a defensive measure for the protection of his market against similar policies of others. Where the practice is undertaken by each of a group of oligopolists, the activities of one in segregating for its own use some of the outlets may be offset by like actions of another, leaving their relative positions unaffected. Where one takes a lead and makes inroads on the market of the others before the latter retaliate, their relative positions may be upset. Perhaps the most important effect of the practice is its weakening of potential competition. The practice works to the special disadvantage of new competitors or financially weak competitors, since the risks of entry into the industry are increased and expensive sales promotion programs become necessary to build up a sufficiently insistent demand to induce dealers to stock the new product.

The significance of an exclusive arrangement to the consuming public lies in the extent to which it limits the variety of choice offered, the effects it has on the costs of distribution, and finally the effect it has in restricting output and investment by enabling the entrenched manufacturers to pursue typical monopolistic policies free from fear of potential competitors. The number of dealers or retailers selling in a given consumers' market is significant. If there is only one local dealer in a small community, an exclusive contract not only restricts the freedom of the dealer but also restricts the consumer since it excludes substitutes from that community. Where, however, there are numerous outlets in a community, various substitutes will probably be carried by the different outlets, especially if consumer preference is rather evenly divided between the several substitutes. Where the product of one producer is in high favor, however, the multiplicity of outlets may not provide assurance of the availability of several substitutes since most or all of the outlets may be constrained to carry only the favored product. Consumers have a like interest in the cost of distribution and the ease of entry of new competitors. As has been suggested above, exclusive arrangements would seem to make the selling costs of new firms higher. This is simply a special application of the theory of monopolistic competition. By cutting off access of competitors to the market and thereby increasing a seller's monopoly power, exclusive arrangements may lead to restriction of output and a malallocation of economic resources such as is typically to be expected from monopolistic power.

To summarize the argument, while public policy tends to fasten its attention on the effect of this practice in injuring rival business interests, the public interest lies in the further consequences of such a policy in affecting the efficiency with which economic resources are used to satisfy consumers' desires, first by affecting efficiency in the narrow sense and second, by interfering with the best allocation of resources.

CHAPTER XI

CONSPIRACY AND COERCION

IT WAS ESTABLISHED at the time of the *Gratz* decision that the Commission may prohibit any competitive practice violating the Sherman Act as an unfair method of competition. As has been seen the Sherman Act applied to two particular classes of practices, monopolistic practices of large firms and collusive activities of loose associations. So far as the monopolistic practices of the large firm are concerned, the more notorious are discrimination and tying and exclusive arrangements, to deal with which supplementary legislation was provided. The activities of the Commission with respect to such practices have been discussed in preceding chapters.

However, one practice by which a large firm may coerce others deserves mention, namely, refusal to buy or sell except on designated conditions. The right of a firm, in all but exceptional industries, to choose its customers and to refuse to sell for any reasons satisfactory to itself has been generally recognized by law, but under certain circumstances this right is limited. The practice of refusing to sell except on condition that dealers maintain suggested resale prices, when combined with an elaborate system for checking violations, is a case in point which will be considered at length in the following chapter.

There are other conditions in which the right to refuse to sell has been curtailed. In several cases the Commission has ordered a firm to cease coercing another by threatening to withdraw its patronage from the other firm in order to induce reciprocal trading. For example, the Waugh Equipment Company, a manufacturer of draft gears used by railroads, threatened to withdraw its large and eagerly sought traffic from a certain railroad in order to secure to itself the patronage of the railroad in the purchase of gears.[1] In a similar case a large meat packing company threatened to withdraw its traffic from a railroad unless the latter purchased certain railroad equipment from a concern in which the packing company was financially interested. The Commission analyzed the significance of this case well when it said:

. . . respondents . . . have created and taken advantage of a competitive weapon, oppressive and coercive in nature, which prevents the customers to whom the respondent corporation and its competitors are trying to sell their products, from exercising their free will and judgment in determining which device is the most efficient and will best serve their needs at the lowest net cost over a period of time, and has thus injected an element in the competitive field . . . which is unfair and abnormal, and tends to reduce the efficiency and economy in the production and sales methods of competing manufacturers and gives to the concern that controls the largest volume of freight traffic an unfair advantage, and thus hinders and restrains the freedom of competition in the natural customary channels of trade in the draft gear industry.[2]

It may be surmised, however, that agreements or understandings involving mutual trading and based on veiled threats are more frequent than the proceedings of the Commission indicate. Such understandings are peculiarly difficult to detect.

More recently a large firm dealing in waste paper and other waste materials whose preponderance in the Southern market made all buyers and sellers alike dependent to a large degree upon it for the purchase or sale of waste was found to be using its power to eliminate its small competitors by refusing to deal with any sellers who sold to its competitors or to deal with any buyers who purchased from them.[3] Thus, by stopping competi-

[1] *In the Matter of Waugh Equipment Co., et al.,* 15 F. T. C. 232 (1931).
[2] *In the Matter of Mechanical Manufacturing Co., et al.,* 16 F. T. C. 67, 74 (1932).
[3] *In the Matter of Letellier-Phillips Paper Co., Inc.,* Docket No. 3434 (order issued August 8, 1938).

tors' sources of supply and access to the market the dealer hoped to eliminate them effectively from the market. Here, clearly, the exercise of the privilege to refuse to sell was being used for coercive and predatory purposes.

The Commission has proceeded against monopolistic policies or policies in restraint of trade most frequently in circumstances where there was joint action by a loose association of business firms. Such joint action has taken many forms.

The purpose of loose associations is generally to further the joint interests of their members. Their activities are varied ranging from joint research and advertising to exchange of price lists, price fixing, control of discounts and other conditions of sale, the control of the channels of distribution, and the elimination or control of irresponsible elements of the trade. In some instances there is simply a voluntary agreement among the interested business parties with no particular injury to other rival business groups. More frequently the group has pursued coercive and exclusive policies with reference to recalcitrant parties or other groups whose practices interfered with the interests of the association in question. In harmony with the general principles developed by the courts in interpreting the Sherman Act the Commission has enjoined all coercive and exclusive practices, policies interfering with the freedom of other parties, however legitimate the purpose which the association wished to accomplish. Moreover, all agreements by which the freedom of competition of business rivals was voluntarily limited were looked upon with suspicion even though no business interests were injured; and whenever it appeared that they had as their purpose the restraint of competition in price or in other terms of sale or the limitation of the freedom of action of business firms in the market, the policies have been enjoined.

To understand many of the practices of these associations it is necessary to visualize the whole conglomerate of customs and practices in the industry. Any one practice may in itself appear to be harmless, yet when associated with other practices and customs it may take on considerable meaning. Nowhere is this more strikingly illustrated than in the case of the circulation of price lists, the introduction of cost accounting systems, or the circulation of standard industry cost formulae.

The types of joint action against which the Commission has proceeded are myriad. Many cases have involved a simple conspiracy to enhance and bring about uniformity in prices. In other cases similar results were achieved by agreement to use standard contracts, or by the compilation of cost data and the circulation of a guide in which standard costs were set forth together with suggested percentages of profit. Price-filing schemes by which the freedom of firms to initiate changes in their prices was restricted, through agreement and appropriate methods of policing, have been frequent.

The Metal Window Institute, for example, an association of 19 manufacturers of metal windows compiled a book of gross or basic prices, from which by use of a formula the price of any product of the industry might be determined.[4] The members then filed discount schedules which were uniform and agreed not to sell at any price below that arrived at by applying the uniform discount schedule to the standard price book. Before making bids on contemplated projects the members of the Institute submitted their estimates to a central bureau to be checked so as to insure uniform bidding. Persuasion and threats were used to induce adherence to price schedules. In areas where "non-coöperating" competitors were threatening to underbid, bidding was declared to be open and the members of the Institute proceeded systematically to undersell the "non-coöperating" competitors. In several cases as a part of a price fixing scheme the country was divided into appropriate zones for the establishing of differentials in delivered prices, and in

[4] *In the Matter of Metal Window Institute, et al.,* 25 F. T. C. 1478 (1937).

others particular basing-points were agreed upon, thereby making it feasible to arrive at uniform delivered prices once uniform base prices had been established.

As an incident to these price agreements it is often customary to standardize other variables to the sale. It is quite usual to agree to eliminate or standardize cash discounts and to control trade-in allowances on used equipment. An association of manufacturers of turbine generators supplemented their agreement on price with an agreement to maintain uniform performance guarantees, an element equally important with price to the buyer in determining the placement of his order.[5] An association of some fifteen manufacturers of tin plate agreed to cease selling or quoting a price on so called "stock plate," which represented over-runs, seconds, and warming-up sizes, and to require buyers of "production plate," which constituted the bulk of their product, to accept seconds up to 25 per cent of their orders.[6] The purpose was to prevent the circumvention of the price filing scheme sanctioned under the NRA code by the substitution of "production plate" for "stock plate," a practice which had the effect of virtual secret price cutting. In another case an association of linen suppliers not only fixed prices but agreed not to solicit or accept the patronage of another member's customer except with the permission of that other member.[7] These will serve to illustrate the variety of ways in which business rivals may voluntarily and by their joint action seek to further their own interest by control of price or other conditions to the sale at the expense of the consuming public.

Joint action which involves coercion of other business groups

[5] In the Matter of General Electric Co., et al., 24 F. T. C. 881 (1937).

[6] In the Matter of American Sheet and Tin Plate Co., et al., 22 F. T. C. 711 (1936).

[7] In the Matter of the Linen Supply Association of the District of Columbia, et al., 21 F. T. C. 667 (1935).

is the occasion for equally frequent action by the Commission. Such practices are significant for their effects on both the other business groups and the consumers. In such cases the customary procedure is for a group to organize a boycott which will cut off the rivals' source of supply of materials or labor or their access to the market for their goods. Such boycotts have been a particularly frequent weapon on the part of certain distributive channels in their struggle for survival.

The struggle between the old and the new channels of distribution is one which has been pursued on many fronts, in the spheres both of industry and politics. In its political aspects it has led to such legislation as the Robinson-Patman Act, the State Fair Trade Laws, and anti-chain store taxes. In the economic sphere it has embraced attempts by the traditional channels to interfere with the access of the newer channels to sources of supply or to the market. Generally this has been done by a joint agreement of the interested parties to boycott or otherwise coerce manufacturers or distributors who were allied with the new and unorthodox methods. In the early 1920's the Commission issued frequent orders of this sort involving the grocery, hardware, fuel, paper, and confectioners' trades. This was part of the struggle of the traditional jobber-wholesaler-retailer channel against the newer chain stores, department stores, and mail-order houses. The traditional channels often combined and threatened the manufacturer with loss of business if he did not refuse to sell the newer channels. In other cases the manufacturer was simply required to sell the newer channels at some fixed price; in the case of chain stores this meant charging the chain the same prices as independent retail dealers.

Such practices have not entirely disappeared from among the orders of the Commission, but the more recent attempts to control the channels of distribution have appeared in different industries. Several of the Commission's orders have involved attempts to control the channels of distribution in the building materials industries. A federation of some 41 associations of dealers in building materials located in 32 states was ordered to cease an elaborate system of control of the channels of trade.[8] The associations were limited in their membership to "recognized" dealers, and the power of the association was devoted to coercing manufacturers into distributing their building materials solely through these recognized dealers. Membership was conditional upon a satisfactory showing by a dealer seeking recognition of an economic necessity for his business in the community which he served; but, as the Commission noted, "practically, it was the arbitrary decision of the officers and leaders representing . . . competitors, . . . of the said dealer seeking recognition. . . ." All direct sales of building materials by manufacturers to consumers, non-recognized dealers, government agencies, etc. were eliminated by the use of the boycott or threats of boycott. When the United States Government in 1935 announced a policy of direct buying of cement for relief projects and asked for bids, no cement company submitted bids. Beyond this the associations proceeded to eliminate the distribution of supplies to dealers by motor truck and to eliminate the function of jobbing. Finally, in some communities they went so far as to foster price fixing by facilitating the exchange of price lists and to limit the sales territory of dealers.

The Commission has issued two orders against glaziers' unions and the manufacturers and distributors of plate glass.[9] In Indianapolis, Indiana there was a conspiracy between the recognized distributors (wholesalers and glazing contractors) and the local trade unions of which the glaziers were members,

---

[8] *In the Matter of Building Materials Dealers Alliance*, 26 F. T. C. 142 (1937).

[9] *In the Matter of Pittsburgh Plate Glass Company, et al.*, Docket No. 3491, The St. Louis case (order issued December 2, 1938); and *ibid.*, Docket No. 3858, The Indianapolis case (order issued January 16, 1940).

by which it was agreed that no union member should work for a glazing contractor who had not signed the union agreement and was not a "recognized" glazing contractor. The conditions which were necessary to establish an employer as a "recognized" glazing contractor were that he keep customarily in stock a reasonable quantity of flat glass products and necessary truck and warehouse equipment for legitimate glazing operation to service the building and replacement trade, and that he employ continuously at least three men. It was with these requirements to qualify as a recognized glazing contractor that the Commission took exception, not to the agreement that no member of the union should work for a contractor who had not signed the union contract. As the Commission pointed out, this definition of a recognized glazing contractor effectively excluded many glazing contractors and glass distributors from seeking business within the Indianapolis trade area.

In the St. Louis area the agreement went further. It specifically prevented the use of union glaziers for setting glass except at the premises of the particular structure for which the glass was being furnished, thus prejudicing sash and door manufacturers in the St. Louis area who might have installed glass in sash and frames in their own factories. Moreover, having eliminated the rivalry of the small glazing contractors and of the sash and door manufacturers, the distributors proceeded to control prices by frequent discussion of prices, employing an agent to check and circulate bids, and conspiring to apportion the business among themselves by designating one of the members to be low bidder on particular transactions. The effectiveness of these schemes for the control of the distributive channels depended upon the control which the union had over glaziers in their particular area. Had the union been weak and the manufacturers unwilling to play ball with the recognized distributors, their scheme would have been ineffective. As it was, labor and the dominant distributors were able to combine to the prejudice of the door and sash manufacturers, the small glazing contractors, and the consuming public.

These various schemes to prevent direct selling or other shortening of the distributive channels, or to eliminate the small distributor are clearly to the prejudice of the public interest, and this quite apart from the injury to such business interests as are prejudiced. In the first place it means the protection of methods of distribution which are technologically and economically inefficient. This is clearly a social waste. Only on the assumption that the resources which would be relieved by the introduction of the new methods would be idle, could any qualification of this conclusion be made. Moreover, if the scheme is used to raise prices, this clearly is to the prejudice of the glass consumers. If the prices are raised so as to raise profit prospects, only to lead to non-price competition or the entrance of new firms, or partial underutilization of old firms, here clearly is an economic waste without gain to the distributors or other interested parties.

If the increased profit prospects do not induce such wasteful practices, but tend rather to reduce output and the quantity of resources associated with the industry, its significance is to be found in its effects on the allocation of resources and the distribution of income. With respect to the former effect, the question arises as to whether there is a diversion of resources to the production of goods of greater or less usefulness, to the production of goods which are more or less desired by consumers. This depends upon the facts of the particular case, though the presumption is that the resources will be diverted to less useful purposes. As for the distribution of income, such a policy would clearly increase the return to capital and enterprise or to labor which remained in the industry. In an industry in which the rate of wages is not fixed by forces beyond the industry but is dependent upon the price of the final product, wage rates might be raised. Where demand for the product is inelastic total income of the factors might be increased by such a policy. If it were true that incomes in the particular industry were unduly low, some justification might be found for such a policy. But it is clear that this is not a policy which can be justified on these grounds by all industries.

The action of the Commission in preventing joint action for the prevention of design piracy is interesting since it involves the question, raised before the courts in the open-price filing cases, as to how far business may go by joint action to eliminate genuine abuses. Design or style piracy is a problem which has long harassed the ladies' dress and millinery industries.[10] It is customary in such industries for certain leaders in the high price brackets to employ designers whose function it is to adapt foreign models or develop new styles. These are the leaders, the fashion originators, in the industry. They offer the new styles, or designs, first. The low price manufacturers generally follow their lead, with adaptations or even imitations. There is, then, continuous rivalry between the originators, who are attempting to differentiate their current offerings from the prevailing styles of the low price manufacturers, and the low price manufacturers, who are trying to duplicate as nearly as possible at a lower price the most popular designs of the originators.

Sometimes this rivalry leads to outright copying to the minutest detail, i.e. to "piracy." The originators who incur the costs and risks of new creations depend upon selling a sufficient volume at high prices to recoup their costs, and when a style is especially attractive they do not like to have its life in the high price trade shortened by piracy. Since it is not feasible to copyright designs and styles in this industry,[11] the

[10] *Cf.* NRA, Division of Review, *Design Piracy — The Problem and Its Treatment under NRA Codes* (Work Materials No. 52).

[11] *Cf.* "Unfair Competition — 1932," *Harvard Law Review*, XLVI (1933), 1196.

originators have sought to develop their own system for protecting their property rights.

The system of the ladies' dress industry is most elaborate.[12] The Fashion Originators' Guild of America (F.O.G.A.), an association of 225 manufacturers of ladies' garments and of textiles used in their manufacture, established a system for registering new styles in women's garments and designs of textiles used in their manufacture and set up a procedure for determining cases of alleged piracy in coöperation with several local fashion guilds. The members of the F.O.G.A. were responsible in 1936 for 39 per cent of the total sales of ladies' garments in the United States in the wholesale price range of $6.75 and up, and 84 per cent in the wholesale price range of $10.75 and up.

The members of the F.O.G.A. agreed not to sell to retailers in cities in which local guilds were located unless the retailers were members in good standing of the local guild. Members of the latter agreed in turn not to purchase from manufacturers who did not conform to the ethics of the F.O.G.A. and particularly not to handle copies of legitimately registered styles. The F.O.G.A. went further and coerced most of the 12,000 individual retailers of ladies' garments in the United States into signing a "Declaration of Coöperation" to the effect that they would not handle garments judged by the piracy committee of the F.O.G.A. to be copies of registered styles or designs. The penalty for failing to coöperate was the refusal of members of the F.O.G.A. to sell their goods to the retailer. The members of F.O.G.A. also agreed to use only textile designs which had been registered with the Industrial Design Registration Bureau of the National Federation of Textiles. The Guild pursued

---

[12] *In the Matter of Fashion Originators Guild of America, Inc., et al.*, Docket No. 2769 (order issued February 8, 1939). *Cf.* also *In the Matter of Millinery Quality Guild, Inc., et al.*, Docket No. 2812 (order issued April 29, 1937).

many other restrictive policies: it limited discounts, prohibited members contributing to retail advertising or making direct retail sales, or selling to persons who conduct business in residences, hotels or apartment houses, etc. Members of the F.O.G.A. violating the rules of the Guild were subject to fines.

These activities the Commission found to be violative of the law and its order has been sustained by the Circuit Court.[13] The attack of the Commission on these practices was not directed at the registering of styles and designs or at the attempt to eliminate "piracy," but rather at the various acts of exclusion, coercion, and agreement not to sell to particular groups, by which the F.O.G.A. was trying to effect its purpose. It is the methods used and their incidence upon particular groups which causes the scheme to run afoul the law. This is quite consistent with the general policy of the courts in interpreting the anti-trust laws, which is more concerned with the methods and practices of loose associations than with the broad results.

[13] *Fashion Originators Guild of America v. F. T. C.*, Circuit Court of Appeals, Second Circuit, No. 312, July 1940.

CHAPTER XII

PRICE POLICY OF THE FIRM

THE COMMISSION has no general power to investigate and issue orders concerning the general price policies of a business firm; specifically it has no powers to pass upon the reasonableness of particular prices. However, it does have certain limited powers for the regulation of business pricing policies. For example, it may proceed against firms for price policies of a deceptive sort. Moreover, it may prohibit the lowering of prices where this is intended to monopolize the trade, and it may prohibit the fixing of prices by joint agreement under any circumstances. It also has jurisdiction over the enforcing of schemes of resale price maintenance, subject to wide exceptions under recent law, and has limited power to regulate the price structure of a firm to the extent of prohibiting discrimination where such practices will injure competition or lead to monopoly. Its powers with reference to price fixing and discrimination have been discussed above. This chapter will be devoted to the others, particularly to resale price maintenance and loss leader merchandising.

SELLING BELOW COST

Despite all the discussion of selling below cost and of its tendency to lead to monopoly, the Commission has issued very few orders in which the practice was alleged. The Commission from the very beginning has held that price cutting is not in general an unfair practice. "Normal competition in prices, whether in cases of resale or otherwise, is in general, a healthy condition of trade and in the dealings in many commodities, even marked reductions in prices are proper where it is necessary to dispose of stocks, as for instance, by reason of seasonal conditions of the trade." [1] But the Commission added that this did not preclude it "from holding certain forms of price cutting as unfair methods of competition, especially where such price cutting has as its aim, either a malicious injury to others, or an attempt to monopolize any branch of trade." [2] Selling below cost is, of course, simply price cutting carried beyond a certain point which is determined by the definition of cost used.

In an early order issued against Sears, Roebuck and Company the respondent was enjoined from selling, or offering to sell, sugar below cost. [3] This practice, however, was joined with another practice, namely, representing falsely that its low price on sugar was possible because of its large purchasing power and quick-moving stock. The Circuit Court in reviewing the order refused to condemn selling below cost except in conjunction with the further practice of misrepresenting the source of its power to sell at those low prices. The court noted that "We find in the statute no intent on the part of Congress, even if it has the power, to restrain an owner of property from selling it at any price that is acceptable to him or from giving it away." [4]

In a later proceeding, that against the Noma Electric Corporation, the circumstances were such as to point to an attempt to monopolize the manufacture of Christmas tree lighting outfits. [5] It was on the basis of this monopolistic action that the Commission proceeded. However, the Commission has consistently refused to limit price competition even when carried to the extent of selling below cost, however cost is defined, in the absence of some showing that such policy is associated with misrepresentations calculated to deceive the consumer or with

---

[1] Federal Trade Commission, *Annual Report*, 1918, p. 7.
[2] *Loc. cit.*
[3] 1 F. T. C. 163 (1918).
[4] *Sears, Roebuck & Co. v. F. T. C.*, 258 Fed. 307, 312 (1919).
[5] 15 F. T. C. 87 (1931).

an intent and effect to eliminate competitors and thereby to monopolize trade. This is clearly indicated by the orders of the Commission and by its careful phraseology of the rules concerning selling below cost and loss leader merchandising which it has permitted to be included among the trade practice conference rules.[6] There is no indication that the recent Wheeler-Lea Amendments have changed this position.

While price cutting is a normal incident to a competitive economy, it is likewise a potent instrument of warfare in conditions of oligopoly particularly where the rivals are of unequal strength. The fear of such price wars is also a potent factor in weakening the effectiveness of potential competition as a regulator of monopoly.[7] It seems that the Commission has in mind just such a distinction between price cutting as an incident to competition and as an incident to monopolistic warfare. It may be questioned whether in our imperfectly functioning markets all degrees of price cutting have the ostensibly favorable results characteristic of purely and perfectly functioning markets, but more of this in Chapter XVII.

FREE GOODS

Another sales policy closely analogous to selling below cost is the giving of free goods. Occasionally the offer of free goods is unrestricted; more often it is made conditional upon the purchase of a certain minimum quantity of the same or some other commodity. When carried through to the consumer, the practice is usually undertaken for promotional or advertising purposes or in order to avoid changing price schedules. When made only to the dealers, free deals are analogous to increased discounts and are merely one means of enlisting dealer support. That the practice is very frequent in industry is shown by a

---

[6] *Cf. post*, p. 275.
[7] C. J. Bullock, "Trust Literature: A Survey and a Criticism," *Quarterly Journal of Economics*, XV (1901), 211–14.

study of the Brookings Institution.[8] Except for two early orders
of the Commission, it has not seen fit to prosecute the giving of
free goods *per se*. In the case of the Fleischmann Company
the giving away of yeast was combined with various forms of
commercial bribery.[9] In the case of the Ward Baking Company, where the respondent was enjoined from giving away
bread, the Circuit Court reversed the Commission's order on
the ground that interstate commerce was not involved. That
no subsequent orders enjoining the giving away of goods were
issued by the Commission may be explained by the *obiter dictum* of the court in the *Sears, Roebuck and Company* decision,
quoted above, to the effect that there was no evidence of the
intent of Congress to prevent the giving away of goods.[10]

The Commission has been led to issue numerous orders
where the circumstances of an offer of free goods were calculated to deceive the public.[11] This has been done in circumstances where the seller making a "free good" offer has raised
the price of a good required to be purchased as a condition of
receiving the free good above its customary level in order
thereby to offset in whole or in part the cost of the free good.
In some cases a seller has been enjoined from making such
offers where he was substituting inferior merchandise for that
ordinarily sold at the price designated in the transaction. In
other circumstances free good offers have been enjoined because
they were conditioned on other purchases or performance of
certain acts which were not divulged. But in the absence of
such circumstances of deceit and misrepresentation the Com-

[8] L. S. Lyon, *The Economics of Free Deals, with Suggestions for Code
Making under the NRA* (Washington: The Brookings Institution, 1933).

[9] I F. T. C. 119 (1918).

[10] This decision was delivered by the court shortly after the second of
the two orders by the Commission enjoining the giving away of a product.
Cf. p. 227.

[11] *Cf.* for example *F. T. C. v. Standard Education Society, et al.*, 302
U. S. 112 (1937). For the Commission order *cf.* 16 F. T. C. 1 (1931).

mission will take no action. The Commission recognizes that an offer of free goods may be used legitimately as a sales method to increase the immediate sale of other goods which must be purchased or to increase goodwill and future patronage. The cost of the free good may be looked upon as a charge to advertising expense, or as a general indirect price reduction on other goods which must be purchased. "Under such circumstances the 'free goods' offer is hardly deceptive, for the purchaser actually does obtain the specified 'free goods' at no additional cost over the ordinary and regular price of the merchandise required to be purchased. . . . In reality the practice in such a case is a convenient and impelling method of calling the attention of the public to price reductions in the goods which must be purchased." [12] Except where used by a large concern to eliminate small competitors, then, the test of the legality of an offer of free goods is whether there is deception of purchasers or whether it is used as part of a lottery device of merchandising.

RESALE PRICE MAINTENANCE: ITS NATURE

The problem of resale price maintenance has probably been the subject of more persistent interest and discussion in the post-war period than any other single trade practice. The Commission has issued numerous orders to cease and desist and has made several reports to Congress on the subject; several of the Commission's orders have been reviewed by the courts. Bills proposing to permit the practice have been introduced in Congress intermittently, and it was the subject of consideration in the drafting of some of the NRA codes. Since the demise of the NRA most of the states have passed bills legalizing the

---

[12] The Commission recently reconsidered at length the question of free goods in an order dismissing a complaint against Samuel Stores, Inc. The position of the Commission is well stated in the *Press Release* concerning this order of dismissal for September 7, 1938.

practice, and finally in 1937 Congress amended the Sherman Act so as to exempt contracts concerning resale prices made under State Fair Trade Laws from the prohibitions of restraints of trade contained in section 1. The question of resale price maintenance, which has become progressively more pressing with the increasing importance of trade-marked products and national advertising, is one of the most controversial in the field of trade practices.

Resale price maintenance is a policy adopted by manufacturers of some patented, trade-marked, or otherwise differentiated products of selling to wholesalers, jobbers, or retailers on the condition that the latter shall resell only at certain specified prices. These specified resale prices need not be the same for all dealers of a given class or in a given territory, although uniformity is the general rule.

The initiative in adopting the policy may come from the manufacturer. Several considerations may induce him to make resale price maintenance a part of his program of distribution. In the sale of a considerable number of branded articles price is an integral part of the advertising program. The manufacturer may fear that the goodwill which he has developed will be impaired or the confidence of the consumer in the announced price will be shaken if the product is sold for a time or through some outlets at less than the specified price; in this event his volume might fall off or pressure might be put upon him by distributors to reduce his price to them. An example may be found in certain cosmetic lines. It appears that often a particular line or brand of cosmetics goes through a price cycle. It starts in the high-priced range where it is sold only to the exclusive trade but is later gradually reduced in price and may finally be sold through mass distributive channels to a more price conscious consuming group. The manufacturer, therefore, is forced to promote new lines or products from time to time. The distributor has it within his power by price cutting tactics to shorten the life cycle of a particular brand, thus destroying the value of the goodwill which the manufacturer has in a given line of the product.

The manufacturer may also have an interest in resale prices in so far as they affect dealers' incentives to handle and push his product. It is reported that often when a department store features a popular book at less than the customary price, the neighboring book stores will either fail to stock the book or put their supplies under the counter. In the case where a branded product is selling in competition with close substitutes the size of the margin which a dealer may receive on one product as compared with the margin on a substitute may be significant in determining the direction of the dealer's sales efforts. Somewhat analogous incentives to maintain resale prices arise where the manufacturer uses a hybrid system of distributive channels. Where he sells to retailers both directly and through wholesalers or jobbers, he may desire to control the price at which they compete in resale in order to control their competitive relations. Finally, where a product is competing in resale with that of a few other manufacturers, the manufacturer in framing his pricing policy must consider not only the price at which he sells to the distributor but also the relation between the price of his product and that of his rivals at the stage where they pass into the hands of the final consumer. This may be particularly important in the sale of expensive items such as cameras, automobiles, or other machinery. In such cases control of the price structure all the way to the consumer may appear to be the most efficacious procedure for an oligopolist in the pursuit of a rational sales policy.

It appears, however, that in most cases the initiative in introducing the policy of resale price maintenance comes from the distributors. One gathers a very definite impression that the pressure behind the recent drive for the passage of State Fair

Trade Laws and the Miller-Tydings Act has come from the dealers' associations. The manufacturers' interest in the policy seems to have been waning.[13]

The distributors' interest in resale price maintenance arises from a conflict in the channels of distribution with respect both to the type of channels through which goods shall flow and to the basis of sales appeal which shall be used. Most retailers find themselves in competition with others in some of their sales, but the intensity and character of the competition vary with the particular product and with different customers. Many products are sold through several channels of distribution and thus the product of a given manufacturer competes with itself in the final sale. The dealer who is reselling is concerned with the price at which the product is being offered through alternative channels. An independent retailer who has purchased through a jobber or wholesaler will frequently find that the demand of at least part of his market is dependent on the price at which the product is being sold by some mass distributor or by the manufacturer direct, as well as by other independent retailers. Lower prices through these other channels may be the result of discrimination by the manufacturer in the prices at which he sells to the various channels; or they may be explained by smaller mark-ups due to the economies of these rival channels or to the fact that these channels are charging lower prices for promotional purposes. In any event resale price maintenance affords one way of giving the various channels security against price competition from one another. There seem to be no limits to this competition between the rival channels for at least short periods of time. Where there is a distributor who specializes in a particular line of products, however, competition in this line with other distributors carrying a diversified line may easily prove ruinous to the specialized

<hr>

[13] NRA, Division of Review, *Resale Price Maintenance Legislation in the United States* (Work Materials No. 16), p. 8.

channel. This factor is a very strong one conducing to diversification in the distributive trades.

Moreover, there are certain products which are customarily used as leaders by a particular class of dealers, that is these products are systematically sold below the manufacturer's designated price, below invoice cost plus cost of handling, or even below invoice cost. This practice has repercussions of a more or less serious nature on competing dealers. While it may not be serious enough to have substantial effects on the competitive relations in distribution, it may well affect the sales policies of rival channels with reference to these particular products. Various distributive groups, therefore, have strong incentives to try to limit the use of price appeal as a sales policy in order to protect their own position in the system of distribution or in order to divert competitive forces to other forms which are more compatible with their own interests.

Manufacturers have in the past tried several methods for achieving control of resale price. In some cases they execute contracts providing for price maintenance; this is the procedure sanctioned under the recent State Fair Trade Laws where contracts satisfying conditions specified in the law are legally binding in all transactions of resale. In other cases, goods are sold with a notice that they are to be resold only at certain prices. In case of failure to abide by the contracts or notices the manufacturer then brings legal action to enjoin violation. In the case of patented or copyrighted goods the manufacturer has sometimes sought relief by alleging infringement of patent or copyright where notices or contracts were violated. As these various methods of enforcing a policy of price maintenance came to be held unenforceable under the common law and even criminally illegal under the Sherman Act, the method of refusing to sell was generally adopted. This method consists in the manufacturer's informing the dealers that he desires certain resale prices maintained on his product and will refuse to sell in the future to any distributor who does not comply with this wish or who supplies anyone who does not comply.

CHANGING LEGAL STATUS OF RESALE PRICE MAINTENANCE

The changing legal status of the various methods of enforcing resale price maintenance forms an interesting chapter in legal history.[14] With one exception, the cases brought to court before 1915 were brought voluntarily by the firms trying to maintain prices. Later the government took the initiative in legal proceedings and charged successfully that the practice constituted a violation of the Sherman Act. Three leading decisions had already established the legal position of resale price maintenance before the courts were called upon to consider whether the practice constituted an unfair method of competition under the Federal Trade Commission Act. In the proceedings against the Dr. Miles Medical Company a system of resale price maintenance by contracts was held to be an unreasonable restraint of trade. The Court argued that the system had the same result as would a combination or a system of agreements between the dealers themselves for the purpose of destroying competition and fixing prices. Such agreements or combinations "are injurious to the public interest and void."

The complainant's plan falls within the principle which condemns contracts of this class. It, in effect, creates a combination for the prohibited purposes. No distinction can properly be made by reason of the particular character of the commodity in question. . . . Nor does the fact that the margin of freedom is reduced by the control of production make the protection of what remains, in such a case, a negligible matter. And where commodities have passed into the channels of trade and are owned by dealers, the validity of agreements to prevent competition and to maintain prices is not to be deter-

---

[14] For more detailed summary of legal history of the various methods for maintaining resale prices *cf.* E. R. A. Seligman and R. A. Love, *Price Cutting and Price Maintenance* (New York: Harper & Bros., 1932) and J. A. McLaughlin, *Cases on the Federal Anti-trust Laws of the United States* (New York: The Ad Press, Ltd., 1930 ed.), pp. 422–24, note 110.

mined by the circumstance whether they were produced by several manufacturers or by one, or whether they were previously owned by one or by many. The complainant having sold its product at prices satisfactory to itself, the public is entitled to whatever advantage may be derived from competition in the subsequent traffic.[15]

The decision in the action against Colgate and Company was the cause of considerable confusion.[16] This did not involve any contracts. The Colgate Company merely refused to sell to price cutters, and when a cutter was detected, it sought promises of future adherence to the suggested prices. The Supreme Court affirmed the judgment of the District Court that the Colgate Company had not been shown to have violated the law. As it later appeared the reason for this decision, apparently favorable to resale price maintenance, was a technical one, a faulty indictment by the trial court.[17] This explanation was given by the Supreme Court after the lower court had intimated that in its opinion the *Dr. Miles* and *Colgate* decisions were inconsistent. In its decision in the proceedings against Schrader's Son, Inc. the Court distinguished, on the one hand, between the policy of indicating a wish concerning prices and declining future dealings if the wish is not respected, and on the other, the further procedure of entering into agreements whether expressed or implied which undertake to bind all customers to observe the fixed resale prices. Although the case itself involved contracts, it was made clear that the requesting of less formal assurances of an intention to maintain prices would violate the law. The contention was that such agreements were "designed to take away dealers' control of their own affairs and thereby destroy competition and restrain the free and natural flow of trade amongst the States." [18]

---

[15] *Dr. Miles Medical Co. v. John D. Park & Sons Co.*, 220 U. S. 373, 408 (1911).   [16] *U. S. v. Colgate & Co.*, 250 U. S. 300 (1919).
[17] *U. S. v. A. Schrader's Son, Inc.*, 252 U. S. 85, 99 (1920).
[18] 252 U. S. 100.

Although the Federal Trade Commission has from the beginning recognized that price cutting may not always be in the public interest and was at one time inclined to recommend legalizing resale price maintenance on condition that price schedules should be filed with some administrative agency,[19] it recommended in 1931 that "no legislation permitting resale price maintenance is at present called for." [20] Meanwhile the Commission had proceeded against the practice as an unfair method of competition by issuing many complaints and orders to cease and desist.

The character of the complaints and findings in the early proceedings of the Commission is significant. It was alleged that the Cudahy Packing Company was pursuing a system of resale price maintenance "with the effect of securing the trade of jobbers and wholesalers and of enlisting their active coöperation in enlarging the sale of its price-maintained product to the prejudice of competitors who do not fix and require the maintenance of the resale prices of their products, and with the effect of eliminating competition in price among the jobbers and wholesalers in its goods, and thereby depriving jobbers and wholesalers of their right to sell such goods at such prices as they may deem adequate and warranted by their selling efficiency." [21] It should be noticed that this complaint alleges three different wrongs. First, it alleges an injury to those competitors of the manufacturer who do not seek to maintain resale

[19] Concerning its report to Congress in 1918 see Federal Trade Commission, *Resale Price Maintenance, Part I* — 1929 (70th Cong., 2d Sess., *House Document* No. 546), p. 4.

[20] Federal Trade Commission, *Resale Price Maintenance, Part II: Commercial Aspects and Tendencies* (1931), p. 6. The Commission also opposed the recent amendment of the Sherman Act (Miller-Tydings Act, August 1937) which exempts contracts made under State Fair Trade Laws from the prohibitions on restraint of trade. *Cf.* 75th Cong., 1st Sess., *Senate Document* No. 58 (April, 1937).

[21] 1 F. T. C. 199 (1918). For similar allegations *cf.* 1 F. T. C. 149; 1 F. T. C. 516; 7 F. T. C. 412; 8 F. T. C. 341.

prices, since the coöperation of the dealers is enlisted in the selling of the price-maintained goods to the detriment of those goods which are not price-maintained. This allegation would satisfy the prerequisite established by Justice Sutherland that to fall under section 5 of the Federal Trade Commission Act, as it stood before the Wheeler-Lea Amendments of 1938, a practice must injure a competitor.[22] The later orders in resale price maintenance cases did not specify this injury to competitors, however. The second allegation of the complaint is that the practice eliminates competition in price among the dealers, which suggests that it involves a violation of the Sherman Act. Finally, it alleges interference with competition based on selling efficiency.[23]

The courts, however, have generally ignored the first and third of these charges in passing upon resale price maintenance under the Federal Trade Commission Act and have placed the emphasis upon the coöperative efforts used to induce price maintenance. Announcing desired resale prices or even refusing to supply dealers who do not maintain suggested prices are not illegal practices *per se*. Rather it is the agreement, formal or implicit, to abide by the suggested prices and the coöperative efforts of various parties helping the manufacturer to enforce his policy which constitute the violation of the law. The leading decision illustrates this well. The Beech-Nut Packing Company had introduced an elaborate system by which it made known its intention to refuse to sell to price cutters. It made a systematic effort to identify price cutters by a system of key numbers

---

[22] *F. T. C. v. Raladam Co.*, 283 U. S. 643 (1931). It appears that the National Industrial Conference Board is in error when it maintains that *no one* contends that resale price maintenance is prejudicial to the interests of other manufacturers. *Cf. Mergers and the Law* (New York, 1929), p. 145.

[23] In this respect the Commission has frequently cited evidence of differences in dealers' cost of operation. *Cf.* 1 F. T. C. 499; 1 F. T. C. 442; 1 F. T. C. 506.

stamped on cases of its products, which numbers enabled it to trace the dealer through whom the product had been obtained. It kept a card system of undesirable price cutters and reinstated dealers only after receiving assurances that prices would be henceforth maintained. The Supreme Court held that:

. . . the Beech-Nut system goes far beyond the simple refusal to sell goods to persons who will not sell at stated prices, which in the Colgate Case was held to be within the legal right of the producer. . . . The system here disclosed necessarily constitutes a scheme which restrains the natural flow of commerce and the freedom of competition in the channels of interstate trade which it has been the purpose of all the anti-trust acts to maintain. In its practical operation it necessarily constrains the trader, if he would have the products of the Beech-Nut Company, to maintain the prices "suggested" by it.[24]

The lower courts have sustained numerous other orders of the Commission where there has been evidence of coöperative effort to maintain prices. In its opinion in the case involving the Cream of Wheat Company the Circuit Court considered at length what a firm might do in the way of suggesting resale prices.[25] The court maintained that a firm might suggest prices and might announce that it would refuse to deal with those not maintaining the suggested prices. Moreover, a firm might act upon information about price cutting received by it without solicitation. However, it might not solicit such information from customers or request price cutters to give assurances of future adherence to suggested prices.

The Commission has consistently disapproved the practice of resale price maintenance and proceeded against it in the usual manner. Moreover, it has refused to recognize the use of leaders or loss leaders as an unfair method unless used in a way calculated to deceive the buyer or used by a firm having

[24] *F. T. C. v. Beech-Nut Packing Co.*, 257 U. S. 441, 454 (1922).
[25] *Cream of Wheat Co. v. F. T. C.*, 14 F. (2d) 40 (1926). *Cf.* also, 9 F. T. C. 43 (1925) for the Commission's proceedings.

significant monopolistic position with the purpose of eliminating a competitor. The pressure of various distributive
groups, however, has wrought an almost complete reversal of
policy in the last decade. California, responding to the drive of
interested parties, began the recent reversal of policy with a
Fair Trade Law legalizing resale price maintenance in 1931.
Under the NRA the distributive groups in many industries
sought to prevent selling below cost and loss leader merchandising by several types of code provisions. Resale price
maintenance was proposed for several industries, but in general
opposition within the NRA was sufficiently strong to prevent its
inclusion in the codes.[26]

Of particular significance in this respect were the proposed
codes of the retail trade and the retail drug trades. The history
of the adoption of these codes is told elsewhere.[27] In the proposed code of the retail drug trade the attack upon price cutting
took two forms. In the first place it was proposed that a producer or dealer in branded articles might specify resale prices,
such prices to be uniform for all producers who were in like
circumstances. Such resale price maintenance arrangements
were to be exempt from the anti-trust laws. The second proposal was a rule providing that no retailer should sell below
"cost sold" plus 5 per cent net profit. "Cost sold" was defined
as the "standard wholesale cost" (i.e. the manufacturer's wholesale list price per dozen) plus the average drug store overhead
as determined by the St. Louis drug store survey of the Department of Commerce.[28] This, then, was a no-sale-below-cost
proposal with a very generous and rigid interpretation of cost.
The proposed codes of the Retail Trade Committee provided

---

[26] Cf. C. F. Roos, *NRA Economic Planning* (Bloomington, Indiana: The
Principia Press, Inc., 1937), pp. 259–275.

[27] Cf. NRA, Division of Review, *Restrictions of Retail Price Cutting
with Emphasis on the Drug Industry* (Work Materials No. 57), *passim*;
Roos, *loc. cit.*

[28] This would have meant a minimum mark-up of 28 per cent.

that with certain exceptions (such as bona fide seasonal clearances so advertised and plainly marked) no sale should be made at less than net invoice delivered cost or current market delivered cost, whichever was lower, plus 15 per cent. This was a loss limitation proposal of somewhat more moderate proportions.

But these were merely proposals. Although the NRA experimented with many types of price control devices, it never permitted the inclusion in codes of either compulsory or permissive resale price maintenance. According to C. F. Roos a decision against the inclusion of a provision for resale price maintenance in the Retail Drug Code was made by General Johnson upon the advice of Alexander Sachs in October 1933; [29] while according to L. S. Lyon, Deputy Administrator of Trade Practices, the Trade Practice Policy Board of which he was a member had recommended to the Administrator that permissive resale price maintenance should not be incorporated in the codes.[30] Although this policy recommendation was never formally adopted, the Office Manual as published by the Division of Review after the demise of the NRA provides among the substantive guides for code making that "No form of price control by the producer or vendor over products of which he no longer holds title is acceptable." [31]

After the conclusion of the NRA, the interested distributive groups turned their attention toward legislative action. By the end of 1936 fourteen states had followed the lead of California in legalizing certain resale price maintenance contracts in intrastate commerce in the case of banded or trade-marked goods. In 1936 in *Old Dearborn Distributing Company v. Seagram*

[29] Roos, *op. cit.*, p. 272.
[30] L. S. Lyon and others, *The National Recovery Administration: An Analysis and Appraisal* (Washington: The Brookings Institution, 1935), p. 729.
[31] NRA, Division of Review, *Policy Statements Concerning Code Provisions and Related Subjects* (Work Materials No. 20), p. 55.

Distillers Corporation the right of a state to pass legislation legalizing such price fixing arrangements was established. The Supreme Court based its decision primarily upon the interest of the manufacturer in protecting the goodwill in his trade-mark or brand name.

> The essence of the statutory violation then consists not in the bare disposition of the commodity, but in a forbidden use of the trade-mark, brand, or name in accomplishing such disposition. The primary aim of the law is to protect the property — namely, the good will — of the producer, which he still owns. . . .

> The ownership of the good will . . . remains unchanged, notwithstanding the commodity has been parted with . . . the act does not prevent a purchaser of the commodity bearing the mark from selling the commodity alone at any price he pleases. It interferes only when he sells with the aid of the good will of the vendor; and it interferes then only to protect that good will against injury. It proceeds upon the theory that the sale of identified goods at less than the price fixed by the owner of the mark or brand is an assault upon the good will, and constitutes what the statute denominates "unfair competition." [32]

Subsequent to this decision most of the states which had not done so enacted Fair Trade Laws. The provisions of the laws show some variation between the various states, though most of them follow the outlines of the California or Arkansas laws.[33]

The California law provides that anyone in the sale of a product which bears the trade-mark, brand, or name of the producer or distributor and "which is in fair and open competition with commodities of the same general class produced by others" may require the signing of resale price maintenance

---

[32] 299 U. S. 183, 193–195 (1936).

[33] This recent state legislation is presented in considerable detail in several sources. *Cf.* E. T. Grether, *Price Control under Fair Trade Legislation* (New York: Oxford University Press, 1939); B. A. Zorn and G. J. Feldman, *Business under the New Price Laws* (New York: Prentice-Hall, Inc., 1937). *Cf.* Arkansas Acts of 1937, No. 92, p. 345 and California Laws of 1931, Ch. 278, p. 583; 1933, Ch. 260, p. 793; 1937, Ch. 843, p. 2364.

agreements. These contracts may provide not only that the buyer agree to maintain price but that he require any dealer to whom he resells to observe the stipulated price. The stipulated price is binding upon all persons whether or not they are a party to the contract; to offer such good wilfully and knowingly for sale at a price less than that stipulated in any such contract is unfair competition and actionable at the suit of anyone damaged thereby. Exception is made for sales below stipulated prices in cases of the closing out of stocks, the sale of damaged or deteriorated goods where notice thereof is given to the public, and the sale of goods by an officer acting under order of the court. The Arkansas law and those modeled after it followed the California law in general outlines but clarify a few points of the latter. The Arkansas law makes it clear that the stipulated prices are merely minimum resale prices, and not maximum. It specifically forbids evasion by offering premiums, combination purchases, or other concessions. Moreover, in the case of closeout sales below stipulated prices the manufacturer or distributor from whom the goods are purchased must be given the opportunity to repurchase at original invoice cost. Finally, following the suggestion of the Supreme Court in *Old Dearborn Distributing Company v. Seagram Distillers Corporation* it is specifically provided that upon removing or wholly obliterating the trade-mark or other identification of the producer's goodwill the product may be sold below the stipulated price.

These state laws were, of course, only applicable to transactions in intrastate commerce. In the case of transactions in interstate commerce or in states not having Fair Trade Laws, the old prohibitions of the anti-trust laws were applicable. However, in 1937 the Sherman Law was amended by passage of the Miller-Tydings Act which exempts from the prohibitions of section 1 resale price maintenance contracts made in interstate commerce on identified products which are in free and open competition with other goods of the same general class, provided such contracts are legal under the law of the state in which resale is to be made.[34] It is specifically provided, however, that the amendments do not legalize any horizontal agreements for the maintenance of minimum resale prices "between manufacturers, or between producers, or between wholesalers, or between brokers, or between factors, or between retailers, or between persons, firms, or corporations in competition with each other."

These legislative changes have, of course, substantially curtailed the scope of the Federal Trade Commission's powers to proceed against policies of resale price maintenance. Upon passage of the Miller-Tydings Act it dismissed several pending complaints.[35] It may still proceed, however, where there is evidence of collusive horizontal arrangements among producers or distributors, where there is not full and free competition with products of the same class, where there is interstate commerce but the contracts are not legal under the law of the state in which resale is to take place, and finally where the provisions of the contract violate in some way the provisions of the particular Fair Trade Law of the state in which resale is to take place.

As a complement to the State Fair Trade Laws providing for resale price maintenance, there have been enacted a large number of State Unfair Practice Laws dealing in particular with sales below cost, the loss leader, and discrimination. These laws, so far as they apply to loss leaders and sales below cost, may achieve in a more flexible way the purposes which are sought by the proponents of resale price maintenance. They apply, of course, to more items, since they are not simply permissive statutes as are the resale price maintenance laws.

[34] Public No. 314, 75th Cong., 1st Sess. (August 17, 1937).
[35] Federal Trade Commission, *Annual Report*, 1938, p. 6; *ibid.*, 1939, p. 50.

They serve, therefore, to limit price competition in the distributive channels where the producers are unwilling or unable to enforce price maintenance contracts. In the grocery trade, for example, the frequency of price changes, the importance of unbranded products, and the sharp buying practices of the customary shopper have made such contracts generally infeasible. On the other hand, if the definition of cost is not too rigid, these laws leave a greater degree of freedom to the distributor in his pricing of particular goods than do the resale price maintenance contracts. But this is not the place to pursue these state laws in detail.[36]

ECONOMICS OF RESALE PRICE MAINTENANCE

The problems of resale price maintenance and loss leader merchandising are but special cases of the problem of distributors' sales policies. The loss leader is a sales policy which uses the attractive power of low prices upon particular lines to increase the sales of others.[37] Resale price maintenance is a policy designed to control one element in the distributor's sales policy by fixing dealers' margins on specific items. Laws providing for minimum mark-ups or preventing sales below cost represent legislative attempts to place less rigid limits upon dealers' price policies. Since these pricing policies are all part

---

[36] The best and most readily available discussion of these laws is to be found in E. T. Grether, *op. cit.*

[37] "The terms 'leader' and 'loss leader' have indefinite meanings and are used by chain-store organizations in widely different senses. A loss leader apparently is variously considered as an article sold below net invoice cost, net purchase cost or net manufacturing cost as the case may be, or it may be applied to goods sold below the net purchase cost of the goods plus operating costs, or simply to goods sold below the usual mark-up. . . . In a broad sense leaders may be defined as merchandise featured or sold at reduced prices to attract buyers and thereby stimulate sales of these leaders and other goods. Such goods may be used more or less regularly and may or may not be advertised." Federal Trade Commission, *Chain-Store Leaders and Loss Leaders*, 72d Cong., 1st Sess. (1932), *Senate Document No. 51*, pp. 2–3.

of the same general problem, the starting point of the present discussion of the economics of these practices will be an analysis of the distributor, especially the retailer, and his pricing problems under the preliminary assumption that he is free from restrictions established by the manufacturer or by the legislature to pursue his own ends of maximum profits.

A retailer, or any other factor in the distributive trades, may be envisaged as "producing" and selling distributive services in connection with the sale of goods. The services which he renders with the sale of different goods or with the sale of several units of the same good may differ in amount or in kind. For the simplification of the subsequent argument it may be assumed that the distributive services of any one dealer are homogeneous and vary from sale to sale only in terms of quantity. The retailer's margin or mark-up is the price at which he sells his services. The difference between the aggregate of the margins received upon the sale of goods and the costs incurred in rendering these services are his profits. It may be assumed that the dealer will offer these services for sale in connection with the sale of different goods in such a way as to maximize his profits. There is no reason to expect him in his quest for profits to offer his services in connection with the sale of different goods or different units of the same good at the same price per unit of service unless there are market forces which make this the most profitable policy.

Two types of dealers should be distinguished, specialized and multi-product dealers. In some lines such as automobiles and radios a dealer specializes in only one type of product. He is interested solely in the size of his margin. His problem is a fairly simple one of maximizing his profits by adopting the best possible price policy. Where feasible this may be a discriminatory policy. The more typical independent dealer who has sponsored the recent legislative drives is one handling several or many different items. His is a problem of so setting his individual margins as to maximize his over-all profits. His is an extremely complicated pricing problem. He is faced with a complex set of demand schedules for various goods of different intensities and above all of different elasticities. Moreover, some of the demand schedules are interdependent, i.e. the intensity and elasticity of the schedule for one item depend upon the price of another. His cost situation is equally complex. The invoice cost of the good is clear and, as shall be seen, can be eliminated from our consideration. But the cost of his services are intricate. There are some costs which are *special* to the sale of particular goods, others are *common* to the sale of several or all goods. Some of these common costs may in turn be joint costs in the technical sense. And if we choose to distinguish between the long and short run, each of these categories may be further broken down into *variable* and *overhead*. Faced with such a complexity of demand and cost conditions the retailer is left with the maximum amount of perspicacity, intuition, or rule of thumb to seek his own interest.

The retailer in effect may consider the consumer demand for any particular good which he offers as a composite of a demand for the good itself plus a demand for his services. The derived demand for his services may be arrived at by subtracting the unit cost of the good to him, that is the invoice cost adjusted for discounts, from the consumers' demand schedule. This unit cost will be a constant for all quantities unless there are discounts or other economies associated with large purchases. The resulting derived schedule is the demand for the retailer's distributive services on the part of customers buying any particular good.

If retailing were a purely competitive industry, the demand for the services of a particular firm by customers buying any one product would be perfectly elastic. That is to say, the retailer could sell at the going price, and at no other. In this case he would sell his services at the same price with all goods;

mark-ups would differ only in proportion to differences in the amount of service or, if services vary in kind, in proportion to differences in cost of different kinds. As it is, however, retailing is not purely competitive. It is a field in which there is service differentiation and consumer preference; the degree and form of competition will vary from product to product. Consequently, the demand for retail services by consumers of various goods will have some finite elasticity, and the elasticity of demand for services of a particular dealer sold in connection with various goods will in general differ.

These factors offer the retailer an opportunity and an incentive to discriminate systematically in the price at which he will sell his distributive services. The principal basis of classification will be the particular good bought, although discrimination as between individuals or sales at different points of time are not unknown. Distributive services will be sold for various prices depending upon the good in connection with which it is sold. Transfer of demand or supply from one market to another, factors which make discrimination difficult in some circumstances, is impeded in so far as one good is not equivalent to the other.[38] We have here a clear case of discrimination. The volume of services offered in each market,[39] i.e. in connection with the sale of each good, will be extended until marginal derived revenue for the service is equal to the marginal cost of the total services sold in all markets. The price at which distributive services will be sold in each market will be indicated by the derived demand price for that quantity.

Moreover, since it may not be feasible for technical reasons to increase and decrease the size of the various departments

---

[38] The reader is referred to chapter VII for discussion of the meaning and prerequisites of discrimination.

[39] By market in this context is meant the complex of forces impinging upon the demand for the distributive services of one dealer in connection with one good.

of a retail store as demand changes and since the firm may be interested in the returns from a department over a period of time rather than at each moment of time, there will be other motives for wide variations in mark-ups which are not matched by differences in cost. Furthermore, the fact that the demand for various goods and therefore the demand for a distributor's services in connection therewith are interdependent serves to explain many differences in margins not matched by differences in cost. So long as distributors even believe that the demands for services in connection with different goods are interdependent, they will follow pricing policies predicated upon this assumption. Certain prices will be low, that is the mark-up will be low or perhaps negative, on the theory that the intensity of demand for other commodities will be increased or that demand for these other goods will become less elastic. In the former case, the "losses" incident to a low price on one product, it is hoped, will be offset by a larger volume of sales of other products. In the latter case, a less elastic demand for other products will enable the retailer to raise his price on these other items, thus increasing his margin.

The loss leader or leader is to be explained in these terms. It is essentially one among several alternative or complementary sales policies which a firm may employ. Whether or not a particular leader or a general policy of leader merchandising will increase the intensity or decrease the elasticity of demand for other goods is something which only experience will show. There is no general formula which enables one to answer this question. It depends on the nature of consumer reaction. What is typical for some consumers or for one period of time may be far from typical for others. Experience would probably differ with different retailers, with different goods, and at different times.

The average price of the retailer's services as sold in connection with different goods, then, will not be equal, nor will there be any relation between the differences in margins and differences in average cost of selling the various goods. If retail selling were a perfectly competitive trade, the rate of return on all lines handled by a particular seller would be equal; margins would be equivalent, allowance being made for differences in the special costs of handling each product and the volume of services rendered. With an imperfectly elastic demand, interdependent demands, and technical obstacles to mobility of resources, this is not to be expected. The above

TABLE II

EXPENSES AND PROFITS [1]

(Based on 7 independent neighborhood stores in St. Louis)

Department	Gross Margins % of Sales Price	Annual Turnover	Operating Expenses % of Sales Price	Net Profit % of Sales Price
Tobacco	20.7	11.9	14.2	6.5
Toiletries	34.3	1.5	40.5	−6.2
Sundries	38.2	1.4	52.0	−13.8
Hospital	55.6	2.2	26.3	29.3
Packaged Medicine	38.2	2.4	27.1	11.1
Store Total	40.7	4.0	34.0	6.7

[1] W. Alderson and N. A. Miller, *Cost, Sales, and Profits in the Retail Drug Trade* (Bureau of Domestic and Foreign Commerce, No. 90, 1934), p. 44.

analysis is verified by the principal available study of retail mark-ups and costs. This study is based on the experience of thirteen drug stores in St. Louis. The data are summarized in Table II which shows that the toiletries and sundries departments, both of which were highly competitive with non-drug outlets, showed a net loss, while the hospital department, the items of which are largely non-competitive, showed the best net profit. The more detailed breakdown contained in the report further verifies the argument.

It is clear, then, that we are dealing with an industry in which discrimination may be considered a typical marketing policy. The implications of discrimination have been discussed in a previous chapter. It is enough to point out here that the marginal costs of distributive services devoted to the sale of different goods will not be proportional to marginal utilities or to price. So far as the size of retailing establishments can with time be closely adjusted to output, there would be in the absence of decreasing costs a *prima facie* case in favor of mark-ups in proportion to costs. Granted the existence of decreasing average costs, sales policies which will increase the intensity of the demands for services of the retailer might be expected to decrease average costs of distribution, especially sales policies which take the form of low prices. On the other hand, if the forces of competition are such as to force demand schedules to a point where there are only normal profits, a particular sales policy will lower costs of distribution only if it makes the demand more elastic. Moreover, if the added profits of discrimination induce additional firms to enter the trade, the average size of the distributive firm may be expected to be less and average cost of distribution to be greater than would otherwise be the case.

The effects of the use of the loss leader are complicated by the difficulty of predicting consumer behavior. A consumer attracted to a particular outlet by a leader may be induced to buy other commodities which he would otherwise have purchased elsewhere. He may do this because of the convenience of dealing in one store or because of ignorance of the values available elsewhere. Presumably a rational consumer will not pay more for an aggregate group of goods in one outlet than he could buy the group for elsewhere under like conditions of service, etc. But consumers are not always well-informed, and even when informed they are not always "rational." If consumers are on balance irrational or ill-informed, the demand for products other than the leader may become less elastic or more intense, with the results outlined in the preceding paragraphs.

Irrational behavior may be induced by another factor, namely a confusion created in the minds of consumers by widely advertised leaders. Some consumers may come to believe that an offer of leaders indicates that the store sells all of its goods at correspondingly low prices. The fact that many goods are not easily compared as between stores because of differences in brands or qualities, or because many goods are not standardized in any respect abets this tendency to confusion of the consumer. The retailer himself may connive to promote this confusion by advertising in connection with his leaders that he is able to present such values because of his buying economies and large turnover. This is charged in the controversy between the department stores and chains on one side and the independents on the other. Thus, as has been recognized by the Federal Trade Commission, leaders may be part of a scheme of wilful misrepresentation and deceit, though this is by no means necessarily the case.

The effects of leader merchandising upon the competitive relations of the retailers may be various. If one dealer adopts the policy, his competitors may be materially injured unless they follow suit or at least adopt some countervailing competitive strategy. If the practice is widely followed by a group of competitors, the efforts of one to stimulate sales may be offset by those of another. The result might then be losses analogous to increased advertising expenses. Such losses can be avoided in the face of the continued use of leaders only (1) by decreasing the number of outlets thus increasing volume per unit, (2) by increasing the mark-up on other goods, or (3) by increasing total volume of sales by all outlets under conditions of decreasing costs. Competitive relations will be affected by the use of this policy, and in the process some may be driven out of the trade if under the new conditions fewer retailers can be supported. However, a practice which can be adopted by all, in a monopolistic market characterized by freedom of entry, may be mutually offsetting. If adopted by all with equal effectiveness, it may result in the sale of the same volume of services at the same *average* price, its only effect being to alter the price of the service in connection with the sale of particular goods. Any effect which leaders have to increase the intensity of demand or decrease the elasticity, thus increasing the profits of discriminatory pricing, may lead to a multiplication of firms and still higher distribution costs. But in so far as rivals are serving similar customers or markets and do not resort to deceit it appears unlikely that leader merchandising will significantly change relative competitive positions over a period of time.

It will not always be true, however, that all competing retailers will be forced into the practice or will find it profitable. The field of retail trade is highly and irregularly imperfect. A dealer whose market is differentiated spatially may find that his net advantage does not lie in following the merchandising policy of a rival. For example, when the policy of employing leaders is adopted by a large retailer in a central market area which is surrounded by a series of interpenetrating marketing areas of lesser importance, the financial benefits to this dealer will be large by comparison with the losses of each of the surrounding dealers taken individually. If so, these latter may not follow suit, since the basis of their sales appeal may lie rather in convenience, personal relations, or better service. At the time that a new centrally located dealer enters the market, the impact of this change may be severe on the local dealers; and since the new rival may find leader merchandising an expedient policy, the local dealers will blame their plight on his price policy when in truth they are the victims of changes of a more fundamental sort in distributive methods.

One of the frequently cited evils of the use of leaders is its effects on the manufacturer. It is claimed first that the goodwill of the manufacturer is destroyed because the consumer loses faith in the product; second, that the dealer loses interest in handling the product and either discontinues it or promotes some substitute. There is doubtlessly some merit in these arguments. The probable effects, however, have often been exaggerated. It is interesting to note that the Federal Trade Commission in its report to Congress stated that "No instance . . . has yet been brought to the commission's attention in which there was conclusive evidence that an article of real merit has been driven off the market by price cutting alone." [40] This is not to say, however, that there has not been some restriction of the market for particular goods due to the use of leaders.

It is frequently claimed that the policy is "ruinous" and "cut-throat." The implications of this charge may well be pursued further. If the local market is dominated by a few retailers of about equal strength, the use of leaders may be an instrument in the warfare of these dealers. The result may be generally ruinous. But this is an inherent potentiality of any oligopolistic market with unused capacity and should be treated as such. It is merely one instrument among many including competition in service and advertising with which an oligopolist may fight. The same may be said where the retailers are of unequal strength. In this case, however, the inequality of financial strength makes it more likely that the result will be the destruction of the weaker and his withdrawal from the market. The use of leaders or loss leaders, i.e. price cutting on a few goods as a way of attracting patronage, is one instrument of economic warfare. It is this type of practice which our trust policy has been designed to correct, and the Federal Trade Commission recognizes the use of leaders in such circumstances as illegal.

The charge that the use of leaders is ruinous is not reserved alone for those situations which are so imperfect as to be classi-

[40] Federal Trade Commission, *Resale Price Maintenance* (1931), Part II, p. 162.

fied as oligopolistic. In one study [41] of the matter, the authors have emphasized the argument that low prices for certain articles used as leaders become established and tend to persist. No dealer can raise prices on these goods so that they cover a due proportion of the overhead, for to do so would give an advantage to his competitors. That certain goods are generally and for long periods sold at costs which do not cover a due share of the overhead is, of course, true. Cigarettes are probably such a product. The fact that each retailer continues to use a particular product as a loss leader is *prima facie* evidence that it pays to do so in the sense that in a market where others are doing so each finds that to do otherwise would mean less profits or greater losses.

The ruinous nature of the practice, however, appears where the burden of the losses is sustained by a few. The retail tobacco store, for example, bears the burden of the use of cigarettes as a loss leader by other distributing agencies. During 1933 the NRA found extreme conditions in the retail tobacco trade. Sales of the popular brands in chain, department, and grocery stores at a dollar per carton were frequent and "in extreme cases there were sales as low as 59 cents a carton. The cost to retailers varied from $1.076 to $1.14 a carton, about 15 per cent of the retailers obtaining the lower price." [42] It is not surprising that the code authority concluded that the retail tobacco dealer was in severe straits. Those to whom tobacco was a minor item might not find conditions serious, but specialized tobacco stores surely could not stand this for long. The consumer of tobacco is an obvious gainer by such a policy, but the specialized retailer bears the incidence of a change in the distribution policies of diversified retailers. Except where there is some such specialized retailer who bears the burden of leader mer-

[41] Seligman and Love, *op. cit.*, p. 156.
[42] C. D. Edwards, *NRA Trade Practice Experience*, chap. II, p. 119. *Cf. post*, p. 318, note 34, for fuller citation.

chandising with particular severity, this policy involves no obvious unfairness as between competing retailers. Of course, certain retailers may use the policy more effectively, or may gain conjunctural advantages by being the first to use it in a particular market. But it is, in this respect, no different from competition by giving additional service or credit or by increasing advertising expenditures. Those who use any sales policy most effectively gain. Once any of these policies is adopted, it may persist.

The interest of the consumer in this practice of leader merchandising is worth consideration. One fact is clear, namely that the use of the leader changes the consumption pattern of the buyer. It will presumably induce him to consume more of the leader and relatively less of other commodities. It is frequently alleged, however, that the consumer does not benefit from the use of leaders since what he saves on them he loses on the unnecessarily high prices of other goods. This charge may mean either that the prices on these other goods are higher in the leader stores than are the prices of comparable goods in other stores, or that these prices in the leader store are higher than they would be if the store followed a policy of making each product contribute equivalently to the overhead and selling expenses. It cannot be said *a priori* whether either of these propositions is true in a particular case. It will depend upon the facts. If the consumer is ill-informed concerning the comparative values offered by various dealers, it is possible that in his ignorance he will pay in the aggregate more for a group of goods bought in the leader store than he could have purchased them for elsewhere. This is very possible in view of the ignorance of consumers in the face of non-standardized and highly technical goods. In those instances where the consumer can and does make a roughly accurate comparison of values (and this is true perhaps of many housewives, who are significantly called "shoppers"), it seems unlikely that he will pay a greater aggregate amount for a given assortment. These other goods *may* individually be priced higher in the leader store than in others, but not so the assortment. If the policy of leaders conduces to large-scale and more efficient retail stores, the aggregate of goods may be sold at a lower price than would otherwise be true. If, however, the use of leaders becomes general so that its effect on the individual store's sales volume is negligible, the "losses" on leaders must be reflected in the higher margins on other goods.

One other factor should be mentioned which complicates the situation even more. Many of the department and chain-stores which follow a systematic policy of leader merchandising sell large quantities of privately branded goods. These private brands are often in active competition with nationally advertised brands. It is impossible to make any generalization about comparative qualities although there are known cases where the private brand is identical (except for labels and other non-essentials) with the national brand and is manufactured by the producer of the nationally advertised brand. Private brands frequently cost the dealer much less than others, thus enabling him to sell them cheaper. So far as the offering of leaders is an instrument in promoting equally good private brands not subject to high advertising expenses, they can hardly be condemned.

The policy of resale price maintenance is sponsored as one method for eliminating the use of leaders, but its proponents usually have the much broader purpose of reducing price competition in general between competitive channels of distribution. The policy of resale price maintenance attempts to limit the discretion of retailers in formulating their pricing policies. It can accomplish this only for trade-marked or branded products. However, various staples such as sugar and butter are also often used as leaders, a practice which price maintenance arrangements obviously cannot prevent. The use of staples as leaders may be limited, of course, by loss-limitation or minimum mark-up legislation, which has been enacted in many states. The present discussion, however, is confined to restraints on resale prices initiated by manufacturers of differentiated products.

The practice of resale price maintenance was attacked under our anti-trust acts as a restraint of trade, a monopolistic practice. In considering whether or not resale price maintenance is itself a monopolistic practice or tends to foster monopoly, its effects on the competitive relations of the manufacturers must be distinguished from its effects on the competitive relations of the dealers.

Consider first the effects of price maintenance on the relations of the manufacturers. In general the market as between the manufacturers of substitute goods has monopolistic elements. The manufacturer may be in a strongly or weakly monopolistic position depending upon the source of monopoly power and upon the freedom of entry into the particular line of manufacture. Granted the existence of monopolistic elements at the manufacturing stage, we may ask whether the introduction of a policy of resale price maintenance tends to promote further monopolistic elements. Such a policy does not of necessity involve any horizontal agreement among otherwise competing producers, and the recent State Fair Trade Laws forbid this. It might, of course, be used as part of such monopolistic agreement among manufacturers to fix prices or production, where it seems desirable to control competitive relations clear through to the point of final sale. The instances which have come before the Commission and the courts, however, have not generally involved such agreements. The manufacturers were free to compete with one another. Of course, in oligopolistic situations, this freedom may not have been exercised. It cannot be assumed, however, that the competitive relations of the manufacturers are not affected by resale price maintenance.

Differences in gross mark-ups may give the dealers more motive for pushing one substitute product than another; and if some products are price maintained while substitutes are not, the dealers may prefer to push the price maintained product and some dealers may even discontinue handling the product which is not price maintained. This does not necessarily mean that the producer of the cut-price product will be forced out of business; he may simply sell a smaller quantity and receive smaller profits.[43]

Nor is it true that dealers will always refuse to handle cut-price products in favor of those which are price-maintained. Dealers may not find it expedient to refuse to handle a nationally advertised product for which there is an insistent demand. The charge of the Federal Trade Commission that the adoption of a policy of resale price maintenance has the effect of enlisting the support of dealers in the sale of price-maintained goods is only partially true. The further charge that it forces other producers to adopt a policy of price maintenance in self-protection is likewise an overstatement. A manufacturer may be so constrained, but it is also possible that he will find it more profitable to continue allowing the resale prices of his product to be free. Vigorous salesmanship on the part of dealers, induced by the maintenance of liberal margins, is one way of attracting customers; low prices and extensive advertising are others.

While the resort to resale price maintenance by some will not necessarily mean the adoption of the policy by all manufacturers, experience under the California State Fair Trade Law shows that to be effective resale price maintenance must be

[43] When dealing with problems in imperfect competition, the rate of profit necessary to force a firm from the industry and the rate which is necessary to induce expansion may be considered to differ by a finite quantity. There is a penumbra within which profits may vary. See Joan Robinson, "What is Perfect Competition?" *Quarterly Journal of Economics*, XLIX (1934), 104.

adopted generally by the manufacturers of rival products. For one or a few to adopt the policy alone involves serious risk that volume will be lost.[44] This means that where there is a high degree of substitution between branded products, successful price maintenance will be achieved only where rivals follow similar policies. If distributors are able and willing to cut off outlets for non-price maintained goods, the manufacturer will be forced to adopt price maintenance. If such is not the case, anyone who undertakes to sell only under resale contracts will be limited in the margins which he can enforce by current practice with respect to rivals' products. Only in the case where consumers are but little affected by a comparison of retail prices will it be possible for one seller to pursue a vigorous policy of resale price maintenance, while rivals sell on an unrestricted basis.

In the case of products for which private brands can be developed by large-scale dealers, the effectiveness of resale price maintenance contracts will be seriously impaired, at least as a protection for independents. Resale prices providing for moderate mark-ups may be acceptable to large-scale dealers, and extreme cases of price cutting may be eliminated: but a manufacturer faces the loss of mass distributive channels if he tries to enforce mark-ups which will protect high-cost independents from loss. It is very probable that the institution of rigorous policies of price maintenance will be a force leading to the realignment of the relations between dealers and manufacturers. In some cases manufacturers will be forced to choose between the price maintenance channels and those where resale prices are not controlled, while in other cases there may be an integration of the mass distributive channels, which customarily resist price maintenance, with manufacturing enterprise.

[44] E. T. Grether, "Experience in California with Fair Trade Legislation Restricting Price Cutting," *California Law Review*, XXIV (1936), 653.

Turning to the effects of resale price maintenance on the competitive position of the dealers, we shall again treat the case of the retailers selling to the consumer, although much of the analysis may be applied to resale prices fixed for the wholesalers or jobbers. The fixing of retailers' margins by a price maintenance system has effects similar to those of an agreement to maintain margins among the dealers themselves. It excludes from dealing in the particular product all who will not maintain established margins and restrains those who continue to handle the product from competing in a certain way, namely, by lowering prices. This is, of course, the essence of the legal argument against the policy. However, the interest of the economist centers on the probable effect of the policy upon profits, volume of sales of the retailers, and upon the number of retail outlets. What may these effects be?

Assume that the policy is adopted for all commodities and results in increasing the mark-up on these commodities. One result would be to check the volume of sales of retail services since the demand function for retail services in general may be considered to be negative. But there are other possible results. Other things being equal, the net profits of the retailers might be increased. However, other things will not be equal. Competition between retailers may take other forms than price. An additional quantity of economic resources may be attracted to retail trade by the additional rewards. The retailers will still be free to compete in service, credit, advertising, sales effort, and window and counter display. All these may be just as ruinous forms of competition as price cutting. In conjunction with the claim that resale price maintenance will protect the little fellow, it may be noted that in the case of some of these other forms of competition, the balance of advantage would seem often to lie with the large dealers and chains. Just as it is often said that the small independent whose resources are limited cannot afford to sustain losses from low prices or leaders, it is also true that the independent often cannot sustain the cost of these other competitive efforts.

Moreover, competition may take still another direction which may make the profits of resale price maintenance equally illusory. This is an increase in the number of retailers with a consequent diminution of the volume of sales per unit. If retail trade were otherwise a perfectly competitive line of commerce, i.e. if retail stores always appeared in large clusters, each without advantage of location or goodwill, and if there were freedom for new stores to enter, the fixing of retailers' margins at a higher level than would be brought about by uninterrupted competitive forces would not lead to any permanent alleviation of the retailers' position. The otherwise excess profits of retailers would be levelled off by an increase in their numbers, decreasing the volume of sales per store, and therefore, increasing average costs. As it is, retail marketing is imperfectly competitive. Assuming that a policy of resale price maintenance were introduced, it cannot be said that competition in service, etc. and competition through the increase in the number of retail units would eliminate for all retailers the advantages of increased margins. Above all it cannot be said that after a period these forms of competition would lead to a situation of normal profits. Retail trade presents a market in which there may be monopoly profits to begin with and in which the competitive forces work unevenly. This unevenness with which competitive forces work in such a market configuration means that the competitive relations of the retailers may be changed, some gaining and others losing. Thus, while a general policy of resale price maintenance may materially affect competition, may reallocate profits, may raise costs of retail trade, may lead to the duplication of facilities, and raise prices to consumers, profits *in the aggregate* may not be substantially affected.[45]

[45] This is a familiar characteristic of monopolistic competition. Chamberlin, *op. cit.*, chap. V.

While it is apparently the hope of the exponents of recent fair trade legislation to induce a general increase in dealers' margins, there may be no such effect. If resale price contracts are limited to only a few lines of products handled by a certain type of retail outlet, the effect may be to induce the retailer to lower his margins on other lines. Were this true, there would be a force at work tending to minimize the degree of discrimination in the sale of distributors' services, a force which would be in a desirable direction. Moreover, this would be a force working against an increase in the average cost of distribution. The real crux of the question of efficiency in distribution depends upon the size of the margins provided for in the contracts, the number and importance of the commodities subject to such contracts, the relation of the established margins to the cost of distribution in the low cost channels, the extent to which the margins on non-price maintained goods are varied, and finally the extent to which various forms of non-price competition are stimulated.

It is not clear that resale price maintenance contracts will mean generally higher margins even on particular products. Grether in his study of the California experience in the drug trade found that although certain habitual price cutters were led to raise their prices, many independents found that the contract prices were below the prices which they had been charging. There were cases where retail prices were actually reduced after the introduction of the contracts.[46] What the net effect of resale price maintenance will be on average mark-up, upon unit store volume, and upon costs of distribution is not at all clear. In part the answer depends upon the size of the mark-up. If it is sufficiently small so that it covers no more than the cost for the lowest cost distributive channel, the system may have no serious effects on the relative position of the alternative channels. Likewise if only a few products are involved, its effects upon costs of distribution may be negligible. It will be significant to the

[46] *Columbia Law Review* (1936), XXIV, 675 *et seq.*

rival channels principally in so far as it limits short-run price wars of a sporadic nature. If, however, the power of independent distributors is sufficient to bring pressure on manufacturers for sufficiently wide margins on enough products so as to protect the high cost channels, competition in retailing will be diverted into other channels than price, such as advertising, service, or trade-in allowances. Except so far as private brands might be developed, forces would be introduced favoring expensive methods of distribution. Moreover, extensive rigid margins would be a factor working toward inflexibility in the economic structure.

RECAPITULATION

This discussion of resale price maintenance and the related problem of leader merchandising serves a twofold function, to show the shifts in our policy with respect to these practices on the one hand, and to show the economic implications and significance of the practices on the other. It has been seen that traditional policy has looked upon resale price maintenance as equivalent to a horizontal agreement among distributors and has forbidden all effective ways of enforcing the maintenance of resale prices as a restraint of trade. More recently, however, there has been a reversal of policy. Loss leader merchandising, on the other hand, has been considered legal unless pursued in such a way as to deceive the buyer or used as a method of monopolizing trade by eliminating competitors. Here, too, many states have recently reversed past policy.

It has been shown that the motives behind price maintenance are complex. In some cases the manufacturer has an interest in controlling the resale prices of his products as part of his general merchandising scheme. In recent times the driving force behind the movement has been the interest of distributors. It was noted that retail specialists have a very keen interest in limiting the use of their specialty by diversified retailers as a leader. More generally, the recent movements in favor of resale price maintenance represent part of the struggle of various groups whose interests are in part antagonistic for control over the channels of distribution. It is in part the struggle of the wholesaler, jobber, and retailer against the mass distributors.

The discussion of the economic significance of price maintenance suffers from the complexity and variety of the market structures in which it is introduced. In the first place, since it is feasible only in the case of differentiated products, the manufacturer must necessarily have some element of monopoly power. Moreover, the retailer whose pricing policies are being limited by the practice is himself selling in a market characterized by monopolistic elements. If retailing were a purely competitive trade, it is quite clear that leader merchandising would not exist and that any limitation on retailers' margins to raise them above the level to which market forces would tend to bring them would increase average margins, induce waste in distribution, and burden the consumer. Since retailing does not satisfy this assumption, the effects of the policy cannot be so easily determined. It is clear, of course, that price maintenance will generally restrict the consumption of particular commodities and penalize consumers whose consumption of these commodities is a greater proportion of their expenditure than is true of the average consumer.

It was argued that the conditions of retailing are such that there is no tendency at work for margins to be equal, or for differences in margins to be related to differences in cost of handling particular products. Retailers discriminate systematically in the price at which they sell their services to different customers according to the goods which the consumer buys; this is the source of some inequalities. Leader merchandising, which accounts for others, is a special case arising from the interdependent nature of the demands for the retailers' services in connection with the sale of various goods. In consequence of the discriminatory nature of distributors' pricing policies it is not clear what the effect of resale price maintenance will be. If applied to a few commodities only and accompanied by lower margins for items which are not subject to price maintenance contracts, there will be a reallocation of consumer's expenditure and a tendency to lessen the inequalities of the ratios of marginal cost to price of services sold in connection with various goods.

Whether average margins or average cost of distribution will increase will depend upon the number of price-maintained goods, the size of the margins provided for in the resale agreements, the effects on the margins of goods which are not price-maintained, the other forms which competition may take, and the extent to which private brands may be developed by mass distributors as substitutes for price-maintained goods. It is possible that moderate resale prices, limited to a few products, will merely result in limiting that price cutting of an extreme type which develops sporadically with respect to many products and more frequently with respect to some. If the wholesalers, jobbers, and high cost independents should develop sufficient power to enforce more liberal resale prices on a wide variety of products, the practice might have serious repercussions upon the efficiency of our system of distribution by increasing costs and seriously affecting price flexibility.

Having sketched the issues we are in a position to ask for the facts which might help to answer the questions which have been raised. The present chapter has done little more than suggest certain hypotheses. It is to be hoped that recent experiences with resale price maintenance will eventually afford sufficient basis for testing these hypotheses against the facts. The author ventures to predict that when this is done, both the hopes of the proponents of the recent legislation on these matters and the fears of the opposition will prove exaggerated.

CHAPTER XIII

TRADE PRACTICE CONFERENCE RULES

THE TRADE PRACTICE CONFERENCE is a procedure which was evolved by the Commission for the voluntary adoption of rules of fair competition by business groups in conference and under guidance of the Commission. The conference and its importance has undergone change during the various phases of the Commission's life. It had its origins in the trade submittals which were initiated by the Commission in 1919.

The first submittal was the result of the Commission's own initiative. It appeared that there was a great similarity in the complaints of illegal practices lodged against members of the creamery industry.[1] The Commission feared that to eradicate unfair methods which were widespread in the industry by individual proceedings might be slow and expensive and might place those who were proceeded against in the first instance at a competitive disadvantage. Consequently, with the encouragement of the Commission the members of the industry held a series of meetings and drew up a list of 13 practices which were held to be unfair. The rules condemned such practices as wilful interference with competitor's contractual arrangements, intentional false report of the quantity of a dairy product, furnishing shippers with cans or dairy equipment in order to gain business, the giving of premiums or other additional compensations. The Commission accepted the rules as expressions of opinion of the industry and agreed to regard the judgment of

---

[1] Federal Trade Commission, *Trade Practice Submittals* (1925), pp. 1–2, 6. Two previous experiments had been made in the case of other industries, but it was the creamery industry which held the first formal submittal.

the trade as conclusive "until testimony to the contrary is produced."

Between October 1919 and April 1926, at which time the new Division of Trade-Practice Conferences was created, some 17 trade submittals were held.[2] The rules included in these submittals were various and completely unstandardized. The butter manufacturers of the Southwest declared it unfair to sell butter in cartons, rolls or prints in weights other than the standard weights of 16, 8, and 4 ounces. The package macaroni industry disapproved the slack-filled package, which it defined as one so large "as to enable it to contain from $1\frac{1}{2}$ to 2 ounces more, net weight, than is actually placed in it." It further disapproved selling macaroni in packages containing less than 8 ounces. It likewise declared that the giving of commissions, bonuses, and premiums to jobbers' salesmen was an unfair practice. The oil industry prohibited a series of practices including the lease or loan of curb-pumps or tanks to dealers and the sale of oil to dealers on a credit basis. The gold-mounted knife industry first undertook to define a gold-mounted knife and then proceeded to condemn the use of various methods of construction by which it might be made to appear that a knife contained more gold of an indicated karat fineness than had been used in fact. The Commission refused to accept this submittal as conclusive. It raised a series of questions with reference to the specific proposals and remarked that these questions "may best be resolved when they arise in connection with concrete cases before the Commission, each case to be judged on the law and the facts as they are adduced in the particular case. The trade practice submittal herewith submitted is informative. It is not conclusive."[3]

In 1925 the rules proposed by the anti-hog-cholera serum

---

[2] Federal Trade Commission, *Trade Practice Conferences* (1933), p. xii.

[3] Federal Trade Commission, *Trade Practice Submittals* (1925), pp. 42–43.

and virus industry precipitated a division of opinion within the Commission. The majority proceeded to divide the rules into two groups. The first group including practices such as false and misleading advertising, disparagement of competitors, and discrimination it accepted as rules defining unfair methods of competition within the meaning of the law. The second group it merely "receives . . . and takes note of the same as the opinion of the industry." These included granting rebates, paying advertising expenses of certain purchases, lavish entertainment of purchasers, guaranteeing against advance and protection against declines in price. The majority noted:

> Fair competition does not mean lessened competition. Fair competition may consist in giving a better price or better terms or better service. A number of practices condemned by the trade consists only in one of these and cannot be condemned by the commission. On the contrary, an agreement not to compete in these particulars, is contrary to law.[4]

The minority protested that certain of these practices were clearly unfair since through use of these competitive methods the financially strong firms were able to dominate the market by driving out the financially weak which were unable to meet the cost occasioned by such practices.

These early submittals, then, were various in content; the rules in each submittal were adapted in general to the peculiarities of the industry in question. Many established rigid standards of product with the intent thereby of reducing confusion of consumers and attendant injury to business interests. Others limited the terms and conditions of sale. The Commission generally accepted the rules as expression of industry opinion without committing itself to the proposition that all violations of the rules were illegal. It reserved the right to consider the effects of practices in particular cases and in some instances

[4] *Ibid.*, p. 54.

specifically warned that the suggested rules might themselves be contrary to law. These early conferences were experimental.

The year 1926 marks the beginning of a new phase of the conference procedure. Changes in personnel had led to a reorientation of Commission policy in 1925.[5] In general the Commission is believed to have become more coöperative with business, especially big-business. " 'Helping business to help itself' wherever and whenever it can be done consistently without prejudice to the best interests of the public as a whole is the principle of this new policy." [6] It adopted new rules of procedure which gave the Commission more discretion in its dealings with complaints and avoided publicity when a case could be settled by stipulation. But at the same time the Commission embarked upon an expanded policy of trade practice conferences and established a special Division of Trade Practice Conferences to coördinate the work. The Commission envisaged this as a great step forward toward the development of industrial self-regulation.[7]

During the next four years the conference procedure flourished. There were on the average about sixteen conferences per year. The Commission continued to divide the rules into two groups, and sometimes even three and four. Rules in Group I the Commission approved as forbidding practices which were definitely violative of the law; Group II rules it accepted as expressions of opinion of the trade, without accepting them as legally binding; Group III rules the Commission disapproved as being themselves illegal and in restraint of trade; rules placed in Group IV were those which the Commission held in abeyance, since the vote at the conference indicated lack of agreement among industry members. During this period the rules in Group I continued to be of a rather diversified sort

[5] Blaisdell, *op. cit.*, chap. IV; *passim.*
[6] Federal Trade Commission, *Annual Report*, 1927, p. 1.
[7] Federal Trade Commission, *Trade Practice Conferences* (1927), p. 1.

and unstandardized in form, the rules in Group II even more so.

In 1930 the movement to develop rules of fair trade received a sudden shock. The Commission announced that it proposed to reconsider and to revise where necessary the rules already adopted. It appears that some doubts were entertained concerning the legality of some of the rules adopted. It was believed in some quarters including the Department of Justice that price fixing had been attempted in some instances "by the misuse of so-called codes of ethics or trades rules." [8] The result of these revisions, despite the protest of industries, was the standardization of many of the Group I rules, the removing of others from Group I to Group II, and finally the elimination of many of the Group II rules.[9] Thus, such Group I rules as those forbidding the making of false or deceptive statements, imitation of trade marks, or the defamation of competitors were formalized and restricted to instances "having the tendency or capacity to mislead or deceive purchasers or prospective purchasers." Selling below cost, consignment selling, and commercial bribery were prohibited only when used "with the intent and with the effect of injuring a competitor and where the effect may be to substantially lessen competition or tend to create a monopoly or to unreasonably restrain trade." Rules concerning discrimination were revised to conform with section 2 of the Clayton Act. Rules forbidding discrimination by absorption of freight and packing costs were eliminated. Rules recommending the adoption of uniform cost accounting were changed to a recommendation that each member install "a proper and accurate" method of cost determination. Group II rules re-

---

[8] Address of John Lord O'Brion, Assistant to the Attorney General, May 1, 1930. Reprinted in Senate, *Hearings before Subcommittee of the Committee on the Judiciary on S. 2626, S. 2627, and S. 2628: A Bill to Amend the Federal Trade Commission Act and to Establish a Federal Trade Court*, 72d Cong., 1st Sess. (1932), p. 306.

[9] For illustration of changes *cf. ibid.*, pp. 298–305.

jected in the revision included prohibitions of guarantees against price changes, antidumping provisions, elaborate provisions for the publication of prices, allowances, and price changes, and elaborate regulations of competitive bidding in those industries where sealed bids are used. The net effect of these revisions was to confine Group I rules to a standardized set of rules which were clearly illegal under existing law, adding nothing new in principle and little in detail, while Group II rules were purged of those which were most likely to be the means of illegal agreement to standardize practices impinging upon price.

Thus, the policy of coöperation with business in order to develop a law merchant and a new era of industrial self-regulation which had been widely hailed in the middle twenties was at an end. The conventional character of trade practice conference rules which were permitted by the new policy can be clearly appreciated by a perusal of new conference rulings adopted in the next two or three years. It was quite clear that there was to be no further development, no pioneering, in the rules of business conduct especially as applied to particular industries. The conference procedure had for the time being lost its momentum; the advent of the NRA meant a further eclipse. With the demise of the latter, however, industry was again dependent upon the Commission for such aid as it might receive in regulation of trade practices. The conference procedure took on new life. From June 1935 to June 1940 rules were promulgated for some 49 industries. This recent period saw several innovations in the character and form of the rules, which it is the purpose of the remainder of this chapter to investigate.

The Group I rules in recent conferences show a high degree of uniformity.[10] There are a series of rules, of a fairly standard

---

[10] For recent rules quoted in the remainder of the chapter see the latest pamphlet of the Federal Trade Commission, *Trade Practice Conferences*, 1940, *passim*.

nature prohibiting practices used "with the tendency, capacity or effect of misleading or deceiving purchasers or prospective purchasers." These include such practices as the use of bogus independents, selling goods as close-outs when such is not the case for the purpose of inducing purchasers to believe they are receiving bargains, concealment of material facts, failure to brand or identify goods, defamation of competitors or the false disparagement of their goods, false or deceptive marking or branding, practices causing an invoice statement to be a false record, misrepresenting the character of a business, substitution of products different from samples or representations made in securing sale without the consent of purchasers, the use of the word "free" where not properly qualified when the article is in fact not free, etc.

The prohibitions of these and similar practices have in general been qualified as was noted by confining the restriction to cases where the practice is used "with the tendency, capacity or effect of misleading or deceiving purchasers or prospective purchasers." It is noticeable, however, that in the rules promulgated as a result of the conferences [11] held since the amendment of section 5 in March 1938, this clause has been omitted with reference to such practices as defamation, false or deceptive marking or branding, making of false or deceptive statements or representations, and the misrepresentation of the character of a business. This change in wording coincident with the change in the law suggests that the Commission now feels that such false and deceptive practices are in and of themselves unlawful quite independent of any specific showing of their tendency or effect in influencing purchasers.

Another series of practices, prohibited by numerous conferences in a rather standard form, concerns practices which unduly interfere with or injure competitors or tend to monopoly.

[11] E.g., in the case of the fur, macaroni, oleomargarine, paint brush, silk, and wholesale jewelry industries.

For example, consignment selling is prohibited in several of the recent conferences when used:

. . . for the purpose and with the effect of artificially clogging trade outlets and unduly restricting competitors' use of said trade outlets. . . .

. . . or with such purpose to entirely close said trade outlets to such competitors so as to substantially lessen competition or tend to create a monopoly or unreasonably to restrain trade.

On the other hand consignment selling is expressly permitted when pursued

. . . in good faith, and without artificial interference with competitor's use of the usual channels of distribution in such manner as thereby to suppress competition or restrain trade.

The inclusion of this carefully worded rule in recent conferences suggests a willingness on the part of the Commission to extend the scope of Group I rules to include practices which in general have not been previously included while restricting the rules to cases clearly violative of the anti-trust laws. Consignment selling has frequently been the concern of industrial groups. On the one side are those who believed it to be a legitimate method of business, on the other are those who believed it to be clearly capable of stifling trade. The rule in the form as recently promulgated undertakes to state those conditions under which the use of the practice may violate the law. While this does not represent any change of the law, it does nevertheless represent a new statement by the Commission of its opinion concerning the applicability of the law to a specific practice. This type of procedure may go far toward extending the concept of unfair competition as well as clarifying its meaning, a process in which many have hoped that the Commission might take a more active part.

Another practice, which is of considerable interest, is the

selling of goods below cost. The customary rule as promulgated after recent conferences is as follows:

The practice of selling industry products below the seller's cost, with the intent and with the effect of injuring a competitor and where the effect may be substantially to lessen competition or tend to create a monopoly or unreasonably restrain trade, is an unfair trade practice; all elements recognized by good accounting practice as proper elements of such cost shall be included in determining cost under this rule.

This rule then establishes three conditions necessary for the prohibition of sales below cost: first, an *intent* to injure a competitor; second, an *effect* of injuring a competitor; third, an effect of lessening competition substantially or a tendency to create a monopoly or to restrain trade. These prerequisites, of course, limit significantly the prohibitions of the rule. It is also significant that the meaning of cost is left to "good accounting practice," but it is insisted in several of the recent rules that these must be the actual costs of the seller, and not some average cost for the industry determined by an industry cost survey.[12] Another interesting rule which has been included in some recent conferences concerns loss leaders. This rule takes one of two forms. The earlier rules read:

The practice of using any product of the industry as a "loss leader" to induce the purchase of other merchandise, the sale of which merchandise is used to recoup the loss sustained on the "loss leader" product so sold, with the tendency or capacity to mislead or deceive purchasers or prospective purchasers and which unfairly diverts trade from or otherwise injures competitors, is an unfair trade practice.

This rule, then, establishes as conditions of illegality that there be a tendency or capacity to mislead or deceive purchasers and that there be an injury of competitors, as by an unfair diversion of trade. More recent rules have deleted this last condition.

---

[12] *Cf.* rules for the marking devices and tuna industries.

Thus, the use of the loss leader with the tendency or capacity to mislead or deceive purchasers is itself prohibited without any necessary showing of injury of competitors. This change has been made since the Wheeler-Lea amendments to section 5 of the Federal Trade Commission Act.

Price discrimination is forbidden in the rules for most industries. In the rules of recent years the prohibitions follow closely the phraseology of section 2 of the Clayton Act as amended by the Robinson-Patman Act.[13] The rules generally include the Robinson-Patman provisions concerning brokerage, advertising or promotional allowances, discriminatory services and facilities. In including these, however, the Commission generally inserted a note to the effect that the paragraph on price discrimination should not be interpreted as embracing the paragraphs on brokerage, etc. This is merely an affirmation of the Commission's opinion that the defenses of the paragraph on price discrimination concerning a lessening of competition are inapplicable to the paragraphs on brokerage, reciprocal purchases, and special services.[14] In several of the recent conferences, rules have been adopted preventing discriminatory returns. The rule prevents discriminating between customers who buy goods for resale, by extending privileges with respect to the return of merchandise to one which are not accorded to all customer-purchasers on proportionally equal terms. This presumably represents an extension of section 2(e) of the Clayton Act as amended prohibiting the discrimination in favor of one purchaser by offering services or privileges not accorded to all purchasers on proportionally equal terms. This interpretation should go far toward eliminating unequal treatment of customers in the matter of returns. It does not deal with an equally significant aspect of returns, i.e. unjustifiable returns which are essentially a wasteful selling method.

[13] *Cf. supra*, p. 143.
[14] *Cf. supra*, pp. 152–53.

These and others having to do with tying arrangements, suppressing of competition, unlawful interference with a competitor's purchase of raw materials, etc. are the more general rules included in Group I. They include many having to do with misrepresentation and deception of purchasers. In some of the more recent rules in this class no showing need be made of injury to competitors. Perhaps the most significant innovation by the Commission with respect to this type of rule has been the prohibition of the loss leader where it is likely to deceive purchasers. Another general class of rules includes those tending to injure competitors, restrain trade, or foster monopoly. With respect to this class the most significant innovations by the Commission lie in its careful statements of the conditions under which selling below cost or selling upon consignment become illegal, and its interpretation of section 2(e) of the Clayton Act to prohibit granting the privilege of returning merchandise to those buying for resale upon other than proportionally equal terms.

In addition to these more or less frequent and standardized Group I rules, there are a large number of rules applicable to specific industries. For the most part these deal with misrepresentation in the peculiar forms in which it arises in specific industries. But in the matter of misrepresentation the recent conferences have taken two interesting steps, first in setting up positive standards for the marking, branding, or advertising of goods and second in declaring the failure to identify products or to disclose material facts to be unfair practices. Positive standards for the identification of products have been established in several industries but with particular thoroughness in the textile industries where rules for the identification of fibre have been developed. Thus, silk and silk noil are defined. Deceptive concealment or the sale of such products under any deceptive or misleading conditions is forbidden. The terms "pure silk," "all silk," etc. may not be used where the material contains any metallic weighting or any other loading materials except dyeing or finishing materials not to exceed 10 per cent or in the case of black 15 per cent by weight. Full and non-deceptive disclosure of the presence of weighting materials together with the percentage thereof is required "in labels, tags or brands attached to the merchandise and in the invoices and in whatever advertising matter, sales promotional descriptions or representations may be used." Such disclosure as to weighting is to "be made plainly and unequivocally, also in immediate conjunction with such representations of content as are used, and shall not be set forth in such manner as to be misleadingly or deceptively minimized, obscured, remotely placed or rendered inconspicuous. . . ." Moreover, all mixed goods are to be marked "by accurately designating and naming each constituent fibre thereof in the order of its predominance by weight, beginning with the largest single constituent. . . ." These are only some of the rules promulgated as a result of the conference of the silk industry.

The rayon industry adopted definitions and established rules for the identification of goods produced thereof. Rules were also adopted for usage of words "pre-shrunk," etc. in the cotton yard goods industry. The tomato paste manufacturing industry established certain minimum contents of tomato solids for tomato paste and heavy tomato paste and declared it to be unfair to fail to disclose the use of artificial coloring in the manufacture of paste. The fur industry condemned deceptive concealment of the true name or nature of the fur, failure to disclose tipping, blending, painting or dyeing of furs, and failure to disclose that garments are made of pieces, tails, or paws.

Rules of similar nature applicable to specific circumstances have been adopted with increasing frequency by recent conferences. This suggests a broadening of the field for Commission action. Whereas in the past the Commission has been confined largely to prevention of positive misrepresentation and the misuse of terms with commonly accepted meanings, the Commission is now giving meaning to terms, thereby establishing standards for the measuring of the truthfulness or falsity of representations; and moreover, it is now maintaining that the mere failure to disclose certain material facts may be unlawful. If these powers are upheld by the courts, we may expect to see a very considerable expansion of the Commission's activities in the way of increasing the knowledge of consumers and protecting their interests.

A brief examination of Group II rules adopted by recent conferences will serve to show practices the violation of which the Commission is not willing to prosecute as unfair methods of competition but which are nevertheless "considered to be conducive to sound business methods" and are "to be encouraged and promoted individually or through voluntary coöperation exercised in accordance with existing law." A rule incorporated by several recent conferences urges that lawful contracts should be performed in letter and spirit and condemns the repudiation of contracts by sellers on a rising market or by buyers on a declining market. Another recommends that disputes between members of the industry and their customers be handled in a fair and reasonable manner and that every effort be made by disputants themselves to compose their differences, failing which it is recommended that disputes be submitted to arbitration. Several industries condemn shipping on consignment goods which have not been previously ordered. This is more sweeping than consignment rules in Group I, which are confined to consignment selling which restrains trade unduly. Others include a rule which disapproves granting the privilege of returning merchandise, *without just cause*, since this "creates waste and loss, increases the cost of doing business to the detriment of both the industry and the public." This is likewise broader than the Group I rule concerning merchandise returns which, as was seen, simply condemns granting the privilege of returns on unproportional terms. Another rule recommends that each member should independently keep proper and accurate records for determining his cost. Still another recommends that each member of the industry publish independently and circulate to the purchasing trade his own price lists fully setting forth his terms of sale. The house dress and wash frock industry recommends that the public be informed on the tag or label of any garment if the fabric may be damaged by certain deodorants or depilatories The rayon and silk industries, each of which provides in Group I rules for the disclosure of the constituents of mixed goods, recommend in Group II that the percentage of each constituent fibres be fully and accurately disclosed. The silk industry further recommends that on tags, labels, and advertisements accurate information be given as to the proper treatment, care, and cleaning of products in order that consumers may enjoy the full benefit of the desirable qualities and services of the products.

A careful analysis of these and other Group II rules suggests that their general purpose and effect would be either to increase the knowledge of products and market conditions, or to reduce wastes by appropriate allocation of risks of business enterprise. That some of the rules, such as those on cost accounting or publication of prices, might in connection with other practices be used to reduce competition or restrain trade is true. But of themselves, they appear for the most part to be directed toward reducing irrational elements in our system or reducing wastes incident to competition. Only where it appears that the other conditions of the industry are favorable to the control of competition is it likely that these rules would have any effect of that sort.

What can be said concerning the achievements and possibilities of the trade practice conference? It is clearly one way to educate competitors quickly and without the conflict incident to litigation concerning the law of trade practices. It is also a more effective and more equitable method for proceeding in the first instance when an unlawful method has become rife in an industry. It may also prove a cheaper method than litigation for eliminating widespread unfair methods. But has the conference added anything more, has it added anything to a clearer or broader interpretation of the concept of unfair trade methods?

It is significant in itself that many practices which have long been clearly illegal have been codified. The conference rules represent a specific list of unfair practices, stated as clearly and precisely as seems possible. Such a list may go far toward satisfying the demands of those who ask that the prohibitions of our trade laws be itemized. More than this, many rules, especially those dealing with misrepresentation in its manifold forms, have been written to apply to the special circumstances of particular industries. This in itself should make the meaning of the law clearer to the interested parties.

But it appears that the achievements may be more far reaching. Tentative steps have been made which offer real potentialities for the future. In the first place, the Commission has recently added to the list of unfair practices selling on consignment where it restrains trade and accepting the return of merchandise on an unproportional basis. These rules represent the extension of the general provisions of the law to new and significant practices. The same may be said of the recent rule with respect to the use of the loss leader where it has a tendency to mislead or deceive purchasers. In accepting these rules the Commission has given new and significant meaning to the generalities of section 5 of the Federal Trade Commission Act and section 2 of the Clayton Act. Finally, acting under the recent amendments to the Federal Trade Commission Act the Commission has begun the task of setting up positive standards of conduct, especially with respect to the use of technical terms and the identification of the character of industry products, which should go far toward reducing confusion and ignorance on the part of intermediate and final buyers. Previously the Commission's activities had been of a negative sort, preventing positive misstatement or misrepresentation where there were accepted standards. Where industrial usage of technical terms was unstandardized or where confusion might be engendered by the mere failure to disclose material facts, the Commission was either powerless or uninclined to act. The recent amendments have apparently opened up new and wide vistas. So far as standards of industrial terminology are necessary the trade practice conference would seem to offer an excellent vehicle for their formulation. The conference rules also offer an opportunity for detailed specification of that sort of information so material to buyers that the failure to disclose it must tend to deceive. If the courts sustain the Commission in the interpretation of the law which is implied in the latter's recent innovations, the trade practice conference should enter upon an era of increasing usefulness. It is not impossible that Group I rules should be extended to cover new practices such as open-price announcements, block-booking, and standardization of credit terms as study determines the type of rule which is desirable in various circumstances.

CHAPTER XIV

INDUSTRIAL SELF–GOVERNMENT: HARBINGERS OF NRA

TRADITIONAL policy with reference to industrial organizations has been based on the assumption that the maintenance of freedom of competition for business rivals will best promote the public welfare, a freedom limited only by restrictions upon the right to exclude others by predatory practices and upon the right to limit competition by voluntary agreement. All coöperation of rival business organizations has not been forbidden, but coöperative efforts to control directly the important variables of price, output, and investment have been consistently prohibited. The anti-trust laws and the trade practice laws do not recognize "ruinous" competition or "excessive" competition as conditions warranting exceptions to the restrictive policy with reference to loose associations.

There was, however, a growing feeling in many quarters long before 1933 that the traditional policy was inadequate. Competition carried to a certain degree was believed to be wasteful, ruinous, and conducive to business instability. The potentialities of coöperative activities by industrial groups were stressed increasingly. The possibility that industry might organize to establish a scheme of self-government and thereby reduce wastes and business instability was envisaged. Voluntary coöperation on a democratic basis it was believed might supersede the unrestricted and ruinous rivalry of the market place.

As General Johnson has noted, the NRA was not "an afterthought or an unexpected brain-storm conceived in the confusion of early 1933." [1] The movements which culminated in

[1] H. S. Johnson, *The Blue Eagle from Egg to Earth* (Garden City, New York: Doubleday, Doran & Co., 1935), p. 157.

the trade practice provisions of the NRA had roots in the pre-war period. One may question the soundness of the scheme. One may even question whether those responsible for writing and passing the act and those appointed to administer it had at the beginning more than the vaguest ideas as to the objectives of its trade practice provisions or the scope of the activities which they might cover. There was surely no general consensus as to the proper scope of the trade practice provisions of the codes. However, one must agree with General Johnson that the record was full of suggestions. An investigation of the proposals culminating in the NRA indicates the forces pressing to expand the ideas of fair and unfair competition.

Suggestions premonitory of the NRA trade practice rules for the regulation of competition may be traced to five different, although not entirely independent, sources. They are: first, the philosophy of the "New Competition" and the correlative trade association movement; second, the proposals to modify the anti-trust laws; third, proposals to give definite recognition to the trade practice conference procedure of the Federal Trade Commission; fourth, the literature on economic planning which came from several sources and was becoming increasingly voluminous by 1932; fifth, our experience with industrial coöperation during the war. These various lines of thought began to converge during the deflation phase of the cycle and the idea of industrial rehabilitation by the coöperative efforts of business, labor, and government emerged.

TRADE ASSOCIATIONS

The trade association is not a new thing in business organization. The mid-nineteenth century saw the formation of associations much like the present trade associations in several lines of industry.[2] Some were preludes to closer associations par-

[2] J. H. Clapham, *An Economic History of Modern Britain* (Cambridge: University Press, 1930, 1932, 1938, 3 vols.), II, 145–153. U. S. Department

taking of the nature of gentlemen's agreements, pools, or trusts; but informal association of trade competitors for their mutual interest has always been an incident of free private enterprise. However, shortly before the war a new lease of life and a new direction was given to the trade association. A leader in this movement was Arthur Jerome Eddy whose writings were of considerable significance in orienting the movement. In his study of the *Law of Combinations* (1901) one may find symptoms of his discontent with our trust policy. Combinations he considered "the inevitable results of economic conditions." Competition he viewed as "piratical" and "merciless" warfare.[3] With the publication of *The New Competition* in 1912 he put forth some concrete proposals for the coöperation of business by the exchange of statistics, especially price statistics. His principal criticism of the existing competition was that it was based on ignorance. He insisted that *true competition* exists only where there are "two or more competitors, competing under conditions that enable each to know and fairly judge what the others are doing."[4]

The essence of competition lies in the element of *knowledge*, it is real, true, and beneficial in proportion to its *openness* and *frankness*, its *freedom from secrecy and underhand methods*.[5]

Under *false* competition the purchaser has every advantage over bidders in the dark; under *suppressed* competition the bidders in combination have every advantage over the purchaser who is in the dark; under *true* competition both deal frankly in the open on a footing of equality.[6]

---

of Commerce, *Trade Associations Activities* (Washington: Government Printing Office, 1923), pp. 303–307.

[3] A. J. Eddy, *The Law of Combinations* (Chicago: Callaghan and Co., 1901, 2 vols.), II, 1335.

[4] A. J. Eddy, *The New Competition* (New York: D. Appleton and Co., 1912 ed.), p. 82.

[5] *Loc. cit.* The italics are in the original.

[6] *Ibid.*, p. 90.

Rivalry — competition in its broadest significance — is the *earnest,
intelligent, friendly striving* of man with man to attain results *beneficial to both*; it is neither relentless nor indifferent; it is neither vicious nor vindictive, it is not inconsiderate, nor is it wholly
selfish; it is not mechanical, but human, and should be therefore,
sympathetic.[7]

The open price policy is the kernel of Eddy's substantive
suggestions. It is based on the proposition that *"Knowledge
regarding bids and prices actually made is all that is necessary
to keep prices at reasonably stable and normal levels."* [8] His
plan provided for filing with the secretary of the association all
inquiries, bids, and contracts. Information contained in the
record of inquiries was not to be exchanged. The secretary was,
however, to interchange all bids as received. But no bidder was
to be bound even morally to adhere to his bid. After ascertaining the bids of others each was to be at liberty to lower his own
bid in order to secure the work provided that he immediately
filed notice of all changes. Nevertheless, Eddy clearly envisaged
a situation where "the man who tries to change his bid will be
looked upon by the customer as on a par with the second-hand
clothes dealer." [9] Finally, the filing of the contract when closed
would enable all other bidders to compare the contract with the
bid of the man who took it. With such a system of open-bidding
Eddy believed there would develop an automatic tendency for
prices to approach a normal level.[10]

Another matter subsequently associated with secret bidding
in many of the NRA codes also attracted the attention of Eddy
in 1912, namely the problem of selling below cost.[11] In a chap-

[7] *Ibid.*, p. 18.
[8] *Ibid.*, p. 121.
[9] *Ibid.*, p. 133.
[10] *Ibid.*, p. 145.
[11] NRA, Division of Review, *Price Filing under NRA Codes* (Work
Materials No. 76), p. 187 *et seq.* It is interesting to note that at this early
date (1912) the mechanism of price-filing and the practice of selling below
cost were associated by the leading exponent of the former.

ter entitled "What Is a Fair Price?" he concluded that prices should cover legitimate cost plus at least some profit. Noting the variations in output of manufacturers with overhead costs he concluded that *"prices should vary with cost and thus ordinarily be higher when the output is low, and vice versa."* [12] The losses due to competition which does not recognize this proposition "are all borne by the community the same as losses by fires"; [13] and the community, Eddy contended, should take as much care to prevent the consequent business failures as it does to prevent fires.

In the post-war period the trade association movement took on increasing significance. It was actively supported by Herbert Hoover and the Department of Commerce. Secretary Hoover's defense of the trade association movement rested on two arguments: first, that it tended to promote the elimination of waste and the achievement of efficiency; second, that it contributed to business stability.[14] The collection and dissemination of data on prices, costs, and production he considered of prime importance in the promotion of business stability. In his introduction to the Department's study of trade association activities, Mr. Hoover recognized explicitly the idea of "rightful coöperation":

The growing complexity of our industrial life, its shift of objective and service, requires the determination of an economic system based upon a proper sense of rightful coöperation, maintenance of long-view competition, individual initiative, business stability, and public interest.[15]

The problem of promoting coöperative action by trade associations Secretary Hoover believed to be primarily the problem of small business.

[12] Eddy, *The New Competition*, p. 246. Italics are in the original.
[13] *Ibid.*, p. 254.
[14] U. S. Department of Commerce, *Trade Association Activities* (1923), pp. 1–8.
[15] *Ibid.*, p. 8.

At a meeting of the Academy of Political Science in 1926 two aspects of the trade association were stressed. Wilson Compton emphasized the difference between ignorant and well informed competition and suggested that this difference "may easily, in practice, become the difference between fair, free and equal competition and unfair, restricted and unequal competition." [16] At the same meeting G. H. Montague hailed the trade association as making possible the stabilization of business by adjusting production to market conditions.[17]

E. H. Naylor writing in the early post-war period reiterated many of the ideas of Eddy, particularly the proposal for open-prices and open-bids.[18] He put much emphasis on the desirability of the knowledge of costs. The trade association he envisaged as a help and necessity for the attainment of the "fair price." It "acts as a stabilizer of the market and naturally tends to prudent and equitable procedure." [19] F. D. Jones writing in 1922 stressed the wastes of competition due to unnecessary duplication of plant, excess capacity, instability of production, unnecessarily large stocks due to the absence of fixed standards, and the duplication of selling efforts and advertising.[20] In considering the ways in which a trade association might remedy this situation he emphasized the dissemination of statistics concerning capacity, current supply and demand, prices, costs, wages, waste, and inventories. He clearly envisaged the stabilization of price as "the natural result of an increased liquidity of the supply and its more sensitive reaction to demand." [21] His exposition of the function of the trade association is closely akin to that of Herbert Hoover. E. L. Heermance suggested that the efforts of trade associations should not

---

[16] *Proceedings*, XI (1926), 586.

[17] *Ibid.*, pp. 579 *et seq.*

[18] E. H. Naylor, *Trade Associations* (New York: Ronald Press, 1921).

[19] *Ibid.*, p. 282.

[20] F. D. Jones, *Trade Association Activities and the Law* (New York: McGraw-Hill, 1922), pp. 30–31.   [21] *Ibid.*, p. 55.

be devoted to price control but rather to production control. He believed that the problem of budgeting which was applied to the firm could be extended to the industry. Market forecasts, production and inventory statistics should be circulated by the trade association, and each individual firm might be expected to regulate its output by consideration of its normal share of the market.[22]

The culmination of the pre-NRA thought on the potentialities of trade associations may be found in the writings of Benjamin A. Javits, especially in his *Business and the Public Interest* [23] (1932), and in the Swope Plan expounded in 1931 by Gerard Swope, President of the General Electric Company.[24] But the proposals made by these two men mark the point of convergence of the trade association movement with the idea of economic planning and with the proposals for modification of our anti-trust policy.

MODIFICATION OF ANTI–TRUST POLICY

In considering the movement for the modification of our trust policy, a distinction should be made between proposals for change in administrative machinery and proposals for change in substantive policy. The former were concerned mostly with the designation of some administrative body which would pass in advance upon proposed mergers or coöperative activities. Their emphasis was upon the uncertainty of the law. Attention in this study is focused upon the proposals for change in substantive policy. With respect to such proposals a fundamental distinction may be noted between the pre-war and post-war agitation. The pre-war proposals seem to have

[22] E. L. Heermance, *Can Business Govern Itself?* (New York: Harper & Brothers, 1933).

[23] B. A. Javits, *Business and the Public Interest* (New York: The Macmillan Co., 1932).

[24] J. G. Frederick, editor, *The Swope Plan* (New York: The Business Bourse, 1931).

been motivated by a fear that a stringent anti-trust policy would militate against the economies of large-scale production. The explicit recognition of the rule of reason in the oil and tobacco decisions in 1911 marked the beginning of the subsidence of this fear. In the post-war period the agitation was for the liberalizing of the restrictions with respect to agreements and the looser forms of combination. It was generally believed that the courts dealt more harshly with these looser combinations.[25] At the same time there was a growing feeling that such agreements would be desirable. On the one hand, it was argued that unorganized industry was at a distinct disadvantage as compared with highly integrated industry in its attempts to avoid the risks of business enterprise. On the other, such highly competitive industries were described as ruinously competitive and conducive to business instability. Professor A. R. Burns has recently indicated the widespread nature of the attempts of various industries to set up informal controls by sharing the market, price leadership, and other means.[26]

As early as 1926 and again in 1928 R. C. Butler in papers before the Academy of Political Science urged recognition of the fact that certain agreements among trade competitors might be legitimate.[27] In 1927 F. H. Levy urged upon the Commerce Committee of the American Bar Association an amendment to permit "reasonable" coöperation and a consideration of producer and worker interests in the results of the competitive process as well as consumer interests.[28] The year 1930 saw a

[25] M. W. Watkins, *Industrial Combinations and Public Policy* (Boston: Houghton Mifflin Co., 1927), p. 257; National Industrial Conference Board, *Mergers and the Law* (New York: 1929), p. 149; J. A. McLaughlin, *Cases on the Federal Anti-Trust Laws of the United States*, p. 374 note.

[26] *The Decline of Competition*, passim.

[27] *Proceedings*, XI (1926), 655; XIII (1928), 156.

[28] *Amendments to the U. S. Anti-Trust Laws*, an address before the Commerce Committee of the American Bar Association, March 23, 1927 (printed in pamphlet form).

renewal of interest in the modification of our trust policy. G. A. Fernley, the secretary of a national trade association, in a paper read before the American Academy of Political and Social Science advocated the permitting of reasonable agreements for the correction of harmful conditions.[29] F. H. Levy at the same meeting urged that public policy should not prevent coöperation to diminish or avert ruinous competition and demoralization of particular industries.[30] At a later meeting of the Academy in May, Benjamin Javits presented a paper which is significant because of its candid defense of profit as the motive for business association and his insistence on the importance of agreements upon price, quotas, territories, and terms of sale for the success of coöperative agreements aimed at stabilization. Profits, he urged, are a prerequisite for stabilization of employment, and elimination of unemployment, yet the law prevents businessmen from working together by agreement to make profits.[31]

Mr. C. W. Dunn in a series of lectures at Columbia University in the same year (1930) proposed modifying our anti-trust laws by the proviso: "It shall be lawful to take any business or trade action the purpose and effect of which shall be to promote constructive competition." [32] Such a proviso, he believed, "would not disturb the prohibition of the act against actual undue restraint of trade." [33]

The American Bar Association and the Chamber of Commerce of the United States likewise presented proposals for modification of our anti-trust policy. While the proposals of

[29] "Special Privilege under our Federal Anti-Trust Laws," *Annals*, CXLVII (1930), 38–39.

[30] "A Contrast between the Anti-Trust Laws of Foreign Countries and of the United States," *ibid.*, pp. 135–37.

[31] "The Anti-Trust Laws," *Annals*, CXLIX (1930), 130.

[32] *The Federal Anti-Trust Law* (New York: Columbia University Press, 1930), p. 16.

[33] *Ibid.*, p. 15.

the Bar Association were, at first glance, only of an administrative type, proposing a commission to approve such contracts in commerce as were submitted to it, there is reason to believe that the proposals were intended to change the criteria so as to allow agreements formerly considered in restraint of trade.[34] In the fourth revised draft of its proposed amendments [35] the provision is made that before rendering its decision, the Commission shall inquire "as to whether or not the performance of such contracts so *lessens competition as not to be in the public interest*, or tends to create a monopoly." [36] The proposals of the Committee on Continuity and Employment of the Chamber of Commerce of the United States were of a similar nature. It proposed the approval by some governmental authority of contracts between industrialists "for the purpose of equalizing production to consumption and so carrying on business on a sound basis," provided that such agreements are in the public interest.[37]

The National Association of Manufacturers added its weight to the movement for modification.[38] In fact its resolutions pointed definitely in the direction of the NRA. While endorsing the objectives of the anti-trust laws in the prevention of private monopoly, oppression of competition, and unfair trade practices, it claimed that the prohibition of coöperative agreements led to an inequality of privilege of producers with consumers in determining the economic levels of price and production. This, the Association asserted, was the cause of social and industrial maladjustment.

Since the producing functions of labor and capital must supply the ability to consume, it follows that protection of pay rolls and investments is the imperative condition precedent to the preservation

[34] J. D. Clark, *op. cit.*, p. 289.

[35] Reprinted in B. A. Javits, *Business and the Public Interest*, pp. 259–262.   [36] *Ibid.*, p. 260. The italics are not in the original.

[37] Reprinted, *ibid.*, p. 262.

[38] Reprinted in the *Annals of the American Academy of Political and Social Science*, CLXV (1933), 83.

of mass purchasing power, to the permanent supply of consumer needs and to the maintenance of the essential source of all taxing power.[39]

Thus, we see in these resolutions the convergence of certain purchasing power doctrines with the proposals for modification of the trust laws. The resolutions called for a Congressional investigation of our trust policy and the enactment of such legislation as might be necessary to permit voluntary agreements between sellers for certain itemized purposes. Its second proposal was that pending the determination of permanent legislation, emergency legislation should be enacted providing temporary relief under the supervision of the Federal Trade Commission. These resolutions clearly presaged the NRA. In connection with this second proposal concerning emergency legislation note should be made of the suggestion of the Attorney General in his *Annual Report* for 1932 that Congress should give "sympathetic consideration" to some measure of relief from the anti-trust laws which might be adopted as a temporary expedient without involving any permanent departure from our traditional policy.[40]

In December 1931 a symposium was held at Columbia University on the subject of our anti-trust laws.[41] At this time Walton H. Hamilton pointed to the possibility of fixing the plane of competition. "Devices must be invented to take up the shock of competition." [42] He also recognized the possibility of contriving for some industries a control from within by the use of such institutions as trade associations, the Chamber of Commerce, trade unions, and coöperatives. Most significant, perhaps, as a commentary on the philosophy underlying the

[39] *Loc. cit.*

[40] *Annual Report of the Attorney General*, 1932, pp. 4–5.

[41] Milton Handler, editor, *The Federal Anti-Trust Laws* (Chicago: Commerce Clearing House, 1932). Another forum was held at New York University in the same year at which several of the same people spoke. See the *Report of the First Session of the National Conference on the Relation of Law and Business*, A. Reppy, director (New York: 1931).

[42] Handler, *op. cit.*, p. 11.

movement for modification of our trust policy was his recognition of the demand of property for its measure of security.[43] As will be suggested in other places this desire of property for security, which takes the form in Javits' argument of a defense of profits and in others of the idea of a fair price, has been a significant force in forming the opinion of the business and legal communities on these matters of competitive practices. It is only in the light of such ideas that much of the movement for the NRA can be understood.

Walker D. Hines, using the cotton textile industry as illustrative, proposed that agreements be made in over-extended industries under the auspices of the trade associations for the purpose of keeping production in balance with demand.[44] M. W. Watkins in the same symposium proposed a tripartite co-operative control of industry by consumer, labor, and capital interests through a reorganized and expanded Federal Trade Commission. As part of his scheme he envisaged industry-wide trade associations, constituted in accordance with statutory standards.

Such associations would be empowered to negotiate, subject to . . . approval . . . , rules of commercial practice, standardized credit terms, standardized grades and specifications of products and even production programs and price policies with other associations representing their trade customers or with coöperative organizations of consumers. . . .[45]

In an address before the American Hardware Manufacturers' Association in October 1931, J. H. Williams urged the legalization of reasonable price and production agreements and the prohibition of selling below cost.[46] At the same time C. R.

[43] *Ibid.*, p. 13.
[44] *Ibid.*, pp. 76 *et seq.*
[45] *Ibid.*, p. 123.
[46] J. H. Williams, *A Cure for Our Sherman Act Troubles*, an address before the American Hardware Manufacturers' Association, October of 1931 (printed in pamphlet form).

Stevenson, a member of an engineering and trade association management firm and later responsible for the management of 19 code authorities,[47] was urging a revision of our laws so as to allow voluntary agreements upon the initiative of 75 or 80 per cent of the members of a trade; the provisions of these agreements were to be binding upon all minorities. These proposed agreements might control production, allocate quotas, or determine fair prices. A "fair price" he considered as one which represented the average normal cost to the industry plus a profit which allowed a return of 10 per cent on capital invested.[48]

It was proposed by Alexander Levene that while the anti-trust laws should be retained, voluntary agreements in violation thereof should be permitted when approved by some appropriate regulatory commission. He believed "ruinous price competition" to be the besetting evil of competition. With this eliminated and upon the establishment by Congress of some machinery to prevent profiteering, "the constructive ability of American Trade will create efficient planning." [49] "Trade without further help will do its planning and coördination, and without the incubus of price competition, will assure to all producers a fair compensation for the capital, time, effort and ability employed by them and a fair uniform cost of the goods consumed by them." [50] Again there is the expressed desire to consider the interests of the producer and the worker as well as the consumer, a desire to be fair to all.

Finally, in an address before the American Bar Association in April of 1932 G. H. Montague made several proposals simi-

[47] NRA, Division of Review, *Minimum Price Regulation under Codes of Fair Competition* (Work Materials No. 56), p. 17.

[48] C. R. Stevenson, *The Way Out* (New York: Private printing, 1931), p. 33.

[49] Alexander Levene, *Does Trade Need Anti-Trust Laws?* (New York: Long & Smith, Inc., 1931), p. 126.

[50] *Ibid.*, p. 133.

lar to those of the National Association of Manufacturers calling for temporary modification of the trust laws in the existing emergency under supervision of the Federal Trade Commission. The substantive change in policy involved in his proposed bill is contained in the following section:

Nothing contained in the anti-trust acts shall be construed as declaring to be illegal an agreement among competitors in commerce regulating competition between them to the extent reasonably needed to prevent destructive competition or wastage of materials or to restore a reasonable balance between production, distribution, and consumption: *Provided*, That the purpose or effect of such agreement shall not be to monopolize . . . the commerce of anyone who is not a party to such agreement. . . .[51]

TRADE PRACTICE CONFERENCES

The third precedent for NRA was the trade practice conference sponsored by the Federal Trade Commission and the agitation for statutory legalization of the procedure subsequent to the revision of the conference rules by the Commission in 1931. The nature and history of the trade practice conference has been discussed in Chapter XIII. As was stated there, in 1930 the Commission undertook a revision and standardization of the conference rules because it feared that some of them contravened the anti-trust laws.

After the revision of the rules by the Commission in 1930 there was considerable agitation in favor of giving this procedure a more definite legal status. This movement took form in the bills introduced in Congress by Senator Nye.[52] These bills seem to have had three distinct purposes. First, to give definite legal status to the conference procedure, thus setting

[51] Reprinted in Subcommittee of Senate Committee on the Judiciary, *Hearings on Amendment of Federal Trade Commission Act and Establishment of a Federal Trade Court* (1932), p. 274.

[52] 71st Cong., 3d Sess., S. 6249; 72d Cong., 1st Sess., S. 2626 and S. 2628; 73d Cong., 1st Sess., S. 14 and S. 15.

at rest the fears of the Commission concerning the propriety of its action. Second, to make the practices approved by the Commission enforceable, i.e. to apply sanctions by declaring it to be an unfair method of competition for a firm to violate any rule adopted at a trade-practice conference by the industry of which he is a member. The unenforceability of the Group II rules had long been considered a weakness of the Commission's work. It is important to note, however, that the proposals implied an intention to make the rules enforceable against all members of an industry whether or not they attended the conference and approved the rules. It was proposed, as later under the NRA, that the "destructive" activities of small minorities should not be countenanced. It proposed rule of the industry by a majority or "representative" group. A third purpose of this movement seems to have been a modification of our trust policy. Among the numerous criteria enumerated to delineate the scope of the agreements which the Commission might approve were the following:

Establishment of any business practice which will tend to keep the channels of commerce free from the use of unfair methods of competition, unreasonable restraints of trade, or monopoly in the particular trade or industry or which would have a tendency to remove incentive from members to enter into unreasonable mergers therein. Establishment or discontinuance of any business conduct or practice which would, in the judgment of the Commission, tend to promote the public interest and the use of fair methods of competition.[53]

It may be presumed that the proponents of these provisions hoped thereby to modify the traditional legal concepts concerning agreements in restraint of trade by permitting a wider range of agreements as "reasonable." It was surely hoped that agreements to abide by Group II rules, which the Commission

[53] Senate Committee on the Judiciary, *Hearings on Amendment of Federal Trade Commission Act and Establishment of a Federal Trade Court* (1932), p. 1.

had consistently refused to recognize as legally binding, would be legalized and enforced as "reasonable" and "in the public interest."

Senator Nye was also sponsor for a bill to make it an unfair method of competition to sell below cost:

> To sell or offer to sell, as a trade incentive or for the purpose of injuring a competitor, any article or commodity at or below his cost price, such cost price to be determined in accordance with the best accounting practice in the trade or business or in accordance with any basis or method prescribed by the Commission.[54]

Exception was made for sales below cost upon a final closing out of business and such sales "made in good faith which in the judgment of the commission were justified by extraordinary temporary circumstances." These proposals, quite generally approved by the witnesses before the Senate subcommittee, definitely foreshadowed much of what was most controversial in the NRA.

PLANNING

A fourth source of thought from which the proponents of NRA drew inspiration was the growing literature on economic planning. The literature had originally been of socialist origin. The Soviet Five-Year Plan was attracting considerable attention. Stuart Chase,[55] Charles Beard,[56] and Jay Franklin[57] were presenting the outlines of plans. The *New Republic* sponsored a study of planning.[58] The slogan of planning, however,

---

[54] *Ibid.*, p. 4.

[55] Stuart Chase, "Harnessing the Wild Horses of Industry," *Atlantic Monthly*, CXLVII (1931), 776–787. "A Ten Year Plan for America," *Harper's Magazine*, CLXIII (1931), 1–10.

[56] C. A. Beard, "A 'Five-Year Plan' for America," *Forum*, LXXXVI (1931), 1–11.

[57] Jay Franklin, "U. S., Incorporated," *Forum*, LXXXVI (1931), 65–73.

[58] *Long Range Planning*, by J. M. Clark, J. R. Smith, E. S. Smith, and

was not confined to personages of such "advanced" attitudes. Dean Donham of the Harvard Graduate School of Business Administration was propounding the idea of planning.[59] Wide interest in planning was evidenced by the meetings of the American Academy of Political and Social Science in 1932.[60] The Swope Plan was offered in an address by Mr. Gerard Swope of the General Electric Company in September 1931.[61] Benjamin Javits proposed a scheme for industrial planning through trade association agreements.[62] Moreover, interest in planning had been sufficient to inspire the introduction of bills in Congress. In 1931 Senator LaFollette sponsored a bill for the establishment of a National Economic Council; [63] hearings on the bill were held by the Senate.[64] This and other similar bills were introduced in the next session of Congress.[65] Another bill evidently modeled on the Swope Plan was introduced in the House.[66] The idea of planning had caught the imagination of widely different groups. It had become a symbol, a symbol of the way out.

From among these plans two may be singled out for detailed comment because they mark the convergence of the idea of planning with the idea of industrial agreements sponsored by trade associations after a modification, if not suspension, of our trust laws. They also mark the convergence of the idea of industrial agreements with purchasing power theories of

George Soule. Published as a separate supplement to the *New Republic*, LXIX (January 13, 1932).

[59] W. B. Donham, *Business Adrift* (New York: Whittlesey House, McGraw-Hill, 1931).

[60] *Annals*, CLXII (1932).

[61] Frederick, *The Swope Plan.*

[62] Javits, *Business and the Public Interest.*

[63] 71st Cong., 3d Sess., S. 6215.

[64] Subcommittee of the Senate Committee on Manufactures, *Hearings on a Bill to Establish a National Economic Council* (1931), 2 parts.

[65] 72d Cong., 1st Sess., H. R. 8933, H. R. 9315, S. 2390.

[66] 72d Cong., 1st Sess., H. R. 7448.

the cycle and with certain proposals concerning labor policies. It was just such a synthesis, or one might say compromise, which formed the basis of the NRA.

The provisions of the Swope Plan fell into two main groups: those providing for stability of business through the control of trade practices and those providing for the security of the workers through the provision for workmen's compensation, life, and disability insurance, a pension scheme, and unemployment insurance, all to be administered by the boards of administration of the individual trade associations. It is with the control of trade practices that we are interested. The plan proposed the formation of trade associations under the supervision of the Federal Trade Commission by all industrial and commercial companies which were doing an interstate business and had fifty or more employees. The possible activities of these associations may be indicated by the words of Mr. Swope:

These trade associations may outline trade practices, business ethics, methods of standard accounting and cost practice, standard forms of balance sheet and earnings statement, etc., and may collect and distribute information on volume of business transacted, inventories of merchandise on hand, simplification and standardization of products, stabilization of prices, and all matters which may arise from time to time relating to the growth and development of industry and commerce in order to promote stabilization of employment and give the best service to the public.[67]

The object, stabilization of business, was clear. The ways and means which Mr. Swope envisaged as necessary to the end were not so clearly indicated. On those matters of special pertinence to this study he was very vague.

Mr. Javits was much more candid in outlining the philosophical implications of his suggestions and the ways and means

---

[67] Reproduced by permission from *The Swope Plan* by Gerard Swope, edited by J. George Frederick (now re-issued as *Readings in Economic Planning*, Business Bourse, New York), p. 25.

necessary to the attainment of his objectives.[68] His starting point was the argument that the keeping of business *profitable* was a necessity since the operation of business at a deficit injures the public in various ways:

The discouragement of new enterprise in necessary industries; the out and out loss of capital through waste; the loss of efficiency inevitably consequent upon such a state of affairs; the possible desertion of these industries by the capital now employed therein in search of more profitable fields of industrial endeavor, with the attendant deprivation of the public and unstabilization of labor conditions, and the tendency to destroy competition; the loss of purchasing power and the consequent economic depression.[69]

He later concluded:

We have seen that at present the bulk of American business is not earning profits but operating at an actual loss; that the courts recognize and protect profits and that even legislatures have done so. I have indicated that profits beyond wages of management, rent and earnings on capital are not only legally defensible but are essential prerequisites of prosperity.[70]

His plan involved the forming of voluntary trade associations. No coercion was to be exercised to induce people to join or remain in the trade association, but during the period of membership the association was to have substantial regulatory power over the business practices of any members. He proposed that the associations should undertake such diverse activities as adopting uniform accounting systems, formulating joint research and standardization programs, provision of a welfare fund to improve the conditions of labor and regularize em-

[68] The following exposition is based on his book *Business and the Public Interest* (1932). These ideas are in line with suggestions made in May 1930 before the American Academy of Political and Social Science. *Cf. supra*, p. 291.

[69] From B. A. Javits, *Business and the Public Interest*, p. 24. By permission of The Macmillan Company, publishers.

[70] *Ibid.*, p. 31.

ployment, enforcement of proper trade practices, and prevention of sales below cost.

There is evidence, however, to sustain the belief that Javits' principal concern was the establishing of the rule prohibiting sales below cost. He painted a glowing picture of the benefits of such a rule, suggesting that it would compel a firm to compete by reducing costs so that the association would be essentially a combination in restraint of waste and efficiency.[71] It is significant to note that in computing cost it was Javits' intention that "interest on investment — or possibly on valuation" should be included.[72]

Upon the question of overproduction Javits seemed to take two positions. At one point he suggested that the dissemination of information regarding inventories, rate of operation, etc. would be effective in correcting the situation.[73] At another point, after presenting the interesting thesis that overproduction is in restraint of trade since it results in unemployment and social instability, he argued for agreements to shut down part of the plant capacity and for the allocation of quotas.[74]

This plan of Benjamin Javits is the most complete and candid exposition of the argument for industrial self-government which the writer has found.

INDUSTRIAL COÖPERATION DURING THE WAR

The fifth and last source of inspiration for the NRA is to be found in our war experience. It is generally believed that during the war the enforcement of the anti-trust laws was suspended. The government encouraged the organization of business competitors in trade associations since such units were more convenient to deal with in attempting to put into effect its program. Coöperation, even planning of a sort, marked the activities of the War Industries Board. This experience has

[71] *Ibid.*, p. 55.
[72] *Ibid.*, p. 137.

[73] *Ibid.*, p. 58.
[74] *Ibid.*, pp. 66–67.

often been cited as an indication of what coöperation in industry could do. The increase in production during the war is pointed to as an example. The depression was characterized as an emergency far more serious than war. Without stopping to contrast the differences in other economic forces as between the two periods, it was suggested that a great coöperative effort of industry acting under a suspension of the anti-trust laws would do the trick. It is significant that Mr. Bernard Baruch, Chairman of the War Industries Board, was active in formulating preliminary drafts of the NRA [75] and that his wartime aide, General Johnson, was appointed its administrator.

CONCLUSION

There were numerous movements emanating from various sources, but each calling for some change in our policy of control of industrial organizations. Each program had its own objectives and its own proposals. Most of them emphasized the need for some elements of coöperation in place of unrestrained competition. Most proposed to allow certain reasonable agreements among trade competitors which were presumed to be contrary to existing law. The purpose of this coöperation and the scope of these agreements were various. Some emphasized the possibilities of eliminating waste and inefficiency. Others were concerned with eliminating ignorance and promoting knowledge as a step in the direction of establishing fair and intelligent competition or for promoting stability. Most proposals stressed the possibilities of fostering stability without, however, considering what stability might mean. Several sought means to avoid the dangers of ruinous or destructive competition. Others proposed to promote constructive competition or equal competition. Several were concerned to prohibit or limit selling below cost, others to establish fair prices. Some proposed to regulate production either by preventing

[75] Johnson, *The Blue Eagle from Egg to Earth*, pp. 113–114.

overproduction or by balancing (or equalizing) production and consumption. Some candidly proposed to protect profits or the rights of property. Finally, the notion became current that the public interest was something different than consumer interest; accordingly it was proposed to control industry with an eye to the interest of the producer and the worker as well as that of the consumer.

We may hazard one or two explanations of this growing interest in such proposals. Many industries in which there was a high concentration of market control or in which there were a few dominant firms had established certain informal controls over competition, especially over price competition. In some instances these controls had been extended to production and sharing of the market.[76] These controls, of necessity incomplete, were subjected to considerable pressure in the face of a prolonged depression.[77] More effective controls, backed by either industrial or governmental sanctions, were sought. Other industries which were highly competitive had long felt that the controls which were open to these highly concentrated industries were unjustly denied to them. Their large numbers and intense rivalries and in many cases the ease of entry to the industry made the establishment of such controls by informal means impossible, while the rigorous interpretation of the Sherman Act with respect to loose combinations prevented formal agreements. The severe recession intensified the drive for relief. These various proposals were aimed more or less directly at some sort of market control, i.e. control of price or production, by action undertaken through individual industries or groups of firms acting as a unit. Those proposals having to do with eliminating waste and inefficiency and with eliminating ignorance and promoting knowledge may appear to be excep-

[76] Burns, *op. cit.*, chaps. I–V.
[77] Witness the allegations of "price shadings" on steel products. *Ibid.*, pp. 80–81.

tions to this thesis. However, the business man's interpretation of eliminating waste often turns out to be a desire to control "product" competition, i.e. competition in service or terms of sale. And much of the movement for the promotion of knowledge may be fairly interpreted as a desire to use knowledge so as to remove incentives to price cutting and to maintain prices at some level above marginal cost. The writer should not be understood as claiming that there are not wastes and inefficiencies of an economic sort, or that there is not uneconomic production based on ignorance, or that discrimination will not be minimized by publicity. There are uneconomic practices of such sorts which warrant the attention of public policy. However, the record indicates that the elimination of these abuses played little part in the proposals.

CHAPTER XV

NRA. I: PASSAGE OF THE ACT AND PURPOSES OF THE CODES

PASSAGE OF THE NATIONAL INDUSTRIAL RECOVERY ACT

PRESIDENT ROOSEVELT in his message to Congress urging the passage of the National Industrial Recovery Act requested the provision of machinery "for a great coöperative movement throughout all industry in order to obtain wide reëmployment, to shorten the working week, to pay a decent wage for the shorter week, and to prevent unfair competition and disastrous overproduction."[1] The whole emphasis of his short message seemed to be on the side of relief and recovery. He recognized the necessity for making the movement a widespread movement since "such action increases costs and thus permits cutthroat under-selling by selfish competitors." The meaning of a "decent wage" was not amplified, although in his statement upon the signing of the bill the President made it clear that he believed that "no business which depends for existence on paying less than living wages to its workers has any right to continue in this country."[2] He made it clear, also, that by a living wage he meant a wage more than sufficient to cover the bare necessaries of subsistence. The scope of the concept "unfair competition" was not indicated. His reference to "disastrous overproduction" was likewise unamplified. Concerning the anti-trust laws he stated in his message that they should be

---

[1] Message to Congress, May 17, 1933. Reprinted in *A Handbook of NRA: Laws, Regulations, Codes* (Washington: Federal Codes, Inc., 1933), p. 1.

[2] Statement by the President on signing the act, published as Bulletin No. 1 by the National Recovery Administration and reprinted in *A Handbook of NRA*, pp. 27–31.

maintained so far as they were designed to outlaw "monopolistic price fixing" and "the old evils of unfair competition." "But the public interest will be served if, with the authority and under the guidance of Government, private industries are permitted to make agreements and codes insuring fair competition." [3] In this the President was proposing a reorientation of our public policy. The codes were not only to prevent unfair competition but to permit agreements insuring fair competition. We shall recur to the implications of this shift of interest from preventing unfair competition to promoting fair competition. Concerning the relation of the anti-trust laws and price fixing, the President stated when signing the act that "the anti-trust laws still stand firmly against monopolies that restrain trade and price fixing which allows inordinate profits or unfairly high prices." [4] This apparently implied, however, that price fixing of some sort would be permissible.

The Congressional hearings and debates add little to an understanding of the philosophy motivating the authors [5] of the bill or of Congressional intent in its passage. With one or two exceptions Senator Wagner and Donald Richberg were the only ones among those who testified before the Senate and House committees to discuss at all the proper scope of the codes of fair competition. One cannot read the hearings without concluding that the principal interest of both centered in the labor provisions. Thus, Mr. Richberg testified "I have felt,

[3] *A Handbook of NRA*, p. 1.

[4] *Ibid.*, p. 29.

[5] According to Mr. Richberg the President appointed a committee of seven to be charged with the writing of a single brief bill. The Committee included Secretary Perkins, Assistant Secretary Tugwell, Assistant Secretary Dickinson, Director of the Budget Douglas, Senator Wagner, and Donald Richberg. After preliminary sessions the first three mentioned ceased active work. D. R. Richberg, *The Rainbow* (Garden City, N. Y.: Doubleday, Doran, 1936), p. 107. For a more detailed statement of the various groups contributing to the drafting of proposals leading up to the bill as finally passed, *cf.* Roos, *op. cit.*, chap. II.

as I said, that the primary unfair competition from which we are suffering here was the unfair competition in the use of labor. I have been peculiarly interested in those clauses of the bill designed to protect labor, to insure the setting of fair standards of work." [6] It is not necessary to illustrate further the preoccupation of many sponsors of the bill with wages, hours of work, and the sweatshop.[7] Our primary interest is in what the sponsors intended in the way of fair and unfair trade practices. Upon what else besides labor practices were the industries to agree?

Senator Connally bluntly asked Mr. Richberg "What is fair competition?" The latter's reply was noticeable for what it did not say. Except to say that custom or common acceptation may determine what is fair and that the exploitation of labor is unfair, he cited only the hackneyed illustration of local price cutting as an unfair practice. In his previous testimony before the House Committee on Ways and Means, Mr. Richberg had painted a picture of trade associations which had enlarged their vision and were desirous of setting up standards of conduct necessary for the common welfare. The effectiveness of such agreements, he pointed out, would be dependent upon the power of someone to force "recalcitrant minorities" into line.[8] But the necessity of any rules beyond certain labor provisions and the already recognized law of unfair competition was not argued.

Senator Wagner emphasized that by passage of the bill "Competition is not abolished; it is only made rational. . . . Com-

---

[6] House Committee on Ways and Means, *Hearings on H. R. 5664, 73d Cong., 1st Sess., National Industrial Recovery* (hereafter cited as House, *Hearings on NRA*), p. 70. *Cf.* also p. 69. Likewise Senate Committee on Finance, *Hearings on S. 1712 and H. R. 5755, 73d Cong., 1st Sess., National Industrial Recovery* (hereafter cited as Senate, *Hearings on NRA*), p. 23.

[7] See statement by Senator Wagner, *ibid.*, pp. 19, 286, 287.

[8] House, *Hearings on NRA*, p. 70.

petition is limited to legitimate and honorable bids for the market and real gains in technical efficiency." [9] His interest in efficiency as the determining factor in business success was recurrent [10] and significant as pointing toward a criterion for code writing of economic import. In discussing the possible scope of the fair trade rules which might be embodied in the codes, he suggested that they might "include devices such as exchange of information, coöperative marketing, simplification of style, standardization of products, and many other features." [11] Those activities enumerated included many which were generally sponsored by existing trade associations and which were legal under existing law. When pressed for an opinion as to whether price fixing would be allowed, he replied "I doubt whether price fixing is going to be a part of that. That is a matter of administration." [12] Mr. Douglas, Director of the Budget, in his testimony before the House committee discounted the idea that it was the intention of the bill to level out natural advantages due to locality, geography, climate, or natural resources. "It is not the purpose of this act to perpetuate a portion of an industry or an industry that should not survive." [13]

Only one witness before the Congressional committees gave some hint as to what he thought might be the interest of industry in the formation of codes of fair competition. Mr. H. I. Harriman, President of the Chamber of Commerce of the United States, expressed the opinion that "the time has come when we should ease up on these laws [the anti-trust laws]

---

[9] Senate, *Hearings on NRA*, p. 2.

[10] House, *Hearings on NRA*, p. 96. *Cf.* also *Congressional Record*, LXVII (1933), 5235.

[11] Senate, *Hearings on NRA*, p. 2. *Cf.* also *Congressional Record*, LXXVII (1933), 5153.

[12] Senate, *Hearings on NRA*, pp. 18–19. *Cf. post*, pp. 312–13, for his remarks on this point on the floor of the Senate.

[13] House, *Hearings on NRA*, p. 16.

and, under proper governmental supervision, allow manufacturers and people in trade to agree among themselves on these basic conditions of a fair price for the commodity, a fair wage, and a fair dividend." [14] He alone suggested the objective of protecting dividends. This trinity of "a fair price, a fair wage, and a fair dividend," which was seen in the preceding chapter to figure in the minds of many of the sponsors of the trade association movement, played a considerable part in many of the subsequent discussions concerning policy under the NRA.

The Congressional debates shed but little more light upon the matter. Representative Doughton, who guided the bill in the House, explained that it guaranteed "equal opportunity to those supplying the jobs, in that the Government will coöperate with industry in maintaining standards of competition in keeping with equity and justice. . . . It sets up flexible machinery which the President may use to prevent monopoly on the one hand and ruinous competition on the other." [15] Senator Wagner reiterated the position which he had taken before the Congressional committees.[16] Senator Borah, however, attacked the bill because it contained no indication of what constituted fair competition. "There is no rule laid down. Anything is fair competition which industry agrees upon and can get approved . . . it furnishes no rule even for the guidance of the President. . . ." [17]

Not only was the debate unilluminating on the general scope of the proposed rules of fair competition, but it was equally vague on those matters of detail to which attention was given. The only significant debate on details concerned price fixing, the prohibition of selling below cost, and the abrogation of the anti-trust laws.

[14] *Ibid.*, p. 134.
[15] *Congressional Record*, LXXVII (1933), 4202.
[16] *Ibid.*, pp. 5153, 5235.   [17] *Ibid.*, p. 5166.

There was a quite general agreement that the bill would make it possible to place some limitation upon freedom of competition in price. Several members of the House expressed the view that the principal objectives of the bill would be destroyed if it were enacted without granting some power over business pricing policies.[18] Control of production was likewise indicated as a probable measure. "The four essentials in any code of fair competition are price, production, wages and hours. . . . There must be agreement as to minimum price. . . . The price must be fair in that it includes a just return to the producer. . . . The code must contain agreement as to production. We are undertaking to establish a balance between production and consumption." [19] The bill was envisaged as a great potential aid to small enterprise and a deterrent to merger and consolidation.[20]

In the course of the debate Senator Wagner insisted on distinguishing price fixing and limiting sales below cost. He contended that "No such thing is contemplated as the fixation of prices," but he added "All that will be provided is that there shall not be any sale at a price below the cost of production." [21] He then explained this policy of selling below cost as one indulged in temporarily by a large firm for the purpose of destroying a small competitor. He indicated no recognition of the problems in defining cost nor of the doctrine generally accepted by economists that the sale of a product at something over variable costs but below total costs may be compatible with the continuation of competition and furthermore may be conducive to an optimum use of our resources. In subsequent debate Senator Wagner put the emphasis on price stability. "Price stability, as distinguished from monopolistic price fixing, is a

---

[18] *Ibid.*, p. 4206.
[19] *Ibid.*, p. 4218.
[20] *Ibid.*, p. 4219.
[21] *Ibid.*, p. 5238. Reiterated, *ibid.*, p. 5245.

universally recognized necessity in order to achieve economic welfare." [22] The general confusion as to the intentions of the sponsors of the bill is well indicated by Senator Reed, who was a member of the Senate Committee on Finance to which the bill had been referred, in his description of the discussion concerning sales below cost.

We spent a long time, both in the Finance Committee and in the conference committee, trying to find out just what this proposal was; and it was impossible to get any definite answer from those who were going to be charged with administration of the bill. First they would say generally, "We are going to prevent sales under the cost of production." Then we would say, "Whose cost of production? If Smith and Jones have adjoining factories and one can produce at a lower cost than the other, obviously the one with the low cost can sell at that figure and run the other man clear out of business by underselling him, and the no. 2 man cannot even compete." When presented with that absurdity they said, "No; we do not mean that. We mean the general cost of production of the industry." Then we said, "Do you mean the cost of production of the highest-cost producer? Is his inefficient management to be the standard?" They said, "No; we do not mean that." [23]

In truth Congress had in hand a problem which it clearly did not understand and with which it is poorly equipped to deal. It sensed the dangers and futility of price competition *à outrance* in certain circumstances, and it recognized the potential evils of price fixing. In the end general reliance was placed upon the statement of objectives of the act to serve as guides to the designated administrators.

Upon the question of the suspension of the anti-trust laws debate was precipitated principally by Senator Borah. Senator Wagner had pointed to the failure of the anti-trust laws in their purpose "to prevent excessive concentration of wealth, and to keep intact the social and economic opportunities of small busi-

[22] *Ibid.*, p. 5840.
[23] *Ibid.*, p. 5842.

ness men, laborers, and consumers." [24] On the other hand, he noted the special severity with which the laws obstructed the attempts of small business at coöperative efforts. "The same law prevented smaller business men from coöperating in order to put competition upon a basis of efficiency, and has resulted instead in a destructive cutthroat competition. We frankly propose to suspend the evil features of the antitrust laws without diminishing their capacity to serve useful ends." [25]

Senator Borah, fearing the codes would foster monopolistic practices, introduced an amendment which provided that such codes "shall not permit combinations in restraint of trade, price fixing, or other monopolies [*sic*] purposes." [26] As reported back by the Conference Committee the proviso omitted all reference to price fixing or restraint of trade. It provided that although the Sherman Act should be suspended, the codes "shall not permit monopolies or monopolistic practices." [27] In explanation of this compromise Senator Wagner stated that the only type of price fixing to which any objection had been raised was that which would result in monopoly or monopolistic practices.[28] It is clear from the record that he believed that certain restraints upon competition which would be in harmony with the purposes of the act and would not be monopolistic might nevertheless be regarded by the courts as in restraint of trade. " 'Restraint of trade' really means restraint of competition, one of the things we want to deal with being the subject of competition." [29] Concerning Senator Borah's contentions that any combination in restraint of trade must necessarily be monopolistic, Senator Wagner replied "That all depends. We may provide for some competitive method which, under the decisions of the courts today, may be regarded as in restraint of trade, which would eliminate cutthroat, sweatshop competi-

---

[24] *Ibid.*, p. 5152.
[25] *Ibid.*, p. 5163.
[26] *Ibid.*, p. 5247.

[27] *Ibid.*, p. 5694.
[28] *Ibid.*, p. 5766.
[29] *Ibid.*, p. 5836.

tion, the thing we are after. Under the provision the Senator [Borah] proposed we could not eliminate or destroy cutthroat competition." [30]

It is quite clear that the words "monopoly" and "restraint of trade" were being used variously by the parties to the debate, with meanings which clearly violated the established interpretations of the courts. The proponents of the bill wished to permit agreements which would violate the Sherman Act, yet they would agree to a stipulation that no code provision should permit monopolies or monopolistic practices. The proposal on its face called for a general reorientation of trade practice policy and for a redefinition of words which had acquired meaning at law. Actually, the proposal was a compromise between several schools of thought and conveniently provided phraseology which might be used to urge any of several policies. The seeds were provided for future confusion and controversy in the execution of the act. With an omnibus declaration of policy and provision for broad discretionary delegation of power, the bill as enacted prepared the ground for action. But the conflicts of view, which were submerged in the consideration of the bill and received very imperfect statement in the debates, were potent forces destined to arise again and again to plague the administrators of the act.

Title I of the National Industrial Recovery Act as passed by Congress was largely permissive legislation.[31] Its objectives, as set forth in its declaration of policy, were stated as:

To remove obstructions to the free flow of interstate and foreign commerce which tend to diminish the amount thereof.

To provide for the general welfare by promoting the organization of industry for the purpose of coöperative action among trade groups.

---

[30] *Loc. cit.*

[31] Text of the act printed, Public No. 67, 73d Cong., 1st Sess., Title II was concerned with public works and Title III with certain miscellaneous matters.

To induce and maintain united action of labor and management under adequate governmental sanctions and supervision.

To eliminate unfair competitive practices.

To promote the fullest possible utilization of the present productive capacity of industries.

To avoid undue restriction of production (except as may be temporarily required).

To increase the consumption of industrial and agricultural products by increasing purchasing power.

To reduce and relieve unemployment.

To improve standards of labor.

Otherwise to rehabilitate industry.

To conserve natural resources.

This declaration provides a truly inclusive catalogue of objectives but, because of its very inclusiveness and the conflicts between its various parts, is of little significance as a guide to or as criteria of fair competition.

The act provided for Presidential approval of Codes of Fair Competition presented by trade or industrial associations, provided the terms of the code would "tend to effectuate the policy of this title" and on condition that the association "impose no inequitable restrictions on admission to membership therein and are truly representative of such trades or industries." A further condition was that "such codes are not designed to promote monopolies or to eliminate or oppress small enterprises and will not operate to discriminate against them." The prohibitions against monopolies were reiterated in the proviso "that such . . . codes shall not permit monopolies or monopolistic practices." The President was empowered to impose as a condition of his approval such conditions as might be deemed necessary "for the protection of consumers, competitors, employees, and others, and in the furtherance of the public interest."

All the provisions of such a code were to be the "standards of fair competition" for the trade or industry involved. The violation of any such standard in trade in or affecting interstate or foreign commerce was declared to be an unfair method of competition within the meaning of the Federal Trade Commission Act.

The essential conditions embodied in the statute were simple. Any provision which would tend to effectuate the policy of the title and which did not promote monopoly, permit monopoly or monopolistic practices, eliminate or oppress or discriminate against small industry might be included in a code. Each such provision was declared to be a standard of fair competition; the violation of any rule incorporated in a code was declared to be an unfair method of competition. However, while the essentials of the statute were simple, their interpretation and administration were far from simple. Broad discretionary decisions had to be made in deciding what policies would tend to effectuate the purposes of the act. Moreover, where there was conflict between the various professed purposes, judgment of the importance or primacy of the conflicting interests had to be made. Finally, the definition of monopolistic practices raised serious problems. The history of the NRA is a record of the unsuccessful attempts to meet those problems.[32]

This history of the discussion of a supposedly epoch-making bill stands in striking contrast to the history of the debate and passage of the Federal Trade Commission Act. The objectives of the new act were not carefully defined. The meaning of the crucial provisions was not subjected to critical study nor to

---

[32] In section 4(b) of the act, licensing powers were given to the President for use whenever he should find that "destructive wage or price cutting or other activities contrary to the policy of this title are being practiced." Other provisions of the act empowered the President to enter into voluntary agreements with various industrial or labor organizations in order to effectuate the policy of the title. Section 7(a) declared the right of collective bargaining and required the inclusion of certain conditions regarding collective bargaining in every code. Special provisions were included for the regulation of the oil industry.

much discussion, although there were reiterated in the debates and hearings most of the purposes mentioned in our summary of the precursors of the NRA. Not only were there no well-defined criteria of public policy expressed in the act, but Congress gave no indication in its discussions that it had in mind any particular content to be given to the general phrases incorporated therein. More than this, it is now agreed that there was a conflict of opinion among the sponsors of the act and its administrators as to whether its main purpose was as a measure of recovery or as a measure of industrial reconstruction and reform.[33] Such expressions of intent as have been found show, however, that the National Industrial Recovery Act was clearly inspired by those diverse lines of thought which have been traced in the preceding chapter.

CONTENT OF THE CODES

The significance of the NRA for this study lies in what the episode may have contributed to the development of criteria of fair and unfair competition or of criteria of the public interest in the field of trade practices. It is no intention of the present study to present in detail a classification and analysis of the code provisions even for the regulation of trade practices, much less for the regulation of labor relations. Nor is it intended to discuss the history of the NRA and its effects on recovery and reform, either in particular industries or in industry in general. These various matters have been dealt with so far as the record permits elsewhere.[34] A general working knowledge of the NRA must be assumed of the reader.

[33] Walter Lippmann, *Interpretations 1933–1935* (A. Nevins, ed.; New York: The Macmillan Co., 1936), p. 89, writing in July 1933. Richberg, *op. cit.*, pp. 11 *et seq.* writing in retrospect with the advantage of close administrative experience.

[34] There are several good studies of the NRA. The most comprehensive and readily available study is that of the Brookings Institution, L. S. Lyon, *et al.*, *The National Recovery Administration* (Washington:

The NRA is viewed in this study as the culmination of a movement for the extension of the ideas of fair and unfair competition. One might reasonably hope that this experiment would make some contribution to the definition of the criteria involved. Unfortunately it did not do so. One commentator has remarked that "In testing trade practice provisions criteria of the public interest were abandoned in favor of recovery," [35] while another has noted that the "criteria which the NRA found it necessary to apply in deciding upon trade practice regulations were the criteria of compromise rather than the criteria of judicially considered public interest." [36] The Staff Report of the President's Committee of Industrial Analysis concluded that "The economic guidance offered by NRA experience in the trade practice field is limited by the fact that NRA contributed little in this field toward determination of the ends of public policy. The trade practice programs as a whole were not based upon a well-defined theory of competitive relations." [37] In the early days of code making the trade practice provisions were in large measure the hostages given to industry in return for voluntary acquiescence in the labor provisions of the code. In truth, the experience with NRA is more significant for the

---

1935). There is also the *Report of the President's Committee of Industrial Analysis on the NRA* (Washington: 1937). More valuable than the report itself are the Staff Studies on which this report was based. Of particular interest for this study is Part III of the Staff Studies, *NRA Trade Practice Experience*, by Corwin D. Edwards. These Staff Studies have not been published but are on file at the Commerce Department in Washington. Another copy may be found at the library of the Graduate School of Public Administration, Littauer Center, Harvard University. An interesting chapter on the NRA is to be found in A. R. Burns, *The Decline of Competition*, chap. X. Another study which is valuable on many points is that of C. F. Roos, *NRA Economic Planning*. A study of the trade practice provisions of the codes will be found in C. A. Pearce, *NRA Trade Practice Provisions* (New York: Columbia University Press, 1939).

[35] E. S. Mason, "The National Recovery Administration," *Quarterly Journal of Economics*, XLIX (1935), 671.

[36] Lyon, *et al., op. cit.*, p. 563.   [37] Edwards, *op. cit.*, chap. VII, p. 32.

light which it sheds on the comparative efficacy of the several techniques and devices for dealing with particular problems than for innovation in conscious criteria of industrial control. During the whole life of the NRA there was a continuous struggle to develop criteria of fair competitive practices which would be acceptable to business and to the public at large. Toward the end of the experiment a set of policies began to emerge, but they were surprisingly similar to the old rules of trade as enforced before the advent of the NRA.

The trade practice provisions of the codes present a bewildering array of regulations. Their significance for this study lies in the purpose of these provisions, the motives of those who urged their incorporation in the codes. However, a brief discussion of the content of these provisions is appropriate as a background for the general argument.

The actual provisions may be conveniently classified under eleven heads:

1. Provisions preventing misrepresentation and deception.
2. Provisions establishing or regulating the standards of product and labeling.
3. Provisions regulating the appropriation of a competitor's "property" values (trade-names, trade-marks, or designs).
4. Provisions limiting the use of coercive or predacious devices (tying contracts, threats of litigation, threats to repudiate a contract, interference with a competitor's contractual relations, blacklisting, etc.).
5. Provisions regulating the relation of prices to different customers (especially discrimination).
6. Provisions regulating the geographical structure of prices.
7. Provisions facilitating the market mechanism (open-price and bid-filing systems).
8. Provisions controlling "product" competition by regulation of the ancillary terms and conditions of sale, services rendered, or quality of the product.
9. Provisions regulating the channels of distribution.
10. Provisions controlling price competition.
11. Provisions controlling the capacity or output of an industry.

Such a classification of the trade practice provisions of a particular code or of codes in general, however, is not very illuminating. The provisions falling in any one of these eleven classes were of various sorts. In some cases the approach was negative, i.e. a certain type of behavior was prohibited; the prohibition might extend to all cases, or exceptions might be made either under conditions specified in the code or at the discretion of some duly constituted authority. In other cases the code provisions were of a more positive sort, i.e. they undertook to specify the market practices or behavior to be followed. In so far as this was true, the trade practice provisions of the NRA constituted a distinctly new orientation in our trade practice policy, since as has been noted in previous chapters, the policy of our anti-trust laws has been merely to prevent certain practices while leaving in most cases a considerable latitude to business enterprise as to the alternatives to be adopted.

A third approach of the codes was permissive, i.e. to give to the Code Authority the power to study a problem or to adopt rules for the regulation of certain practices either with or without administrative approval. Illustrative of this approach were many enabling provisions or discretionary rules. For example, more than 130 codes had provisions empowering the Code Authority to undertake subsequent work for the establishment of standards of product and labeling. Most of these provisions, unfortunately, led to no significant results.[38] Some industries were empowered at their discretion to establish a price-filing system, with appropriate details to be established by the Code Authority. Among the discretionary provisions may be grouped many of the price control provisions. In most cases price controls could be instituted only upon a finding of an "emergency,"

---

[38] NRA, Division of Review, *Information Concerning Commodities: Part B, Standards and Labeling* (Work Materials No. 38B. Hereafter cited as *Standards and Labeling*), p. 92.

or of "wilfully destructive price cutting," or of a practice of selling below "cost." It is significant that many of these enabling provisions were never used. This is especially true of provisions incorporated at the instigation of the government for the protection of consumers, such as those establishing product standards or providing for their labeling.

Moreover, to understand the significance of a code provision it is not sufficient to consider the particular provision in isolation. It is a virtue of the treatment of trade practices under the Sherman Act that a practice is considered not in and of itself, but rather in the light of the general market structure in which it is used and of other trade practices characteristic of the industry. It was an unfortunate error of those responsible for the policy of NRA that, at least until late in the days of code revision, attention was too often focused upon a type of code provision as such, rather than upon the significance of the code provision in conjunction with other conditions in a particular market. This is well illustrated by the controversy over the price-filing systems in general and the waiting period in particular. Only late in the history of the NRA was it realized that the question was not whether or not price-filing would promote the public interest but rather under what conditions and in what types of markets price-filing would promote the public interest.

A systematic study of the NRA experience with particular code provisions would demonstrate clearly that a particular trade practice may have as its purpose any of a large number of purposes. Or to reverse the proposition, a particular purpose may be effected by any one of several types of code provision. For example, the establishment of standards of product and labeling had as one of its purposes the protection of consumers by enabling more rational choice. But it had other purposes. It was seen above that in the lead pencil industry an attempt was made to establish standards of product as part of a scheme to protect the four dominant firms of the industry from newly developing price competition. In the fertilizer industry, however, a standardization of product was fostered in order to reduce the number of grades produced, thus reducing costs of production and wastes of excessive inventories.[39] In other codes standards were established for first and second grade products with the hope thereby of preventing discrimination or the evasion of price control features of the codes. The latter seems to have been the motive for standardization provisions in the floor and wall clay and the cordage and twine industries.[40]

Price-filing systems offer another excellent example of a trade device which was put to various uses. The traditional argument for such systems has been the promotion of more accurate knowledge in order to insure rational market adjustments. In particular it has been urged that publicly published prices by which it is either mandatory or customary for a seller to abide would enable sellers to resist the activities of the "lying-buyer." It is frequently argued that such systems will prevent discrimination. This was alleged to be the purpose of the system established by the Sugar Institute.[41] Leading members of the iron and steel industry have in recent years announced a policy of publishing open-price lists to which they will adhere. The reason advanced for this policy was the desire to avoid discrimination and the granting of secret concessions, practices which were revived after the demise of the NRA.[42]

In some industries, open-price provisions seem to have had the effect if not the purpose of disturbing the relative volume positions of rival sellers to the disadvantage of those whose product had less consumer acceptance.[43] This developed be-

[39] NRA, Division of Review, *Standards and Labeling*, p. 79.

[40] *Ibid.*, pp. 35, 46.

[41] 297 U. S. 553.

[42] *New York Times*, March 8 and 11, 1936.

[43] This was true in the coal, business furniture, automobile tire and luggage industries. *Cf.* Edwards, *op. cit.*, chap. II, pp. 52 *et seq.*

cause such sellers customarily depended for the attraction of buyers upon the attractive power of a price below that of their competitors. However, with publicly announced prices from which it was illegal to deviate, the sellers of the product with most consumer acceptance often found it feasible to sell down to the filed price of the lowest priced seller. By doing this they could append a large part of the patronage formerly belonging to the seller of the low priced product. In the corrugated and solid fiber shipping container industry an open-price filing system was used as one element in a scheme for sharing the market. Price-filing in conjunction with the exchange of statistics of production and sales and a gentlemen's agreement to adjust output to demand was intended to distribute the burden of unused capacity among the members of the industry on a "fair" basis.[44]

In some cases it was believed that the principal purpose of price-filing was to reduce the incentive to price cutting, especially that of a temporary sort.[45] By identifying the initiator of a price decline or by removing the advantage of being first in making a price concession, as is true where provision is made for a waiting period, it was hoped to decrease the frequency and the amplitude of price changes. In the fertilizer industry there were special problems. In this industry it had been customary to pay for all purchases at the end of the season and to allow the customer on all his sales the lowest price at which he had bought at any time during the season. Temporary price cuts at the end of the season, in consequence, were very costly. The open-price system was designed to prevent this guarantee against price declines.[46] In some industries the

---

[44] NRA, Division of Review, *Price Filing under NRA Codes* (Work Materials No. 76. Hereafter cited as *Price Filing*), pp. 318–320.

[45] *Ibid.*, pp. 218, 223; NRA, Division of Review, *Fertilizer Industry, Price Filing Study* (Work Materials No. 67), p. 48.

[46] Edwards, *op. cit.*, chap. IV, pp. 11–12.

price-filing system was used to police conformance to other code provisions. Thus, in a code which provided that there should be no selling below cost, the price file might be used by the code authority to challenge members believed to be violating the cost provision.

The many provisions controlling the ancillary terms and conditions of sale had a similar variety of purposes. In many cases they were inspired by a desire to insure that product competition would not develop in an intensified form where price competition had been eliminated. In some instances the standardization or regulation of the terms and conditions of trade seems to have been necessary to make the filed prices intelligible.[47] In other cases the professed purpose was to simplify the problems of business management by reducing the secrecy and confusion in industries where the possible variables were many.[48] In still other industries the purpose seems to have been consciously to affect the competitive positions of rivals in an industry by limiting the range of competitive weapons, thereby favoring those who were best equipped for competition within that range and penalizing those whose best prospects of success lay in the use of the proscribed competitive weapons. Consignment selling, installment selling, or the use of missionary salesmen necessitate financial resources. Code provisions preventing or limiting these practices act as a protection to those whose resources are limited. Finally, in matters such as consignment selling, returned goods, credit terms, and guarantees against price declines the purpose in some cases was to control the incidence of business risk by limiting competition in risk taking.

[47] NRA, Division of Review, *Price Filing*, pp. 2, 230, 231.
[48] Lyon, *et al.*, *op. cit.*, p. 698.

PURPOSES OF CODE PROVISIONS

An analysis of the record of the NRA experience with the trade practice provisions of the codes suggests that these provisions were motivated by one or more of seven purposes.

The promotion of rational consumer choice was one purpose which was frequently urged by the industry groups but proved in practice to be more useful as a means to promote good public relations than as a motive to action. Rational choice was to be achieved by the prohibition of misrepresentation and deception and by rules providing for standardization and labeling. In some instances the rules concerning standardization and labeling were considered useful for establishing norms for the determination of misrepresentation and deception. It was frequently urged that price cutting along with the deterioration of the quality of products had misled the consumer. Thus, one argument for control of standards of product in the macaroni and the mayonnaise industries was to protect the consumer against deception.[49] These are products in which the average consumer finds it very difficult to detect the sale of an inferior product. Quality deterioration which is deceitful or misleading to the consumer must, of course, be distinguished from the sale of inferior products at lower prices under conditions where the consumer makes a free and informed choice.

A second purpose of many of the code provisions was so to control competition as to protect a particular concern from the impact of policies of rivals which were specifically directed at the value of its property rights. This was the type of protection which in general was afforded by the common law of unfair competition. The particular innovation in the NRA episode was the attempt to extend the scope of existing patent and copyright laws to the prohibition for a certain period of time

[49] NRA, Division of Review, *Standards and Labeling*, pp. 19–22.

of design and style piracy.[50] This represented an attempt to create a new property right. For the rest there were a large number of provisions designed to protect going concerns from direct injury by competitors by such means as simulating a competitor's trade-name or trade-mark, interfering with a competitor's contracts or contractual relations, tampering with a competitor's property, and retention or use of a competitor's identified containers.

A third purpose, one which likewise followed in the path of traditional policy, was the protection of business enterprise against certain restrictions upon the freedom of competition. It is not meant that any pretense was made of maintaining complete freedom of competition, whatever that may mean. Rather the aim was to protect enterprise against coercive and predacious devices such as tying and exclusive contracts, blacklisting, boycotts, or collusion with an awarding authority in industries where competition for a contract is done by a system of sealed bids. Such practices had been held illegal in general under the Clayton and Federal Trade Commission Acts, but the tests of monopolization or injury to competition which had been adopted by the courts were stringent. In many cases the code provisions went further in their limitations of a practice than the preceding law. The most significant activity in this line was the attempt of the NRA to limit the use of block-booking in the motion picture industry, a practice which previous law had been unable to restrict.[51]

A fourth purpose, which the record shows was a very minor one, was the elimination of waste. The term "waste" as used by the exponents of industrial self-government is an ambiguous

---

[50] NRA, Division of Review, *Design Piracy — The Problem and Its Treatment under NRA Codes* (Work Materials No. 52). For a summary of the law on design and style piracy *cf.* "Unfair Competition — 1932," *Harvard Law Review*, XLVI (1933), 1197 *et seq.*

[51] NRA, Division of Review, *The Motion Picture Industry* (Work Materials No. 34), pp. 83–97.

one. In some cases it appears that devices designed simply to change the burden of risk or expense as between different groups without minimizing in any way the total burden of the risk or the expenditure of resources have been urged in the name of "eliminating waste." On the other hand, simplification schemes such as those sponsored by the fertilizer industry may decrease total costs and may, therefore, be considered as genuinely reducing waste. This is true, likewise, of provisions concerning the charge for and allowance on containers. Moreover, agreements to make charges for the furnishing of estimates and appraisals or for the furnishing of plans and specifications may, by reallocating the burden of such costs, reduce their aggregate. Likewise, a limitation upon the number of consignment points may serve to check the unnecessary and costly duplication of such points which otherwise would result from the competition of rivals to expand their volume by offering better service.

A fifth purpose was to aid business enterprises in the transaction of their daily business by reducing secrecy and confusion and by simplifying administrative problems in general. Every business enterprise has an interest in knowing the prices of its competitors. Its own administrative problems are simplified if it can be sure that published prices are being observed. This gives business competitors an interest in a system of price publicity. It also gives rise to attempts to foster uniform procedures with respect to the introduction of price changes. It often happens that the buyer and seller alike are less interested in the actual level of prices than in the relation between the prices of sales concluded by different sellers. A seller wishes to be able to meet a rival's prices and asks only that he may know what price it is that he has to meet. Buyers, especially dealers who are buying for resale, wish to know that they are buying at a price which is the same as that which rival dealers are receiving from other sources. This interest in prices extends to an interest in price structures. Buyers are especially interested in the classification of customers and in discount schedules; buyers and sellers alike are interested in the geographical price structure. Finally, there is the problem of the variations in the ancillary terms and conditions of sale such as credit terms, guarantees, discounts, and delivery terms. The very number of these variables in many industries is conducive to secrecy and confusion. By standardizing or publicizing the price and the "bundle of utilities" for which a price is charged, it was hoped thereby to simplify the administrative problems of business and to promote more rational business decisions.

A sixth purpose, which may be inferred from the record (although not expressly stated therein), was to regulate price and production policies so as to control the impact of the competition of rival groups within an industry whose interests or policies were antagonistic or incompatible. This was perhaps the dominating purpose of many codes, though obviously the intentions of the sponsors of these codes were not baldly stated. In the coffee [52] and rubber tire [53] industries an attempt was made in connection with a prohibition of selling below cost to define cost as market or replacement cost. This was intended to remove the advantage of some of the large manufacturers who because of their more adequate financial resources were able to buy supplies at low prices in the fluctuating raw materials markets. In some cases the question was raised as to the fairness of estimating depreciation on the basis of cost when assets had been purchased at a bankruptcy or distress sale.[54] It was argued that the owners of such assets had an unfair advantage and would depress the market unduly.

[52] NRA, Division of Review, *Price Control in the Coffee Industry* (Work Materials No. 55), pp. 23–30.

[53] NRA, Division of Review, *The Rubber Industry Study* (Work Materials No. 41), pp. 102, 130 *et seq.*

[54] NRA, Division of Review, *Minimum Price Regulation* (Work Materials No. 56), pp. 101, 104.

A very frequent objective was the favoring of particular groups in the distributive channels. Price protection in the retail rubber tire industry [55] and the tobacco retailing trade [56] was motivated by fears for the small independent dealers. These latter were frequently specialized dealers in competition with other retailers to whom the particular product was only one among many items. In consequence the latter frequently took less than a "normal" mark-up on the particular item. In several industries the codes provided for protection of wholesalers by prohibiting manufacturers from giving equivalent discounts to others. In the plumbing fixtures industry the provisions were designed to protect legitimate wholesalers against the inroads of mail-order houses.[57] In the lumber and timber industry the problem was that of direct-selling by manufacturers.[58] In other instances the purpose was the protection of elements among the manufacturers which were dependent upon the use of certain channels of trade. For instance, in the lead pencil industry [59] customer classification together with product standardization and minimum pricing was proposed in order to protect the big-four against the newer elements in the trade which were selling to chain and mail-order houses.

Another type of conflict among rival groups arises from differences in the basis of sales appeal. In the cleaning and dyeing industry there was a conflict between the cash-and-carry and the call-and-deliver elements, the former making a price appeal which during the depression proved disastrous to the latter.[60] In other industries factional differences were

[55] NRA, Division of Review, *The Rubber Industry Study*, pp. 145 *et seq.*

[56] NRA, Division of Review, *Minimum Price Regulation*, pp. 92–98.

[57] NRA, Division of Review, *Manufacturers' Control of Distribution* (Work Materials No. 62), p. 62.

[58] *Ibid.*, pp. 57 *et seq.*   [59] *Ibid.*, pp. 27 *et seq.*

[60] NRA, Division of Review, *Minimum Price Regulation*, pp. 33, 57 and 196.

caused by the existence of a significant fringe of small and perhaps temporary "fly-by-night" or "hall-bedroom" competitors. This fringe seems to be an ever present element in some industries, but its effects are particularly noticeable during times of bad trade. Ease of entry due to low investment costs or to easy diversion of unemployed capital equipment generally used elsewhere are characteristics of such situations. Thus, it was stated that in the canvas goods industry the capital required by the handicraft operator was only $52.00, "$50.00 for sewing machines and material, and $2.00 for a marriage license to get a wife to do all the work." [61] This seems to have been also a characteristic of other industries.[62] Finally, in some industries there was a conflict between those firms which were attracted by the long-run advantages of price stability and those interested in the short-run advantages of price changes. The activities of the latter, if unchecked, interfere seriously with the policies of the former. Price leaders in markets characterized by price leadership are especially vulnerable to the activities of "chiselers" since their position as leaders makes retaliation especially dangerous. This conflict between those interested in price stability and those desirous of disposing of their product at any price is especially evident where the by-product of one industry comes into competition with the principal product of another.[63]

The seventh purpose which lay behind many of the controls was the desire to mitigate the impact of competitive forces upon a whole industry or group of allied industries. In part the purpose was simply to redistribute the burden of the depression as between different industries. Certain industries had felt the burden of the price declines more than others, partly because

[61] NRA, Division of Review, *Minimum Price Regulation*, p. 221.

[62] E.g., fur dyeing (*ibid.*, p. 204) and commercial relief printing (*ibid*, p. 214).

[63] Edwards, *op. cit.*, chap. I, pp. 10–11.

of their inability to curtail production in view of the absence or ineffectiveness of formal or informal controls which were in use by other industries. These industries looked with envy upon those which had more effective controls and welcomed the NRA as an opportunity to redress this inequality. But more than this, there was a desire to give security to property, to assure the profitability of existing firms and equipment. Often this objective was imperfectly described as a desire for a "fair" profit or a "fair" return upon investment.

As Mr. Richberg has noted, "It is a curious fact that private price fixing agreements appeal to most of their makers as simply protective measures to which even customers should not object." [64] Thus, at the Open Forum sponsored by NRA in March 1934, one code authority executive claimed that "it is right to get back that which it costs you to produce and distribute that article, plus the little extra." [65] Then there is the case of the small confectioner of New York City with a capital investment of only $10,000 who desired simply to be able to meet his payroll, material costs, taxes and rents and to earn for himself an annual salary of $5000.[66] Vested interests seek security against the risks of industry; they seek to be protected against changes in the general business situation, against the effects of innovation, against their own follies. They seek the preservation of the capitalized values of their concerns. They seek in the face of general business fluctuation or of particular disequilibrium to maintain "normal" price, "normal" market areas, and the "normal" distribution of volume. The responsibility for disturbing these relationships is placed upon the fly-by-night, the less farsighted, the uninformed, the panicky, or the wilfully predatory minorities, i.e. the so-called chiselers.

[64] *The Rainbow*, p. 32.
[65] *United States News*, March 16, 1934, Special Supplement, p. 37.
[66] Roos, *op. cit.*, p. 243.

These are the principal purposes of the code provisions sponsored by the industry representatives. Above all, the codes were intended to control competitive forces within industry groups and between industry groups so as to enable various groups to improve their relative position in the economic order and to decrease their risks. This might be done by limiting the intensity of competition, by changing its form (price, quality, service, or advertising), by reallocating its incidence as between business rivals in the same industry, as between industries, or as between labor, capital and consumers. Other purposes, such as the development of more rational markets, the simplification of business procedures, the reduction of waste, the protection of property values, the elimination of coercive and exclusive policies, are reflected in many code provisions; but, except as they served to further the paramount purposes of enabling an industry or business group to improve its relative position in the economic struggle, they provided little real incentive to action.

CHAPTER XVI

NRA. II: POLICY AND SIGNIFICANCE

IMPLICIT CONCEPTS OF FAIR AND UNFAIR COMPETITION

THERE are several contrasts between the old approach to the regulation of trade practices and that implied in the code provisions. Traditional policy had emphasized the interest of the individual enterprise in the freedom to pursue its own aims. This freedom was limited only at the point where it tended to injure other business rivals by deceit or misrepresentation, or by coercion or exclusion. The interference *by a group* with the freedom of the individual enterprise in the pursuit of its business was considered a restraint of trade and an unfair method of competition. While the traditional policy recognized that there was a legitimate sphere for coöperative action in order to purge industry of fraudulent, misleading, or wasteful practices, it was insisted that such coöperation be reasonable in the sense of being confined to the elimination of clearly recognized abuses. Furthermore, such coöperation was to be entirely voluntary and to eschew any interference with the freedom of the individual enterprise by binding it in advance to a given pattern of behavior. Such a policy offered the greatest possible scope to innovation and experimentation. Another consequence of this policy was a great diversity in pricing policies and other trade practices in any one industry and a frequent change in such practices. The freedom of the individual in determining his trade practices, provided such practices were not clearly unconscionable, was considered paramount to the interests of others, especially business competitors, in these practices.

One contrast of the new policy with the old lay in a shift in emphasis from a set of negative rules to a positive program. Traditional policy revolved around the concept of *unfair competition*. The approach was negative in so far as it was confined to the proscription of certain practices which were assumed to transgress unduly the freedom of others. For the rest, the individual was free in the choice of his practices. In no case, however, might he bind himself to abide by any particular policy with reference to production, price, or the terms of sale. The codes reversed this. They provided a program of *fair competition* by specifying in considerable detail the precise pattern of behavior which competitors were to follow. Any departure from this prescribed behavior was an unfair method of competition.

The traditional policy had been based on the assumption that the public welfare would be best served through the independent action of the individual enterprise. But the NRA reversed this likewise. It gave precedence to the collective action of the group. For the individual to interfere with this group interest or purpose was deemed unfair. The impact of the policies of the individual firm upon the purposes of the group became the dominant consideration. The group through which the NRA operated was, in general, the "industry," i.e. a group with relatively high cross-elasticities of demand. It was the industry's interests and purposes which dominated the code making process in the early days. The industry was conceived to have legitimate interests as against the individual, and it was the purpose of the codes to implement the group in furthering its purposes. The possibility that there might be irreconcilable conflicts of interest or purpose between members of the group or between groups was ignored. The group was interested in the type of competition pursued by the individual, whether in price, in the terms of sale, in the product, or in advertising. It was concerned likewise in the aggressiveness of competition. In the matter of price competition the group was interested as much in the structure of prices and in the way in which price changes were introduced as with their level. The group was interested in the entrance of new firms, the building of new capacity, the introduction of new products or of different grades or qualities of old products.

It should not be supposed that there had merely been a shift from a desire to protect the individual to a desire to protect the industry group. It was a shift in opinion of how best to promote the public welfare. There had been a shift in control from those who believed that the public welfare is best promoted by giving the individual enterprise the maximum freedom to pursue its interests to those believing that industrial groups acting in their own interests, subject only to a minimum of government supervision, might best promote the public welfare. This view lay behind the whole movement for self-government. It represented the inarticulate assumption of the NRA. In testing the code provisions some gestures were made indicating a concern for the public welfare. The connection between price competition and wage-rates was stressed. The social significance of price disparities was urged. The waste of capital resources due to declines in capital value, to the abandonment of enterprises which were in temporary financial difficulties although economically sound from a long run point of view, to the impact of temporary fly-by-night firms on established firms — the consideration of these and many other factors was urged. Moreover, certain of the crude purchasing power theories of recovery gave credence to the view that joint action aimed at increasing prices, wages, and profits might further the public welfare. But while some respectability was sought for code provisions by reference to these broader considerations, fundamentally the real drive behind the code provisions of a particular industry was their relation to the collective interests of the dominant group in the industry, not to the collective interests of some wider public.

IN SEARCH OF POLICY

The history of the NRA is in large measure a history of the struggle to evolve some policy, and in particular some criteria of fair trade practices. It is fair to say that except for the undigested and often conflicting views of the many sponsors of the NRA idea, the Administration began without any consciously formulated policy with respect to trade practices. Although there were some who recognized at an early date the need for thinking out fundamentals in this field, the formulation of such policy was long delayed. Moreover, as policy with respect to certain matters crystallized, it became obvious that there was serious conflict between the content of the codes and the policy later developed. A statement of policy with respect to many practices considered in the writing of the codes was not made; in fact, there is no evidence in the published record of any very serious consideration of policy with respect to several types of code provisions. However, on those matters in which the innovations of the NRA were greatest and around which the controversy turned, such as price-filing, and the control of price, output, capacity, and the ancillary terms or conditions of sale, the development of policy was imperative.

Open-Price Filing. In the matter of price-filing, as in other matters, NRA policy was slow in crystallizing. In urging passage of the act, Senator Wagner had clearly indicated that he thought an exchange of price schedules was one of the things to be encouraged. It was for this reason that he objected to the Borah Amendment concerning restraint of trade.[1] From an early time, however, there seem to have been certain groups within the Administration which looked with suspicion upon

---

[1] *Congressional Record*, LXXVII (1933), 5840. C. F. Roos says that D. I. Podell and M. C. Rorty, both of whom assisted in drafting the NRA, intended to free business from the anti-trust laws to the extent of permitting price-filing (*op. cit.*, p. 279, note 4).

the inclusion of price-filing systems in the codes. The earliest statement of policy was contained in a confidential memorandum of the Policy Board,[2] October 25, 1933. This did not go far, however, toward delineating a consistent philosophy. At the Hearings on Price Changes held by the NRA in January 1934, substantial charges were made that price-filing systems were in many cases being used for purposes of price control by either coercive or collusive methods.[3] After the Hearings, the Administrator directed that all provisions for waiting periods should be suspended in codes approved thereafter on the theory that the waiting period was frequently used for coercion and collusion.[4] Subsequently, studies were undertaken and suggestions made by the Research and Planning Division, the Consumers' Advisory Board, and the newly established Policy Group.

Office Memorandum No. 228 (June 7, 1934) represented the first fruits of this study and criticism.[5] This memorandum declared it to be official policy to permit open-prices by the filing of prices, terms, etc., with a confidential and disinterested agency. Such data were to be relayed immediately upon receipt to all members of the industry and to those customers who should apply and defray the cost thereof. Prices when filed were to be effective immediately upon receipt by the designated agency. This implied a waiting period equal only to the time necessary to notify the agency. It was provided, however, that requests for a longer waiting period in particular industries would be considered on their merits. Once a member had filed a price revision he might not file a higher price within 48 hours. This provision was designed to eliminate "price-raiding." Mem-

---

[2] NRA, Division of Review, *Price Filing*, p. 450.

[3] Senate Committee on Finance, *Hearings Pursuant to S. Res. 79: Investigation of the National Recovery Administration*, Parts 1–6, 1935 (hereafter cited as Senate, *Investigation of NRA*), pp. 351, 923 *et seq.*

[4] NRA, Division of Review, *Price Filing*, p. 454.

[5] For a reprint of this memorandum, *cf.* Senate, *Investigation of NRA*, p. 137.

bers were forbidden to sell on any other terms than those filed. Finally, all attempts to fix or maintain prices by combination or conspiracy, or to coerce or intimidate a member of the industry into changing his price were prohibited. Under this statement of policy the status of price-filing differed from its previous status under the Sherman Act only in that a seller was required to abide by any price filed, while under the Sherman Act any agreement not to depart from a published price was illegal.

Perhaps most significant was the announcement of the purpose of the declared policy as the promotion of a "free and open market."

> The objective is to achieve fair competition, based on knowledge of competitive factors to the fullest extent possible without unduly curtailing private initiative or destroying incentives to any individual legitimately to extend his business.[6]

Price publicity which would promote the establishment of a competitive market similar to that of an organized exchange was the direction toward which NRA policy was working.

Furthermore, the Administration came to the realization that a price-filing system could not be used appropriately in all industries. Those industries where the nature of the product is such as to make identification difficult, where commodities differ widely in character from sale to sale, where market changes usually take the form of non-price competition, where the commodities are highly perishable and supply fluctuates rapidly, or finally, where the number of concerns and products is very large were considered unfavorable for price-filing. Moreover, it was recognized that in some industries "the need is to preserve competition against attack, rather than to foster it" [7] and that in such cases an open-price system is liable to

---

[6] NRA, Division of Review. *Policy Statements Concerning Code Provisions and Related Subjects* (Work Materials No. 20. Hereafter cited as *Policy Statements*), p. 49.

[7] *Ibid.*, p. 51.

serious abuse. In short, the final conclusion of those responsible for policy of the NRA was that open-price filing is appropriate in only a limited number of industries and that where used, the system should be so devised as to promote the objective of publicity and thus to foster a "free," "competitive" market.

It is interesting to speculate on the extent to which price-filing under these conditions is feasible. Clearly those industries in which a product is standardized, where competition centers primarily upon price, and where the number of firms are not too large to make price-filing infeasible or too small to make it unwise must be few. And it is to be questioned whether the incentives of business to adopt it would be great. Stripped of its potentialities to standardize trade practices or to limit price competition, the cost and inconvenience of such a policy might well offset the gains. Moreover, in many industries where there are significant differences in consumer acceptance of rivals' products or where there is a diversity in relative importance and financial strength, it is possible that the price publicity would so seriously upset competitive relations as to make enforcement difficult.

Price Control. A previous chapter indicated the widespread interest of business men in respite from price competition or in some sort of protection of prices from falling below cost. The hearings before Congressional Committees and the debates in Congress indicated that some proponents of the National Industrial Recovery Act, hazy though their ideas were, envisaged the inclusion of such provisions. Industry clearly expected to be allowed to incorporate such provisions in its codes. Although the President warned against the raising of prices as fast and as far as wages, General Johnson made it clear before the end of June 1933 that codes might contain agreements not to sell for less than cost of production.[8] During the first six

[8] Johnson, *op. cit.*, p. 224. NRA, Division of Review, *Minimum Price Regulation*, p. 22.

months of the NRA minimum price provisions and cost protection formulae of numerous sorts were adopted in many
codes.[9] With the gradual development of opposition to the
price provisions within the ranks of the NRA, among members
of Congress, and on the part of the public, the problem of developing a definite policy with respect to pricing practices was
undertaken.

The principal problems revolved around three types of provisions. First, those providing for the fixing of definite minimum prices. Here the questions were under what conditions an
industry should be allowed to fix such minima and what the
criteria for such minima should be. The second type of provision was one setting a lower limit to price by reference to
cost. The problems here were what elements should be included
in cost, whose costs should be used, and what exceptions should
be made. Finally, there was controversy about the code provisions for the installation of uniform cost accounting systems.

From a very early period certain members of the NRA staff
had recognized the need for a general policy with respect to
price and cost accounting provisions.[10] Opposition to such
code provisions was made in part on the basis of principle and
in part on the basis of administrative expediency. In January 1934 some general approval seems to have been given to
a formula which would prevent sales below "lowest reasonable
cost," such cost to be determined by an impartial agency.[11]
This, of course, raised more problems than it settled. The first
open step in retreat is to be found in an NRA Office Memorandum (February 3, 1934), in which the idea of emergency price

[9] *Cf.* G. W. Terborgh, *Price Control Devices in NRA Codes* (Washington: The Brookings Institution, 1934), for a summary of price provisions in
the first 250 codes.

[10] Roos, *op. cit.*, pp. 86–87, 95 *passim*, 244–46, 249–59.

[11] *Ibid.*, pp. 254–58.

regulation was evolved.[12] This was a compromise between those who were asking for broad powers to fix minimum prices and those who would eliminate all such provisions. This memorandum provided that when a code authority should determine that an emergency exists and "that the cause thereof is destructive price-cutting such as to render ineffective or seriously endanger the maintenance of the provisions of this code," the code authority might cause to be determined the "lowest reasonable cost" below which, if it is approved by the Administrator, it should be an unfair method of competition to sell. This statement of policy was intended to limit minimum price provisions to circumstances characterized by emergency, thus acknowledging the undesirability of general minimum price provisions.

Price policy was further delineated in Office Memorandum No. 228, issued June 7, 1934.[13] This was one of the results of the appointment of Dr. L. S. Lyon as Deputy Assistant Administrator for Policy on Trade Practices.[14] In addition to its provisions concerning open-price filing and cost accounting, this memorandum contained important statements of policy on the matters of cost protection formulae and the fixing of minimum prices. It provided that except in cases of a declared emergency, there should be no fixed minimum basis for prices. On the other hand it declared that "Willfully destructive price cutting is an unfair method of competition." It would seem that in the category of destructive price cutting was included price cutting "imperiling small enterprise or tending toward monopoly or the impairment of code wages and working conditions."

In determining whether or not an emergency existed, the Statement directed that the Administrator should consider

---

[12] This memorandum is reproduced in Lyon, et al., op. cit., p. 605; and NRA, Division of Review, Minimum Price Regulation, p. 27.

[13] Reprinted in Senate, Investigation of NRA, pp. 137–40.

[14] Lyon, et al., op. cit., p. 719.

whether there were conditions tending (1) to impair employment or wage scales, (2) to induce especially high mortality of enterprise especially among small firms, (3) to create panic within the industry, or (4) to promote other special conditions which were thought to require stabilization by minimum price control. In the event that an emergency was found to exist the code authority was authorized to cause an investigation of costs and to recommend to the Administrator a stated minimum price which, if approved, should become effective. No criteria were established for determining the minimum price except that it should be "reasonably calculated to mitigate the conditions of such emergency and to effectuate the purpose of the National Industrial Recovery Act." This statement of policy with respect to minimum price fixing and destructive price cutting was controlling at the time that the Supreme Court brought the NRA to a close.[15]

As for policy with respect to the prohibition of sales below cost, the so-called "Substantive Guide" in the NRA Office Manual in May 1935 stated:

> The great majority of cost provisions employed to delimit prices are unwise and unenforceable. In most cases the difficulty is not basically a problem of cost or even of price, but of industrial maladjustment. It rests upon a disparity between the capacity of the industry to produce and of the market to absorb.
> Analysis shows little justification for attempting to secure a simple and continuing relation between the cost and prices. A pegging of prices on the basis of cost can neither establish economic justice nor restore industrial prosperity. For these reasons . . . the use of a cost formula to limit price may be allowed only in the case of loss leaders, natural resource industries, and emergencies. In other instances, the necessity for its use and its practicality must be established beyond reasonable doubt.[16]

[15] Cf. NRA, Division of Review, *Policy Statements*, pp. 52 et seq., 85–86.
[16] *Ibid.*, p. 54.

In short, the Administration had repudiated all direct attempts to fix prices except in certain natural resource industries, in instances of declared emergency, and in the use of loss leaders; [17] and it found the other cost formulae which would limit prices to an individual firm's own cost, except where rivals were selling at lower prices, inexpedient and unenforceable.

In the matter of cost accounting the Administration moved gradually from provisions enabling the code authority to impose mandatory systems embodied in the earlier codes to a policy of encouraging voluntary systems. Office Memorandum No. 228 recognized the desirability of proper cost accounting methods and provided that these might be developed and, after approval by the Administrator, be made generally available to the industry. It likewise recognized that "sound cost estimating methods should be used and that consideration should be given to costs in the determination of pricing policies." But the adoption of suggested methods was to be voluntary and under no condition was the code authority "to suggest uniform additions, percentages or differentials or other uniform items of cost which are designed to bring about arbitrary uniformity of costs or prices." This was essentially the policy incorporated in the Office Manual at the demise of the NRA.[18]

The official policy had, then, moved away from attempts at price control. Natural resource industries were recognized as presenting extenuating circumstances. In general, however,

---

[17] Resale price maintenance was forbidden in the policy statement as it stood in May 1935 (*Ibid.*, p. 55, § 1791.) However, some control in order to limit the use of loss leaders was countenanced experimentally. (*Ibid.*, pp. 53–54, §§ 1770–1772.) For a recommendation by the Assistant Administrator for Policy urging on economic grounds that all prohibitions of loss leaders be eliminated from codes *cf.* Lyon, *et al.*, *op. cit.*, p. 733; H. F. Taggart, *Minimum Prices under the NRA* (Ann Arbor: University of Michigan, School of Business Administration, Bureau of Business Research, 1936), pp. 50–52.

[18] NRA, Division of Review, *Policy Statements*, pp. 54–55, 86. *Cf.* Taggart, *op. cit.*, pp. 457–59.

price control was to be confined to emergency situations where the maintenance of labor standards or the maintenance of the volume of employment were threatened, where an undesirable mortality of small enterprises or monopoly was imminent, or where panic threatened the industry. This was in line with the general assumption of those responsible for policy that the objective should be "the establishment of conditions under which in a free and open market competition may determine a fair price." [19] It is significant that price control for the relief of destructive competition, from which business had hoped for so much, should come to so little. The theory had been that destructive competition was at the root of many of the difficulties, that price control or cost protection would prove a boon to industry and to the general welfare. On this basis the early codes were written, but bit by bit policy was enunciated which pushed back the frontiers of the domain of price controls, so that price fixing and cost protection were recognized for the most part only in "emergency" situations, of which the Administration eventually recognized less than a dozen. Truly this shows an amazing reversal in direction of policy. It was in the control of price competition that reform was sought, but it was just this that the policy makers eventually refused.

Ancillary Terms and Conditions of Sale. NRA policy in the early days seems to have shown itself sympathetic to restriction on the ancillary terms and conditions of sale. In early codes were incorporated innumerable restrictions upon discounts, upon guarantees against price declines, consignment selling, offering of free goods, premiums or other services, etc. But a study of the development of NRA policy indicates a tendency away from such restrictive policies.

Policy statement as it stood at the time when the Supreme

[19] Taggart, *op. cit.*, p. 444.

Court intervened to terminate this experiment held that "The field of merchandising is one which should be invaded hesitantly, if at all, for the purpose of limiting individual practice and initiative." [20] The statements concerning particular practices showed a similar caution. Terms of payment were to be restricted only upon "adequate showing of abuses, or possibility of abuses." [21] The restrictions were to be "reasonable" and "consistent with the custom of the industry." They "must be no more than a maximum," permitting a member of the industry to adopt stricter terms if he desired. Consignment selling was recognized as not inherently bad although possible of abuse if used by "large, well-financed concerns to take customers away from weaker competitors." [22] Moreover, the practice might in a few instances have "unduly burdened the cost of distribution." Restrictions on the period of contracts for future delivery were recognized as "well outside the normal area of code regulation." [23] Uniform sales contracts were "in the shadowland of policy," the burden of proof for the incorporation of such a provision being upon the industry.[24] Trade-in allowances were recognized as a possible source of deception and might constitute a definite unfair trade practice, but "Any casual, unconsidered limitation . . . would offend against the policies respecting price fixing." [25] Any limitation should at most set a maximum. The basis of such limitation should be "a factual showing of the prices of actual sales of such second-hand products in the open market." [26]

Advertising allowances, it was recognized, might breed suspicion, secrecy, confusion, and misrepresentation.[27] The solution lay, however, not in their prohibition since this "would

---

[20] NRA, Division of Review, *Policy Statements*, p. 40, § 1610.
[21] *Ibid.*, § 1611.
[22] *Ibid.*, § 1613.
[23] *Ibid.*, § 1614.
[24] *Ibid.*, p. 41, § 1615.

[25] *Ibid.*, § 1620.
[26] *Ibid.*, p. 42, § 1622.
[27] *Ibid.*, § 1630.

not change the basic facts that sellers must price their goods to buyers and that certain buyers have promotion services which they desire to render and for which the sellers are willing to pay." The remedy proposed was to establish clearly the facts concerning the activities involved and to cause that part of the allowance which is actually a price reduction to appear as such, and cause that "which is actually a payment for service rendered to appear as such with a definite description of the service and with such publicity, where practicable, as will render less likely the payment of more than the competitive worth of the service." [28] Premiums and free-deals, likewise, were not to be prohibited except where used so as to involve commercial bribery, lottery, misrepresentation, fraud, deception, or discrimination.[29] The guarantee of one's product was held to be "at once one of the solidest of sales devices and a grateful protection to the consumer" and was to be limited only where abuse was shown.[30] Finally, guarantees against price declines, it was stated, should be prohibited rarely, exception being made for "an industry where the practice of refraining from guaranteeing against price decline is well established, where it has aroused little or no opposition among customers, and where the business is largely spot." [31]

To summarize the eventual policy of NRA on these matters it may be said that the Administration was in general opposed to entry into the field of limiting the ancillary terms and conditions of trade. Moreover, in those cases where exception might be made, it was opposed to blanket prohibitions and to the fixing of limits which would be more than maximum limits and which would restrict the freedom of the individual firm to im-

[28] *Ibid.*, § 1631. Lyon, *et al.*, *op. cit.*, pp. 700–704, 730.
[29] NRA, Division of Review, *Policy Statements*, pp. 43–44. On the formulation of this policy *cf.* Lyon, *et al.*, *op. cit.*, p. 724.
[30] NRA, Division of Review, *Policy Statements*, p. 46.
[31] *Ibid.*, p. 56.

pose terms and conditions below this maximum. Exception to these rules were to be allowed only where there was proof that the limitation was necessary to prevent deceit, misrepresentation, confusion, discrimination, or abuse of strength. In the case of consignment selling, restrictions might be allowed to prevent burdening the cost of distribution. Guarantees against price declines might be prohibited where the practice of refraining from such guarantees was a well established custom of the trade. The filing of all such ancillary terms and conditions along with price under an open-price system, without any restrictions upon the freedom of the individual firm to vary these terms, was favored as sufficient in most cases for effecting all legitimate aims.

The NRA favored freedom, diversity, and flexibility in these matters of the terms and conditions of sale. Even as it refused ultimately to grant inflexible price controls, so it refused to accede to the demands of industry to standardize these other variables in a transaction. Their standardization or limitation was, of course, a necessary condition for successful control of the intensity and impact of competition. Price control alone would have been inadequate. Price-filing likewise would have been materially facilitated by such standardization. But the doctrine of the free market precluded such restrictions.

Control of Channels of Distribution.   The problem of the control of the channels of distribution was not considered in detail, but the statement that "The field of merchandising is one which should be invaded hesitantly, if at all, for the purpose of limiting individual practice and initiative" [32] was significant of its attitude. Customer classification was declared to be a legitimate activity, but it was not to be used to fix prices, discounts, or differentials, or to establish resale price maintenance. Moreover, such a classification was not to be used so as to interfere

[32] *Ibid.*, p. 40.

with any member of the industry in so far as he sought to classify his own customers in accordance with his own judgment. Furthermore, the codes were not to incorporate provisions which would restrict the sale by manufacturers to certain dealers or forbid the sale to others. "It is not the function of codes to limit the judgment of members of industry as to the persons to whom they should sell." [33] Finally, the Trade Practice Policy Board had recommended that resale price maintenance, which represents a type of control of the distributive channels, should not be sanctioned by the codes,[34] a recommendation which was incorporated in the final Manual of Policy.[35]

Control of Output and Capacity.   Beginning in the spring of 1934 NRA policy turned away from control of output and capacity.[36] In February 1934 limitations of this sort which had been incorporated in the early codes were attacked by the Consumers' Advisory Board in a memorandum to General Johnson.[37] Their propriety was questioned at the meetings of the Conference of Code Authorities and Trade Associations held in Washington on March 5–8, 1934.[38] The Trade Practice Policy Board recommended that it should be contrary to NRA policy to permit the limitation of machine hours or restrictions on new capacity.[39] No declaration of policy, however, was made. At the time when the Supreme Court terminated the NRA, the Office Manual stated that no general policy had been formulated respecting measures designed to control production. It concluded that none of the experimental measures already embodied in the codes had demonstrated a right to permanence.

[33] *Ibid.*, pp. 47, 82.
[34] Lyon, *et al., op. cit.*, p. 729.
[35] NRA, Division of Review, *Policy Statements*, p. 55, § 1791.
[36] Senate, *Investigation of NRA*, p. 941.
[37] Reprinted, *ibid.*, p. 849.
[38] *United States News*, March 16, 1934, Special Supplement.
[39] Lyon, *et al., op. cit.*, p. 732.

It recognized that the best showing for production control can be made for the natural resource industries. "Without any commitment as to policy," the statement continued, "any application for production control must be accompanied by strong factual evidence of the necessity of the limitation." [40] Some indication of the direction which official opinion was taking may be found in the bill which was being considered in Congress in 1935 for the continuation of the NRA at the time of the *Schechter* decision.[41] This proposed to prohibit code provisions providing for price control or production control where they would be "restrictive of fair competition." Exception was made for circumstances in which such controls should be necessary to protect small enterprise, to provide correctives for emergencies and for public utilities and natural resource industries.

APPRAISAL OF SELF–GOVERNMENT IN INDUSTRY

The NRA was the answer to those who had been urging the virtues of coöperation in the place of unlimited competition in the industrial sphere. It was a broad experiment in the practice of industrial self-government, an attempt to apply to economic matters the principles of democracy and representative government. It attempted to establish by voluntary action of industrial groups, functioning through delegated representatives, rules for the conduct of their business affairs, rules of fair trade to circumscribe them in the conduct of their rivalry. In this attempt the interested groups were subjected to the supervision of the government which stood as the guardian of the interest of minority groups and the public at large. This attempt broke down on several bases. The Supreme Court found that the act provided an undue delegation of authority. Even before the *coup de grâce* of the Court, however, the NRA had bogged down due to unwieldy administrative problems and a

---

[40] NRA, Division of Review, *Policy Statements*, p. 44.
[41] 74th Cong., 1st Sess., H. R. 7121.

conflict between its statements of policy as they developed and the desires of industry. But above all the NRA was destined to failure because of certain inherent weaknesses in its logic.

The movement for coöperation and self-government in industry is a response to the increasing risks of modern business. The use of heavy capital investments, the rapidity of technological and organizational innovation, the dangers of shifts in demand due either to changes in the general business situation or in the forces affecting a particular industry, these are factors making for insecurity of capital, labor, and enterprise. The existence for long periods of unutilized capacity of capital and other factors stands as a potential source of danger to the price structure of an industry. Decline in the rate of growth of particular industries, and perhaps of the economy as a whole, accentuates the risks incidental to error in particular commitments of resources quite apart from its effects upon the general level of economic activity.

In these circumstances joint action is urged to control the competitive process, to make it more effective. Traditional policy had been concerned with insuring the preservation of competitive forces by preserving the maximum freedom of individual action. The theory of self-government proposed various limitations upon this competitive process in order to mold it into a more effective instrument. It was proposed to increase the selective nature of the competitive process, thereby insuring survival on the basis of efficiency rather than chance or financial strength. It was proposed to reduce many of the wastes of competition, the wastes of duplicative investment, product differentiation, and advertising. It was proposed to eliminate secrecy and discriminations, and to promote a rational and orderly process of adjustment of economic matters. Finally, it was proposed to limit "cutthroat" competition and to promote economic stability.

Behind this theory of self-government lie two assumptions:

first, that there is sufficient cohesiveness of interest within
the industry to make it a vehicle for joint voluntary action; and
second, that the group interest and the public welfare are compatible. If these assumptions were true, industrial self-government would prove feasible. But the fact that these assumptions
are to such an extent the opposite of the truth complicates
matters enormously.

Consider first the cohesiveness of the group interest. The
first problem raised is a question of defining the industry
group. Generally for practical administrative purposes the
industry is defined in terms of the physical characteristics of
the product. Firms often produce many products, and most
industries produce several products. The usual classifications
are arbitrary. But to be effective for purposes of industrial
control the group must include all those firms the cross-elasticities of demand of which are great, i.e. all those firms which are
such close rivals that the action of one affects significantly the
action of others. Such a test for inclusion in an industry group
makes it possible to classify in different groups producers of
the same physical product which are so separated geographically as to be of little significance to one another. On the other
hand, even though the physical characteristics of the product
may be different, two firms producing products which are close
substitutes may desire to be classified in the same "industry,"
or at least may require careful correlation of policy between the
"industries" in which they are classified. The industry is a
convenient concept, but it has its problems.

Now among rivals within any group there are clearly wide
communities of interest. They have an interest in developing
consumer demand for the product, in limiting the entrance of
new firms, in preventing price from going below a point where
net revenues of the group decline, and in keeping items of cost
as low as possible, whether by affecting the prices of factors
of production or by achieving economies in their use. But

there are equally important, if not more important, conflicts which may make agreement on joint action difficult. There is the conflict between those whose basis of sales appeal is price and those whose basis is service. There are those with a national market and those with a local market. There are those for whom a particular product is their principal source of revenue and those to whom it is merely a by-product in which their interest is subsidiary. There are firms whose interest in a particular market is temporary in contrast to those whose interest is of the long-run. There are high-cost firms and low-cost firms, integrated and non-integrated, unionized and non-unionized. There are optimists and pessimists. And finally, as though these conflicts were not enough, there are the innovators whose every action is upsetting to the *status quo*, whose interest lies in being first and in some way different from the others.

With such conflicts, the problems of voluntarily agreeing upon joint policy are patent. If the decisions of the majority are made binding upon the minorities, the problem may be resolved; but this is accomplished only by curtailing seriously liberty of action in the industrial sphere. Moreover, this places within the hands of a majority the power to create or destroy property values, to decree life or death for rival enterprises. Finally, it makes very important the decision upon the basis of representation. A common characteristic of many industries is the existence of a few large firms together with a fringe of numerous small firms. Proportional representation on the basis of output, sales, etc. places the small firms at the mercy of the large; equal representation places the large at the mercy of the small. Those responsible for public policy in this country have been reluctant in the field of economic life to place these powers in the hands of majorities. The alternatives to majority rule are to compromise the conflicts or to fight them out in the market. Now it is this last which self-government of industry is intended to avoid. But compromise is often difficult to achieve. Inevitably, recourse must often be had either to the arbitrary power of the government or the matter is left undetermined, which is to say to the determination of the market. If the government assumes the responsibility for effecting a compromise of the issue, it must choose between the rival interests or some other interests, and thereby the theory of self-government itself is seriously jeopardized. From such responsibility democratic government shrinks. It is not surprising that during the NRA voluntary action by industrial groups was not easily effected in many circumstances.

The validity of the second assumption is equally open to serious question. There are certain areas within which the interest of the industry group and the public welfare may be coterminous. The elimination of genuine wastes is a case in point. Likewise joint action may so allocate risks as to conduce to a more effective organization of industry. But consider the problem of reducing monopoly power and the effects of monopoly power. Do not the interest of the industry and the welfare of the public conflict at this point? Where there are significant monopoly powers, it is not likely that joint action will be used voluntarily to diminish it. The codes did not attack the fundamental bases of monopoly power where it was most entrenched. The problems of patent control, ownership of raw materials, manufacturers' control over the distributive channels, these controls were not lessened. Nor were those elements which make for price leadership or for restrictive policies in oligopolistic markets weakened. As a matter of fact basing-points and price-filing, both of which may tend to strengthen monopolistic action, were sponsored and made more effective. It is significant, also, that for all the talk about the necessity for price control in order to curb a monopolistic pricing policy aimed at the elimination of competitors, the record of the NRA shows only one unmistakable instance of this policy.[42] One student of the subject has stated that "One who studied the situation could not fail to be impressed by the fact that most of the provisions, with the exception of the 'loss-leader' provisions in the retail codes, were aimed at price cutting by 'little' fellows." [43] Price cutting as promotive of monopoly was not the aim of the price protection features of the codes. The experience with the NRA lends little support to the theory that the expansion of concepts of fair and unfair competition and the regulation of trade practices by voluntary codes offer a feasible solution to the monopoly problem.

In many areas it appears that the group interest and the public welfare are as likely to be in conflict as they are to be compatible. For example, innovations in organization or technology are matters which cause considerable loss; and it is not inconceivable that joint action might so channelize innovation and so regulate the rate of introduction of change as to reduce the wastes of resources, of duplicate investment, and of technological and frictional unemployment. But joint action affecting new investment and innovation may go far beyond this. It is in the nature of entrenched groups to resist the innovations of new firms and of minorities; history shows a strong bias of entrenched interests against innovation. Yet it is these innovations which constitute the basis of change and progress in a capitalistic society. It cannot be assumed that the policies resulting from the compromise of interested parties will be the policies which will further the public welfare by inducing the optimum rate of innovation with least cost. Because of the nature of innovation a rational control of it in the public in-

---

[42] This involved the lead arsenate and calcium arsenate industry where it appears that one concern which was in a strong financial position wished to force distress prices upon the industry in order to destroy its weaker rivals. Edwards, *op. cit.*, chap. I, p. 16.

[43] Taggart, *op. cit.*, p. 420.

terest is difficult; to attempt it is to attempt to foresee the outcome of new and untried things.

Consider likewise the interest of the group in the control of the short-run price policies of the firm. No one can deny that there is a good deal of competition in price which is injurious to both the public and private interests, which serves no significant function, and which in some cases accentuates fluctuations in the rate of business activity. Price as we know it is a very imperfect instrument for organizing economic life. The competitive process is not as selective an instrument as it might be. The survival of firms is determined only roughly on a basis of economic efficiency. Chance and financial strength are equally important. During periods of business recession serious economic loss may result which *selective* price protection might mitigate. But price protection by the joint action of the group is not likely to be confined to promoting selective survival. The effect of price protection fostered by group action is indeterminate.[44] But one thing is clear, the bias of group action is likely to be in favor of protecting firms which should be weeded out. The voluntary price cartel has never proved to be especially selective.

Another argument frequently urged for price protection is that the spiral in prices incident to a business recession and the price disparities which result therefrom far from inducing economic adjustments accentuate the maladjustments. It is no doubt true that the slow downward spiral of prices tends to induce speculative withholding from the market. It is also true that price disparities arise which have no other explanation than differences in the power of the various industries to control price. Moreover, price cuts may be reflected in wage cuts, and in the face of an inelastic demand the effects may be deflationary. Consequently, there may be *a* price policy which would be

[44] J. A. Schumpeter, *Business Cycles* (New York: McGraw-Hill, 1939, 2 vols.), II, 537–38.

more conducive to full employment than that which now results from the free play of individual action in our imperfect markets. But it is not at all clear that the price policies which would result from the compromises of the interested parties acting jointly are the price policies which would promote full employment. So far as price adjustment is of significance in the business cycle, it is a question of relative price changes. It may be true that price controls which prevent whole segments of the price system from collapsing are desirable, but the problem of engineering *relative* price changes remains. Such relative price changes are necessary in order to promote full employment in the short-run and to serve for the allocation of resources in the long-run. But this means that *certain particular changes in relative prices* must be engineered. There is no *a priori* reason to believe that the interests of a particular group or the compromise which it may effect will lead to a pattern of prices more conducive to full employment or to the optimum allocation of resources. Quite to the contrary. If the industry group is fairly homogeneous, the price policy which it follows will depend upon the elasticity of demand for its product and upon its supply or cost conditions. The less homogeneous the conditions, the less predictable the result but the more likely is price control to be ineffective. Joint action simply increases the resources of particular groups to protect their relative position. Demand, capacity, and cost factors set the conditions within which the industry must operate. Within a given set of such conditions and at a particular level of business activity the relative position of the industry may often be improved by joint action. But there is no magic in the interjection of joint action with reference to price which makes the interest of the industry group and the public interest in full employment or optimum allocation of resources coterminous.

This is not to say that the results of free competition as we know it are the best possible or that action taken through the trade association or industry group might not improve upon the situation. But it must be recognized that there is a difference between self-government of industry, i.e. joint voluntary action by associations of business firms, and the use of associations of business firms for the purpose of executing the policies directed from above by some centralized body of control. This is the difference between the voluntary and the forced cartel. In a controlled economy, where fundamental decisions are made from above, the association may prove an effective arm of administration. It is conceivable that associations of firms in various industries could be induced to follow a specific policy believed by those in control to be in the public interest. In this case policy comes from above. The association is merely a convenient administrative unit. Its action is not voluntary and may well not be in its own interest. But this is the trade association or the cartel adapted to totalitarian purposes.

While free competition, particularly in markets as imperfectly organized as many are, is vulnerable to criticism on several bases, it clearly cannot be demonstrated that voluntary joint action of industry groups, with or without equal consumer representation, will promote better results. Much good may come from the association of business firms; but if left to their own devices, particularly with reference to matters of price, production, and capacity, much that is contrary to the public welfare will result. Those responsible for the formulation of articulate policy in the later days of the NRA were aware of this. As we have seen in the preceding section of this chapter, they eventually fell back upon the idea of a free market. With proper exceptions for situations involving "emergencies," monopolistic action, or natural resource industries freedom of action in the matter of price, production, and the ancillary terms and conditions of sale was to be reserved to the individual firm. The policy makers recognized that so-called "destructive competition," i.e. a condition in which large parts of an industry are experiencing unprofitable operation, is symptomatic of certain difficulties in underlying conditions. In the short-run in modern industry price is as much a result of conditions as it is a cause. Policy which does not operate to change these basic conditions is doomed to failure, and it appeared to the policy makers that many of the purposes which the industry groups were pursuing failed to recognize and deal with these basic conditions.

CHAPTER XVII

UNFAIR COMPETITION AND THE PRICING SYSTEM

THROUGHOUT the agitation for revision of our policy with respect to industrial organizations and trade practices there runs the argument that some limitation is needed on the free play of market forces in price changes downward. It is asserted that there are certain characteristics of the pricing mechanism which induce undesirable results when the price and production policies are left to the discretion of the individual firms acting independently in the market. These arguments have little to do with the familiar analysis which demonstrates that monopoly elements result in a maldistribution of resources by raising price and restricting output in the monopolistic industries. This latter analysis is primarily concerned with lowering prices while the arguments in question are concerned with raising them, or at least limiting certain downward movements. The proposals for limiting price competition are concerned with current or short-run price and production policies in conditions of either partial or general disequilibrium. It is proposed to control the downward movement of prices, thereby preventing "wasteful," "ruinous," or "uneconomic" competition. The suggested methods include various techniques for control of price, output, and capacity. This raises the general question, to what extent and in what sense may the determination of price by the individual firm acting in what it believes to be its own interest be "unfair" or undesirable from the point of view of public policy?

Conventional price analysis indicates that under static conditions and upon the assumption of full employment, the most effective utilization of our economic resources is that in which the output of each product is extended to the point where marginal cost is proportional to price.[1] This assumes that the relative prices of various products reflect the relative marginal utilities of the products to each buyer. It also assumes that the cost of production of a given product truly reflects the value (in a price sense) of the best opportunities forgone for using the factors of production in alternative employments. This analysis further demonstrates that in a society in which all industries are purely competitive and in which there are no imperfections in the form of restrictions on movement of resources or ignorance this ideal situation will be attained, subject only to the exceptions made clear by Professor Pigou.[2] Where there are isolated monopolies in a sea of competitive industries, the best utilization of resources will be obtained by expanding production in the monopolistic areas to the point where price is equal to marginal costs. In a system characterized by a sea of monopolistic competition, the best utilization of resources will be attained by shifting resources from those industries which are least imperfect to those which are most imperfect so that marginal cost and price (marginal utility) are proportional.[3]

This in brief outline is the analysis in its most recent and acceptable form of the type of allocation of our economic resources which will satisfy the maximum number of effective desires in the order of preference, i.e. will yield the greatest satisfaction or utility. It is to be noted that this analysis ignores the question of the distribution of income. It either starts with the demand functions (and therefore the distribution of income) as given data, not subject to analysis, or assumes that the problem of just distribution of income has

[1] In a society of purely competitive industries, marginal costs would not only be proportional to price but equal to price as well.

[2] *The Economics of Welfare*, Part II, esp. chap. IX. For a simpler exposition see his *Socialism versus Capitalism* (London: The Macmillan Co., 1937), chap. III.

[3] R. F. Kahn, "Some Notes on Ideal Output," *Economic Journal*, XLV (1935), 1–35.

been dealt with by means external to the pricing mechanism, or finally assumes as desirable the distribution of income implicit in the pricing arrangements associated with such an allocation of resources.

This analysis of the optimum distribution of our economic resources has implicit in it certain price relations. These are equilibrium price relations. In a purely competitive economy they are the "normal" prices under static conditions. They are predicated upon assumptions of perfect knowledge, a degree of mobility of resources, full employment, and rational (i.e. profit-seeking) behavior. They imply a given relation between price and marginal cost. In the case of pure and perfect competition from which so many of our popular notions of economic matters are derived, there is implied an equivalence between average cost and price. This "normal" price is featured in many of the proposals for price control as the "right" price, the level to which current price *should* conform in the large.

Actual prices, however, are current or short-run phenomena. Prices and price changes are incidents in the stream of the ever changing present of an economy which is characterized by the growth and decay of particular firms and industries, by changes in consumers' tastes and in the technique of production, by changes in the volume of our economic resources and the effectiveness with which they are used, by cyclical fluctuation and unemployment, and by some varying degree of ignorance and uncertainty. It would not be surprising if in these factors should be found some explanation of the phenomena which induce dissatisfaction on the part of business with a free pricing system and give rise to an attempt to expand the concept of unfair competition. Any significant public policy with respect to pricing practices must recognize these phenomena since public policy must deal, if it deals at all, not with "normal" prices but with current prices.

COSTS AND THEIR RELATION TO PRICE

The starting point of an analysis of business price policies lies in an analysis of costs. We are concerned with costs as seen by the individual firm, but not necessarily costs as calculated by the accountant or as represented by cash expenditures. The cost of production or sale of a given commodity may be defined as the value of the alternatives displaced by that production or sale.[4] Cost then is the value of the opportunities lost, i.e. the opportunity cost. It is significant to note that the value of displaced alternatives may vary according to the point of view. For example, an individual concern might visualize the cost of a given output as either greater or less than would a calculation from the point of view of the whole economy. This is true, for example, where the individual is able to force others to bear some of the costs of goods or where the individual sacrifices some opportunity to make future monopoly gains.

The costs which enter into a current decision include the price of factors of production which it is proposed to purchase, the alternative value of assets or factors which are already owned or contracted for ("user costs"),[5] and any losses in future income (or any gains figured as negative costs) which would result from the decision. This latter element requires explanation. Present price may affect future income through its effect on future demand or future costs. For example, a present lowering of price may spoil the market, thus decreasing future demand; it may on the other hand increase future demand by serving to change consumers' tastes or by developing new uses; or finally, it may prevent a future decrease in de-

---

[4] Cf. Fraser, *Economic Thought and Language*, p. 103 for the "displaced alternative" concept of cost.

[5] J. M. Keynes, *The General Theory of Employment Interest and Money* (New York: Harcourt, Brace, 1936), pp. 53, 66–73.

mand which would result from the breaking of consumer contacts. Likewise, future expenditures may be affected by current decisions with respect to price and production in several ways. A present decision not to produce currently may mean future costs of reopening a plant, or it may affect future efficiency adversely. For a firm to which the supply of labor is not perfectly elastic at the going wage, present price policies which have repercussions on the present level of employment may have various effects on future wage rates; present price cuts may induce wage cuts which would persist, thus lowering future costs, or the present wage cuts may by shifting the future supply curve of labor negatively, by inducing unionism, or by decreasing the morale and effectiveness of labor increase future wage rates. These factors are merely illustrative of the considerations entering into costs; they are not an exhaustive list.

Costs may be broken down into the two categories of *variable* and *overhead*. Variable costs may be defined as those costs whose aggregate depends upon or varies with the volume of sales. Overhead costs are those costs whose aggregate is independent of current sales; they are the difference between the total value of displaced alternatives and variable costs. It will appear that the magnitude and content of these two categories depend upon the decision which is being made. We are taking what might be called an operational view of business decisions.

It should be clear that this concept of cost has little or nothing in common with accounting concepts. Nor has this distinction between overhead and variable much in common with similar accounting categories. The latter categories are frequently based on a distinction between fixed and variable factors and upon the accounting costs associated therewith. Or again the accounting distinction may be between those accounting costs which can and those which cannot be allocated. However, it is the categories of costs as defined above and not the accounting categories which will be important to a rational, profit-seeking firm in determining its pricing policies.

Furthermore, it should be clear that classification of particular costs will depend on the problem in question. In deciding whether or not to make an investment or to disperse the assets of an investment already made, the opportunity costs of the investment (at their current valuation) is variable. If the investment has been made and there is no question of dispersing the assets, capital and depreciation charges, in so far as the life of the assets is independent of use, will be classed as overhead. The case of expenditure on labor and raw materials is equally complex. For a firm which produces only on order and contracts for labor and raw materials only after the receipt of an order, these costs are variable. If the firm produces in anticipation of demand, the classification of these costs depends upon the decision in view. In considering whether or not to produce, these costs are variable costs. In making a decision, once the goods have been produced, as to the price at which they shall be sold, the content of the variable cost category takes on a new complexion. If the product is perishable, variable costs of sale are independent of the costs of production. The variable costs of a *sale* are simply the additional selling expenses necessary.[6] If the goods can be stored, the variable cost of present sale is equal to the discounted expected future value of the goods, minus the cost of storage (including insurance etc.), and plus the present costs of sale and delivery.

It should not be supposed that overhead costs are simply a short-period phenomenon. They might persist in equilibrium conditions provided units of investment or management are lumpy and cannot through time be closely adapted to the equilibrium scale of output.

Finally, it should also be noted that variable costs and

[6] With additions noted below for the effect of present sales on future profits through affecting future revenues or cost.

current *out-of-pocket expenditures* are not identical categories. Not all out-of-pocket expenditures are made in payment of variable costs, and likewise not all variable costs are matched by current out-of-pocket expenditures. For instance, in general it is not feasible to adjust the managerial and salaried staffs to current changes in output. This may be due to discontinuities in the supply of managerial units, or to the fact that it is not feasible to expand and contract the managerial and salaried staffs with merely temporary changes in output. However, convention or convenience has in many instances led to a method of remuneration which makes expenditure independent of the volume of production. Here is a stream of expenditures which does not enter into current calculations of the cost of current production. As an example of a variable cost which does not necessarily involve out-of-pocket expenditures we may consider the opportunity cost of current utilization of a plant the life of which is not solely a matter of years but rather of use as well. The present discounted value of the anticipated values of the future services of the plant, if not used now, is a variable cost of current production. It represents the value of the opportunities lost due to current production and is dependent upon the volume of present output. It is a variable cost involving no *necessary* current cash expenditure.

These facts suggest the necessity of making a sharp distinction between two sets of problems with which the business firm is faced. On the one hand are its considerations of sales. This is the pricing problem in which costs must enter, and upon this depends its revenues. The second set of problems are its financial problems, the problem of marshalling assets and determining the form which they shall take. On these decisions depend its expenditures. In an analysis of long-run situations it is not necessary to consider this distinction. In an analysis of current business decisions and their significance, such a distinction is of great importance.

SHORT–RUN PRICE IN PURE COMPETITION

What is the most general theorem concerning price and output in the short-run? The generally accepted theorem is that on the assumption of a desire to maximize profits production will be extended to the point where marginal cost is equal to marginal revenue and price will be that indicated by the demand curve for that quantity. Where production is undertaken in anticipation of sale or variable costs are incapable of precise determination, this theorem might be recast to read, production will be extended to the point where the expectation of marginal revenue to the firm equals its expectation of marginal cost. As often interpreted this theorem would have serious limitations due to a failure to consider the factor of clock-time. It might be objected that the purpose of a firm may not be to maximize profits at any given moment of time, but rather to maximize profits over some period of time.[7] However, a definition of cost so as to include the effects upon future demand and expenses saves this theorem as stated from condemnation on this ground. Our definition of cost makes this theorem synonymous with another theorem, namely that the individual firm, acting at any moment of time in terms of the conditions then existing (including its liquidity preference) and its expectations as to all factors likely to affect it in the future, will act so as to maximize the present value of the firm, i.e. to maximize the discounted value of expected future net incomes. To explain what

[7] It might be further objected that a firm may not be interested in profits in any sense or over any time period. This objection has validity. They *may* not. We shall ignore this objection and the alternatives which it suggests, however. The writer does this in part because to open the question of non-profit motives in pricing policies is to open up a bewildering array of alternatives and a crop of unexplored problems, in part because he believes that when the concept of cost is defined as it is in this chapter, the assumption of a desire to maximize profits will be found to be more fruitful in explaining business phenomena than is sometimes supposed.

is meant more fully, the firm looking into the future is faced on the one hand with a choice between a series of alternative expenditure streams and likewise a choice between a series of revenue streams. It will choose that combination of associated streams of expenditure and revenue which will maximize the net profit or difference at its present value.

Applying this theorem to a purely competitive industry. the short-run pricing considerations are comparatively simple. The profits of one period are independent of the action of an individual firm in another, since an individual firm cannot affect the price of its product nor the price of the factors at any point of time. The future enters into the present price considerations of the firm only in so far as expectation as to the future price affects present "user cost" of the equipment, raw material, and inventory. The individual firm produces and sells an amount such that its estimated marginal cost equals the expected price. The firm will continue to produce so long as the expected price is above its lowest average variable costs. If for any reason price becomes less than this, it will suspend operations whether it expects this situation to be permanent or temporary.[8] Where there is a substantial interval between the decision to produce and the time at which the product is ready for sale. an erroneous expectation may lead the firm to reconsider policy after the goods are produced. Willingness to sell at the market price will be made in terms of costs as defined; these costs will depend upon the alternative of storing for sale at a later date.

It is sometimes argued that some firms may cease production because of inadequate financial resources, even though the aggregate revenues exceed aggregate variable costs. We have seen that out-of-pocket expenditures may exceed variable costs

[8] Our definition of costs is such that in those cases where it is expected that price will only be at this level temporarily, it will balance the expenses of closing and reopening the plant against temporary loss of revenues through selling at low prices.

because of the necessity for paying certain overhead, such as salaries, or certain fixed charges on indebtedness. Or current capital may be impaired due to unwarranted expectations in the past. This may be true. It is arguable, however, that if financial resources in such a condition cannot be replenished, there is *prima facie* evidence either that the investment market is imperfect or that the expected return due to additional investment in this firm is not as great as can be hoped for elsewhere. Under conditions of general equilibrium but partial disequilibrium of one industry or firm, if the investment market is perfectly informed and if there are no prior contractual obligations, investment funds should be forthcoming for the replenishing of a firm's financial resources unless the expected future income discounted to present value is less than the funds necessary. Failure to receive funds would indicate that the investment is unprofitable in a pecuniary sense. If the prices of the factors reflect not only the value of alternatives forgone from an individual but also from a social point of view and if markets including investment markets were free from monopoly elements or other imperfections, this inability to secure funds would indicate that the continuation of the firm or industry would be uneconomic.

Of course, difficulties may arise where there are conflicts in expectations in getting assent to the rearrangement of priorities in the financial structure.[9] The owners may be reluctant to give priority to those supplying the new funds, or there may be legal obstacles to satisfactory adjustment. That some firms can obtain funds on more favorable terms than others is indicative either of greater risks or of an imperfect capital market. If the capital market is functioning perfectly and proper adjustments of the financial structure can be made, survival will depend upon whether the prospect of return on additional

---

[9] This is the economic basis of many of the difficulties faced in corporate receiverships and reorganizations.

funds in one direction is as great as the prospect in alternative directions involving equal risk. The fact remains, however, that in our imperfectly functioning world financial difficulties may be responsible for the withdrawal of firms from the market where considerations of efficiency would warrant their survival.

From a social point of view price changes in an industry which is characterized by partial disequilibrium are significant because of their effects on the allocation of current resources between alternative uses, and upon the utilization of the fixed equipment and other factors which are attached to the industry for a period of time. So long as there is any elasticity to the demand, a lower price means a greater current employment of labor and materials in an industry and a greater current output than would result if the price were higher. It also means a greater current use of the fixed factors. So far as the services of the fixed factor become unrecoverable with the passage of time, as is true in part of the services of the salaried group and of equipment which depreciates with time, a low price means a greater output of product by these resources through time. In so far as the services of these fixed factors are exhausted only with use, the period of time for adjustment by withdrawal of firms is shortened by lowering the price to marginal cost over what it would be if prices were maintained at some higher level by any means, and the amount of services received from these factors in the present is increased at the expense of the future. Provided the lowering of price has no adverse repercussions on the total expenditure and through that on the total amount of employment, provided likewise it has no serious repercussions on income distribution, the optimum utilization and distribution of economic resources would seem to dictate a policy of allowing price to seek the level of marginal cost in an industry characterized by pure competition, a level which in the absence of interference it tends to seek.

The long-run flow of investment and labor depends on the

expectation of return in the future. The current price and the firm's current income dependent thereupon are significant only in so far as they color the future expectations, or in so far as current income may affect the efficiency of the labor concerned through affecting its standard of living. This latter factor may be significant in those cases where the supply of labor to the firm is inelastic downwards for a considerable period of time. The problem of adjustment will be prolonged in this case, because as the financial reserves of labor become exhausted mobility decreases. To what extent present prices and incomes as such are projected into the future it is hard to say. Apart from short-period cyclical fluctuations this factor is probably not so important.[10]

Where prices are below "normal" and demand may reasonably be expected to remain at the existing intensity, a contraction of investment is in order. The incidence of the burden of adjustment will depend upon broad economic factors. Other things (such as labor supply, technical efficiency, relation to the market) being equal, the incidence will fall on those firms whose plant needs replacement first and on those whose estimate of the future is most discouraging. Those firms which are most pessimistic about the future will tend to withdraw for two reasons: first, their pessimistic estimate lowers their opportunity cost of present production, which means that they will liquidate fixed factors faster and thus face replacement sooner; second, when facing the question of whether to replace equipment, these are the firms which are the least likely to decide affirmatively. The smoothness of adjustments will depend very much upon how the partial disequilibrium develops, whether it develops suddenly or more slowly, whether it comes from shifts on the demand side or on the supply side, and whether the demand and cost situations are stable or highly fluctuating.

[10] Mordecai Ezekiel, "The Cobweb Theorem," *Quarterly Journal of Economics*, LII (1938), 277.

So far as the recession in demand is viewed as only temporary, current price policies will affect the flow of investment and labor in various ways by affecting the relative profit prospects. Market conditions or programs of control which may be reasonably expected to keep price above marginal cost would make any particular industry more attractive than it would otherwise be. It should in consequence attract more investment funds than otherwise, provided there are no restrictions to new investment. If all industries have some prospect of controlling price in the short-run so as to keep it above its purely competitive level, the expectations of profit and in consequence the flow of investment and labor will depend among other things upon the relative expectations concerning the success of the schemes of control.

Of equal importance with the effects of price cutting incident to partial disequilibrium on the output, employment, and incomes of the industry as a whole is the incidence of the competitive pressures on particular firms. The effects of competitive pressures in an industry characterized by something approaching pure competition cannot be identified as the result of the unchivalrous or predatory action of one or a few firms. The current conditions are the results of the policies of innumerable rivals, the action of any one not being discernible in the total. However, not all members of the industry feel the impact of the disequilibrium equally, nor do they view it in the same light.

In the first place, in conditions of partial disequilibrium the accounting costs of the firm are often not covered. The extent to which the individual firms in an over expanded industry will suffer accounting losses will depend among other things on valuation policies and their accounting procedures, factors which vary between firms. More significant are differences in their estimated marginal costs. Those firms whose cost functions are highest and most elastic will contract output most. These costs depend on the technical conditions of production to which the firm is subject at the time, upon the current price of variable factors, and upon its "user costs." Firms with newly established and highly mechanized equipment will have lower marginal cost functions and will continue production longer than those using a high proportion of variable factors. On the other hand, if the supply of variable factors is not infinitely elastic at the going rate, those to whom the supply is most inelastic downward have a chance to decrease their variable cost curves most when employment declines. This means that the burden of loss will tend to fall upon those to whom the supply of variable factors is most elastic.

The matter of "user costs" is more complicated; these represent an estimate of the loss of future income through the use of fixed assets in the present for production. This is an estimate which depends on expectations as to the future and the present values of these assets and depends further on the rate (or rates) of discount applied. The better the prospects for a recovery of prices and the less the rate of discount, the greater will be the user cost of current production and the smaller the current output. Those who are most pessimistic about future prospects and those whose rate of discount is greatest will sell the largest quantities in the present; those who are least pessimistic and whose rate of discount is least will tend to bear the burden of current contraction in volume. The action of the pessimistic will be a factor tending to accentuate present price declines; on the other hand, by using up assets in the present the pessimistic tend to hasten the adjustment of capacity in the industry.

Note should be taken of the significance of financial obligations and financial resources for this process of adjustment. So long as there is something approaching a perfect capital market the financial problems will not affect the outcome significantly. When financial obligations cannot be adjusted and necessary additional resources cannot be obtained, a firm is forced to go through bankruptcy and perhaps to disperse its assets. In the interim the rate of discount which is used by the firm in its calculation of "user costs" will be higher than otherwise, and in consequence there will be a tendency to depress the market by liquidating fixed factors at a faster rate. Finally, it should be noted that costs will vary and the burden of disequilibrium may be markedly uneven where for some sellers the product is a by-product while for others it is the sole or principal product, since the action of those producing it as a by-product will be largely determined by conditions in the market for their other joint-products.

The introduction of elements of monopoly into the market makes the picture more complicated. If we assume that the current actions of monopolistic firms are dominated by a calculus of profit, a desire to maximize the present value of the firm, the principles are the same although new elements for consideration are introduced and the results may be different. It should be recognized, however, that it is just in this field of monopolistic industries that there is the greatest scope for industry action which is not motivated by pecuniary calculations of profit or loss. Where the elements of monopoly power are strong and freedom of entry is restricted, a firm may systematically pursue a non-profit seeking policy. Where the monopoly elements are associated with other highly competitive elements, persisting non-profit seeking motives will be possible only if the firm is willing to take losses systematically. However, even here, in its current decisions, there is a wide penumbra in which the firm may exercise choice with respect to production and sales policies. The introduction of monopolistic elements multiplies the factors affecting a business decision.

In the first place, in a monopolistic market, the current conditions no longer have the appearance of being independent of the action of any one firm. There are elements of control exercised by each over the market. Where the numbers are large and the impact of the action of one on each of the others is imperceptible, the effects of the action of one may not be identifiable although price, quality, and conditions of sale of each seller's product are, within limits, in his control. On the other hand where the sellers are few or where a larger number are connected in a "chain" relationship, the effects of the action of one upon another become quite identifiable. In consequence, dissatisfaction with current market conditions, which in a purely competitive market would take the impersonal form of a lament over the "destructive" or "ruinous" nature of competition, is turned into personal recriminations against the "chiselers" who are identified as responsible for current conditions.

Where sellers are few, the effect of any one on the market becomes clear; and, in making its decision as to current policy, a firm may take more or less account of the indirect effects of its policies through considering the reactions of rivals.[11] The weight given to such considerations will depend upon the foresight of those responsible for a firm's decision, the certainty with which they are able to predict competitors' reactions, past experience in these matters, and upon whether the particular industry or industry in general is faced by an increasing or decreasing demand.

In some industries leadership in price changes may customarily be taken by one or a few. Upon them will rest general responsibility for current competitive relations. On the other hand, at times the initiative in price changes may be taken either openly or secretly by those who customarily follow. These are the "chiselers." Their independent action may be predicated on a difference in interest; or it may be predicated on the temporary advantages which accrue to one who starts a price or product concession which it is believed the leaders

---

[11] Cf. Chamberlin, op. cit., chap. III.

will not find it advantageous to meet immediately. In some industries in which the leaders have built up a consumer acceptance for their product, there may be certain customary price differentials which are upset in the day to day adjustments, a change of the differential being the first step in a situation likely to initiate a new equilibrium. Changes in relations between leaders and followers, between dominant firms and independents are the source of many complaints. Equally important are the conflicts between a few sellers where there are no disparities between the firms as to importance or leadership. In these markets the objective of each may be conceived as the maximization of the present value of the stream of future net income. This involves certain assumptions concerning the action of others. There may be conflicts in these assumptions. An adjustment may be predicated upon one of several expectations as to rivals' reactions; but the final outcome will depend on the precise reaction, and a rival may not react as expected.

In making decisions as to current policy, expectations concerning the future are of equal importance with expectations concerning the reactions of rivals. In a purely competitive market future expectations enter into current decisions principally through their effects on estimates of user costs. Estimates of user costs enter into current decisions of an industry with monopolistic elements as well. But in a purely competitive market the future price is independent of the present action of the individual firm. Each firm looks upon the present and future prices as given, i.e. as independent of its action. Not so with monopolistic firms. A seller recognizes that future demand is dependent upon present price and production policies in various ways. There is the problem of "spoiling the market." Present sales, especially of durable goods at low prices, may decrease the future demand. Goods selling largely on their prestige value are protected in their goodwill, in part, by their high price; temporary sale at low prices may destroy their prestige value. A monopolistic firm may find continuity in customer relations of considerable value; to break those contacts by temporarily withdrawing from production or by failing to meet rivals' prices may seriously decrease future demand for its product. Finally, so far as consumption patterns are a matter of habit and consumer preference can be built up only by overcoming inertia, present prices are obviously significant for future demand.

Current pricing policies in monopolistic industries may, then, be based on considerations far removed from any accounting concepts of cost or any concept of cost as applied solely to variable factors and user costs. Prices and production are the result of decisions. Often the initiation of changes in prices or the terms of sale is traceable specifically to a particular source. It is inevitable that differences of opinion should arise between rivals as to desirable policy. In part this may be due to a conflict of interests between the rivals.[12] On the other hand these conflicts may arise from uncertainties or differences of opinion concerning present or future conditions, or concerning the way in which rivals will react.

These are the types of market situations, briefly sketched, which business men face in many markets where there are monopolistic elements. The existence of monopolistic elements among the buyers accentuates only further the amount of uncertainty and the element of estimate in the making of current decisions. Each firm has a certain degree of control over his buying and selling policies; there rests upon each a certain very definite responsibility for market results. Yet each is to a greater or less extent circumscribed in his action by competitive elements.

It is not surprising that there should be some attempt at agreement upon uniform policy or that there should be developed certain customary practices which seek to limit the

[12] *Cf. supra*, pp. 351–52.

uncertainty in these matters and bring order out of chaos. Thus it is that price leadership develops; that a standard performance guarantee becomes customary in a trade; that it becomes a custom to use prices published in a trade journal for bidding on public projects; that price lists are issued or open-price filing develops with a greater or less tendency to adhere to the published prices; that a basing-point is adopted; that new models and new prices are introduced at a customary time such as the annual fair or show. These and other trade practices develop either by plan or by chance, usually by a curious mixture of both. The practices are seldom universal and are often in the process of change or of being perfected.

Limited adherence to these practices and the fact that the practices themselves are subject to evolution give rise to further conflicts, conflicts between those who are playing the game and those who are not. The fact that these practices are ever in the process of change, that they are experimented with and perfected, makes a determination of the identity of those who are not playing cricket difficult. Some of the "chiselers" may be motivated by a real difference of interest. On the other hand the dissenter's policy may simply be to take advantage of the others by making profits through systematically undercutting the terms of sale as established by custom. The atmosphere may be highly charged with personal recriminations concerning responsibility for the state of the market. No longer does it appear that the impersonal forces of the market are responsible for current conditions. The individual firm because of its monopolistic position has an element of responsibility for its own action. However reasonable this action may appear from its own point of view, its direct and indirect effects on others are more or less obvious.

The traditional problem of price cutting in markets characterized by few sellers has been that of ruinous competition, that is, temporary price cutting with the intent and effect of eliminating rivals. It is significant to note that for all the discussion of such practices in connection with the NRA only one case was found which clearly fell in this category.[13] Nevertheless, the potentiality is there. It has been noted that the individual firm in its current policies may consider the effect of present policies on future demand. A policy which would lead to the collapse of a competitor and the withdrawal of its assets from the industry might, where competitors are few, increase the intensity and perhaps decrease the elasticity of future demand significantly. These potential future gains may be set off against loss of revenue due to current low prices. If the financial resources or connections of a rival are significantly worse than those of the firm initiating a predatory price policy, the latter might pursue such a course with some confidence provided it has sufficient capacity to satisfy the demand, provided future revenues seem sufficiently alluring, and finally provided the risks deterring the development of new competitors are sufficiently great. There is a wide penumbra here for competitive battle in the outcome of which market strategy and financial resources will be determining factors. There is no limit to the period during which conditions of low price may persist provided only investors can be found with conflicting views as to who will win in order to finance both sides of the battle.[14]

This is the pricing mechanism as it appears at its work, a continuing process resulting from the current decisions of business firms. It should now be quite plain that current prices need have no relation to accounting costs as generally calculated. Moreover, prices may be quite different from the expecta-

---

[13] *Cf. supra*, pp. 353-54.

[14] Both sides of the battle might conceivably find their resources periodically replenished by individuals who looking into the future take different views of the prospects of survival. After all, losses on past investment need not determine future prospects.

tions which formed the basis of past investments. However, this is no proof that prices are not based upon a rational calculation of profit and loss as the firm visualizes the situation which it faces.

EFFECTS OF SHORT–RUN PRICE CHANGES

What is to be said for allowing price to seek its level unimpeded by voluntary agreement or by government control? What would be the effect of such agreements or controls? On these questions something has already been said particularly in relation to purely competitive markets, but the problem may be explored further.

Consider first the effects upon current output and employment at any given time with the given capacity. It is clear that if we take the demand for various products to be given and if there is any elasticity to the demand for a particular product, current output and employment in the industry will be greater the lower the price. If then we are dealing only with partial disequilibria in a few industries and can assume money incomes and demand to be independent of pricing policies, it follows that output in an industry will be less with a policy of price control. Such a decline in output means either unemployment for the released resources or their absorption in some other line. If the disequilibrium is presumed to be temporary and an increase in demand seems likely to make possible their reabsorption later, unemployment in the interim is probable. Temporary unemployment is also probable at the time the disequilibrium develops even though there seems to be no chance of their reabsorption by an increase in demand later. Price control with a consequent smaller output would, then, mean less current employment of resources in the industry.

The current rate of output affects the utilization of equipment and other fixed factors as well. So far as the services of these resources are exhausted with a mere passage of time, a policy of price control means a sacrifice of some of these services. To the extent that the services of these factors are exhausted only with use, the enjoyment of these services is postponed into the future. In either case present goods are not being produced, even though demand is such that additional goods of a sort are valued at more than the variable costs of their production. The variable costs are the value of the displaced alternatives as seen by the firm. Unless there is a divergence between the social value of the displaced alternatives and the value as envisaged by the firm, it follows that additional units of the product which would follow from free pricing are valued more than the additional units of alternative products. In a purely competitive economy at full employment in which the prices of the factors represent the value of their marginal productivities elsewhere, the optimum distribution of economic resources for the satisfaction of existing wants would be attained in general by allowing price to seek the level of marginal cost. In these circumstances the presumption would be against interfering with the decline in the level of prices in an industry in cases of partial disequilibrium.[15]

Next consider the long-run effects which current price policies have upon the allocation or flow of economic resources between alternative employments, that is the effect of current prices upon the "capacity" of the industry in terms of equipment, managerial staff, and specialized labor.

Assuming that there is freedom of entry for new investment

---

[15] Such interference would lead to an uneconomic utilization of our resources in three respects: it would lead to a waste of services of fixed factors, where the use of these services is lost by the mere passage of time; it would lead to the postponement of the use of fixed factors whose services are exhausted only with time into the future even though the present valuation of these services used in the future is less than the valuation of these services used in the present; finally, it means the shifting of current factors to other uses in which they are valued less than they would be in producing more units of the product in question.

and factors into every line of industry investment will depend on the relative expectations of return which are entertained for the various industries. This expectation depends upon the expected relation between revenues and expenditures for some period into the future. A price policy which holds price above the level of marginal cost to which it would tend in the absence of price control would, if foreseen, increase the expectation of revenue. Unless there were some offsetting increase in expenditures or unless the expectations of profit in other directions were increased correspondingly, the industry would appear to be a more attractive direction for investment. Price protection as applied to a particular industry, in consequence, may reduce the risk of loss and increase the expectation of profit. This would probably lead to a greater investment, a diversion of investment from other uses. On the other hand, a policy of price control which is instituted after the development of disequilibrium and without any expectation that the policy will be continued may have no such effect. In fact, so far as the services of equipment and fixed factors are exhausted only by use, such a price control scheme would simply lengthen the period necessary for adjustment, thereby tending to discourage additional investment.

If the power to control price competition were granted to all industries and the prospects of its effective pursuit in all industries seemed equal, there would be a neutralizing effect. From the point of view of particular disequilibrium the risks of loss due to partial maladjustments would be reduced in all directions. As applied to the risks of the business cycle, if the degrees of monopoly power in the various industries were thought to be the same, the relative attractiveness of the various fields would not be altered. If there were variations in the relative degrees of price control to be anticipated, a greater proportion of the resources might be expected to flow into those areas in which price protection was expected to be most effective.

Where industries are characterized by monopoly elements in the sale of their product, there is no longer the same presumption that free pricing will promote the optimum current allocation of resources between alternative uses. The marginal costs as viewed by the firm no longer represent the value of the alternatives foregone from a social point of view. This is true for two reasons: [16] in the first place, marginal costs are no longer proportional to marginal utilities, or prices; [17] secondly, marginal costs as viewed by the firm reflect not only the value of factors being used but also future losses or gains which it may expect from the exercise of monopoly power. Mr. Kahn has demonstrated that with given conditions of demand and under conditions of long-run equilibrium with full employment, a curtailment of output in those industries which have less than an average degree of imperfection or monopoly and an application of these resources to industries which have more than an average degree of imperfection would be desirable.[18] This theorem, however, is applicable to equilibrium conditions, while our interest is equally in current prices and output with the actual capacity in existence. It has been seen that given the physical capacity to supply the demand, there is no limit to the lower level to which competition may take price where there are only a few rivals. Also, where there is product differentiation, prices may go far below the marginal cost of the variable factors of production used even though rivals are many. What can be said concerning the public interest in free and controlled pricing policies in such industries?

Consider sales at a price below the marginal costs of variable factors for the purpose of maintaining customer contacts and

---

[16] If there are monopsonistic forces in the buying of factors, this will be another force leading to a difference between marginal costs to the firm and to society.

[17] Except in rare cases.

[18] Kahn, *op. cit.*

protecting goodwill. It is difficult to see wherein the losses involved in such sales differ from investment in advertising or introductory offers made at the time of the establishment of a new concern. The losses are made in the expectation that the recession in demand is temporary, in anticipation of a recovery in price due to an exodus of some firms, or in anticipation of a fall in variable costs. Entry into such an industry is restricted to those with resources sufficient to make such original investments; unless there is some countervailing interference, survival will be dependent, among other things, on ability to follow up this investment with other investments for the protection or extension of goodwill. If there were no imperfections of the capital markets, funds would be equally available to all and survival would be determined by the comparative expected efficiencies through time, including not only efficiency in production but also efficiency in attaching consumer demand to a particular product. As it is, success often goes to those who are financially strongest.

There is no obvious reason why public policy should distinguish between the original investment in consumer goodwill and subsequent investment to maintain that goodwill. It may be desirable to detach business success from ability to attract consumer demand by financial outlays and place it entirely on a basis of efficiency in production. But this is an argument for radical change in existing practice; it would eliminate by the roots much consumer preference based on advertising as well as selling temporarily at low prices for the purpose of acquiring or retaining goodwill. However, given a society in which product differentiation and consumer preference based on advertising are countenanced, it would seem the better policy to encourage the establishment of goodwill by methods which mean low prices to the consumer rather than by other means such as an intensified advertising campaign, the public benefit from which is to say the least dubious.

Of course, in markets characterized by a few sellers, not all sales below the marginal cost of variable factors are made merely for the purpose of maintaining consumer contacts or developing goodwill. Price wars develop partly because price cutting gets out of hand and partly because of an intent to drive a competitor out of business or to capture part of its market. The incidence of such price cutting by one firm is not necessarily spread evenly over its rivals but may fall with special severity on one or a few. This is particularly true where a series of firms are in a "chain" relationship, each competing primarily with the two closest to it and only remotely with the others. In all situations of oligopoly there are inherent possibilities of great instability of price in the short-run. Clearly it is advantageous from the point of view of the current utilization of resources that prices should be allowed to decline to the marginal cost of variable factors. But in these markets there are no limits to which prices may not go for a period while firms remain in the industry. There can be little doubt, in consequence, but that success in these industries often depends as much on financial strength as upon efficiency. Current output is not necessarily produced by the firm which has lowest costs, nor is survival dependent upon ability to achieve lowest costs over time. Moreover, there can be little doubt but that there is a considerable waste of investment in the building of capacity in such industries. Such capacity may be built for either offensive or defensive purposes in oligopolistic warfare. The competitive process, in short, is not an extremely selective instrument of control.

It is clear, consequently, that it is technically possible to increase the effectiveness with which resources are used in such industries. But it is questionable whether price control is the indicated direction of action. Broad powers of price control are not likely to be more selective than price competition in such circumstances. They are very likely to be used to obstruct innovation and to impede fundamental adjustments. Moreover, price cutting is only one weapon which may be used in oligopolistic warfare. Costly advertising campaigns and improvement in quality or service are others. Is there any reason to limit the one if the others are not limited? If such markets are allowed to exist and no restriction is placed upon the building of new capacity, is there any reason to restrict the use of such capacity? Back of the practice of selling below the cost of variable factors lies a market structure which gives rise to it. As will be suggested in the next chapter public policy might go far toward reducing the oligopolistic forces which give rise to such price policies, but the difficulties of evolving and administering selective price controls preclude such measures, unless the situation calls for elaborate controls of the public utility type.

One further proposal for the use of price control as a corrective of monopolistic forces may be mentioned. In so far as the economy is at any given time composed of industries with varying degrees of monopoly control, the extension of the power of minimum price control to the more competitive industries might force resources out of the most competitive and into the monopolistic industries, and might induce thereby such a reallocation of resources between industries as would reduce the spread in the degree of monopoly power between industries and make marginal costs more nearly proportional to prices. If this were achieved, the results would be on the whole desirable, since the goods sacrificed in the highly competitive industries are desired less than the additional goods which might be produced with these resources in the highly monopolistic industries. This is a simple extension of Mr. Kahn's theorem. It necessitates, however, not only a restriction on price and output, but a restriction on investment as well. This restriction on output and investment would release factors of production and induce their absorption in other industries. In this respect it should be noted that the program might have serious effects on the distribution of income.

This proposal so far as it has any merits calls for selective price controls. It is not an argument for a complete reversal of policy with respect to voluntary agreements on prices and production. A blanket withdrawal of the Sherman Law restraints on loose agreements might increase the powers of monopolistic action of the highly competitive industries, but it is equally likely to increase the monopoly power of the less competitive industries, since it would remove the last obstacle to the perfection of the informal controls which many of them have already developed. It is common experience that the problems of effectuating voluntary controls where the numbers are even moderately large are very great. A general withdrawal of our prohibitions to loose agreements might well strengthen monopoly powers in those areas already characterized by a high degree of monopoly power even more than in the highly competitive industries, thus increasing rather than decreasing the range of degrees of monopoly power. So far as this proposal has merit, it points toward selective controls of the type now associated with bituminous coal and agricultural industries.

We are inevitably led to a consideration of price policies and the business cycle. In most of the previous discussion the effects of price policies on total output, employment, and investment have been ignored. Attention has been devoted to the allocation of employment, output, and investment between various alternatives. The business cycle, however, is an all pervasive fact; more or less synchronous price changes in many industries are a familiar characteristic of the cycle. For purposes of the allocation of employment, output, and investment between alternative employments the question is one of the comparative expectations of profits. On the assumption of continuous full employment or of a given cycle of employment, there are very definite *price relations* which will conduce to an optimum allocation of resources. The effects of short-run price controls on the allocation of resources has been discussed above. The present problem concerns the desirability of some control of the short-run level of prices in general, or of groups of prices. Thus, although control of a particular group of prices in a depression while others are free may induce an undesirable allocation of both current employment and the flow of investment and develop certain strains in the system which intensify the cycle,[19] a completely flexible pricing system is not the only alternative to the present mixture of flexible and inflexible prices. It is possible that the whole pricing system be made less flexible or that specific groups of prices be induced to behave in a specified manner.

So far as the function of price is to change the direction of employment and investment, this purpose will be served by changes in relative prices. It is not clear that generalized changes of the whole price level are necessary.[20] Price, however, has other important functions in so far as it is one of the elements which is important in determining the level of employment. During the course of the cycle prices of products, of labor, and of other factors fluctuate widely. These changes have innumerable effects. They react upon the level of employment in so far as changes in prices induce changes in money incomes and changes in money expenditures. They also affect the level of investment through their effects on profit prospects.

---

[19] For the classic exposition of this view, *cf.* G. C. Means, *Industrial Prices and Their Relative Inflexibility* (74th Cong., 1st Sess., 1935, *Senate Document* No. 13).

[20] *Cf.* Schumpeter, *op. cit.*, Vol. II, chap. VIII for a distinction between the system of prices and the level of prices which is analogous to the distinction made above between price levels and price relations. Schumpeter also explains the reasons for changes in the level of prices during the cycle in terms of his model. It is his contention that certain price declines are inherent in the process of business recession in our capitalistic society.

They induce changes in the timing of employment in so far as the expectations of price changes lead to speculative buying or speculative withdrawal from the market. The expectation of price changes not only works through its effects on the demand side but through its effects on supply conditions as well, since the cost of present sale is affected by the expectations of the value of the alternative of sale in the future. Price changes react upon wage rates and wage incomes. They react upon the value of assets and, therefore, upon the willingness of individuals to spend. Finally, price changes which affect the value of inventories, the size of the wage bill, and the need for circulating capital react upon the demand for loans and the volume of circulating media.

In the post-war decade the problem of the control of the price level has been in the forefront of economic discussion. The principal proposals in the early post-war period were for a control of the quantity and velocity of circulating media, particularly by central bank policy designed to ease or tighten credit conditions. More recently the emphasis has been upon public spending and the inducement of private investment. There is implied in much of the contemporary wage and price discussion, however, an alternative method. This discussion contends that price and wage flexibility in the face of business recession is either undesirable or at least desirable only within limits.

The argument may proceed in various ways. In the first place it is argued that a price fall leads to a fall in wage-rates; and unless there is a high elasticity of money demand, this reacts in the form of lower money incomes and a further decline in the money demand for commodities. There is, of course, no question but that a business recession will in the absence of wage control put a pressure on wage rates, since in the face of a business recession the industry and firm alike are not faced with a perfectly elastic supply of labor. In fact the supply curve of labor may become less elastic and even assume a negative elasticity. It is true that a mere protection of the price of final products might not protect wage rates. On the other hand, in a society in which wage rates are subject to determination by trade unions or in which there are strong inhibitions to wage cutting except as a last resort, price control in times of unemployment may serve to relieve the pressure on wage rates. If this is true, it may be argued that money incomes will be greater and the money demand for goods greater than they would be in the absence of price control. While this may not mean greater output, because of greater costs, it will avoid the difficulties and maladjustments engendered by the cumulative downward spiral.

Another attack on free pricing in the face of business recession centers around the effects of expected price declines on the willingness of consumers to buy finished products, of the investors to buy capital goods, and of producers to renew inventories. The sudden change in the outlook of business which characterizes the turning point at the peak sets loose certain forces of a cumulative nature. The price changes which follow are not all equilibrating. In the first place as the expectations concerning the future prices become less favorable the willingness to sell in the present, to liquidate inventories or fixed investment, increases; i.e. marginal costs decline quite independently of any change in the price of present variable factors. This is a force which in itself induces further price declines. At the same time buyers are more cautious. The slightest sign of a weakening of price will induce a tendency to postpone purchases if there is an expectation that further declines will follow. Merchants will tend to postpone the renewal of inventories. Manufacturers faced with a less intense demand and expecting a decline in the price of labor and raw materials will delay production. These postponements have the effect of further decreasing the demand since incomes are reduced due to a decline in employment and output.

The proposal, then, is to alleviate the cumulative effects of a recession by limiting price and wage declines. It is hoped thereby to mitigate the depression. The cycle will take the form of a cycle of production and employment, with only a limited change in prices. It is argued, however, that the production cycle will be less intense or of shorter duration than under a free pricing system.[21]

It is not our intention to pursue this argument further. Business cycle theory is still in a state of flux and the present book will not venture to tread more than lightly on this ground. However, there seems to be a general agreement that there are cumulative forces at work which tend to accentuate the intensity of the cycle. It is likewise clear that there is an intimate relation between wages and prices in the course of the cycle. The suggestion that some limitation on price fluctuations might be introduced by group action is worth consideration, although it must be weighed against the proposals of others that public policy should seek to make prices more flexible. It is to be noted, however, that the proposal for limitation on price declines implies not only the granting of the right to control price declines, but successful control of such price declines. It is, of course, not the intention to prevent price adjustments which are dictated by the peculiar conditions of the industry, those incidental to technological change, to secular decline in demand in a given industry, etc. Changes in price relations are necessary. It may be found that adjustments in relations of particular groups of prices, such as a change in the relation of prices of consumers' and investors' goods, are called for to

[21] Appeal to the well known fact that those industries which have the greatest degree of price control are the same industries which experience the greatest decline in output is beside the point. This may be explained by the character of the industries in which price control is most frequent, industries involving capital goods. Moreover, the effects of a system in which all prices are controlled may be quite different from one in which only some are controlled.

induce the return of the prospect for profits upon which recovery hinges.

The argument is one in favor of preserving the price level or limiting its changes, not necessarily in preserving price relations. The successful application of this policy implies the determination of what adjustments of price relations are desirable and the development of some techniques which will make it possible to adjust individual price and wage relations without seriously affecting the level of prices. This is an argument for price and wage control of a very selective sort. It is not an argument for price control of any sort whatsoever or at all times. Its success cannot depend upon the hazards of voluntary agreement. The author would venture the guess, however, that other methods for alleviating depressions would prove more feasible, especially from an administrative point of view, in particular government spending financed by budget deficits.

The emphasis in the discussion so far has been primarily on the effects of price changes on the allocation of resources and upon the intensity and efficiency of their utilization. However, a very important consideration for public policy is the impact of price changes upon the distribution of income. Much of the agitation for the NRA and the principal force back of the subsequent schemes for price control in bituminous coal and cotton textiles was a belief that it was desirable to protect the wage scales and wage income. It is quite clear that for most industries in the short-run the supply of labor is not perfectly elastic downward, and in a period of recession the elasticity becomes less and may remain so for a considerable time. In the absence of strong collective bargaining there will be a strong pressure on wages. In a highly competitive industry this pressure on wages is inevitable. Price protection may serve to diminish this pressure, or it may be the necessary condition for the development of a strong industry-wide system of collective bargaining. If the question is simply one of partial dis-equilibrium, there is something to be said for wage protection if the impact is likely to be large and of considerable duration. Otherwise there may be a force at work tending toward extremes of inequality in the social structure. In the case of general disequilibrium incident to the business cycle, it is likewise true that the impact of change may be felt more seriously in some industries than in others. Price control might serve as one means to alleviate the particular impact of the cycle. This again implies a selective price control. Questions of the extent to which an alleviation of income inequalities shall be sought at the expense of employment, of a change in the size of income, or of a change in the composition of the income arise. Such considerations are not easily resolvable except by a careful consideration of the magnitudes involved, which are themselves not comparable in any economic terms. Here we strain at the limits of economics. Considerations of public policy must enter to resolve these conflicts.

This same concern for the impact of disequilibrium and change on the income of investors is seen in the movement which we have traced for greater security to property. It would not be without good reason if public policy should be less concerned with the impact of change on investors and entre-preneurs than with its impact on labor, if only because the numbers of investors and entrepreneurs whose security is at stake in the condition of a given industry are less than in the case of labor and their capacity to withstand particular losses greater. Actually we find that because of the power of business interests to bring pressures to bear upon the legislative process, protection to investment in the form of tariffs, anti-chain store legislation, etc. is quite common.

This survey of the economics of current price policies should serve to explain the economic basis of many complaints about free or uncontrolled price making and to throw into relief the principal economic factors to be considered in formulating public policy with respect to price. It is clear that current prices bear no immediate relation to costs in any accounting sense. A firm in determining upon its current policies may consider to a greater or less extent the indirect effects of its action upon the market both in the present and in the future. Estimates of present and future prices and costs and individual discount schedules will all have their effects on current prices. In monopolistic markets there will be a sphere of individual responsibility for current conditions, a responsibility which becomes greater as the numbers become less or monopoly controls become greater. The risk that action will be precipitated which is unfavorable to some or all is great. Responsibility for precipitating such action may be determined. From this arises an increasing concern with the "ethics" of market behavior. A policy undertaken with an intent to destroy and one designed merely to increase the profits of a particular concern are difficult to distinguish. Their effects are similar. Faced with these conditions industry has devised a threefold program: first, to prevent price policies designed to destroy rivals; second, to set up informal controls designed to minimize risks in such markets; third, to restrain action which might impair the effectiveness of such controls. Increasingly the concern of business has been with the latter.

Prices and price relations serve several functions in our society. Upon them depends the allocation of employment and resources between alternative uses. They are responsible for the distribution of income. They are a more or less perfect regulator of the rate at which our economic system adjusts itself to change. They are responsible in part for determining the magnitude and incidence of loss which accompanies such change. They may be more or less conducive to full employment. The previous argument suggests that certain price changes and certain price relations to which free pricing gives rise may not be for the best. Price changes may set loose cumulative forces of an inflationary or deflationary character. Free pricing in an economy with industries of varying degrees of monopoly power might be superseded by *selective* price and investment controls with beneficial results upon the allocation of capacity and output. Price control might be a way for minimizing the impact on particular groups of the burdens of partial disequilibrium. On the other hand, it has been suggested that failure to allow a change in price relations in the face of changes in underlying conditions may lead to an uneconomic allocation of current output between various products and may induce an uneconomic flow of investment and resources.

The argument could be elaborated. To be of any significance as a guide to policy it would require a very extensive factual investigation. Its significance for the present study, however, is the light it sheds on the fundamental forces lying back of much of the distrust of free price policies. There are elements of truth in the claims of those who urge that free pricing, production, and investment policies are not in the public interest. It does not follow, however, that the blanket extension of the right of voluntary agreement to industry groups would have effects which were systematically better.

May not the problem of excessively low wages, where it is acute, be better approached directly? Is the question of securing the survival of efficient firms faced by temporary financial reverses best attacked by the blunt instrument of protecting price? May not this problem be better attacked by improving credit facilities, perhaps by direct government loans, by revision of tax laws, or by revision of corporate financial structures? So far as this problem becomes acute it is during periods of depression. A policy designed to protect efficient firms at such times must be integrated with other policies with respect to the cycle.

It has been suggested that the price level might be strengthened by granting power of price control to industry and that this might mitigate the cumulative process of recession. Judgment on such a proposal must await more general agreement on the significance of price policies for the cycle. It is clear that this calls for selective price controls, not merely the grant of voluntary powers to industry to agree on prices. This raises the serious question as to where the power is to be located so as to get the desirable degree of flexibility in price relations while at the same time changes in the price level or segments of the price level are limited. Granted that free pricing as it works in many fields is characterized by secrecy, by misrepresentation, and by unsystematic price discrimination how far can we go toward eliminating these factors without eliminating the forces which make for competitive pricing? These questions face anyone who urges that the concepts of fair and unfair competition should be extended very far in the field of pricing.

CHAPTER XVIII

THE PROBLEM REORIENTED

THE CONCEPTS of fair and unfair competition are not economic, they are essentially regulatory concepts indicating a distinction between what is and what is not countenanced by public policy in the way of competitive practices. The law of unfair competition and the law of fair competition, so far as any such has been developed, are essentially laws applying restraints to competition. The one forbids the use of certain competitive practices, and the other forbids the conduct of competition in any way other than that specified. There has been an attempt in recent years to change the content of these two concepts. The change in emphasis which was signalized by the NRA codes from a law of unfair competition to a law of fair competition is a striking example of such a change. Similar attempts are to be found in various suggestions to broaden the concepts, or to redefine and give more economic significance to them. It has been said by one political theorist that "The business of a legal system is to make the postulates of a society work."[1] This suggests that the various proposals for redrawing the line between the lawful and the unlawful in competitive business relations may represent either a recognition of the need for change in the postulates of the system or a change in the rules which it is believed will make the postulates work. It is clear that much of the discussion of the inadequacy of current concepts of unfair competition arises out of a belief that the postulates upon which the theory of a freely competitive society is based are inadequate.

[1] Harold Laski, *The State in Theory and Practice* (New York: Viking Press, 1935), p. 154.

LEGAL APPROACH TO COMPETITION

The concept of "competition," which occurs so repeatedly in discussions of public policy with reference to industrial markets is ambiguous. Most generally the term implies rivalry, and as applied to business matters rivalry between firms in the purchase, production, and sale of goods. Sometimes the term "competition" is used as descriptive of our present economic system or of the norm at which we aim. But rivalry is only one characteristic of our economic mechanism; there are many other equally important characteristics.[2] But frequently the term "competition" is used in conjunction with other terms such as "freedom of competition," "pure" competition, "perfect" or "imperfect" competition.

The legal concept which has dominated public policy in this country has been that of free competition. The object has been to insure the freedom of competition, the freedom of rivalry. Public policy has not insisted upon the *fact* of competition, i.e. it has not insisted that there *must* be rivalry, or that rivalry must take certain forms or lead to certain results. Nor have steps been taken to insure that market conditions shall be such that rivalry will exist. The object of traditional policy has been to insure that firms, whether actual or potential, shall be free to enter a market and compete with others by any means they choose so long as the means are not unfair or in restraint of trade. The Sherman Act and the legislation of 1914 have been concerned with the practices and methods of firms as they affect rivals. Business must not be diverted from rivals by misrepresentation or deceit; rivals must not be injured by coercive, exclusive, or other predatory practices; rivalry must not be eliminated voluntarily by agreement between independ-

[2] Thus, our system is corporate, capitalistic (capital-good using), acquisitive (profit-seeking), free (i.e. relatively free); it is characterized by private property, exchange, and credit.

ent firms. Injury to competitors by deceitful and predatory methods and joint agreement to eliminate rivalry are the signs of illegality. Joint agreement in restraint of trade aside, the protection of private business interests from injury by fraudulent, coercive, or predatory practices was the task of the legal system. The preservation of *the freedom to compete in any manner short of unfair or predatory practices*, this was the ideal of policy.

This concept of free competition is one which was concerned but little with the basic market structure. Trusts might be unscrambled if they had been formed with an illegal intent and by predatory methods, or where in the case of a combination technical conditions made potential competition impossible. Interlocking directorates and stock-holdings were prohibited where they substantially lessened competition. But mergers, large size, predominance in the market were not attacked directly. In fact many institutional and legal arrangements favored such developments. Moreover, traditional policy gave little attention to the results of various policies or market conditions. Neither close combinations nor loose associations were considered in terms of the results of the conditions and trade policies in the particular markets. Agreements by loose associations on prices or production were illegal however reasonable the prices or production quotas might be. Mergers, combinations, and firms with predominant position in the market were legal in the absence of an intent or effect to exclude others by predatory practices. No questions of price, output, investment, or profits were raised.

Underlying the traditional policy was the inarticulate assumption that the maintenance of the freedom of competition as previously defined will produce *desirable* results, or at least the *best possible* results. In dealing with particular situations before the courts or the Commission a showing of desirable or undesirable results was an irrelevant consideration. "Good" results could not save an illegal method, nor "bad" results convict an otherwise legal practice. Traditional policy was concerned not with the market structure nor with economic and social results but with business methods and practices as they impinged upon competitors. Certain methods of rivalry were forbidden; public policy restrained certain *positive acts* in competition or in restraint of competition, but it did not penalize the failure to compete nor specify the pattern which business practices should follow.

CHANGES IN THE CONCEPT OF UNFAIR COMPETITION

As indicated by the trade association literature, the writings of contemporary economists, and recent legislation, there has been an attempt by redefining unfair competition to change the scope and emphasis of our public policy. The NRA and the several currents from which it stemmed shifted the emphasis from the individual enterprise to the group, especially the group as represented by the industry. The predominant purpose of the codes of fair competition was to give security to the interests of the industry group by setting up defenses against actions of the individual firms which might injure the group interest. Restrictions were placed upon the individual enterprise in the interest of the group. This was industrial self-government as conceived by its most ardent business exponents. Whereas the traditional policy had forbidden the interference by an individual with the legitimate interest of another individual, the proponents of the early codes sought to prevent the interference by the individual with the legitimate interest of the group.

The emphasis upon group interest which dominated much of the early code making was gradually repudiated by policy makers. This attempt to shift the emphasis from the protection of the individual from injury to the protection of the group represented an attempt to change the basic postulates of our economic system. In large part the postulate that the interests of the industry group and the public interest are compatible has been repudiated by official policy, although the philosophy and technique of the NRA has been applied to isolated parts of the system, notably in the control of the bituminous coal industry and in the legislation permissive of resale price maintenance. Nevertheless, this represents a significant direction in which the concept of unfair competition was developing: from the interest of the individual enterprise to the interest of the industry group; from the protection of the individual against the group, to the protection of the group against the individual enterprise; from the interest of the employer group to the interest of employers, employees, and consumers alike.

Coördinate with this development, in fact as an integral part of it, has been a shift of emphasis from the prevention of unfair competition to the promotion of fair competition. This idea of fair competition has a legal basis in the law with respect to loose combinations. Several court decisions have acknowledged the doctrine that there is a legitimate sphere for coöperative action in order to eliminate unethical practices. The emphasis on fair competition as it developed under the NRA involved a shift toward the prescription of the precise trade practice to be followed. Traditional policy had merely forbidden certain acts; the new developments would go further and detail the practices to be followed, prohibiting all alternatives.

A further development of the concept of unfair competition has been the extension of the idea to include consideration of the effects of trade practices and competitive methods upon other stages, forward and backward, in the productive process. The traditional concept was for the most part concerned with competitive methods only in so far as there was direct injury to competitors on the same plane in the competitive process. Evidence of an expansion of the concept to include the effect on purchasers or consumers, who lie forward in the productive process, or on labor or others, who lie backward, is to be found in several directions. The recent amendments to section 5 of the Federal Trade Commission Act have just this as one of their purposes. Moreover, the sections of the Wheeler-Lea Act forbidding the dissemination of false advertising of food, drugs, devices, and cosmetics seem to have opened the door to an increasing emphasis upon the buyer-seller relation. Another example of such a concern with buyer-seller relations is to be found in the recent Robinson-Patman Act. The whole history of the agitation leading to the passage of the Robinson-Patman Act shows a dominant concern with the effects of manufacturers' sales policies on the competitive relations of distributors.

Perhaps the most controversial attempt to extend the range of interests to be considered in delineating unfair competition has been the attempt to consider the repercussions of selling practices on labor located earlier in the productive process. One of the elements which it was most frequently urged should be considered in determining policy with respect to trade practices under the NRA was the effect upon the wages, hours, and conditions of employment. The elaborate procedure by which bituminous coal prices are now controlled and the terms and conditions of sale standardized was adopted, not primarily for the purpose of controlling prices as such, but rather in order to relieve the competitive pressure of price cutting upon wages and conditions of employment in a market with excess capacity. This development is a recognition of the fact that at least for short periods there is in many industries an intimate connection between competitive relations in the selling market on the one hand and wages and other labor conditions on the other. It is recognized that neither for the industry nor for the firm can the price of labor be considered an independent variable; that is, the supply of labor is not always infinitely elastic at the going wage. Just as the idea of unfair competition has been extended to consider the effects of competitive practices upon the security of the employers' investment, so it has been extended to include a consideration of the economic security of labor. It is to be noted that an alternative approach was to be had in the direct regulation of wages and conditions of employment.

Policy dealing with competitive practices seems to be moving in several directions. The theory of industrial self-government, which involved a repudiation of the postulates of our system, has been itself repudiated. But there appears to be a gradual broadening of the groups whose concern with competitive practices are being recognized by public policy. The traditional law of unfair competition was concerned with the protection of business rivals from injuries by certain methods. Increasingly the interest in trade practices of industrial buyers, final consumers, and labor is gaining recognition.

ECONOMIC APPROACH TO COMPETITION

The economist has a different view of competition from that of free competition which dominates public policy. Where the legal distinction is between free competition and restraint of trade and uses as its criteria business methods or policies, the economic distinction is between degrees of competition (pure, perfect, imperfect, monopolistic, etc.) and types of competition (price, service, product, advertising, etc.) based primarily upon a consideration of conditions and results but with an increasing concern with policies. In its limiting cases, perfect competition and perfect monopoly, the economist posits a rigid series of conditions with which conditions a unique set of determinate results are associated. In the situations intermediate between perfect monopoly and perfect competition the relations between conditions and results are not so clear. In such circumstances the existence of some degree of monopoly power and various types of other imperfections afford to business firms a penumbra of choice within which conscious administrative policies become important. Economists have increasingly recognized the importance of administrative policy making in such markets for the results to be expected, but the classification of market situations has not been carried sufficiently far to be useful for purposes of public policy. The difficulties seem primarily to be in the inadequacies of existing information for a determination of the quantitative significance of the results.

In the past, deductive reasoning has been relied upon for a determination of results; and while it is probable that deductive reasoning will continue to be of importance, this is a field in which quantitative study might make a considerable contribution. However, the fact remains that many possible quantitative measurements are of little pertinence, while many pertinent measurements are not feasible. Moreover, even if the task of measurement of results were surmounted, public policy questions would remain in balancing against one another considerations of technical efficiency, the continuity of employment, the level of employment, the rate of innovation, the political and social repercussions of alternative policies, etc. However, it is fair to say that the economists have been working in the direction of a study of markets in terms of results.[3]

This contrast between the economic and legal approaches is unfortunate but understandable. The economic emphasis upon results stresses the direction in which public policy should develop, but such an approach was hardly sufficiently developed to have served as a guide to public policy in the past. Analysis of results had not been sufficiently conclusive for the intermediate cases which are the most frequent, and the classification of markets had not been sufficiently detailed and realistic. Moreover, as has been suggested, an analysis of economic

[3] *Cf.* Wallace, "Industrial Markets and Public Policy: Some Major Problems," *Public Policy*, pp. 59–129.

results leaves the question of desirable results unsettled. Finally, the economists have devoted all too little attention to the question of the rectification of market conditions or the control of business policies so as to improve upon the results, problems which depend upon developing techniques both of quantitative measurement and of administration.

The fact that public policy has revolved around a control of competitive practices rather than a consideration of economic and social results is not to be explained entirely by the fact that materials were not at hand for a successful policy based upon a consideration of results. In the first place, there was a fairly widespread presupposition that the results which might be expected to follow from free competition as legally conceived were on the whole good. Moreover, policy based upon a control of competitive practices, i.e. a control of business policies as they affect rivals, was a natural response of the political and legal system to the most articulate and obviously interested groups. Business firms sought protection from the deceptive and predatory practices of their rivals, they sought this quite apart from the interest of any other groups and quite apart from its effects on the operation of the economic system. Finally and probably most important, the political and social context in which policy was developed was oriented toward "freedom." The legislatures and courts were not equipped to deal with the intricate problems of market structures and market results. The political and social context was antagonistic to the imposition of controls upon business which would insure the existence of the conditions and policies necessary for desirable results.

PLACE OF THE REGULATION OF TRADE PRACTICES IN A SCHEME OF CONTROL

Traditional policy has aimed at making free business rivalry work. It has aimed at establishing a law of trade practices which would make competition effective and efficient. It did so, in the first place, by protecting to a degree the consumer in his exercise of free choice through preventing misrepresentation and deceit and, in the second place, by curbing the grossest forms of coercive and exclusive practices which were used by business concerns to impede rivals in approaching the market.

In 1914 it was sensed that the doctrines of unfair competition and restraint of trade which had developed at common law and by legal interpretation of the Sherman Act were inadequate. It was recognized that the regulation of business practices was necessary, but the reasons upon which this belief were based varied. The Wilsonians sought the regulation of competitive practices together with certain controls of market structures (e.g. interlocking directorates and intercorporate stock-control) as a means of maintaining competition, while the Progressives proposed the control of trade practices as a way of regulating monopoly. The logic of these divergent groups called for different types of regulation of trade practices, but both agreed upon the necessity of an administrative commission which should have powers to deal with these problems.

That it was not and is not feasible to draw up a list of unlawful practices is understandable, particularly when it is acknowledged that the significance of most practices depends on the general market structure and the other practices in conjunction with which they are pursued. The Commission was given a general mandate to prevent unfair methods of competition which it was hoped would enable it to deal with new situations as they arose in the light of its supposedly expert knowledge and understanding of the matter. Difficulties arose on several fronts. The courts by giving a narrow interpretation to the statute and by applying common law criteria of unfair competition and restraint of trade immobilized the Commission for a long while in its attempts to widen the concept so as to cope adequately with the problem of promoting an effective and efficient competition. There was in general an inadequate understanding of the issues by the courts, the Commission, the legislature, and the public.

Moreover, inadequate powers were given the Commission to deal even with those problems which were understood. The Commission might forbid misinformation; but it could not require the giving of all pertinent information, nor could it establish standards of labeling and branding. The Wheeler-Lea Act of 1938 made tentative steps in this direction by declaring unfair and deceptive acts to be contrary to section 5 and by prohibiting misleading advertising of foods, drugs, cosmetics, and devices. Recent innovations in the administration of the Trade Practice Conference Division of the Commission, however, point toward a promising method of developing standards of labeling and informative advertising. The Commission was granted no powers to deal with the price structure of the firm, in which the public has a clear interest, except in so far as the price structure of the firm interfered with free competition; and only with the passage of the Robinson-Patman Act in 1936 was the law adequate to deal with this limited aspect of the problem. The Commission was given no powers to prevent the development of monopolistic market structures in the absence of the use of predatory practices nor to regulate the use of such power once it was acquired. Oligopoly, price leadership, wasteful forms of non-price competition are matters beyond the scope of its mandate.

There was an almost complete failure to see the need for positive controls of market structures or trade policies except to prevent injuries of private business interests by deceptive and exclusive methods. It is not inconceivable, however, that by a proper combination of policies much might be done toward developing a reasonably workable and effective competitive system. A revision of the law of trade practices must be part of the approach, but only a part of the approach. Experience indicates that the problem of making competition work is not solely or primarily a question of controlling unfair methods or other trade practices.

An effective policy with respect to trade practices must consider the significance of each practice in the general milieu in which it is pursued. To isolate and define a practice and to develop a rule of policy with respect to it without any regard to the industries and market structures in which it may be used is to simplify the problem beyond recognition. Moreover, the significance of a trade practice will vary according to other general policies which are being pursued. This means, for example, that a practice which may be desirable in an economy in which the emphasis is on freedom of competition may impair the efficiency of a controlled competition. An effective policy will, therefore, analyze any given practice in its particular setting and in terms of the postulates of some broader policy with respect to the control of industrial organizations.

It is one merit of the Sherman Act as it has related to trade practices that the emphasis has not been upon the practice *per se* but rather upon the practice in relation to other practices and conditions in a particular market situation. It is true that the Sherman Act as it has been interpreted has distinct limitations. The emphasis, at least until recently, has not been on industrial efficiency in any sense. The tests have not been those of results. The emphasis has been rather on restraints of trade which impaired the freedom of competition. The emphasis was admittedly on intent rather than results. Monopoly position was countenanced, and even the exercise of some monopoly powers. Such practices as resale price maintenance, discrimination, the basing-point, freight absorption, and tying contracts were not considered illegal *per se* but were illegal in certain circumstances. These practices, however, could arise only in markets characterized by some element of monopoly power in the economic sense. With the possession of this power, public policy has not been primarily concerned. It was concerned rather with how the power was attained and with the intent which led to its acquisition. Nor was there a concern with how this power was used, provided only it was not used to exclude competitors. Given the general philosophy inherent in the law as interpreted, however, the general *method* adopted by the courts with respect to trade practices seems to have been a wise one, i.e. in view of the general postulates to consider the particular practice in the particular market structure.

The experience of the NRA seems to have been leading those responsible for its policy toward a similar *method* for distinguishing desirable and undesirable code provisions. In formulating policy declarations with respect to such practices as price protection, price-filing, and production control, it became increasingly clear that a general declaration to permit or prohibit a given practice was inadequate. It was deemed appropriate to make distinctions in the light of the general characteristics of each particular market. A basing-point formula of price quotation used in the lumber industry is one thing; used in the steel and cement industries it is another. Price-filing where the product is completely standardized and sellers are few is one thing; where the product is differentiated or sellers are many, it is another; unsystematic price discrimination in industries where buyers are of equal strength may be tolerated as necessary to induce price flexibility, while between unequals it may become an undesirable practice.

Policy with respect to a particular practice will often be largely determined by the general policy, the general postulates of industrial policy in a given sphere of industry. If in a particular industry, for example, price control by industrial groups, by the government, or by the joint efforts of both is found to be necessary, control of the product, advertising, and all ancillary terms and conditions of sale may inevitably follow. Norms of "fair" practice may be established, any deviation from

which will be termed an "unfair" interference by the individual
with the group policy. In industries where the sellers are scat-
tered and freight is a significant item, the geographical pattern
of prices must likewise be fixed if the control of the level of
prices is to be made effective. If, on the other hand, free pricing
policies are favored, policy with respect to the geographical
structure of prices might take another direction.

These remarks should serve as a warning that the problem
of separating practices which are to be forbidden or regulated
from those which are to be encouraged cannot be pursued without reference to general economic policies, i.e. the postulates
of the system, on the one hand, and their specific application
on the other. For this reason an exhaustive listing of the rules
of the game is not feasible. Moreover, in dealing with a practice
it is important to consider whether the practice which interferes
with the efficiency of the economy is pursued systematically or
whether it is merely an incidental concomitant of the way of
doing business. For example, competitive selling as we know
it gives rise to much incidental price discrimination. Advertising often leads to misunderstanding which diverts consumers
from a rational pursuit of their desires. Price-fixing by any
authority is likely to introduce elements of unsystematic discrimination. Control of product may deprive some consumers
of a degree of differentiation which they genuinely value. But
these incidental effects should be distinguished from systematic
misrepresentation or systematic discrimination. The grant of
broad powers of compulsion which may be used with wide
discretion would seem, in consequence, to be the most fruitful
approach to the problem.

Finally, it is not enough to prove that a practice may on
balance be undesirable in some cases, or that regulation of price,
production, or investment might improve on free determination of these matters. Discretionary powers to deal with these
factors, whether given to a government agency or to some in-

dustry group, should be granted and exercised only where the nature of the practice and surrounding conditions are such that the regulatory body may reasonably be expected to distinguish correctly on balance those cases in which the practice should be regulated from those in which the practice is best left untouched. The complexities of administration, the interests of the regulatory body or other group to which power is given, the political forces which would be brought to bear upon the duly constituted authority are also relevant considerations.

With these remarks we face the major question: What place will the regulation of competitive methods and trade practices have in a policy of industrial control which is based upon a consideration of economic results?

The task of making a system of private enterprise work is one which must be attacked from many angles. It is necessary to determine those areas in which it is feasible to develop a workable type of competition and those in which controlled monopoly is the better alternative. The establishment of a workable type of competition [4] calls for a substantial change in the structure of industry, on the one hand, and a control of its trade practices on the other. It is relatively easy to eliminate the restraints on trade resulting from voluntary agreement between rival firms. These agreements leave their traces. Moreover, it should be possible to do much more toward fostering rational consumer choice through a more vigorous program for developing standards of product and of labeling and for the control of advertising copy. These are matters in which the powers of the Federal Trade Commission might be strengthened. It is a field of endeavor, however, in which many other organizations might participate, such as the Food and Drug

[4] For a discussion of workable competition cf. J. M. Clark, "Toward a Concept of Workable Competition," *American Economic Review*, XXX (1940), 241–56.

Administration, the Bureau of Standards, various consumer organizations, and the relevant industrial groups and trade associations. Much competition which takes the form of product differentiation and advertising is not only costly but confusing and misleading to consumers. As such, it interferes seriously with rational consumer choice.

But the eradication of the effects of monopolistic conditions based, not upon agreement, but upon the existence of large firms, oligopoly, and price leadership presents a more perplexing problem.[5] It is conceivable that much might be done by a revision of policy with reference to corporate law, patents, mergers, the ownership of natural resources, and manufacturers' control of the channels of distribution. While it would not be feasible to pulverize industry sufficiently to approximate pure competition, it might be feasible to increase the number of firms and decrease their average size in many industries so as to increase the competitive forces. To what extent this would be feasible without interfering with the attainment of the optimum scale of plant and rate of operation is conjectural. Knowledge concerning the relation between efficiency and the scale of plant and operations is peculiarly scarce, though there have been no dearth of so-called authorities who have been willing to make extreme claims on both sides of the argument. However, it should be possible to acquire such information. It must not be assumed that present firms are of optimum size from anything but a profit point of view. It is very probable that in many cases they have passed an optimum size from the point of view of costs, in which event it is not sufficient to prove that smaller firms would be of less than optimum scale. It is necessary to weigh this inefficiency against the inefficiency and other results of monopolistic conditions resulting from firms which are larger than the optimum. To

[5] *Cf.* C. D. Edwards, "Can the Antitrust Laws Preserve Competition?", *American Economic Review*, XXX, Suppl. (1940), 164–179.

change the market structure of established and matured industries may be more difficult than to influence the structure of new or expanding industries. A revision of the rules may be sufficient to lead the latter to evolve in a desired manner, while trust-busting in the traditional manner might be necessary to effect desired changes with reference to the former.

The control of competitive methods and trade practices will have an important place, however, in the development of a workable competition. In the first place by continuing a control of exclusive and predatory practices as in the past the channels of trade may be kept clear to innovation and adjustment to economic change. This has been done reasonably effectively by traditional policy. But it should be recognized that there are many practices which, while it would be difficult to prove that they are injurious to competitors or are directed at the exclusion of competitors, do nevertheless work to the advantage of large and established firms and impede the entrance of new firms. Block-booking and other sales practices in the moving picture industry, some forms of consignment selling and competitive advertising, pump leasing arrangements in the gasoline industry are apparently cases in point. It is not sufficient simply to prevent these practices. If it is desired to foster a workable competition, it is necessary to devise alternative business arrangements which will favor the entrance of new firms and permit the survival of smaller firms.

There are many practices which affect significantly the structure of industry by favoring the expansion of established firms and the survival of firms with access to large financial resources. These practices are a real obstacle to the effective use of a technical freedom to compete, although they appear to have been countenanced by public policy in the past. A revision of the statutory law or a modification of the judicial tests applied in cases involving the Sherman Anti-trust and Federal Trade Commission Acts is in order. Initiative in the revision of trade practices of this sort must come from some government agency. Industry is not likely to coöperate without the threat of the imposition of rules from above or the threat of penal action. However, this is a task which must be done industry by industry and will necessitate the coöperation of the various industrial groups. It is conceivable that a procedure could be developed by which the Federal Trade Commission, the Department of Commerce, and the Anti-trust Division of the Department of Justice could each take an appropriate part in developing and enforcing such practices. Once approved they might be included among the Group I rules promulgated by the Trade Practice Conference Division of the Commission.

It is hardly conceivable that structural changes by these various means would be sufficiently far reaching to so reduce monopolistic elements as to make competition workable. There is likely to be a substantial residual of monopolistic positions, and there is a public interest in how the power which this monopoly position affords is used. Does the seller discriminate between various groups of final consumers? Is the geographical price structure of the industry conducive to efficient location of production? Does the seller allow buyers to take delivery at the factory where this would prove economical? Will the seller use the cheaper forms of transportation such as waterways or trucks where the buyer so desires? Are price changes made openly, or are they made secretly? Are pressures for reciprocal dealing imposed upon buyers? Are there certain trade customs which lead to uniform bids on government contracts, or to rotation of the lowest bid among several sellers? Are there practices in the industry which foster inflexible prices?

There is a public interest in such practices. The conventional approach through the idea of unfair competition is inadequate to deal with them. The practices are not shocking to the ordinary sense of business morals. Nor are many of them contrary to public policy as previously conceived. Only when the monopoly problem is conceived in broader terms to include the regulation of the practices of monopoly, i.e. the exercise of monopoly power, as well as the ways in which monopoly power is acquired, will such practices be dealt with adequately. There must be developed a control of the trade practices of monopolistic industries aimed at inducing practices which will lead to good results in terms of the level of employment, efficient production, the allocation of resources, the distribution of income, etc. Rules of behavior, often very detailed rules, must be developed in terms of the particular conditions and practices found to exist. This may be done by specific legislation such as that embodied in the Robinson-Patman Act or in proposed legislation dealing with basing-point policies. Or again it may be done by granting new and general discretionary powers to such bodies as the Federal Trade Commission, the Department of Commerce, and the Department of Justice. At present the powers of the government to specify the practices to be followed by business firms is practically non-existent, although the Anti-trust Division of the Department of Justice has recently been trying to use its powers to enter consent decrees for this purpose. Again, it must be insisted that the initiative in these matters must come from some government agency implemented with positive powers to act. The contribution which business through its trade associations can make to this task, however, should not be minimized. These associations may serve as very effective agencies to negotiate with the appropriate government body in drafting effective rules of trade practices and even to aid in administering such rules. Such associations have coöperated quite effectively with the S.E.C. in its attempts to control security markets.

There is, however, a third attack on the monopoly problem, an attack from the direction of the excessively competitive industries. By strengthening the controls in industries in which competition is most keen, there may be a tendency towards just such a redistribution of economic resources as is desired. Legislation for our sick industries, legislation favoring agreements and controls in highly competitive industries might have this effect if it were accompanied by a limitation on investment or other policies which forced resources out of these industries and into others. This implies fostering by permissive legislation, by voluntary agreement, or perhaps by extensive regulation certain practices which will increase the degree of control in aggressively competitive industries.

These seem to be the limits to our power to deal with the monopoly problem by the regulation of trade practices. A redefinition of the monopoly problem in the terms 'suggested would open a wide field of trade practices with which it might prove wise to deal in an attempt to reduce the injurious effects of monopoly power.

The discussion so far has been concerned with the acquisition and exercise of monopoly power on the assumption that the problem is to introduce more competitive elements into such markets and increase output. However, one of the complaints frequently raised in markets with monopolistic elements is that the competitive pressures are too great; competition where sellers are few is apt to become disastrous or ruinous. In a previous chapter some of the factors which give rise to such conditions have been indicated. The only limit to the depth to which one or more sellers can take price if they so choose is determined by their capacity to supply the demand. Granted that there is often unused physical plant which can produce the product at some cost, there is the power to precipitate a price war. Conditions may then become chaotic. Price changes may be large and disorderly. They may prove financially embarrassing to particular firms. Prices may be far less than variable costs measured in terms of the accounting costs of the factors employed, although perhaps not as viewed by the firm which considers the various effects on future demand for its product. We have no clear idea of the importance of such situations quantitatively speaking.

It is not simply a question of competition in price; competition may take the form of changes in the terms of trade, the product, or advertising. Nor is it simply a question of competition with the intent and effect of driving a competitor out of business. Such a statement of the problem is too simple. The question is rather whether such competitive situations with respect to price and other conditions promote the best utilization of current resources and the best direction of investment, and whether they are conducive to selective differentiation between those firms which are to survive and those which are to fail. If it developed that they do not and that such situations are quantitatively significant, there arises the problem of how to deal with them. The problem is that of putting a bottom to competitive forces. The experience with minimum pricing during the NRA was not encouraging. Seriously disruptive pricing policies are usually either ephemeral or indicative of extensive changes in underlying conditions. The grant of powers to industry to deal with such situations by group action runs into the danger that symptoms will be mistaken for causes and that necessary adjustments will be impeded. If this problem proves to be one limited to a few situations, it might be dealt with by granting to some body such as the Federal Trade Commission discretionary powers to encourage voluntary agreement or to impose a mandatory minimum level below which competition should not be allowed to go.

What of the problem of economic waste? To what extent may the regulation of trade practices be used to eliminate waste and thereby increase the efficiency of the economic system? The meaning of economic waste as used by exponents of the trade association movement is not too clear. There are the wastes or costs of inventory incident to an unnecessary duplication of sizes, types, or colors of product. Much may be done toward simplification and standardization of product by voluntary agreement. Moreover, much of the waste resulting from competition in industries where competition is blended with monopoly might be eliminated by control of the trade practices of monopolistic industries as suggested above.

Often it is the reallocation of risk which is meant when it is urged that waste be reduced. It is true that economic efficiency can often be increased by an appropriate allocation of risk. A guarantee against price decline may be conducive to uneconomic inventory practices. The liberal policy adopted with respect to the return of product in the clothing trades may be conducive to over-buying. The form of a contract which results from unfettered or free bargaining may not be best designed to stimulate economic efficiency. In this respect the contrast may be noted between the stability of monthly output in the bituminous coal industry in Germany where the terms of the sales contract have forced dealers and consumers to assume certain functions of storage, with the monthly instability of output in our own industry.[6] It is, of course, true that the allocation of such risks by an agreement on the part of rival sellers will not necessarily result in such an allocation as will be conducive to economic efficiency. Business groups are, as we have stressed repeatedly, only too eager to reduce business risks; and in the absence of control risks will be located on the basis of the relative power of the interested parties, not on the basis of their effect upon economic efficiency. There is here, however, an area in which voluntary agreement subject to some check might be used to regulate the terms of sale with the purpose of reallocating risk so as to reduce wastes. This is the type of function which the trade practice conference of the Federal Trade Commission might well perform. Where the wastes are serious, sanctions might be imposed by incor-

[6] A. H. Stockder, *German Trade Associations: The Coal Kartells* (New York: Henry Holt, 1924), pp. 65, 243–44.

porating regulations among Group I rules. It will be necessary, however, to distinguish between markets where the elimination of freedom in the determination of these terms will eliminate the last vestiges of competition from markets where other forms of competition may be expected to continue undiminished. In the former, efficiency in allocating risk may be sacrificed in favor of weakening monopolistic controls.

Another waste which is often deplored is the waste of unutilized capacity. What can the regulation of trade practices do about this? In part unutilized capacity is a natural concomitant of the business cycle. There is, however, such a thing as a volume of capacity in a particular industry which is greater than would appear useful in the visible future. Capacity control would be the only cure for the evil, but this involves foresight. What are the probabilities that action by either the industry group or by government would generally be better able to assess the desirability of new capacity? To what extent does capacity when made seem reasonable from the standpoint of profit and loss considerations? If the difficulty arises from ignorance of knowable facts, publicity and joint action might alleviate the malallocation of investment. But much of the unused capacity would appear to result from the shift in consumer preference between firms selling differentiated products. This can be avoided only by steps which would strike at the roots of product differentiation and competitive advertising. This realm of problems is relatively unexplored, and we must for the present leave it with these remarks.

Another problem which has been associated with that of excess capacity is that of the excessive number of firms of less than optimum size.[7] Professor Chamberlin has demonstrated that in the markets for differentiated products it is very improbable that the size of the firm will be optimum.[8] In a

---

[7] *Cf.* J. M. Cassels, "Excess Capacity and Monopolistic Competition," *Quarterly Journal of Economics*, LI (1937), 426–43.

[8] *Op. cit.*, pp. 88, 97, 161, 166.

market without advertising but with free entry, he shows that the size of the plant will be less than the optimum. Where there is advertising, the plant may be either larger or smaller than the optimum; but only by chance will it be the optimum. Mr. Harrod has shown that not only will the firm be of other than the optimum size, but the output of the firm will not be the optimum for the actual plant.[9] These characteristics it seems are inherent in a system of enterprise which encourages product differentiation. If consumers' demand as determined by market forces is to be taken as given, there is little that can be done about it except as was suggested above by programs fostering more rational consumer choice. So far as consumer demand is due to ignorance or misrepresentation, some improvement might result from descriptive labeling, publishing of formulae, or revision of advertising copy. Such changes in current practices might tend to increase the elasticity of demand for the individual firm and minimize the effects of product differentiation and advertising.

What of trade practices and the problem of the distribution of income and the allocation of the burdens and gains incident to change? That the burden of disequilibrium and of adjustment to change falls arbitrarily upon investors and management is quite clear. But that an attempt to minimize these burdens by protecting investment is worth the costs involved is not so clear. The burdens of change must be borne; price control schemes can at most spread these burdens, and it can do this only at a sacrifice to effective satisfaction of consumers' desires. The rationale of private enterprise assumes that industry shall bear these burdens just as it participates in the conjunctural gains of change. The principal public concern in the impact of competition in industry on the distribution of income is in its effects upon wage income. An elaborate control of competitive selling practices which will reduce the rigors of competition

[9] R. F. Harrod, "Doctrines of Imperfect Competition," *Quarterly Journal of Economics*, XLVIII (1934), 44.

may relieve significantly the pressure on wages in a particular industry. This may aid labor organizations in their attempts to protect wage scales, or it may mean that management will be less inclined to cut wages. This relation between competitive selling relations and wage conditions bulked large in the philosophy of NRA. It appears, however, that the recent trend is to attack the problem of distribution more directly. By setting minimum standards of wages and hours, through trade union action or through government regulation, a level is set below which competitive selling cannot force labor conditions. Such direct action is the surest way of effecting such ends. Except in the case of especially sick industries which warrant special legislation, it is improbable that the regulation of trade practices will be depended upon to deal with the distribution of income or to control the incidence of change.

Finally, what of the trade practice problem and the cycle? Here we are on tenuous ground. The principal problem lies in the relation of price flexibility to the business cycle. There are certain price relations which are conducive to the best utilization of our resources and which are most conducive to full employment. There is, however, a difference of opinion as to the degree of flexibility of *price levels* which is most conducive to full employment. Trade practices are significant in so far as many of them are designed primarily to strengthen short-run controls of price. It does not seem probable that a blanket grant of powers to industry groups, even if price controls of some sort would be beneficial, would be conducive to that selective type of price control which some believe desirable. At the present juncture a regulation of trade practices so as to break down specific controls seems to be the trend of public policy. Were it concluded that the cycle could be best dealt with by limiting price flexibility to a change in price relations while the cumulative spiral of price levels is curtailed, a rather elaborate regulation of pricing practices would be called for.

Voluntary controls of short-run cyclical changes in prices might be strengthened rather than weakened. How this could be done in such a way as to keep price relations flexible is baffling. Business seems to have such a bias in favor of existing price relations, at least for its own products, that it would appear necessary to supervise closely the use of such powers as might be granted.

In the preceding pages has been traced the development of the idea of unfair competition as a concept for regulating the competitive practices of industrial concerns. We have seen the gradual broadening of the concept from one which was concerned primarily with the morals of business to one which is increasingly concerned with the economic effects of business practices. This changing use of the concept is indicative of shifts in presumptions as to the efficacy of private enterprise. The postulates of traditional policy are questioned by many. With a weakening of faith in the efficacy of unfettered competition, a change in view as to the need for limiting trade practices arises. It should be clear that recent thinking on the form which our regulation of competitive practices should take has not been systematically in one direction. The content which it is proposed to give to the concept of unfair competition by different groups varies. Some are concerned to develop additional defenses to private enterprise. Others are concerned to use the power to regulate trade practices as a weapon for the more effective functioning of our economic system, as an approach to the problems of economic efficiency, stability, and the distribution of income.

With this shift in emphasis from a concern with the ethics of business to a concern with results, i.e. with the economic efficiency of business in the broadest sense of the word efficiency, the problem becomes one of public policy in its broadest sense. Such policy should be based on broad considerations of social good in which economic considerations are only a part, though a very important part. The negative approach to competitive practices which characterized traditional policy can no longer be viewed as the sole or even primary approach to the problem of industrial markets. Basic market structures must be remodeled, and positive types of trade practices must be prescribed. The choice of such policies must be tempered by a consideration of the problems of administration. To what groups shall the power to make decisions on these matters be allocated? How shall it be divided? To whom shall the execution of such decisions be entrusted? What parts of the general problem can be entrusted to voluntary action by industry groups? What aspects must government deal with by use of its coercive powers? Public policy with respect to trade practices cannot be dissociated from these problems.

It is a merit of economic theory that by ignoring many trade practices it has been able to simplify its problems so as to be able to see the forest from the trees. With the help of this technique economic theory has made important contributions to an understanding of the functioning of industry. However, public policy must deal with the realm of brute reality, with industry working through markets in which there are many customs, many ways of doing things, many trade practices in the broader sense. Some of these practices are of little significance to the general outcome. Some are of more importance. The trade practice problem in its broadest sense is to reëxamine these ways of doing things, to assess their significance against the background of specific conditions, and to establish a policy where considerations of social good so demands.

SELECTED BIBLIOGRAPHY

SELECTED BIBLIOGRAPHY

A. BOOKS AND ARTICLES

Blaisdell, T. C., *The Federal Trade Commission: An Experiment in the Control of Business* (New York: Columbia University Press, 1932).

Burns, A. R., *The Decline of Competition: A Study of the Evolution of American Industry* (New York: McGraw-Hill, 1936).

Cassels, J. M., "Excess Capacity and Monopolistic Competition," *Quarterly Journal of Economics*, LI (1937), 426–43.

Chamberlin, E. H., *The Theory of Monopolistic Competition* (Cambridge: Harvard University Press, 1933).

Clark, J. D., *The Federal Trust Policy* (Baltimore: The Lord Baltimore Press, 1931).

Clark, J. M., "Basing Point Methods of Price Quoting," *Canadian Journal of Economics and Political Science*, IV (1938), 477–89.

—— *Social Control of Business* (2d ed.; New York: McGraw-Hill, 1939).

—— "Toward a Concept of Workable Competition," *American Economic Review*, XXX (1940), 241–56.

Daugherty, C. R., De Chazeau, M. G., and Stratton, S. S., *The Economics of the Iron and Steel Industry* (New York: McGraw-Hill, 1937, 2 vols.).

Davies, J. E., *Trust Laws and Unfair Competition* (Washington: Government Printing Office, 1915).

De Chazeau, M. G., "Public Policy and Discriminatory Prices of Steel: A Reply to Professor Fetter," *Journal of Political Economy*, XLVI (1938), 537–66.

Dunlop, J. T., "Price Flexibility and the 'Degree of Monopoly'," *Quarterly Journal of Economics*, LIII (1939), 522–34.

Eddy, A. J., *The New Competition* (New York: D. Appleton and Co., 1912).

Edwards, C. D., "Can the Antitrust Laws Preserve Competition?", *American Economic Review*, XXX (1940), 164–79.

Edwards, C. D., "NRA: Trade Practice Experience," Volume III of the Staff Studies submitted to the President's Committee of Analysis on the NRA, 1937. Not published. Available at the Department of Commerce in Washington and at the Littauer School of Public Administration at Harvard University.

Fetter, F. A., "Rejoinder to Professor de Chazeau's Reply," *Journal of Political Economy*, XLVI (1938), 567–70.

—— *The Masquerade of Monopoly* (New York: Harcourt, Brace & Co., 1931).

—— "The New Plea for Basing-Point Monopoly," *Journal of Political Economy*, XLV (1937), 577–605.

Gaskill, N. B., *The Regulation of Competition* (New York: Harpers, 1936).

Grether, E. T., *Price Control under Fair Trade Legislation* (New York: Oxford University Press, 1939).

Haines, C. G., "Efforts to Define Unfair Competition," *Yale Law Journal*, XXIX (1919), 1–28.

Handler, M., "Unfair Competition," *Iowa Law Review*, XXI (1936), 175–262.

Harrod, R. F., "Doctrines of Imperfect Competition," *Quarterly Journal of Economics*, XLVIII (1934), 442–70.

Henderson, G. C., *The Federal Trade Commission: A Study in Administrative Law and Procedure* (New Haven: Yale University Press, 1925).

Herring, E. P., *Public Administration and the Public Interest* (New York: McGraw-Hill, 1936).

Javits, B. A., *Business and the Public Interest* (New York: The Macmillan Co., 1932).

Johnson, H. S., *The Blue Eagle from Egg to Earth* (Garden City, New York: Doubleday, Doran, 1935).

Kahn, R. F., "Some Notes on Ideal Output," *Economic Journal*, XLV (1935), 1–35.

Kaldor, N., "Market Imperfections and Excess Capacity," *Economica*, II New Series (1935), 33–51.

Knight, F. H., "Ethics and Economic Reform. I: The Ethics of Liberalism," *Economica*, VI New Series (1939), 1–29.

—— *The Ethics of Competition, and Other Essays* (New York: Harpers, 1935).

Lerner, A. P., "The Concept of Monopoly and the Measurement of Monopoly Power," *Review of Economic Studies*, I (1934), 157–75.

Lyon, L. S., and others, *The National Recovery Administration: An Analysis and Appraisal* (Washington: Brookings Institution, 1935).

McFarland, Carl, *Judicial Control of the Federal Trade Commission and the Interstate Commerce Commission, 1920–1930* (Cambridge: Harvard University Press, 1933).

Marshall, Alfred, *Industry and Trade: A Study of Industrial Technique and Business Organization* (London: The Macmillan Co., 1919).

Mason, E. S., "Monopoly in Law and Economics," *Yale Law Journal*, XLVII (1937), 34–49.

Meade, J. E. and Hitch, C. J., *An Introduction to Economic Analysis and Policy* (New York: Oxford University Press, 1938).

Means, G. C., *Industrial Prices and Their Relative Inflexibility* (Senate Document No. 13, 74th Cong., 1st Sess., 1935).

National Industrial Conference Board, *Mergers and the Law* (New York, 1929).

—— *Public Regulation of Competitive Practices* (Revised ed.; New York, 1929).

Pearce, C. A., *NRA Trade Practice Programs* (New York: Columbia University Press, 1939).

Pigou, A. C., *The Economics of Welfare* (4th ed.; London: The Macmillan Co., 1932).

—— *Socialism versus Capitalism* (London: The Macmillan Co., 1937).

Robinson, Joan, *The Economics of Imperfect Competition* (London: The Macmillan Co., 1933).

Roos, C. F., *NRA Economic Planning* (Bloomington, Indiana: The Principia Press, Inc., 1937).

Rublee, G., "The Original Plan and Early History of the Federal Trade Commission," *Proceedings of the Academy of Political Science*, XI (1926), 666–72.

Seager, H. R., and Gulick, C. A., Jr., *Trust and Corporation Problems* (New York: Harpers, 1929).

Seligman, E. R. A., and Love, R. A., *Price Cutting and Price Maintenance* (New York: Harpers, 1932).

Stevens, W. H. S., *Unfair Competition* (Chicago: University of Chicago Press, 1917).

Taggart, H. F., *Minimum Prices under the NRA* (Ann Arbor: University of Michigan, School of Business Administration, Bureau of Business Research, 1936).

Terborgh, G., *Price Control Devices in NRA Codes* (Washington: Brookings Institution, 1934).

U. S. Steel Corporation, *The Basing Point Method of Quoting Delivered Prices in the Steel Industry* (October 30, 1939; prepared under the direction of T. O. Yntema).

Wallace, D. H., "Industrial Markets and Public Policy: Some Major Problems," in C. J. Friedrich and E. S. Mason (Editors), *Public Policy* (Cambridge: Harvard University Press, 1940).

Watkins, M. W., *Industrial Combinations and Public Policy* (Boston: Houghton Mifflin, 1927).

Wilson, Woodrow, *The New Freedom* (Garden City, New York: Doubleday, Doran, 1913).

B. GOVERNMENT DOCUMENTS

Bureau of Corporations, *Annual Reports of the Commissioner*, 1904–1914.

Department of Commerce, *Trade Association Activities* (1923).

Department of Justice, *Bills and Debates in Congress Relating to Trusts, 1888–1913* (3 vols., 1903, 1914). Compiled by the Attorney General; first volume published as Senate Document No. 147, 57th Cong., 2d Sess.

Federal Trade Commission, *An Analysis of the Basing-point System of Delivered Prices as Presented by the United States Steel Corporation* (Report to the TNEC, January 26, 1940).

—— *Annual Reports*, 1915–1939.

—— *Cement Industry*, 73d Cong., 1st Sess. (1933), Senate Document No. 71.

—— *Chain-store Leaders and Loss Leaders*, 72d Cong., 1st Sess. (1932), Senate Document No. 51.

—— *Decisions*, volumes 1–29.

—— *Final Report on the Chain Store Investigation,* 74th Cong., 1st Sess. (1934), Senate Document No. 4.

—— *Monopoly and Competition in Steel* (Report to the TNEC, March 7, 1939).

—— *Price Bases Inquiry: The Basing-point Formula and Cement Prices* (1932).

—— *Resale Price Maintenance,* Part I (70th Cong., 2d Sess., 1929, House Document No. 546), Part II (1931).

—— *Trade Practice Rules* (1940).

National Recovery Administration, *Report of the President's Committee of Industrial Analysis on the NRA* (1937).

—— *Report on the Operation of the Basing-point System in the Iron and Steel Industry* (November, 1934).

NRA, Division of Review, *Control of Geographic Price Relations under Codes of Fair Competition,* Work Materials No. 86.

—— *Design Piracy: The Problem and Its Treatment under NRA Codes,* Work Materials No. 52.

—— *Information Concerning Commodities, A Study in NRA and Related Experience in Control: Part A, Misrepresentation and Deception; Part B, Standards and Labeling,* Work Materials No. 38.

—— *Manufacturers' Control of Distribution,* Work Materials No. 62.

—— *Minimum Price Regulation under Codes of Fair Competition,* Work Materials No. 56.

—— *Policy Statements Concerning Code Provisions and Related Subjects,* Work Materials No. 20.

—— *Price Filing under the NRA Codes,* Work Materials No. 76, 2 vols.

—— *Resale Price Maintenance Legislation in the United States,* Work Materials No. 16.

—— *Restriction of Resale Price Cutting with Emphasis on the Drug Industry,* Work Materials No. 56.

U. S. Congress, House Committee on Ways and Means, *Hearings on H. R. 5664, A Bill to Encourage National Industrial Recovery,* 73d Cong., 1st Sess. (1933).

U. S. Congress, House Committee on Ways and Means, *Hearings on the Extension of the National Industrial Recovery Act*, 74th Cong., 1st Sess. (1935).

——Senate Committee on Finance, *Hearings on S. 1712 and H. R. 5755; Bills to Encourage National Industrial Recovery*, 73d Cong., 1st Sess. (1933).

—— Senate Committee on Finance, *Hearings Pursuant to S. Res. 79; Investigation of the National Recovery Administration*, Parts 1–6, 74th Cong., 1st Sess. (1935).

INDEX

INDEX